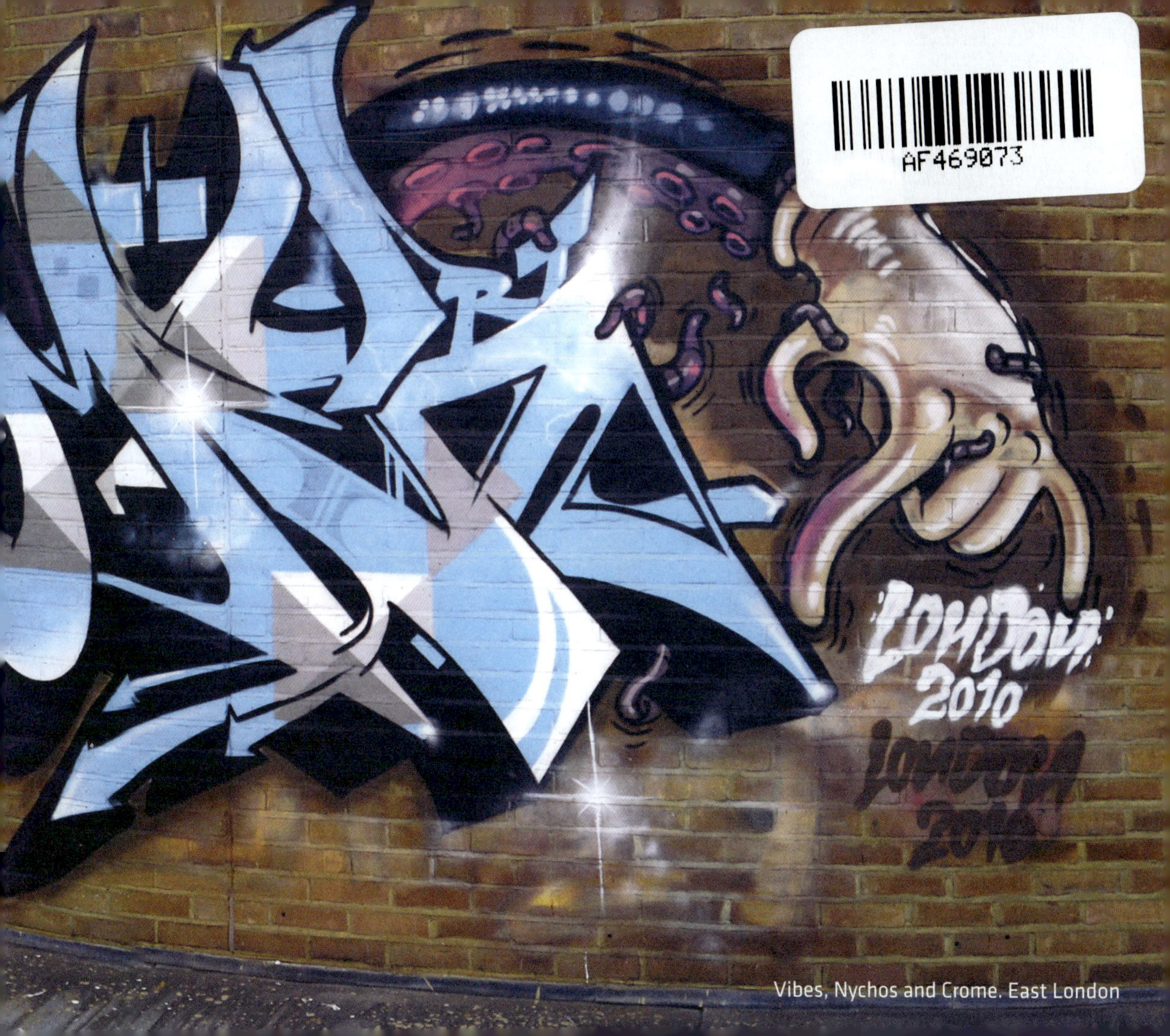

Vibes, Nychos and Crome. East London

LONDON Graffiti and Street Art

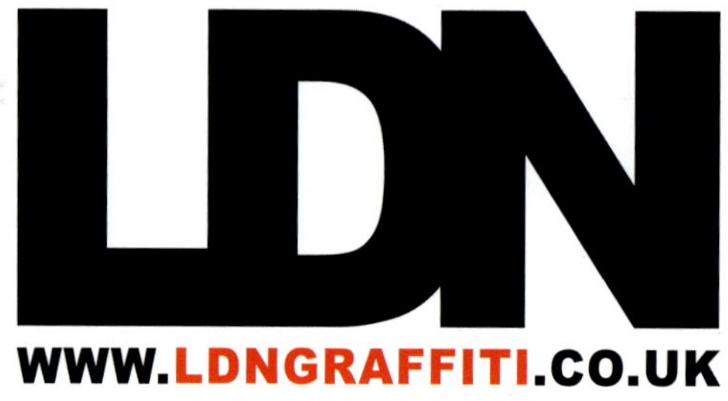

COVER: Mighty Mo & Cranio. East London

LONDON Graffiti and Street Art

Unique artwork from London's streets

LDNGRAFFITI

Joe Epstein

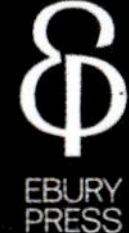

EBURY PRESS

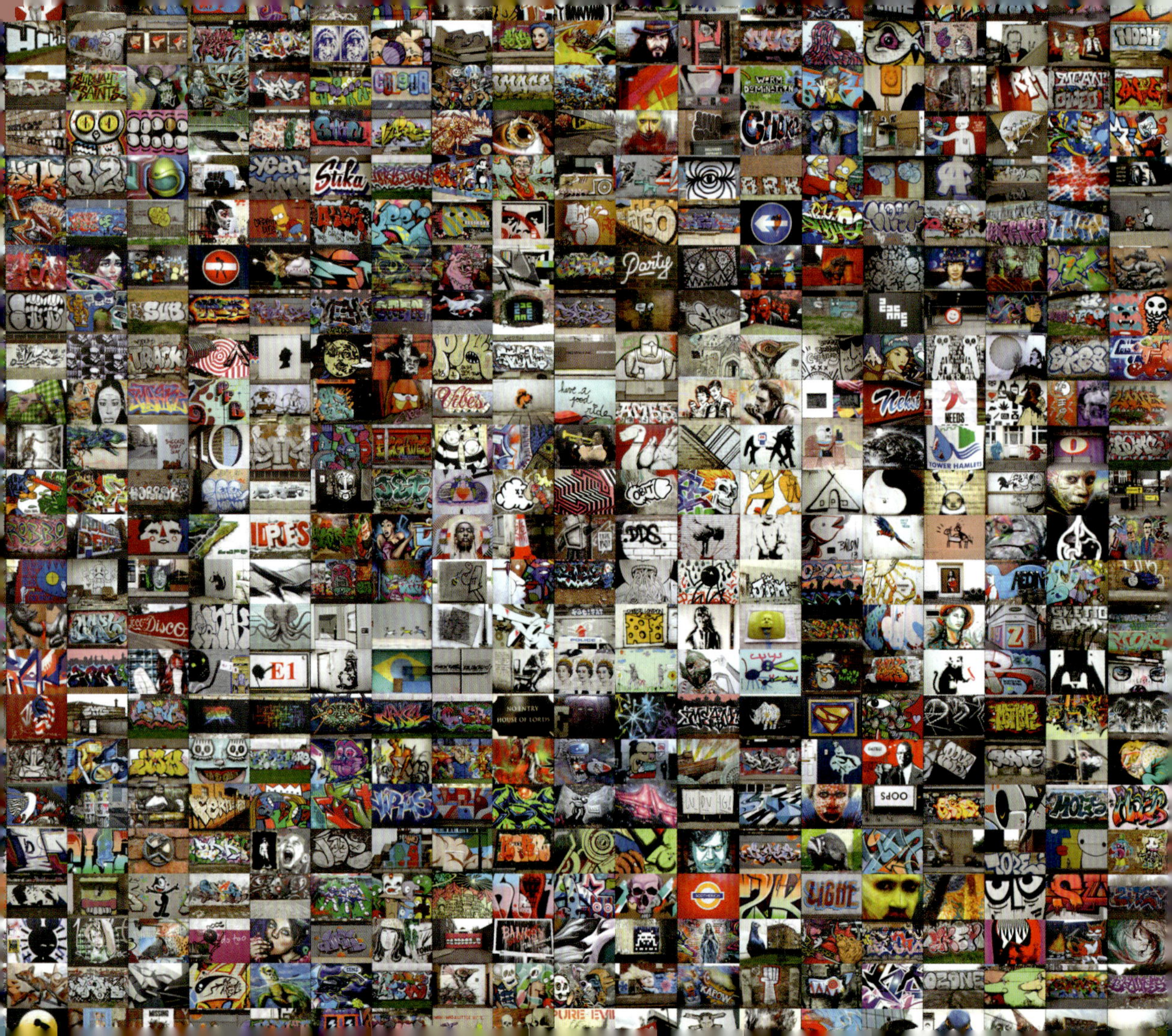
Stika
Party
Vibes
NEEDS
TOWER HAMLETS
E1
Disco
NO ENTRY
HOUSE OF LORDS
LIGHT
OZONE
PURE EVIL

In no way can my photography featured in this book represent an ever-changing London in its entirety, but I hope it will express some of the best talent, diversity and creative output found within the great capital. From the graffiti halls of fame, derelict buildings, illegal interventions, permissioned artworks, and the streets themselves, it documents how the landscape has changed, and the motivations behind the graffiti writers and street artists working in London today. Many of those artists have responded to the question, 'What does London mean to you?' in an attempt to give an insight into the inspirations and experiences they draw on to create the work I continually document.

What does London mean to me?
The artworks I see, and photography I take, all over London, are an inspiration to me. They break the visual monotony instilled in the grey streets I experience on an everyday basis. London has become my lifeblood. As much as I sometimes hate the place, I know the winding streets, open green spaces and the fantastic people, somehow will always be my heartfelt home.

I do not condone or take part in any form of vandalism, trespassing or criminal damage to public or private property. All the photographs I have taken and selected for this book have been recorded in legally accessible circumstances.

Thanks to everyone, especially Esther and Mark, for helping me compile this book. This project, and my website LDNGraffiti.co.uk, would not be possible without the considerable support and eternal patience from my son Josh, my love Line, developers TonyO and Bram, my family and all my very dear friends wherever you are!

For now... Street art is the new pub, so take to the streets, Londons walls are waiting!

Joe Epstein
Producer, LDNGraffiti, 2014

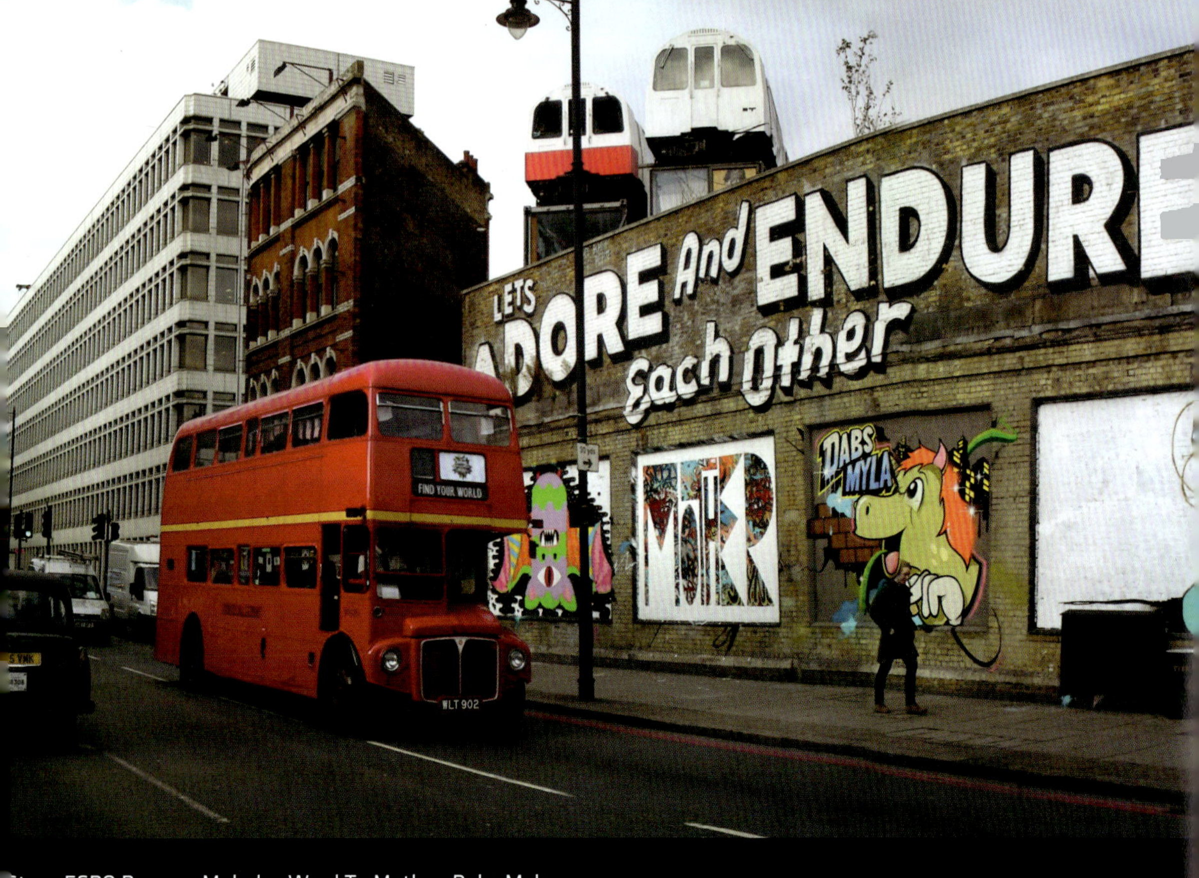

Steve ESPO Powers, Malarky, Word To Mother, Dabs Myla, Best Ever, InkFetish 40HK, Txemy, Muro & Matem, Cadi, Ronzo and more, Great Eastern Street, East London

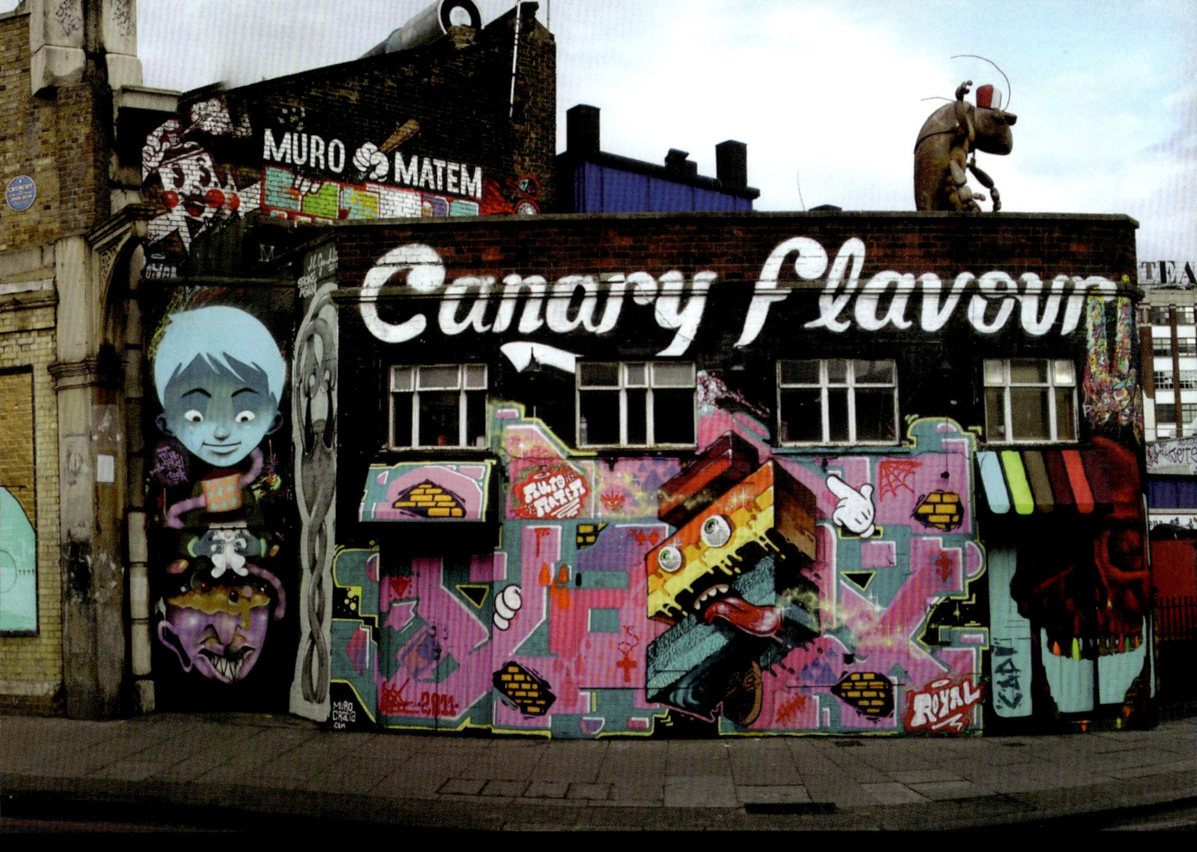

- FOREWORD BY PURE EVIL
- INTRODUCTION BY LDNGRAFFITI
- LONDON GRAFFITI
- LONDON HALLS OF FAME
- LONDON SITES
- LONDON STREETS
- ENDWORD BY DAVID SAMUEL/RAREKIND
- ARTIST CREDITS

WELCOME TO THE NEW YORK GRAFFITI RE-ENACTMENT SOCIETY 2014

GRAFF AT ITS VITAL BEST, CAN STOP YOU IN YOUR TRACKS, MAKE YOU WALK INTO TRAFFIC, ALMOST GET YOU KILLED BY A BUS – JUST BECAUSE YOU WANT TO GET A BETTER LOOK AT THAT PIECE.

~~N.Y. GRAFFITI RE-ENACTMENT SOCIETY~~

THIS IS BECAUSE THE ARTIST IS YELLING AT YOU THROUGH THAT PIECE, SHOUTING:

"LOOK AT THIS! LOOK AT THE LINES, THE COLOUR, LOOK WHERE IT IS, HOW ON EARTH DID I GET THERE AND DO THIS!"

ARTISTICALLY, GRAFFITI IS LIKE WALKING A TIGHTROPE, WHERE OTHER TYPES OF ART SEEM MORE LIKE EATING A BISCUIT IN A COMFY CHAIR. IT TAKES RISKS. IT STICKS IT TO THE MAN. IT IS DANGEROUS...

AND I LOVE IT.

PURE EVIL

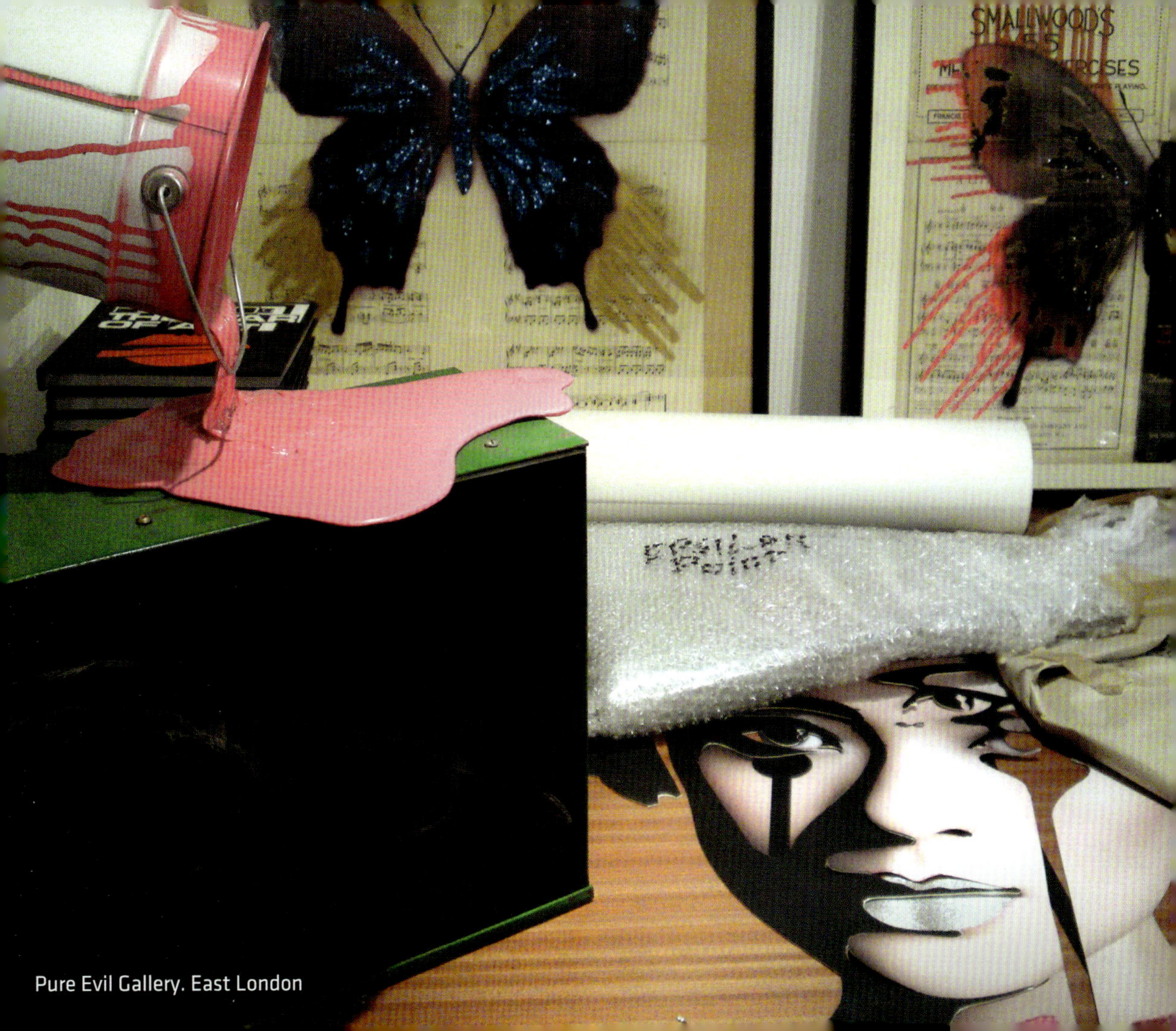

Pure Evil Gallery. East London

INTRODUCTION

'Old school' graffiti has certainly evolved over the decades. Some of the original aspects – hip hop, style, fashion, culture – have eroded, but at the heart is still a way of life. The days of painting whole trains and watching them roll around the city are lost, in New York and London at least. Those unique canvases, however illegal, inspire generations of writers and artists to develop a creative style, and engage in an expressive and creative art form.

The early pioneers Cornbread, Taki 183, Jean-Michel Basquiat, Keith Haring, Blek le Rat, are all considered. The important documentation of the early eighties graffiti scene in New York by Martha Cooper and Henry Chalfant meant the original works by Dondi, Cap, Blade, Duster, Futura, Iz The Wiz, Kase2, Min1, Seen, et al would not be lost and modern graffiti history washed away.

They enabled a fresh, new medium to be communicated to a global audience – with profound effect – and continue to inspire generations of creative people around the world. Through the work they published in the seminal book *Subway Art* and the film *Style Wars*, people found a new direction and connection with a positive, lifestyle movement.

"Old's cool!" - **Doze WRH**

Prime, Choci Roc, King Robbo and Doze - We Rock Hard (WRH). The Battle of Waterloo, 2010

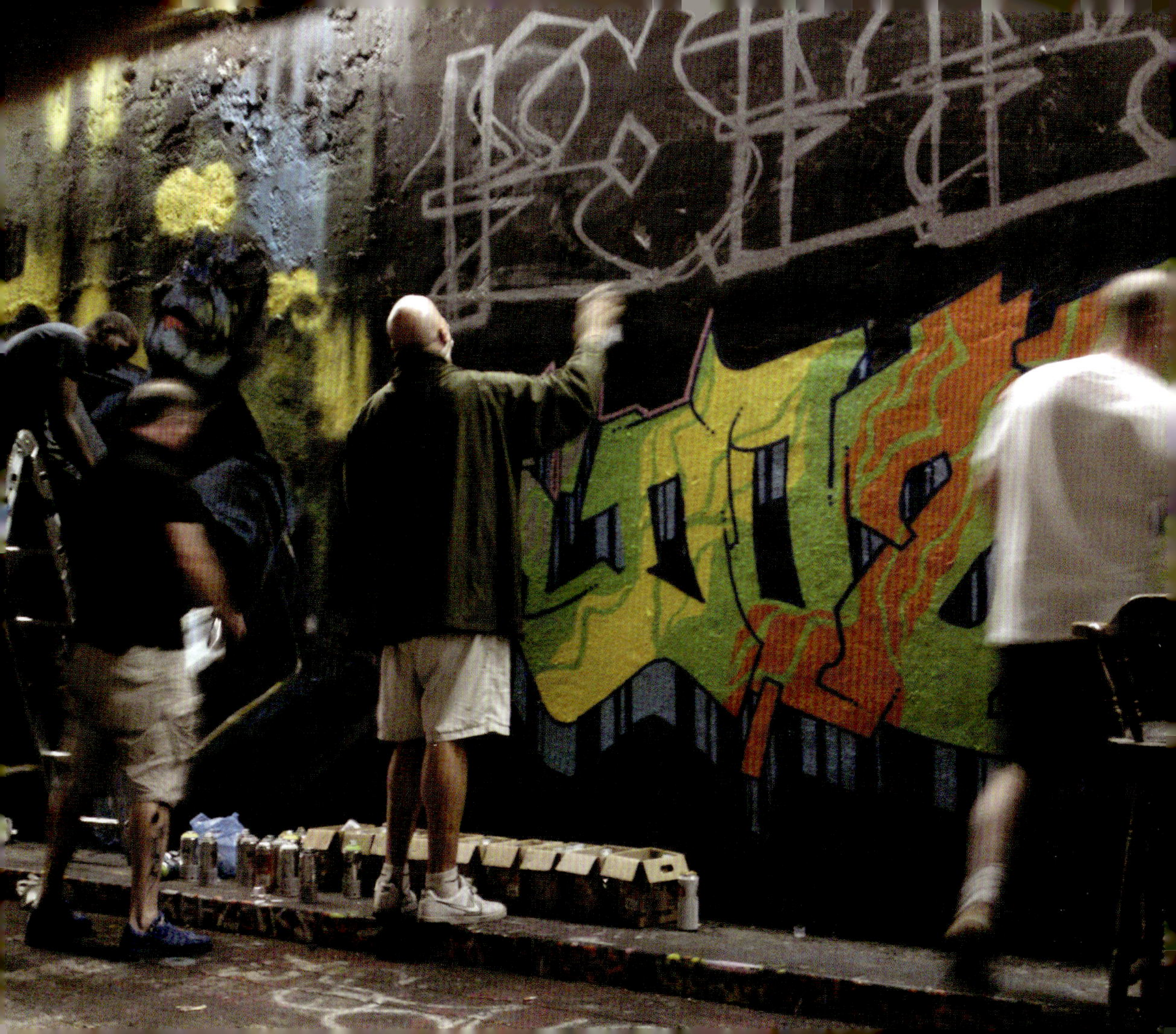

London's urban and cultural landscape has continually evolved, ever since the city walls were breached and the scope of the capital was established. The city spread out its many creative possibilities across a relentlessly developing environment, providing an ever-changing platform for graffiti writers and street artists.

Graffiti writers tend to direct their work to a minority – their peers, close knit friends and crews – within secluded halls of fame, or derelict and decaying wasted spaces. Street artists evolve from many diverse backgrounds. From art schools, design studios, or just a sincere desire to create, they have a need to express themselves and their personal creative endeavour. Either way, they are all communicating something creative.

"Being born and bred in London makes it an integral part of who I am. I know London intimately. I see it from above and below ground. For what to some might just be a busy high street, is to me a street full of history and multiple memories. The majority have no say in the way the city looks. In that way I've always found it a very controlling environment. For me, London's tall buildings have always felt intimidating, peering over you with their conservative architecture. For this reason, I like to conquer buildings as if they were mountains leaving my flag on top. It's a reminder to myself that I am free, and I am part of my city in a very real way." - **Mighty Mo**

Mighty Mo. Central London

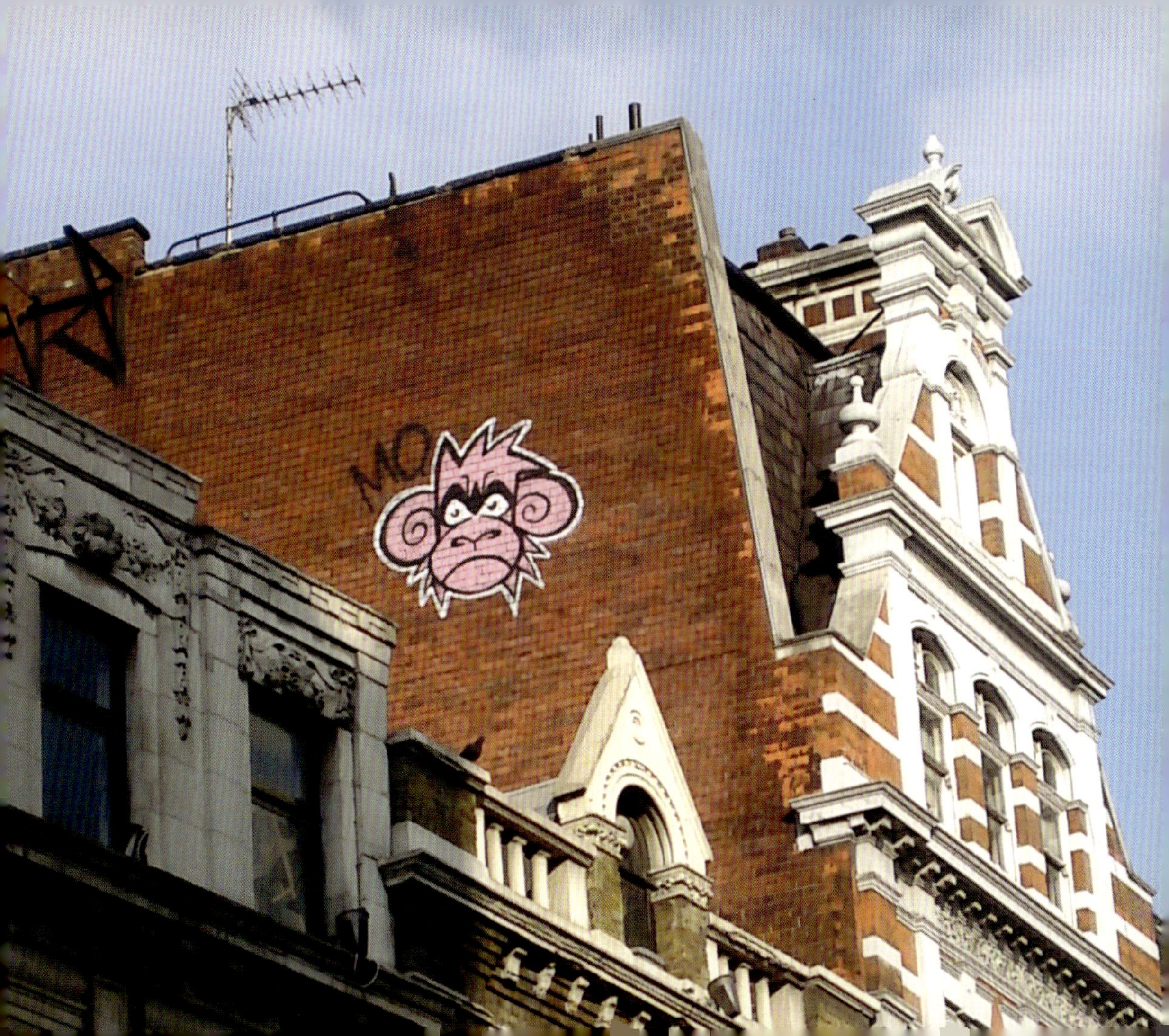
MO

LONDON GRAFFITI

Every city has its own unique landscape for the graffiti writers and street artists to interact with, but they all see the environment in a very different way. The nooks and crannies hidden within streets become dynamic canvases for them to play with, reconsider or leave their mark.

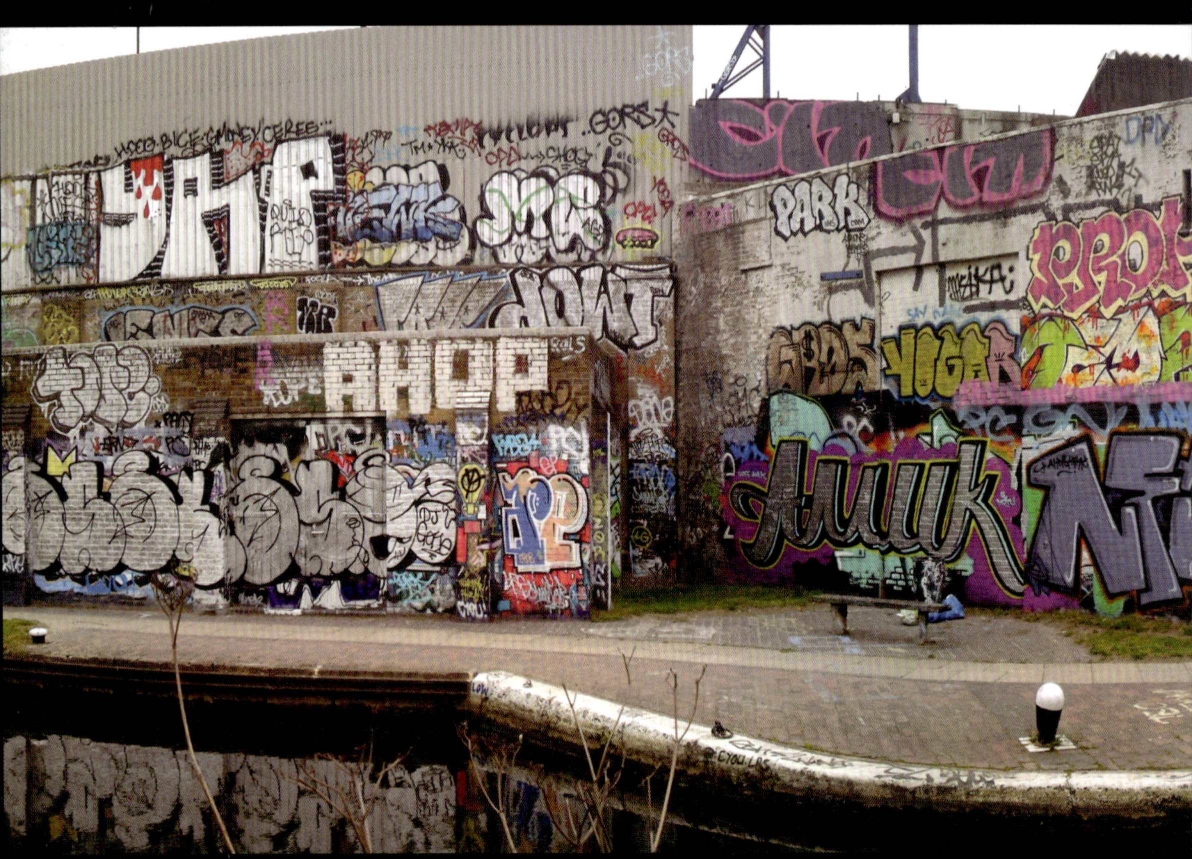

But London – one the greatest cities of all time – has long held a creative tradition and its artistic dynamics have served many different generations, and no doubt will continue to do so. The desire to 'get up' will always be a factor for our society…

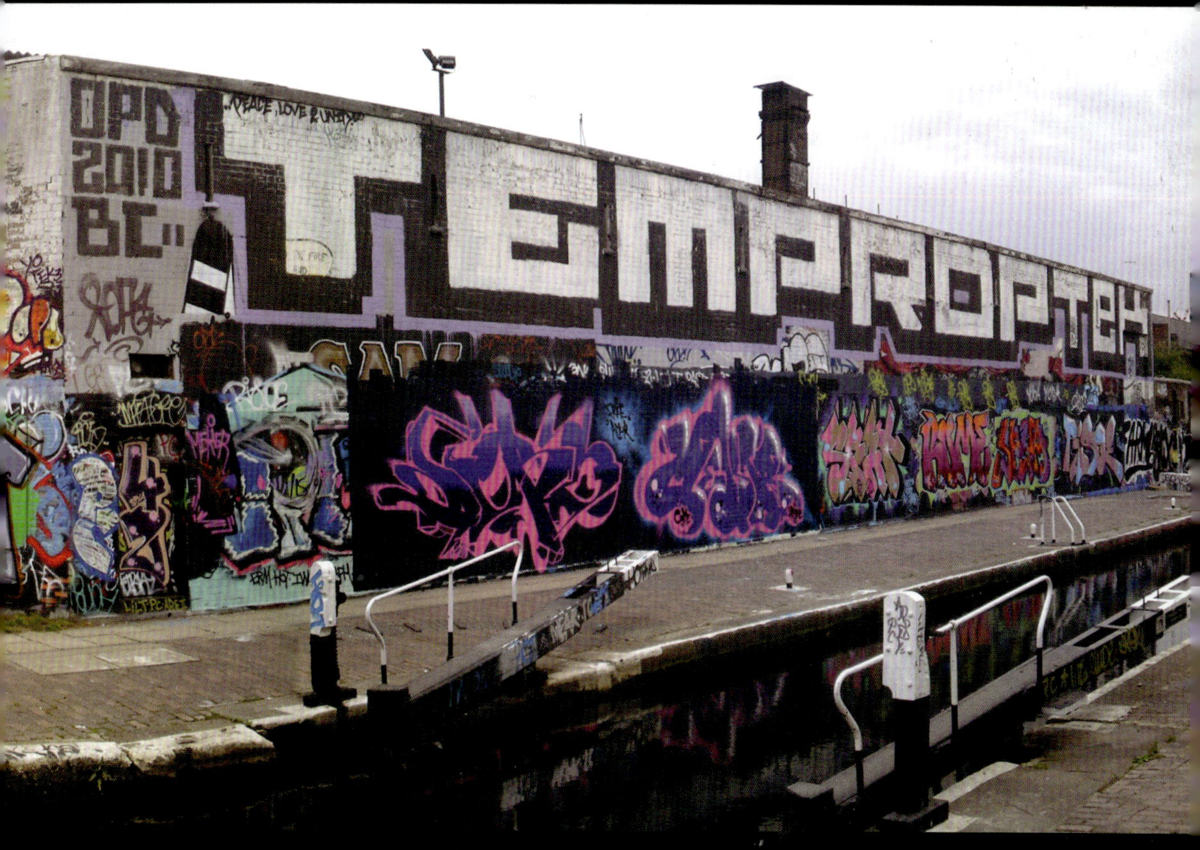

Regent's Canal, Hackney, East London

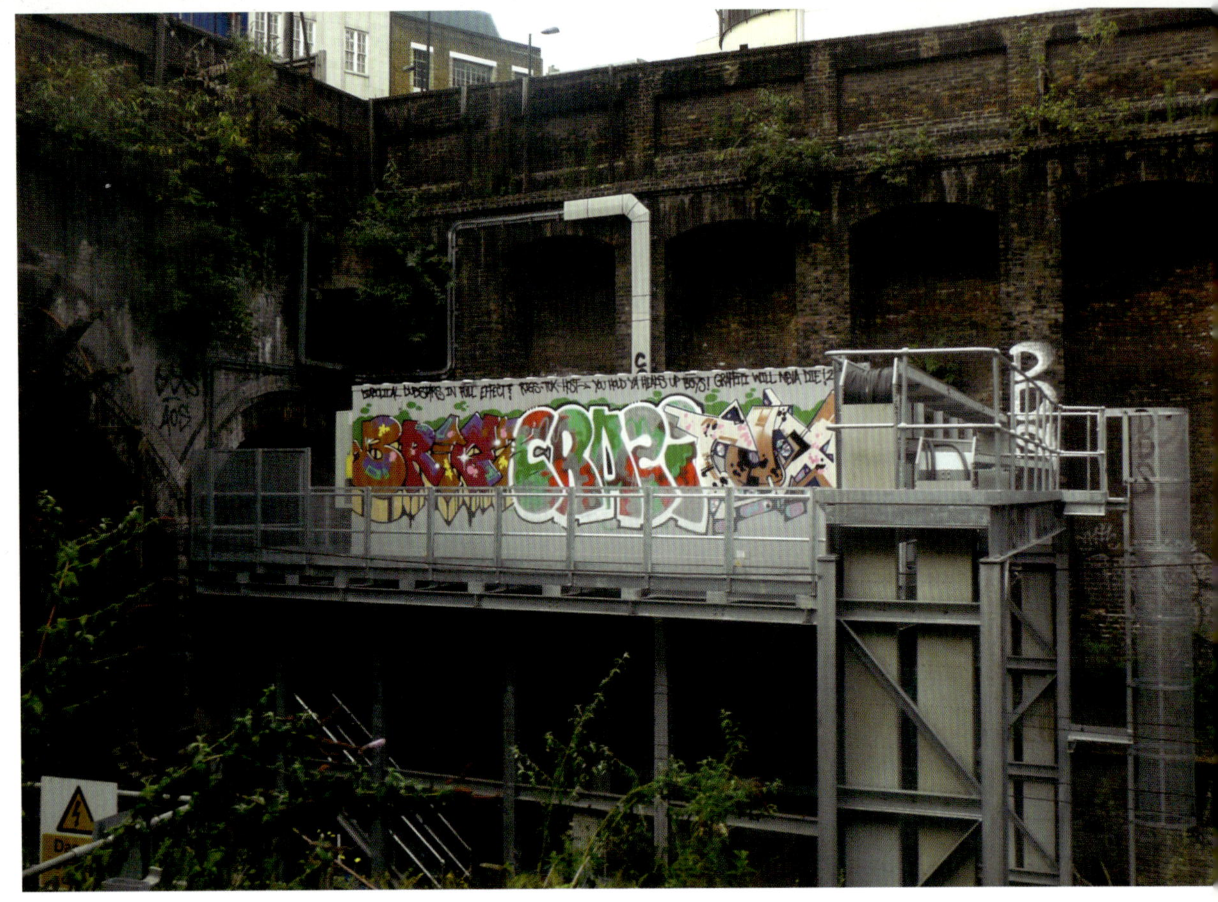

3Rigs, Crazi and Tox - This piece located between King's Cross and Farringdon train stations was one of the trickiest photos I have ever taken. It took me 16 attempts, travelling between the two stops, back and forth, over three lunch breaks. Armed with a DSLR and a compact camera, the best image was captured on my mobile phone!
The pieces are dedications to imprisoned writers. The use of '3' translates to free.

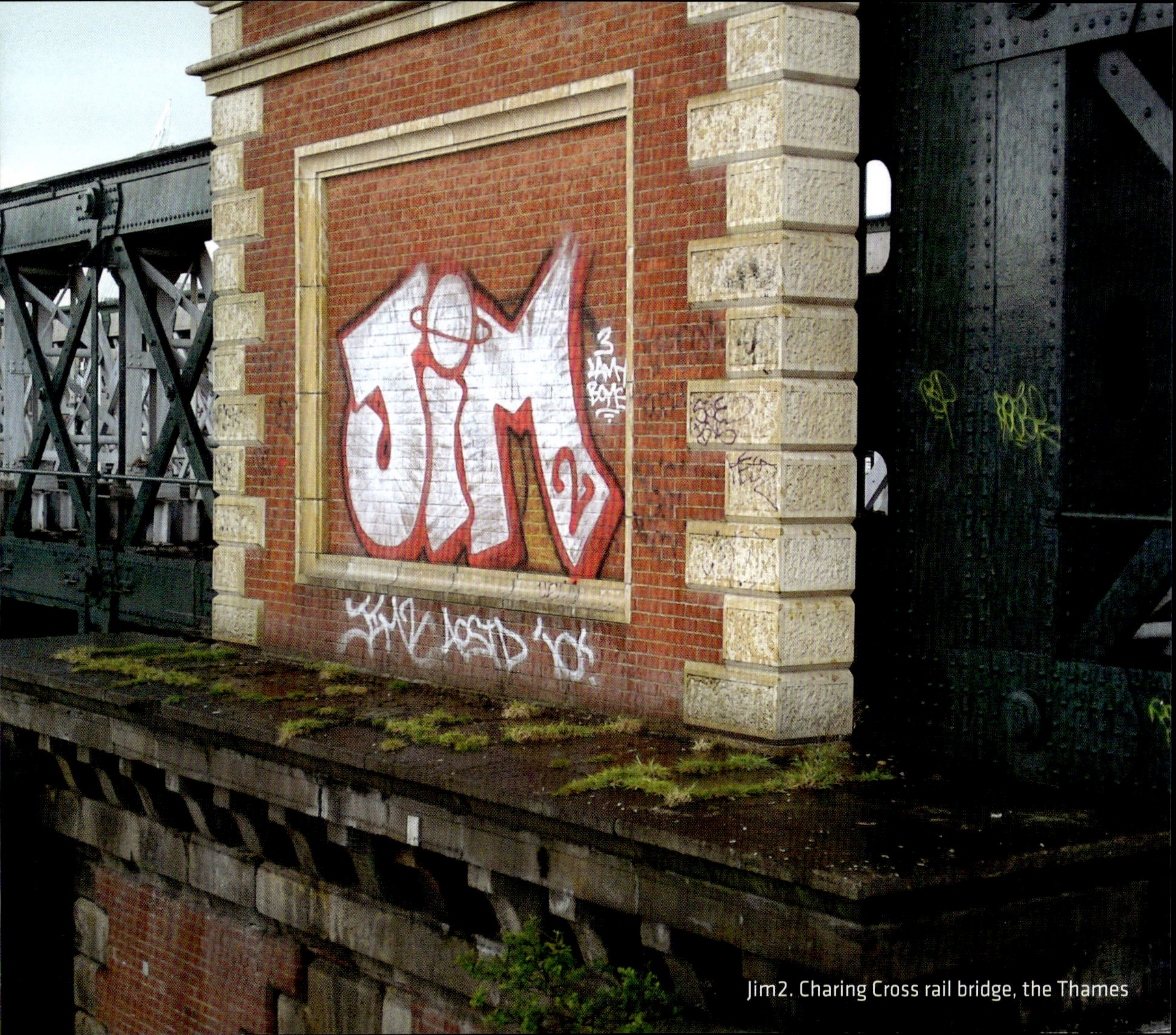

Jim2. Charing Cross rail bridge, the Thames

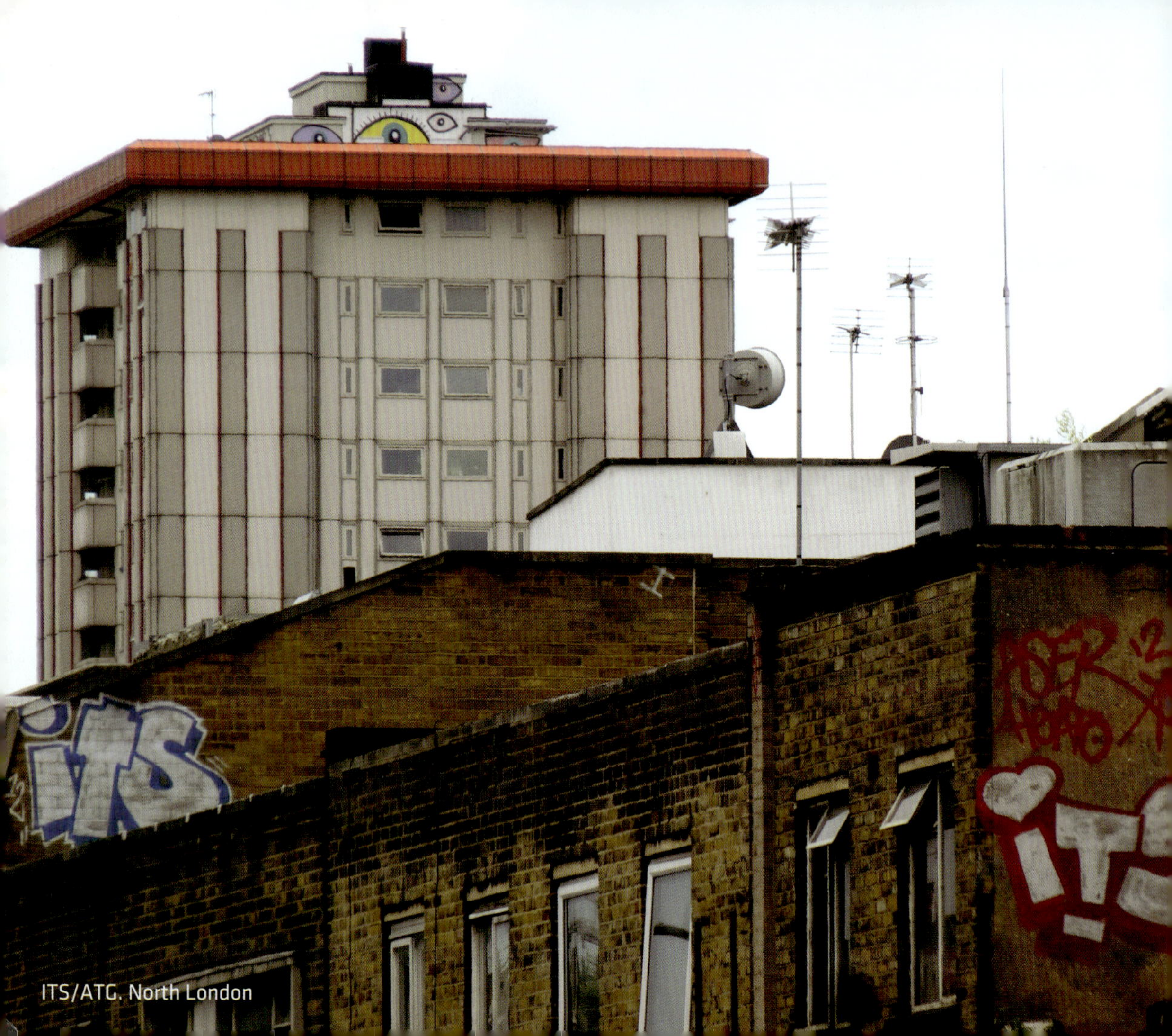

ITS/ATG. North London

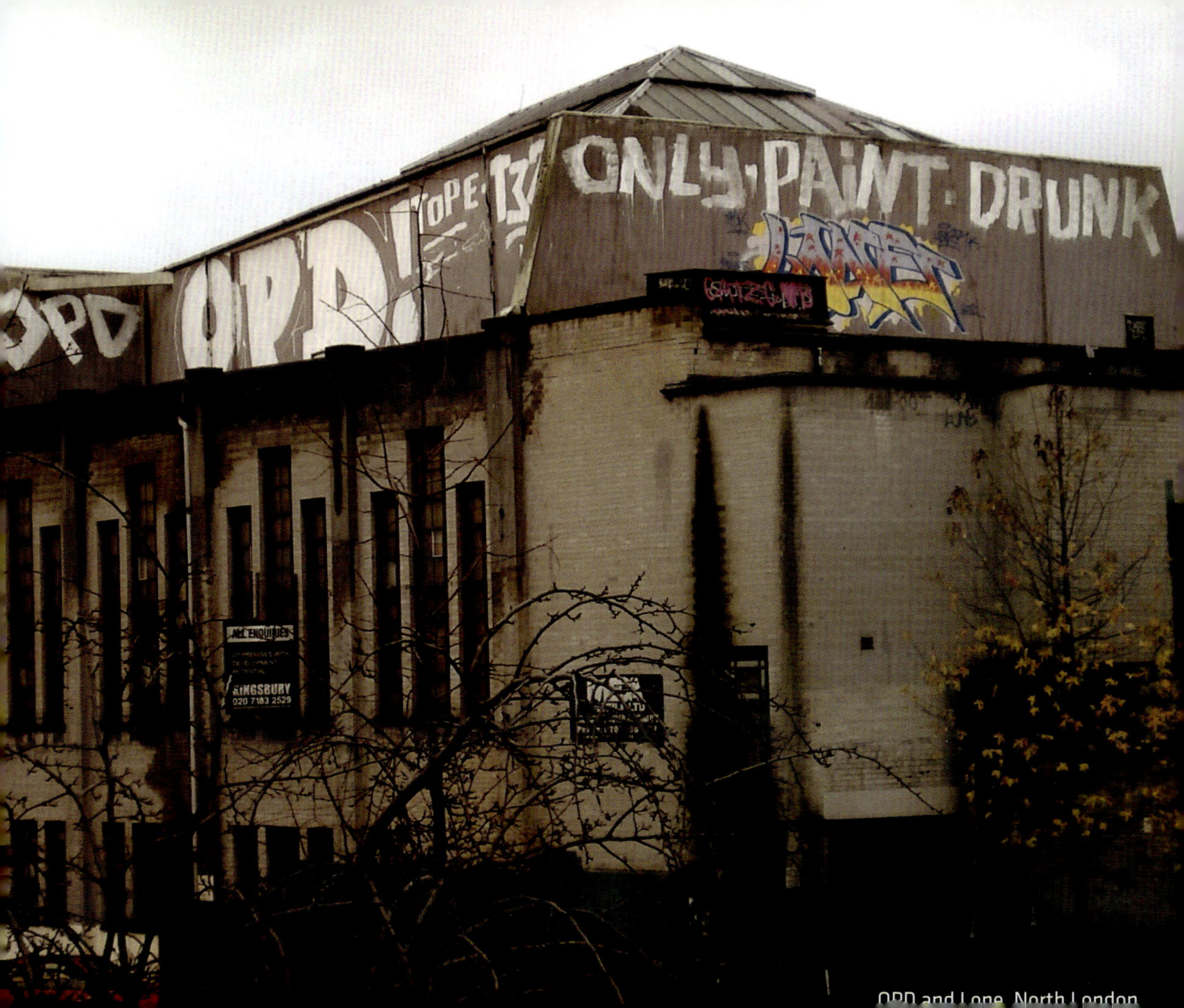

OPD and Lone, North London

LONDON HALLS OF FAME

The legal/tolerated halls of fame in London are a testing ground for graffiti writers. This is where they can invest time to develop their styles and techniques – from tags, 'throw-ups', letterforms and characters, to 'burners' and full productions. These halls are the birthplaces of many, very adept and talented graffiti writers and artists.

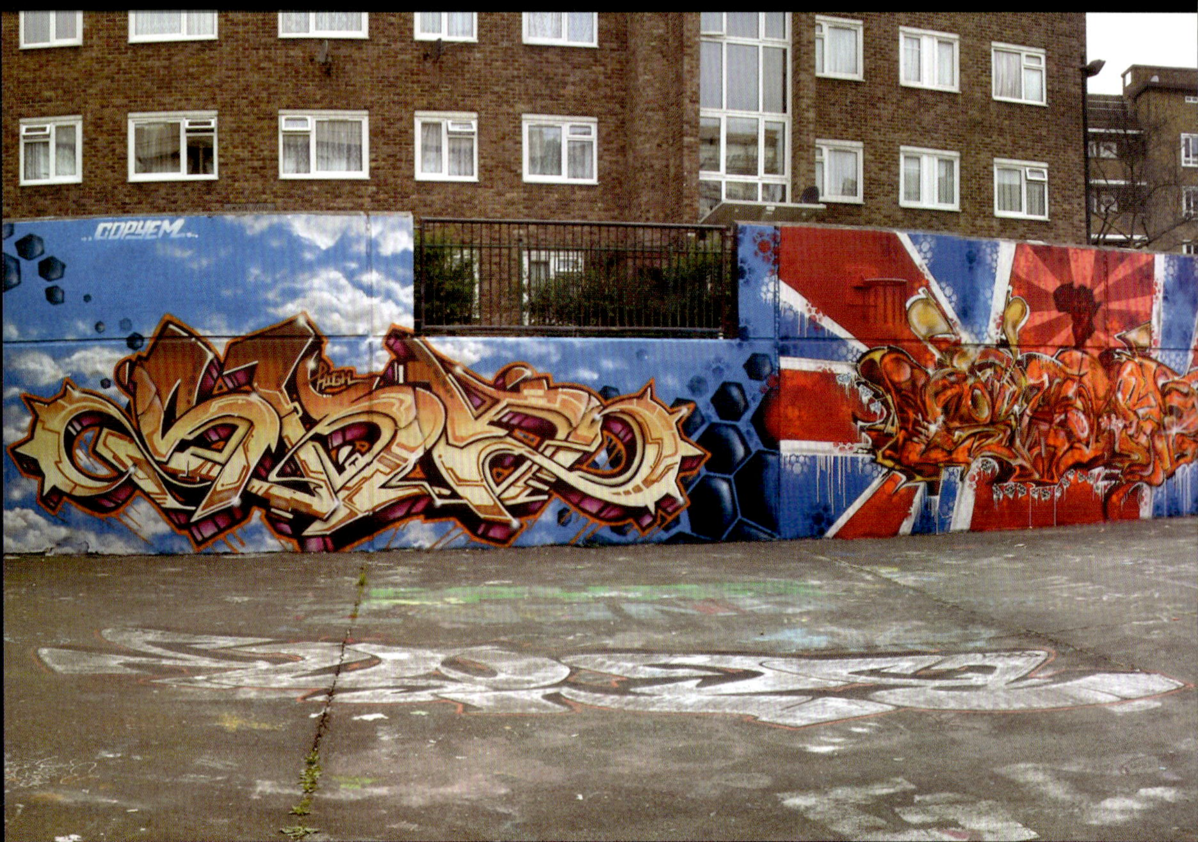

Sadly though, most of these spaces are not protected in the interests of the art, but being neglected by local councils, or eyed-up by greedy developers circling the skyline of London. Despite protests from local artists and residents, these important spaces are being redeveloped into sterilised play-spaces, privatised housing and desolate car parks.

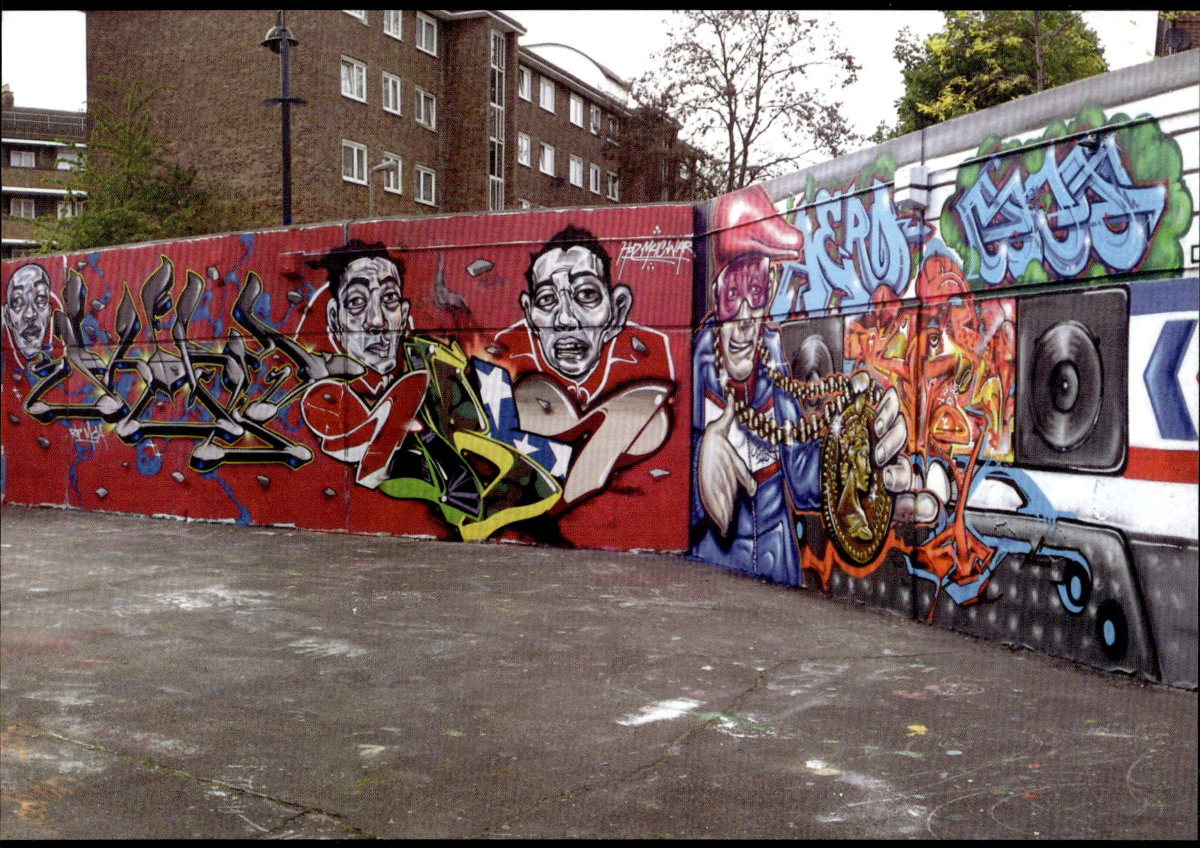

SkyHigh, Solo One, Phorm, Sares, Tizer, Aero and Mr Cenz. Stockwell, South London

THE PIT, WEST LONDON (DEMOLISHED)

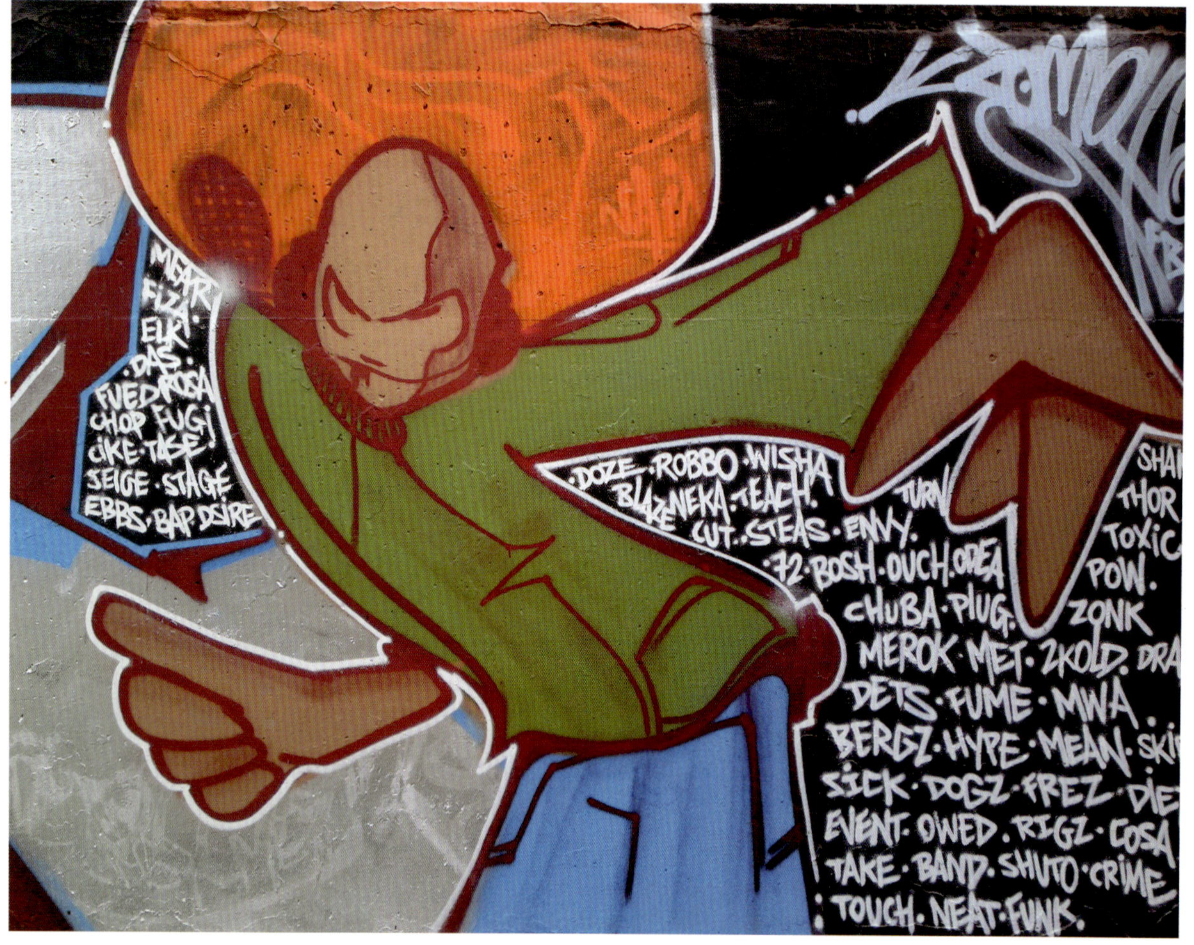

“London means edgy cool with a twist of cultures and adventure.” - **Zomby**

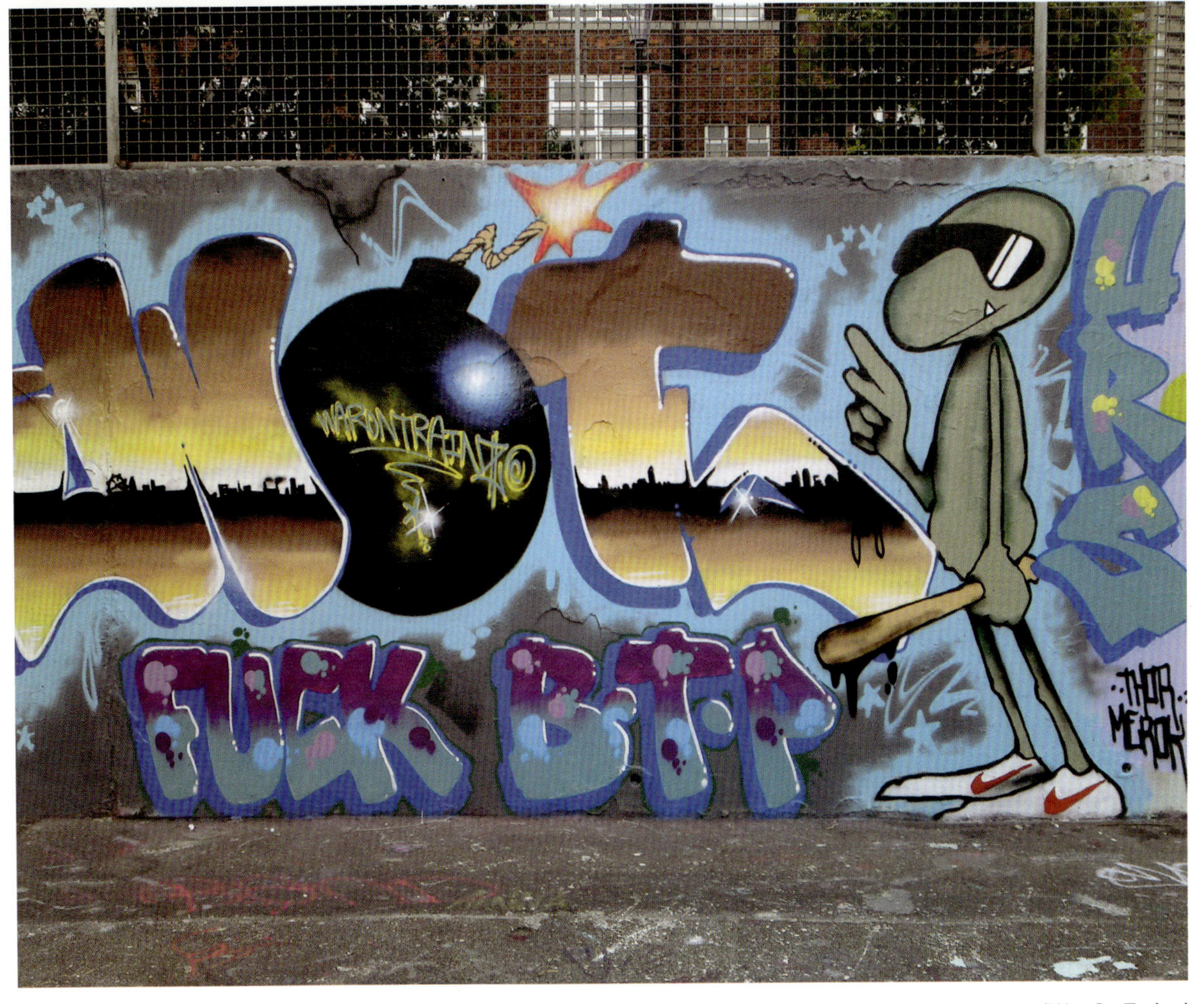

'War On Trainz'

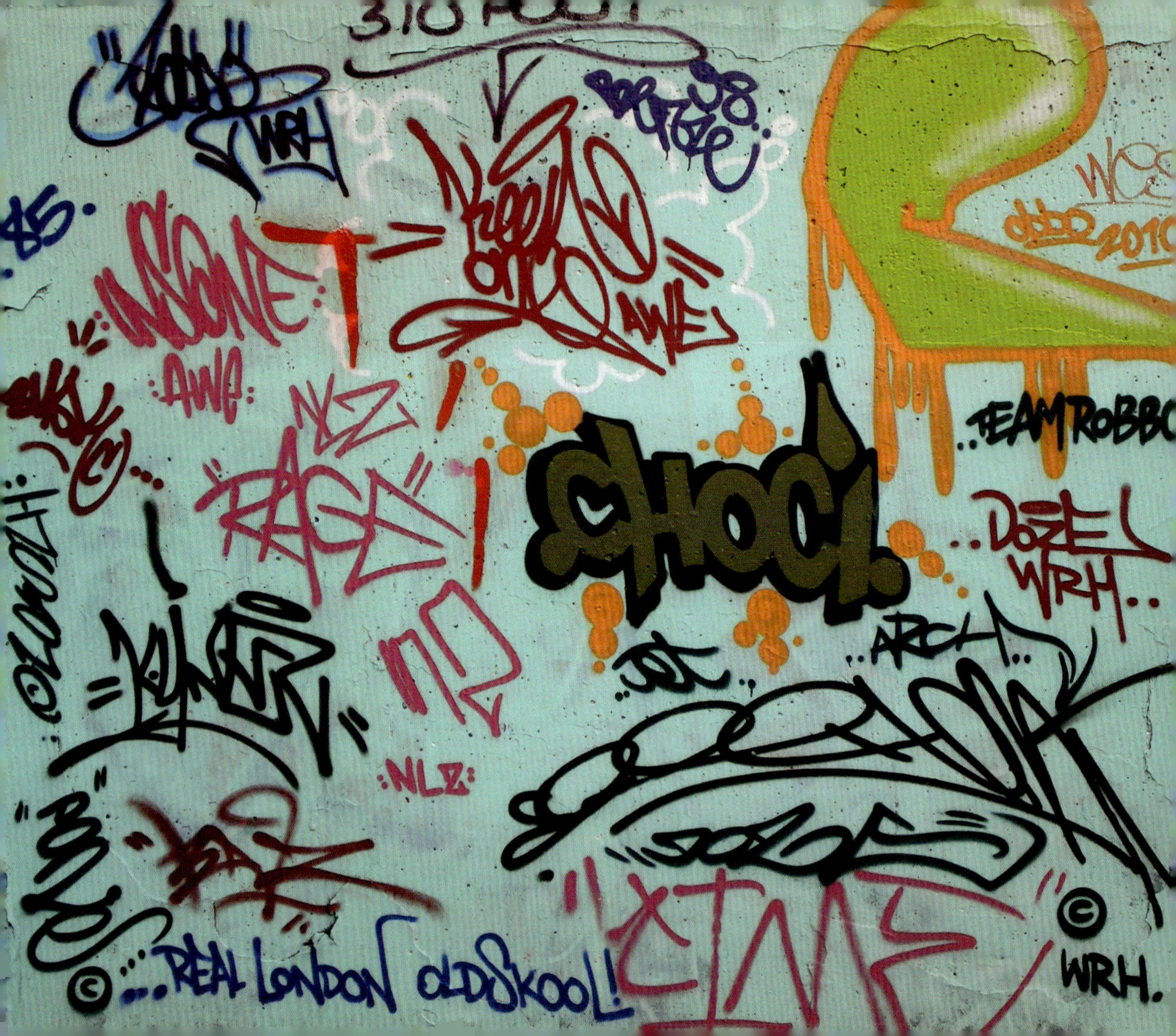

CHOC!
TEAM ROBBO
DOZE
WRH
ARCH
NLZ
AWE
...REAL LONDON OLDSKOOL!
WRH.

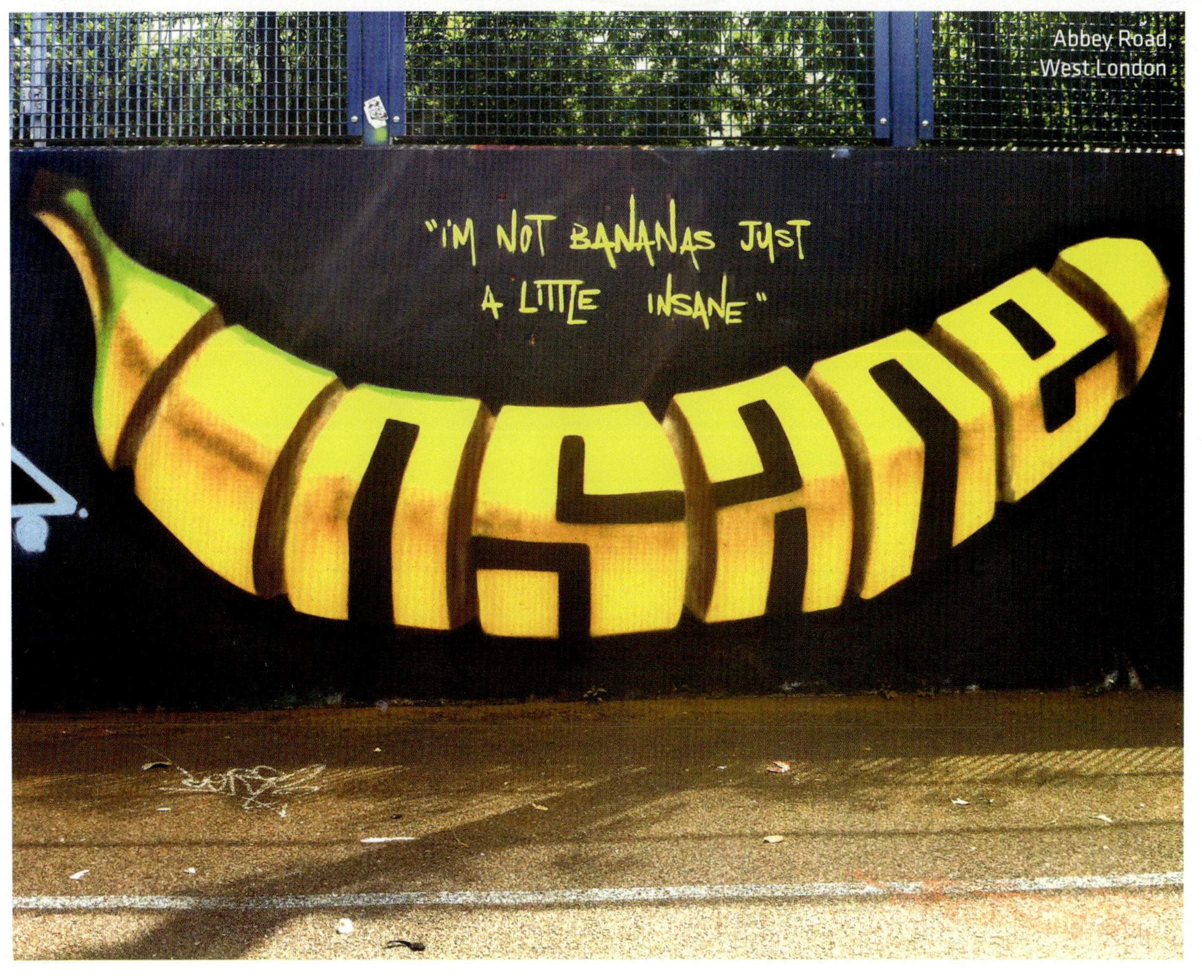

"This is not New York and I am not a New Yorker - I am from London and this ever-changing, beautiful, organic city is for me where all of this started. It's where I draw my inspiration and it's where I call home" - **Insane FM & NLZ**

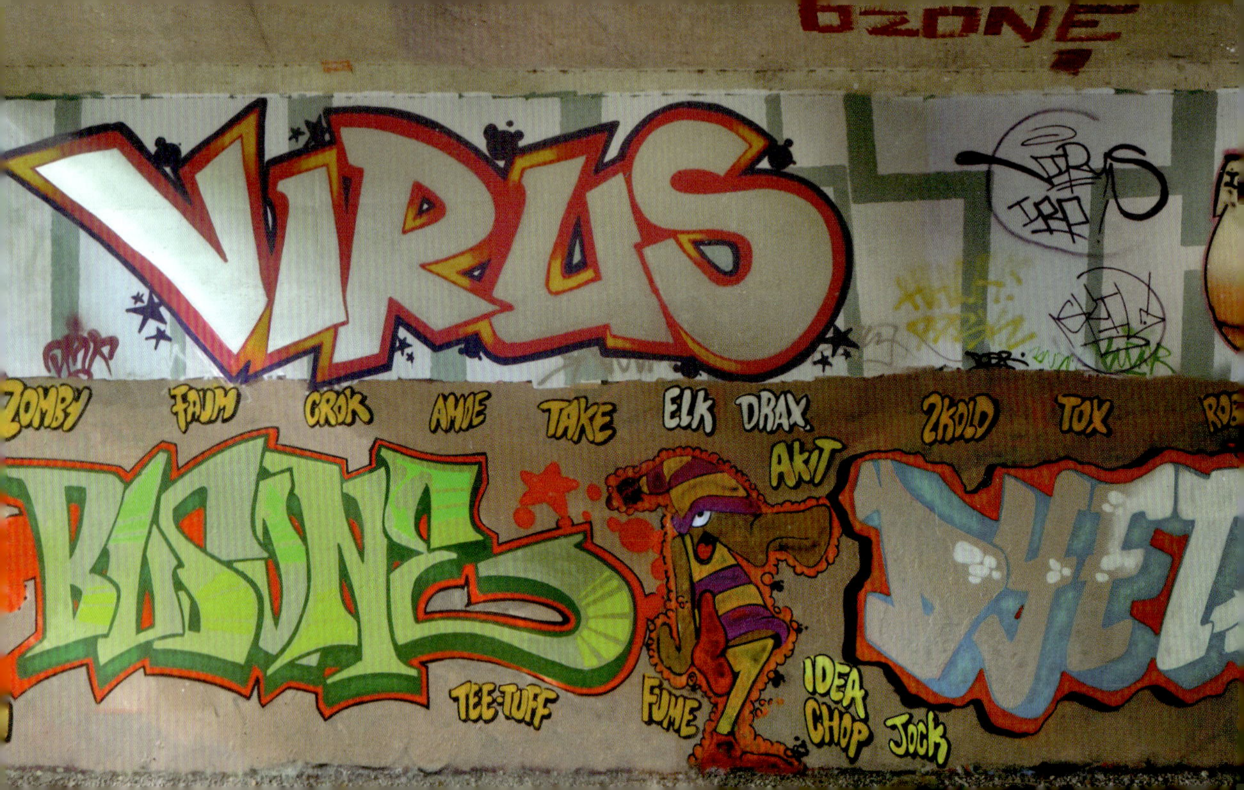
VIRUS
ZOMBY
FAUM
CROK
TAKE
ELK
DRAX
2KOLD
TOX
AKIT
TEE-TUFF
FUME
IDEA
CHOP
JOCK

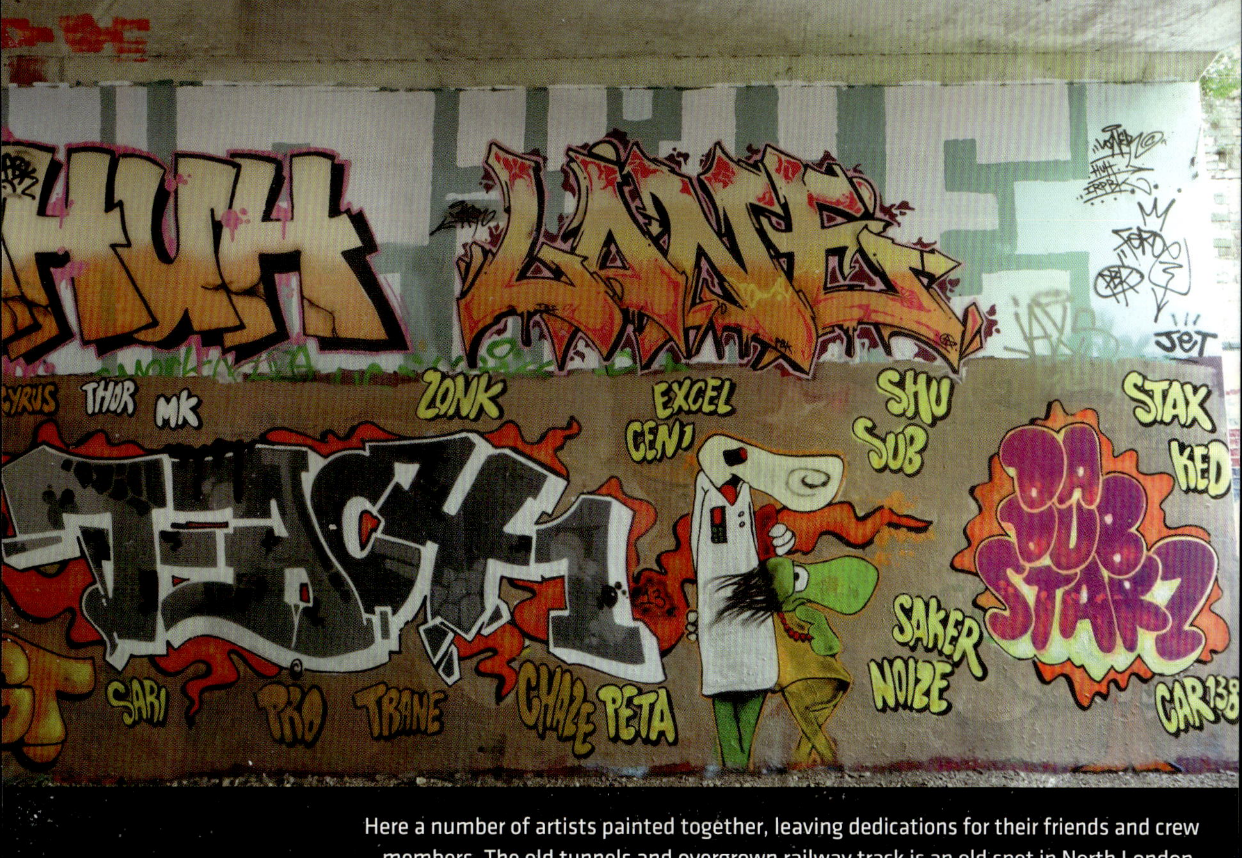

Here a number of artists painted together, leaving dedications for their friends and crew members. The old tunnels and overgrown railway track is an old spot in North London.
Ozone RIP, Virus, Uhuh, Lone, Busone, Dyet, Teach1 and DDS

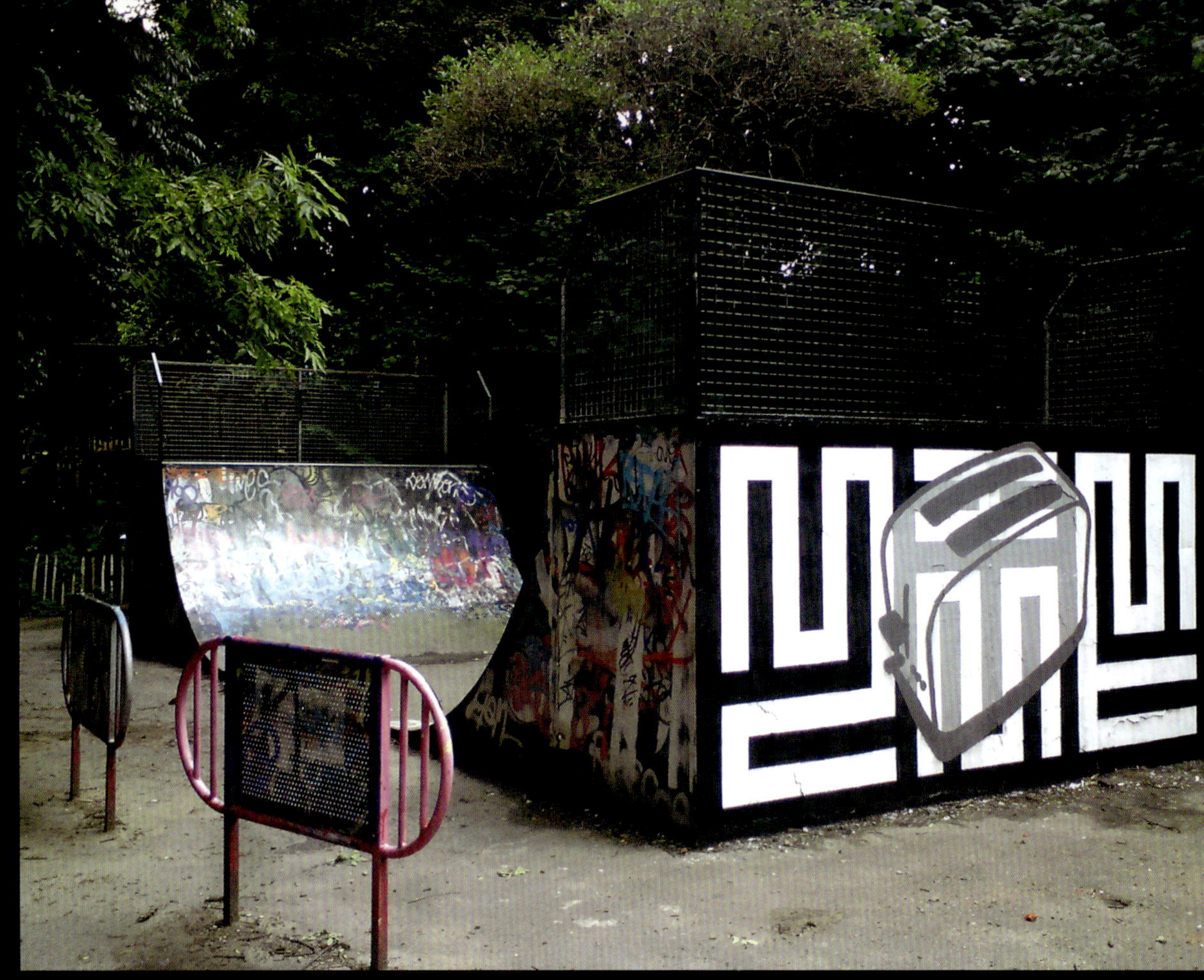

Zime (SOL) and Toaster. 2008

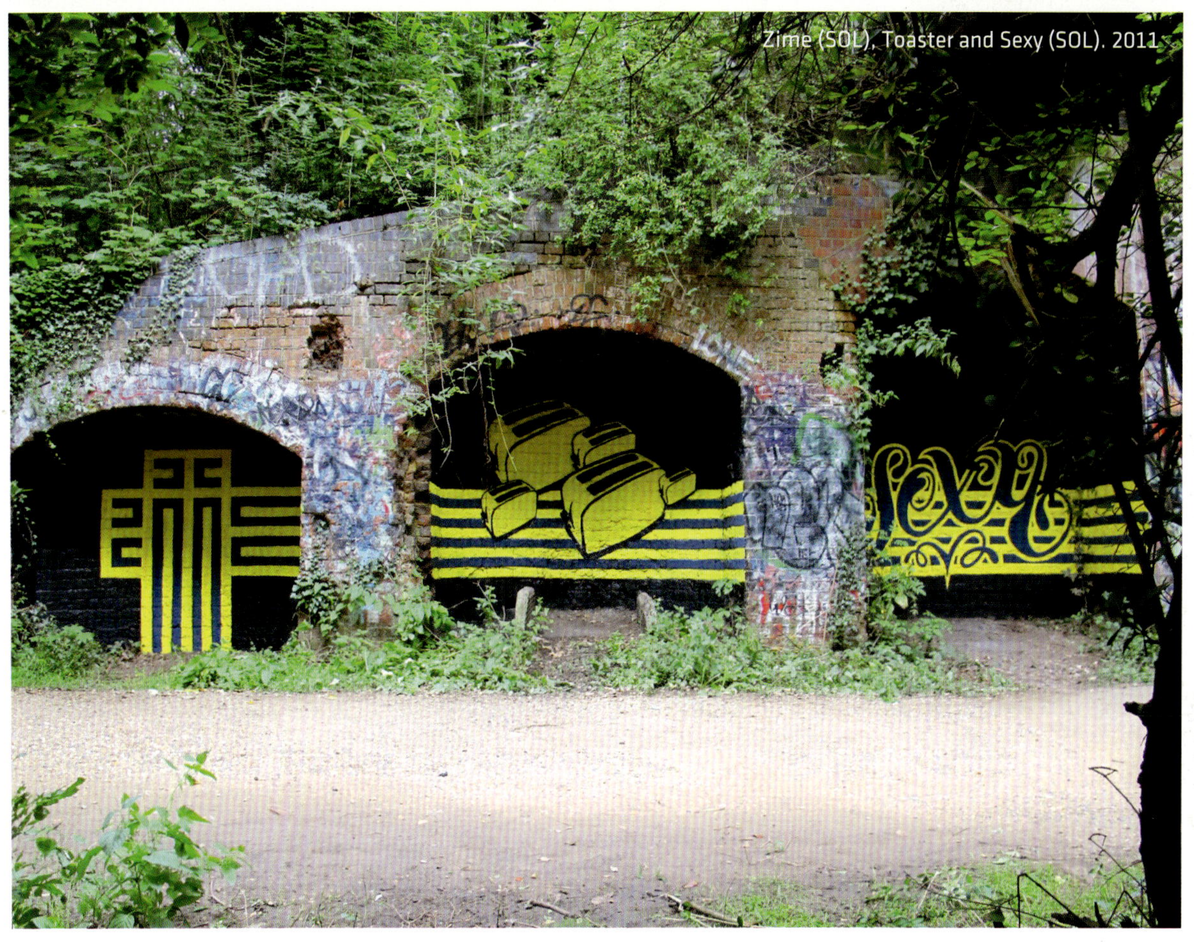

Zime (SOL), Toaster and Sexy (SOL). 2011

"Parkland Walk is my favourite spot in London. Especially where Crouch End railway station was located. Next to the old platforms are some great old brick walls with arches. Rough walls, so not easy to paint with emulsion paint and rollers, but I like walls with character. Plus, the natural setting is really beautiful." - **Zime - SOL crew**

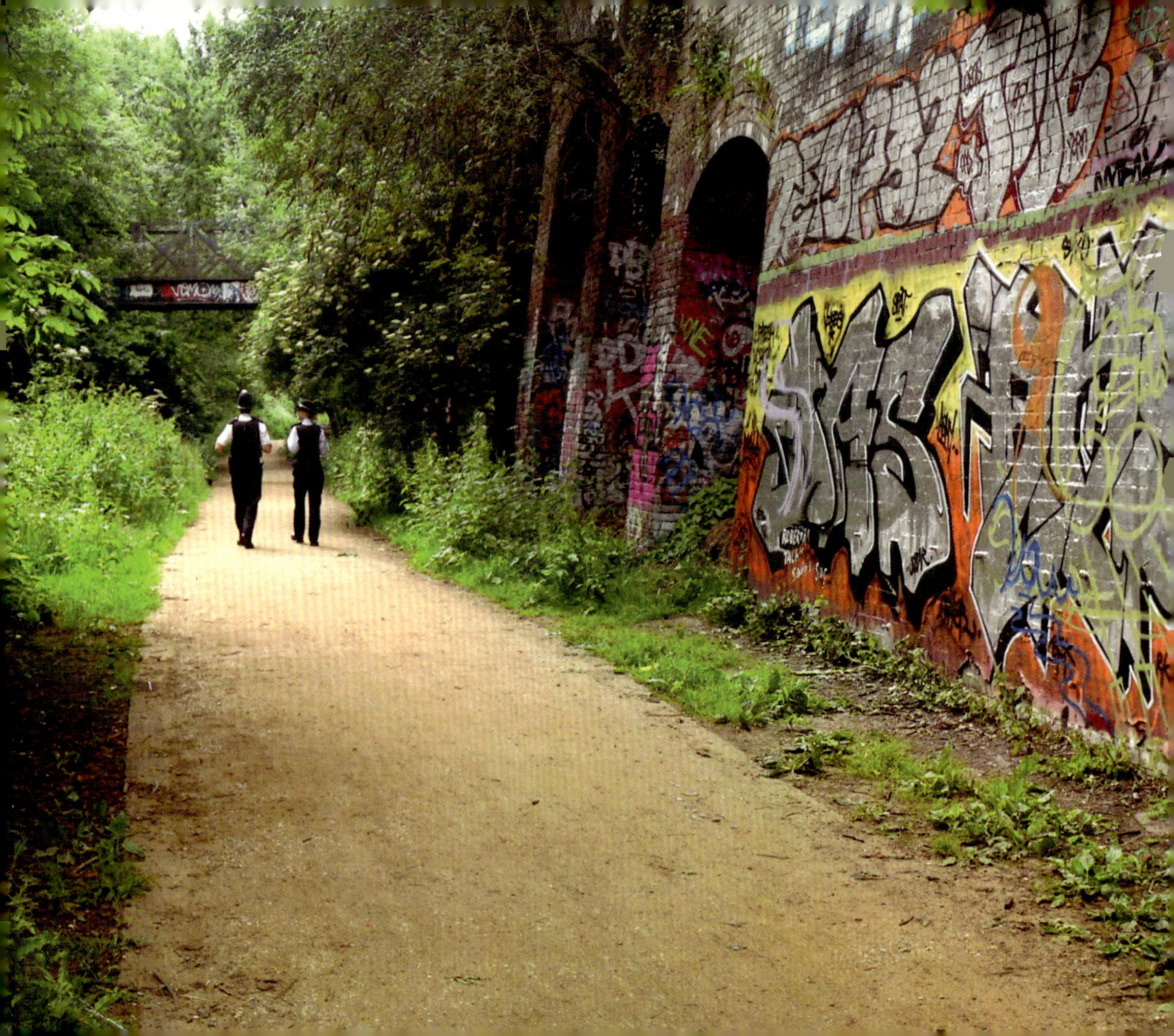

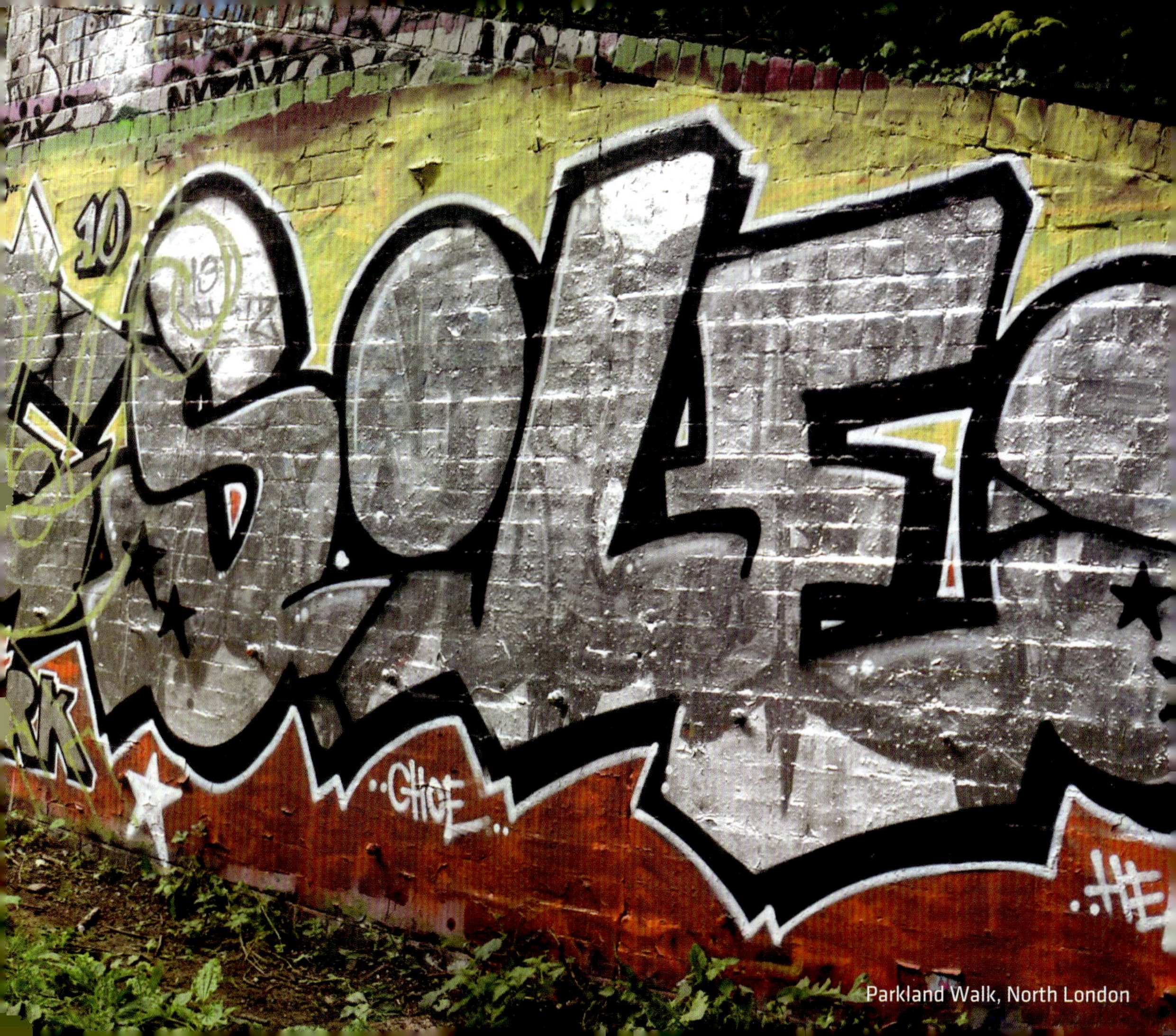

Parkland Walk, North London

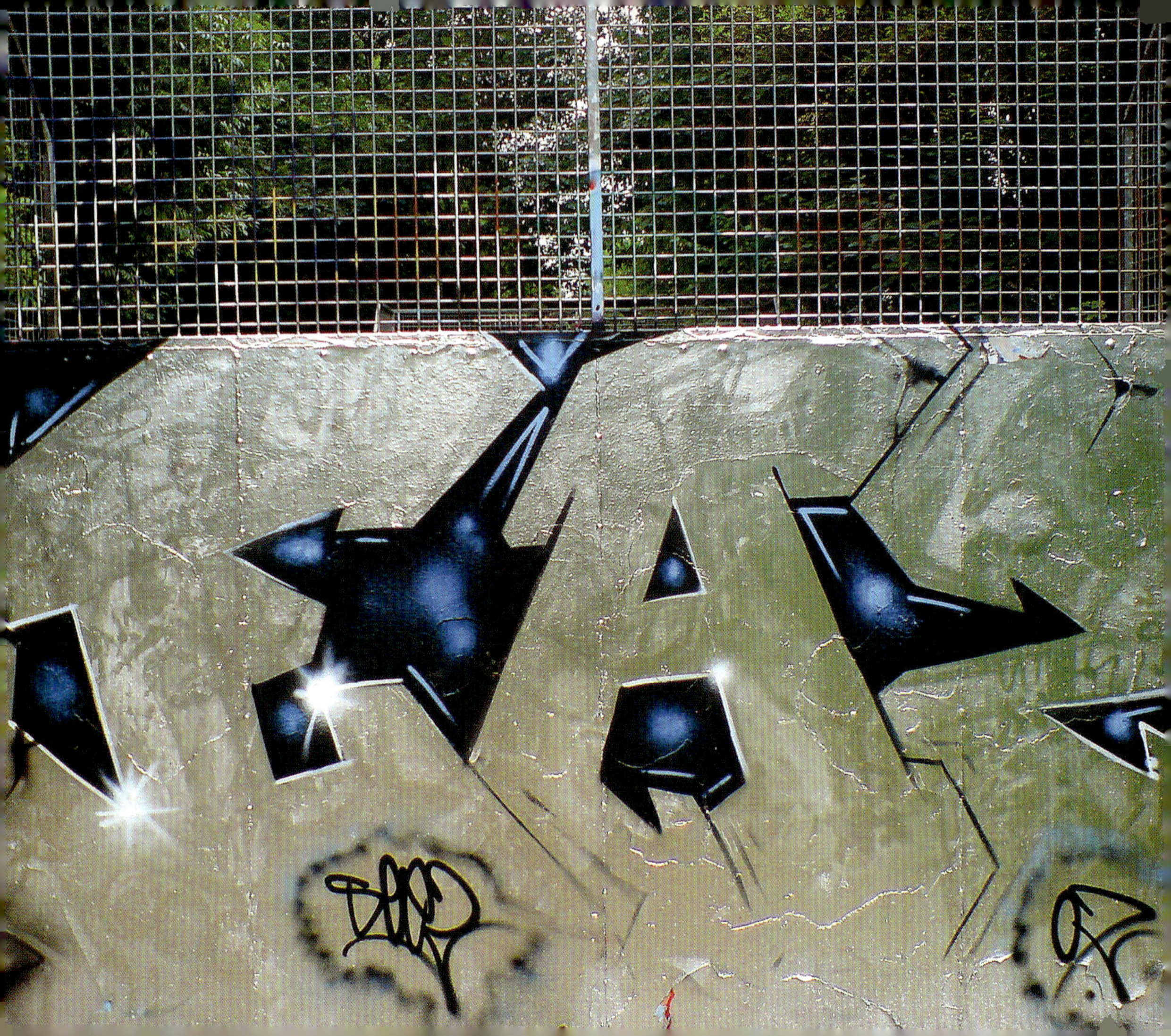

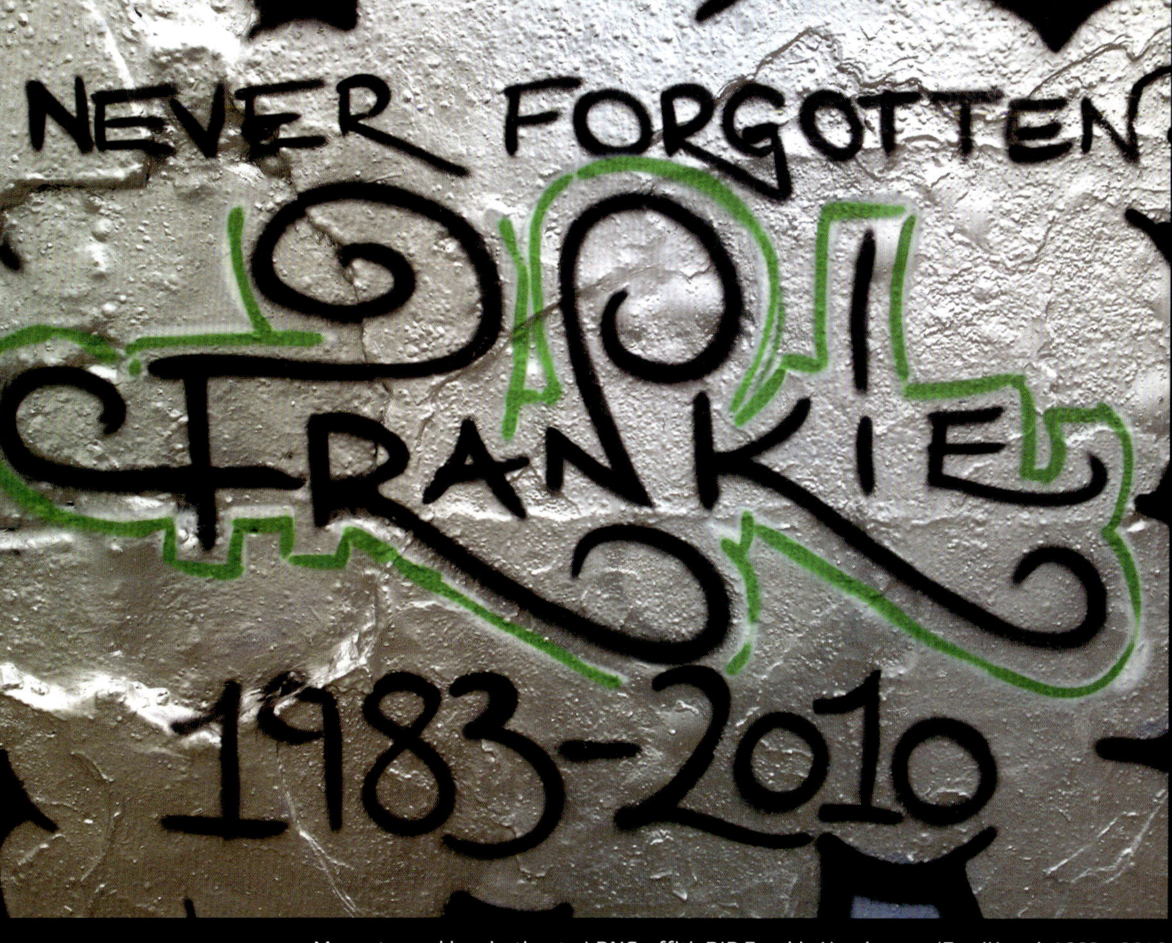

My mate, and inspiration to LDNGraffiti. RIP Frankie Hemingway 'Eaz/Kong', 1983 - 2010

‘THE SPOT’, MARKFIELD PARK, NORTH LONDON

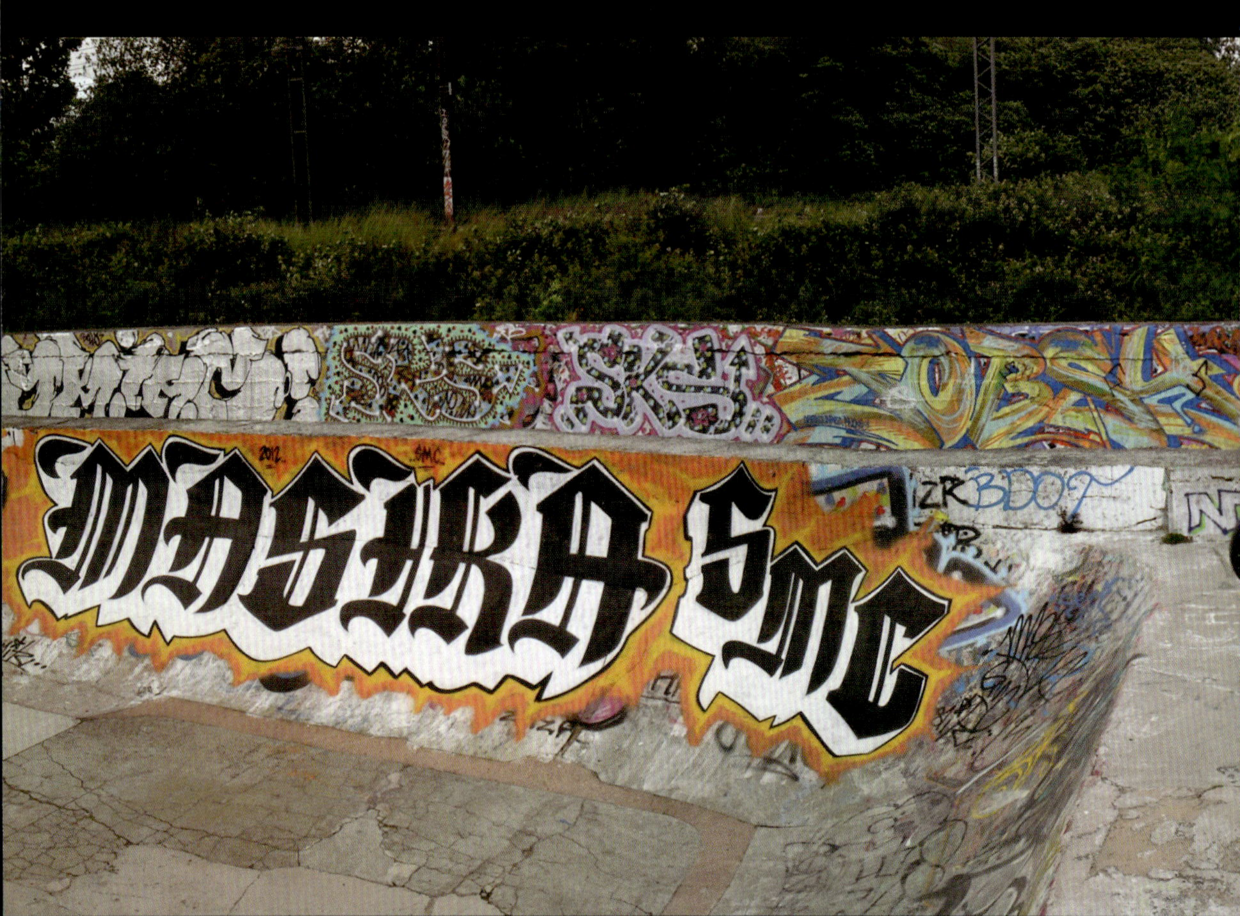

Located next to a railway line, this spot in North London is painted regularly and has been for many years.

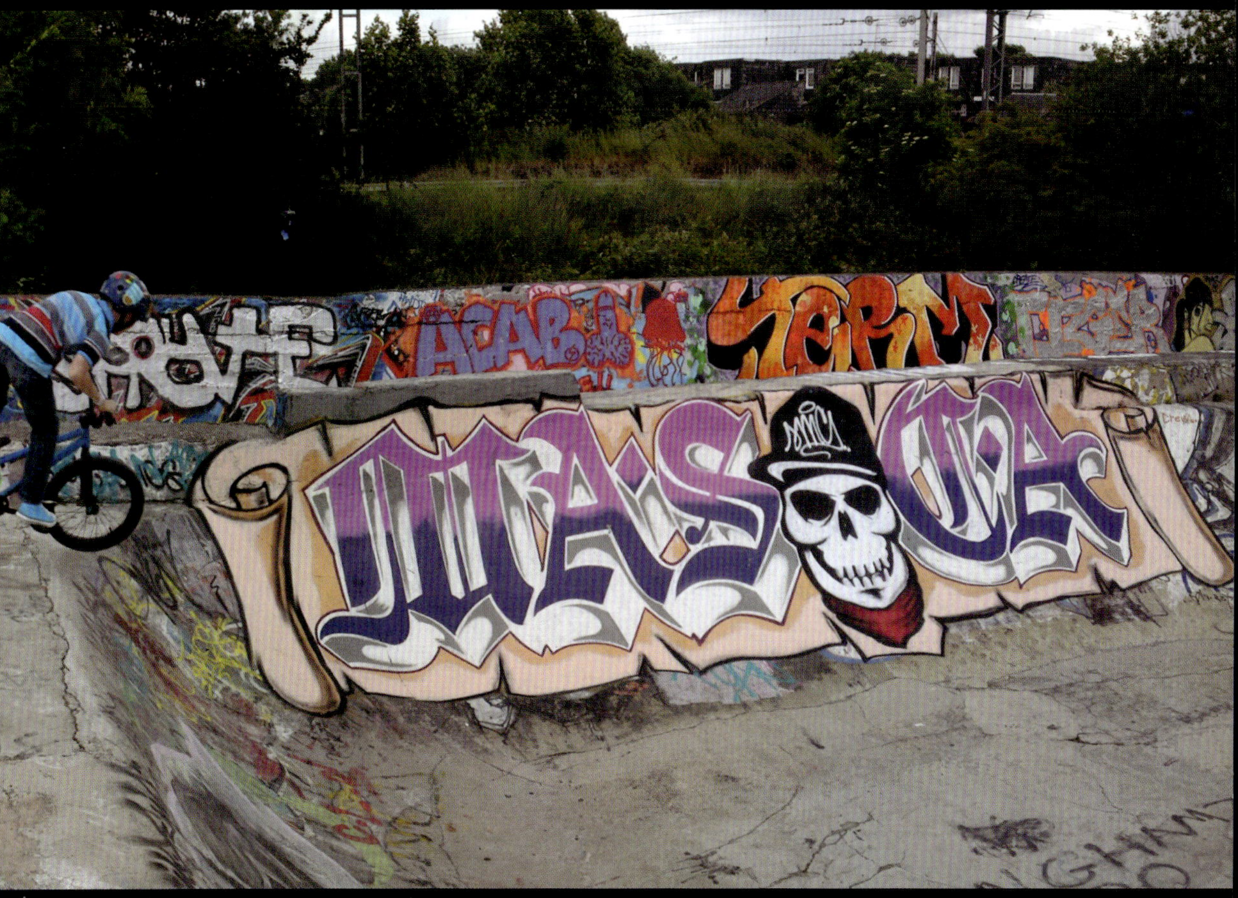

"London is a place of intricacy and intrigue, of variety and wonder, of choice and chance, but above all, there are places for people to live and to interact, to produce, to consume and to generate ideas." - **Masica SMC**

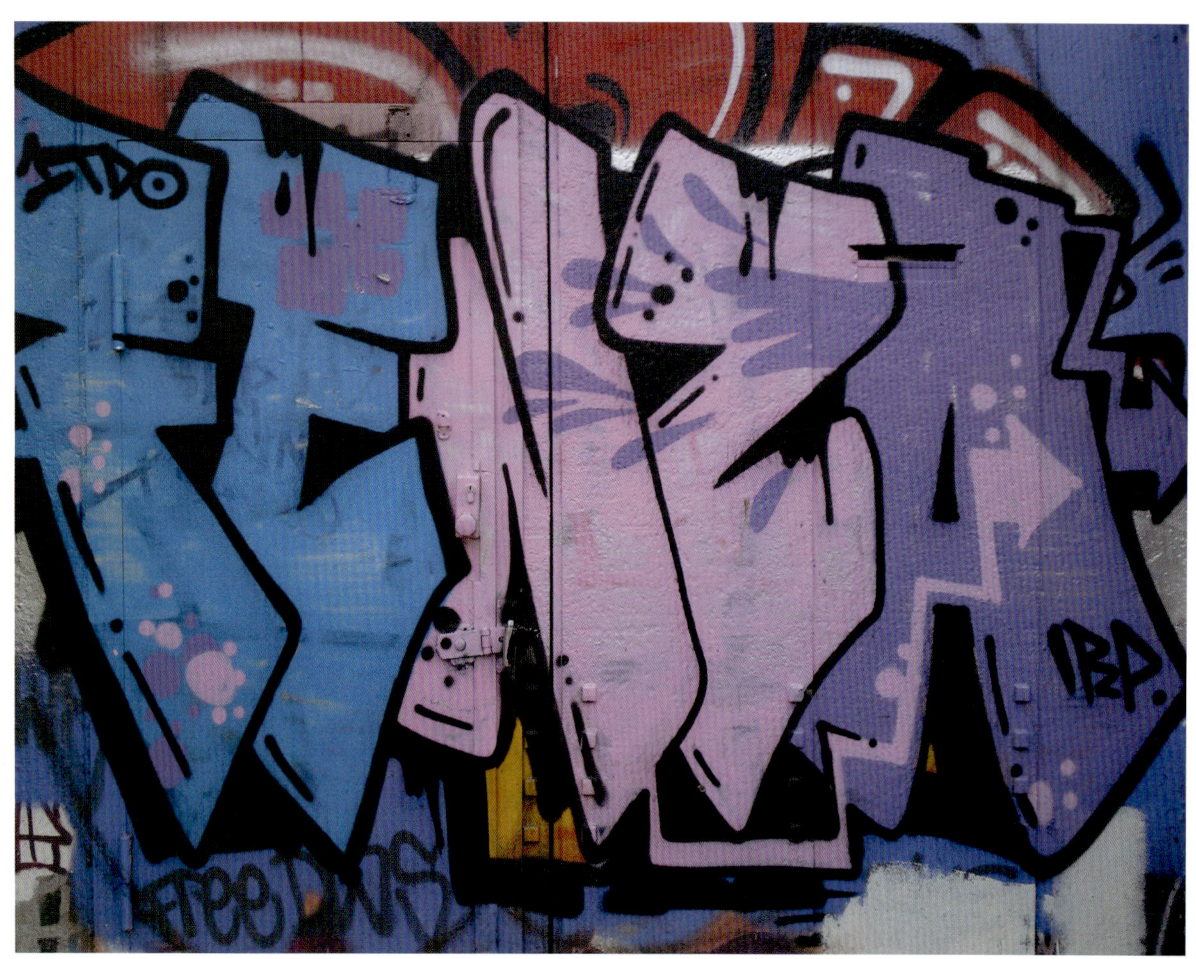

“A lot of madness, a lot of graff.” – **Fenza**

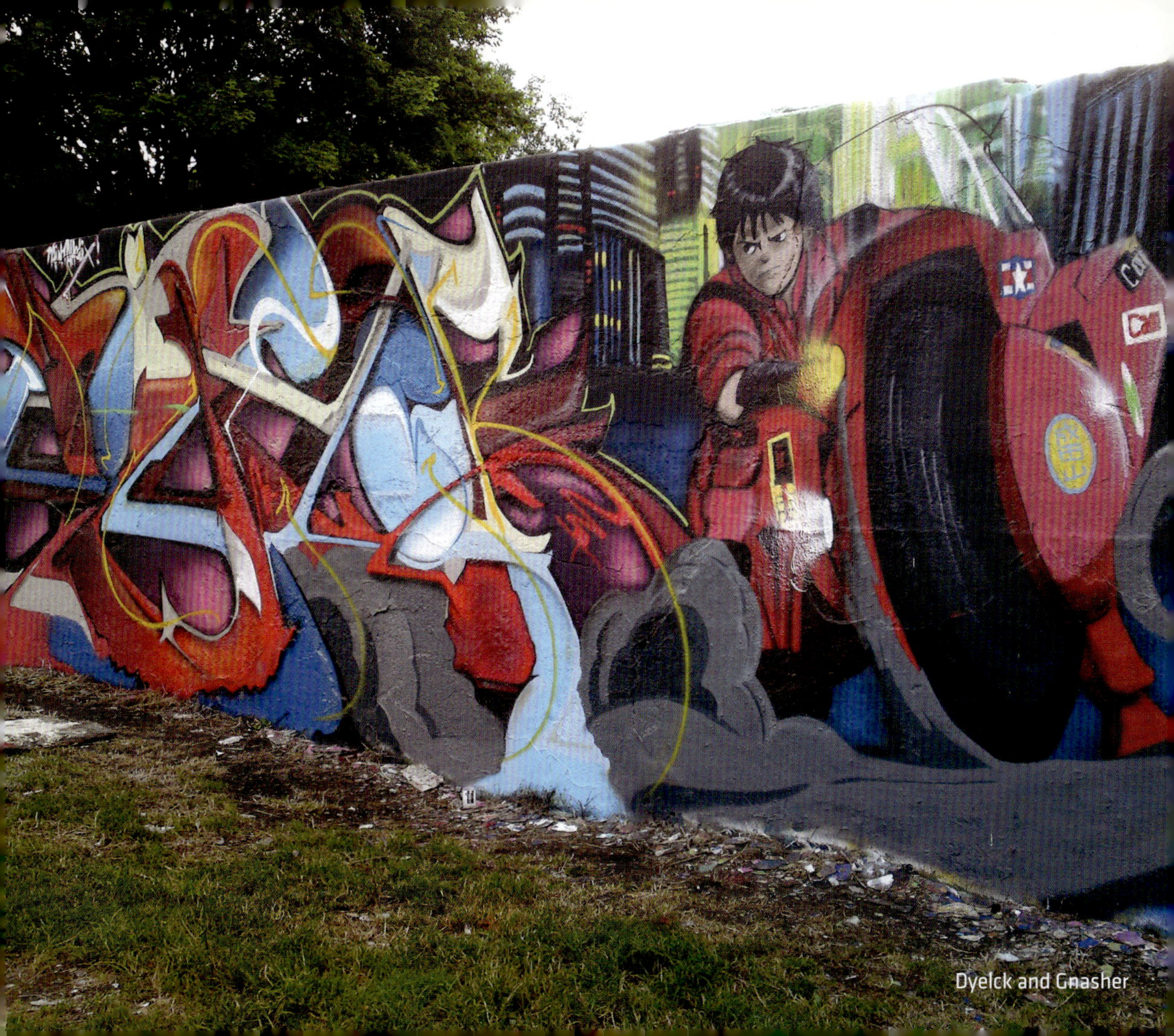
Dyelck and Gnasher

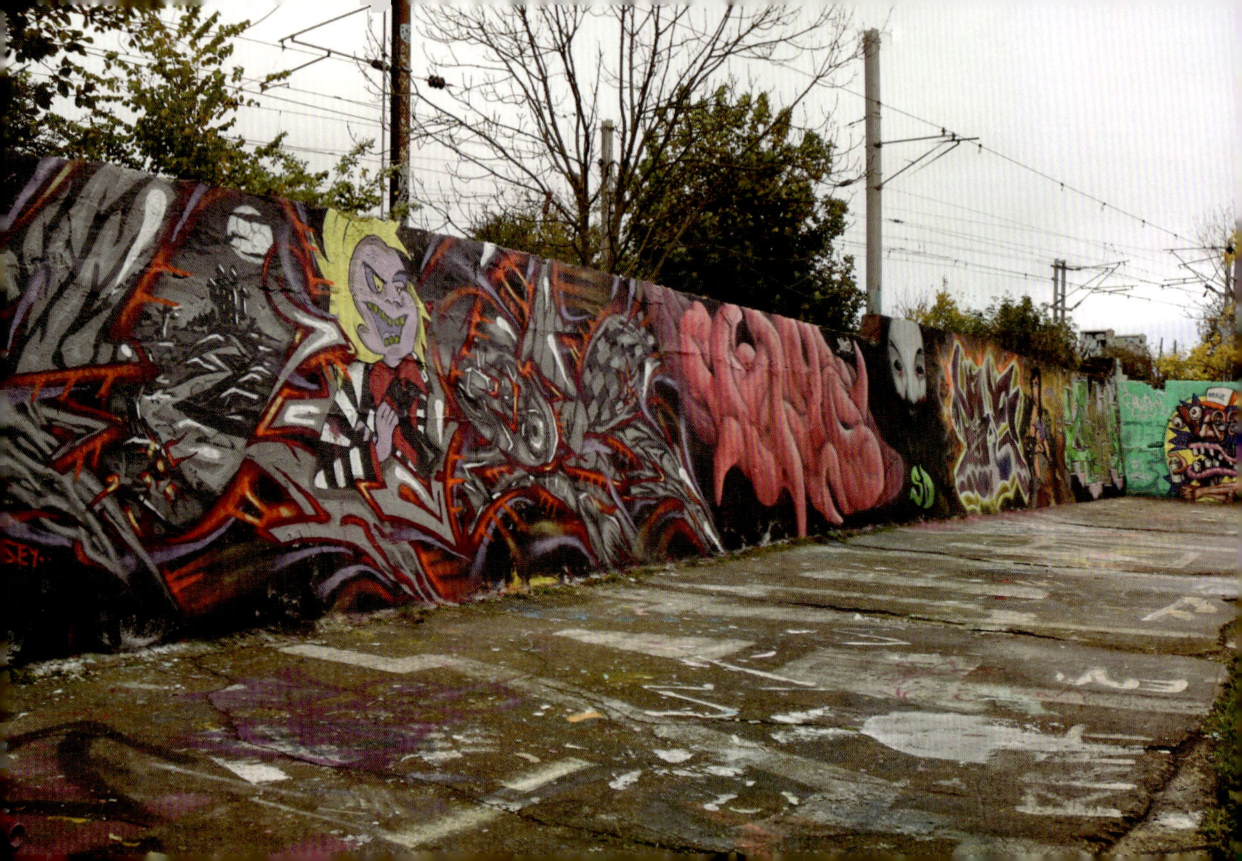

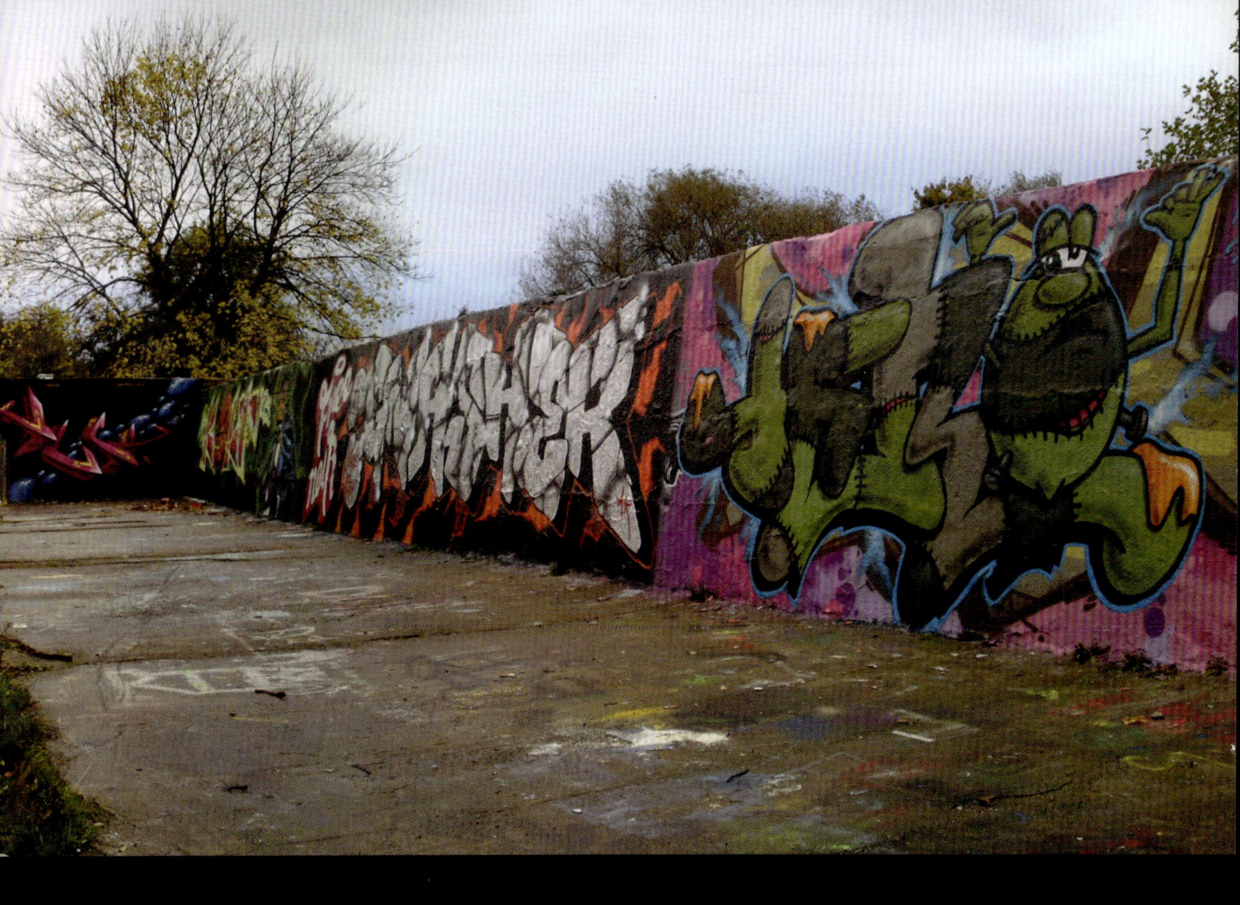

Faver, Blavoe, Basik, Roe, Pedro, Daps, Brave1, Hush, Colt45, Gnasher, Neyec, Hero32 and more

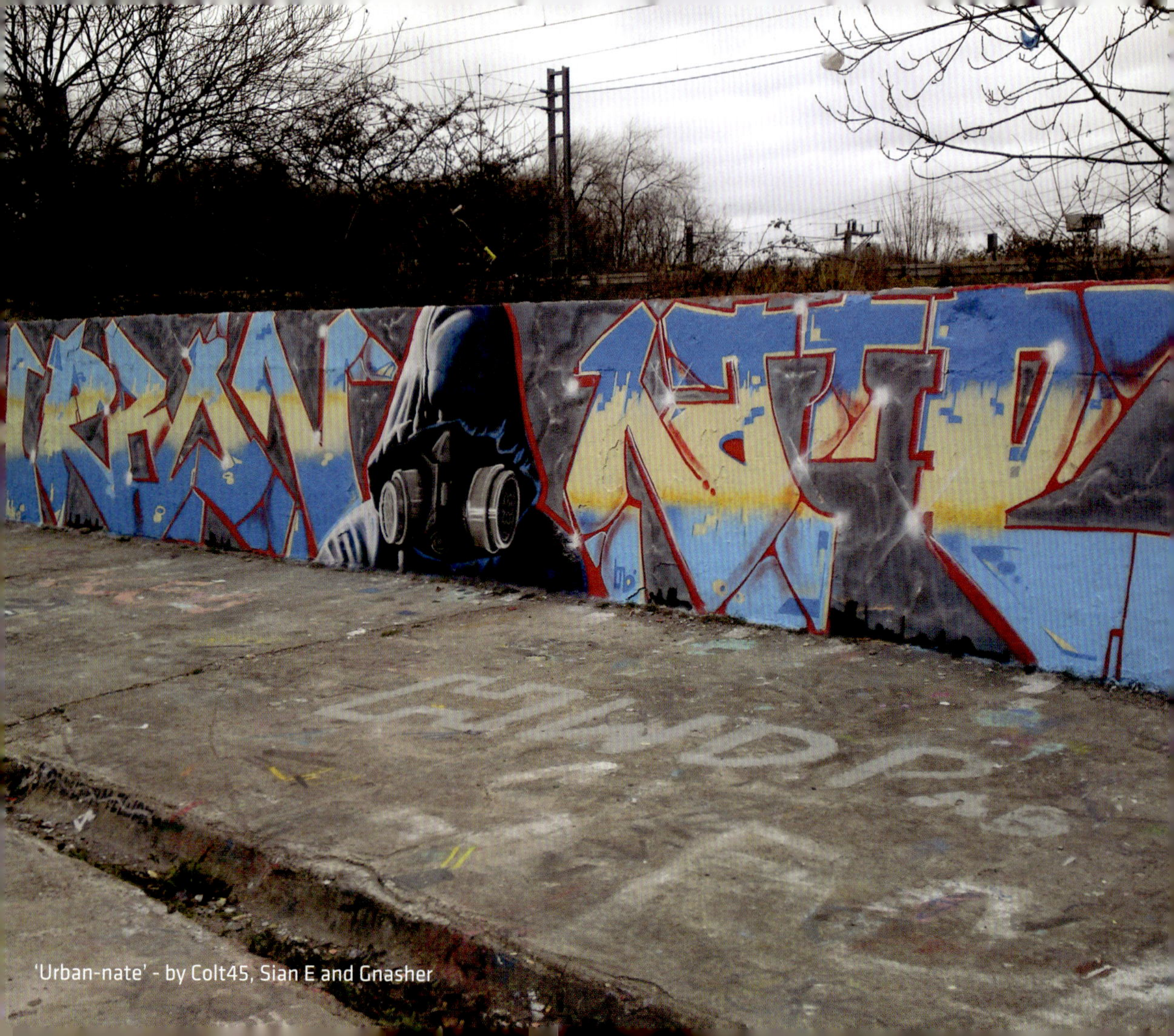

'Urban-nate' - by Colt45, Sian E and Gnasher

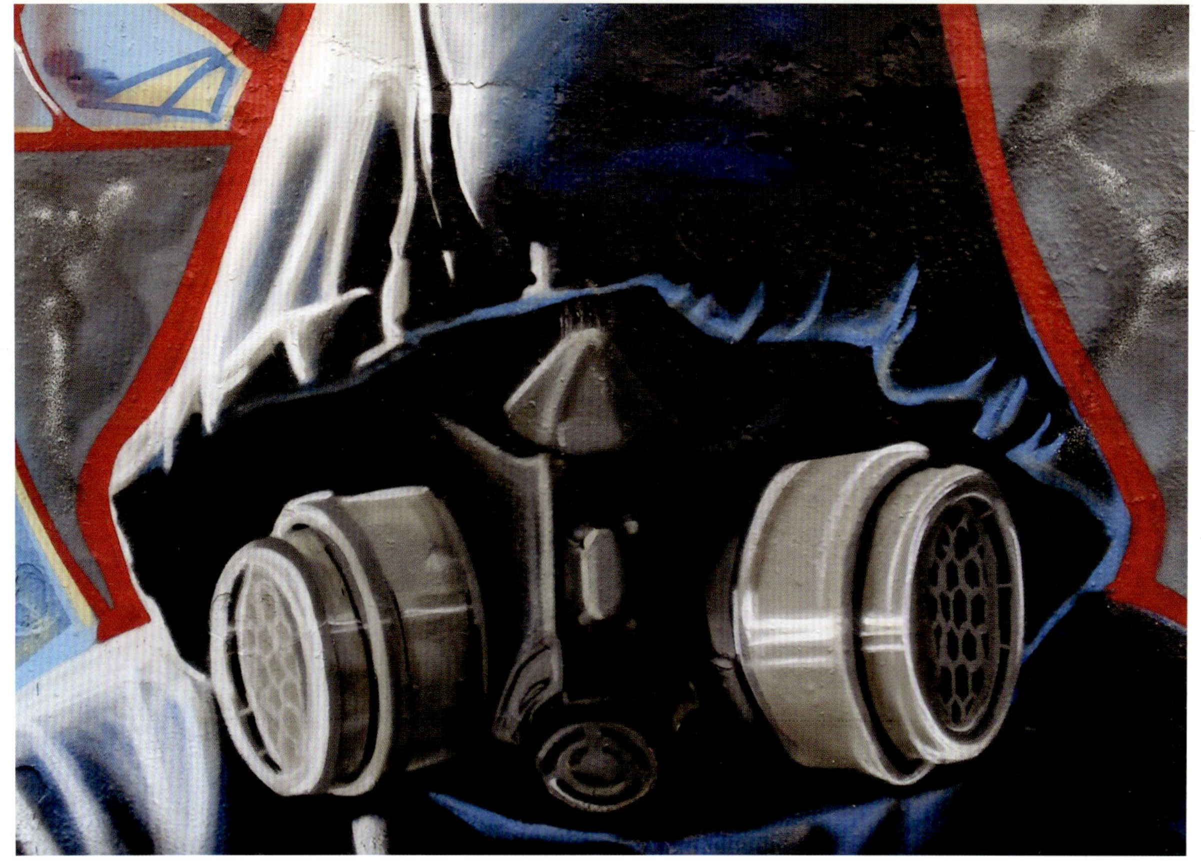

"London has always been diverse, and I think this comes across in the graff/art scene. People come from all over the world to paint in London; it has some excellent locations such as Shoreditch, 'Milf city' i.e. Ally Pally and Mile End. My favourite spot was Markfields, not just because it was 5 minutes from my house and I could sneak out from the Mrs to paint it. But also because it has character, oh and a wicked cafe. I'm not a street artist or a graffiti artist, I was allowed to do my own thing in London." - **Gnasher**

TRELLICK TOWER, WEST LONDON

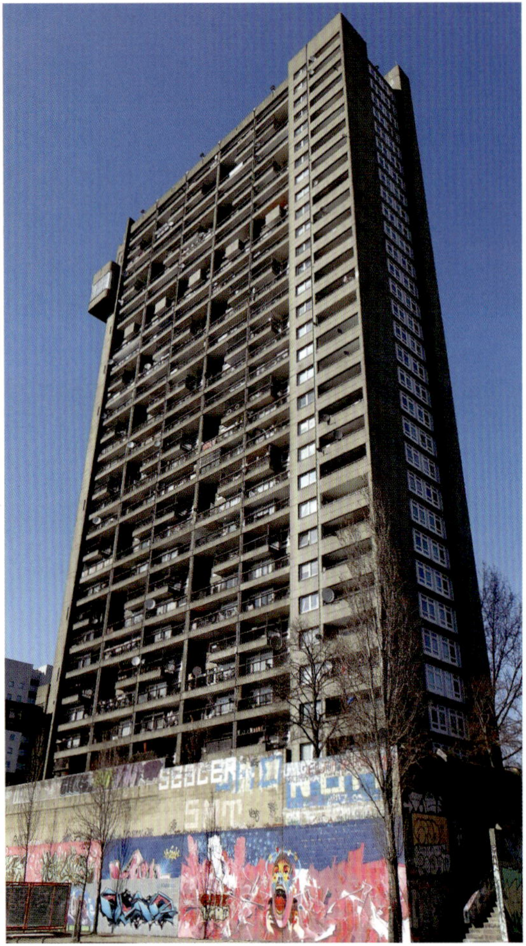

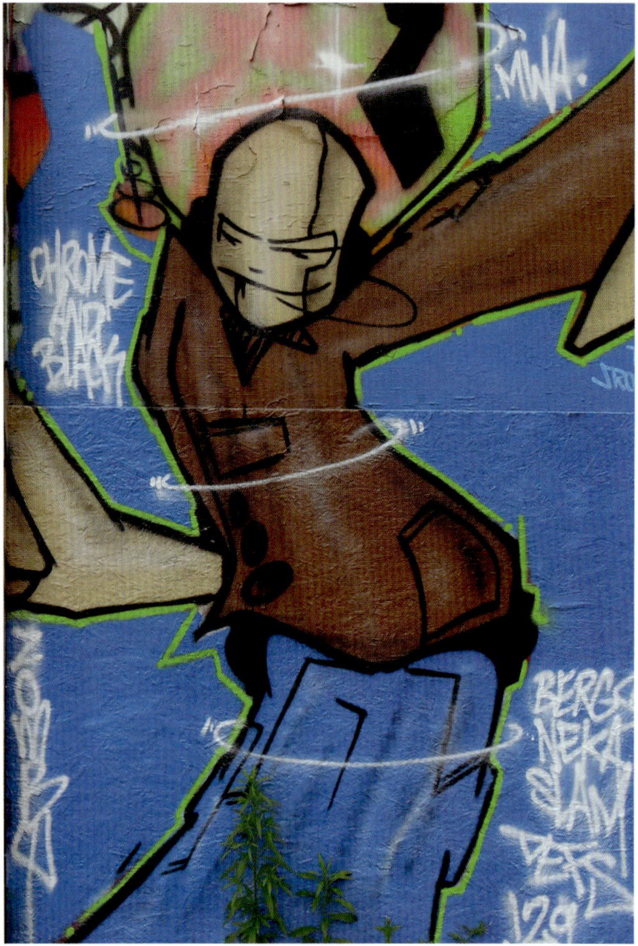

Zomby

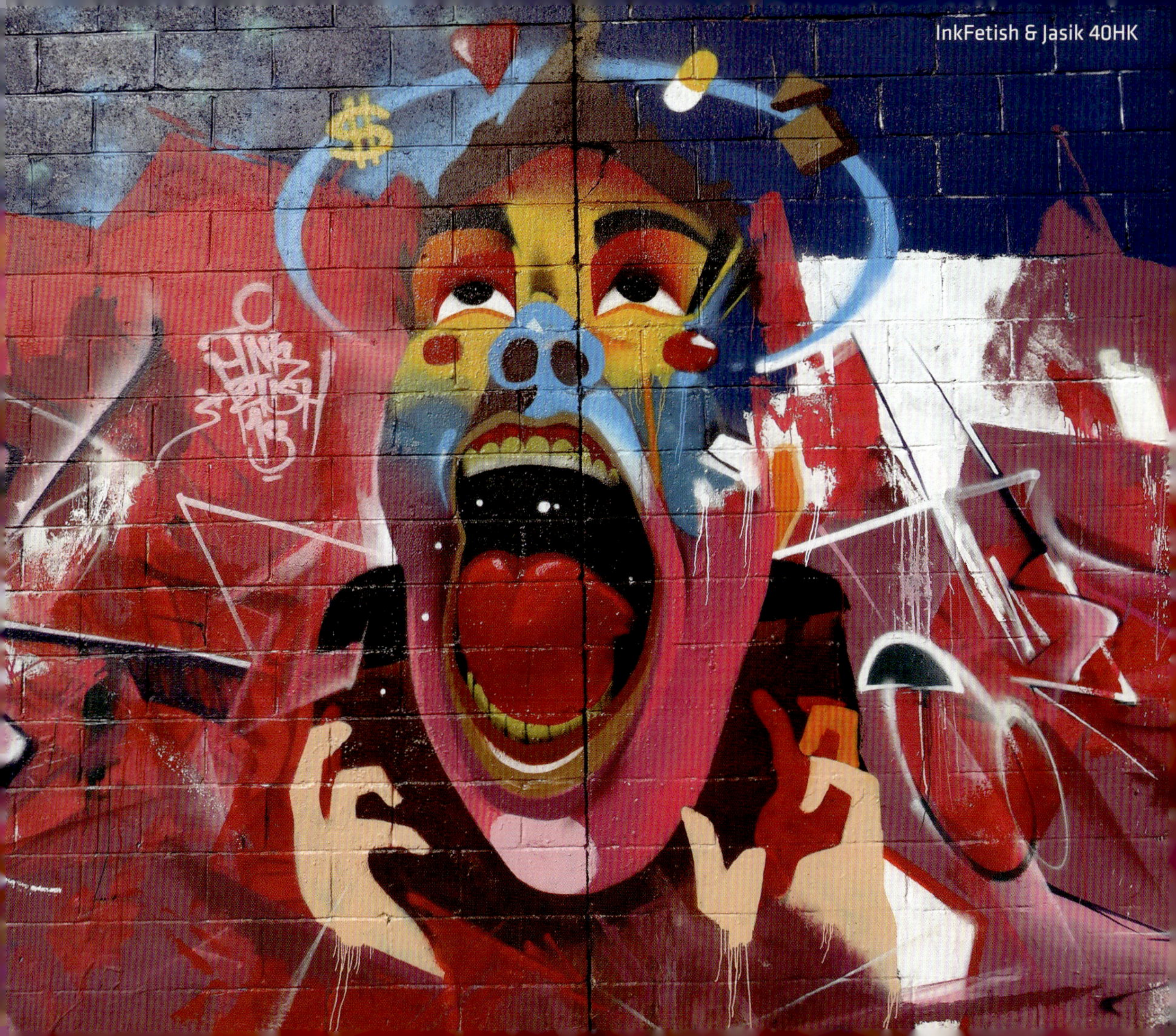

InkFetish & Jasik 40HK

Owed's Birthday Bash!

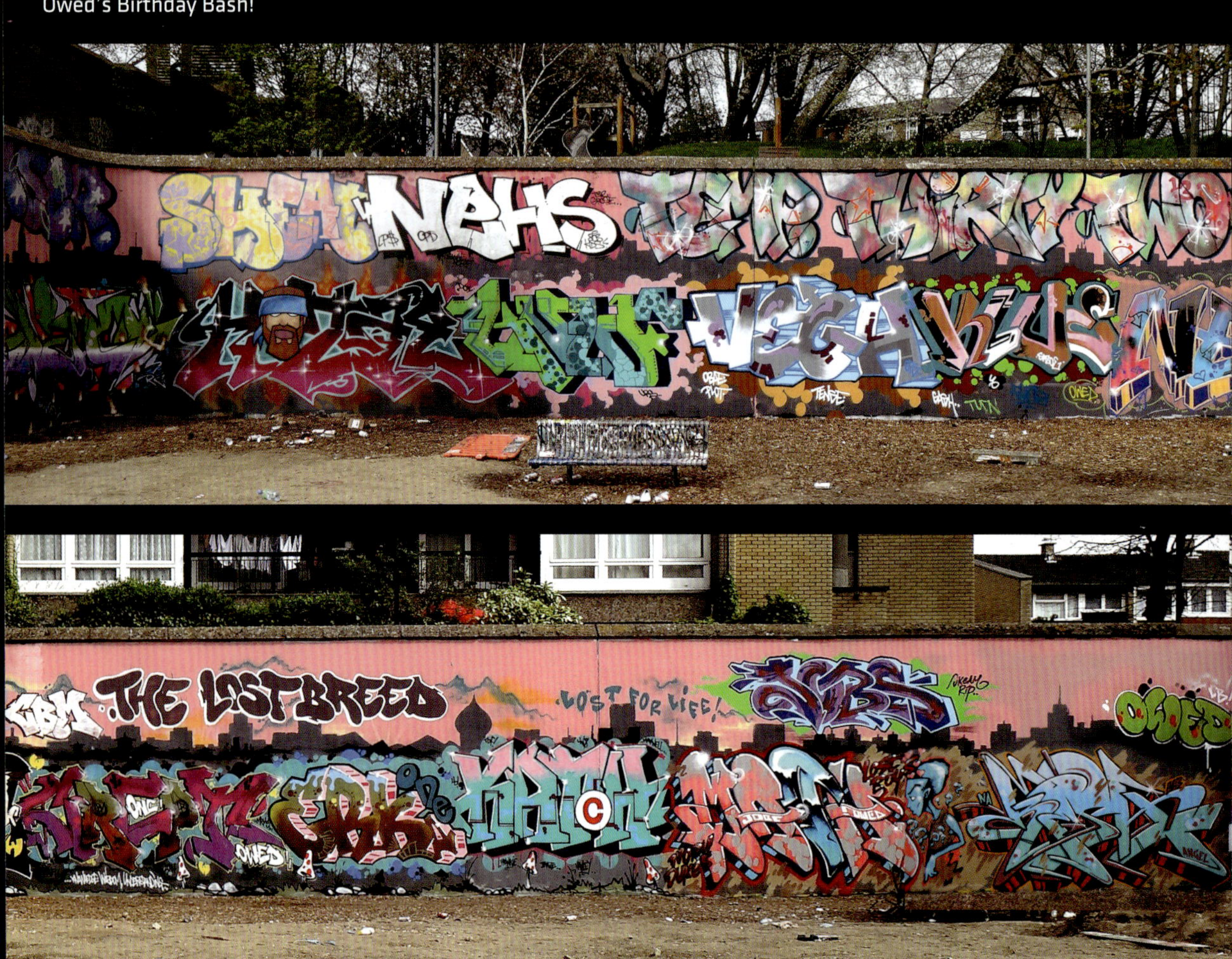

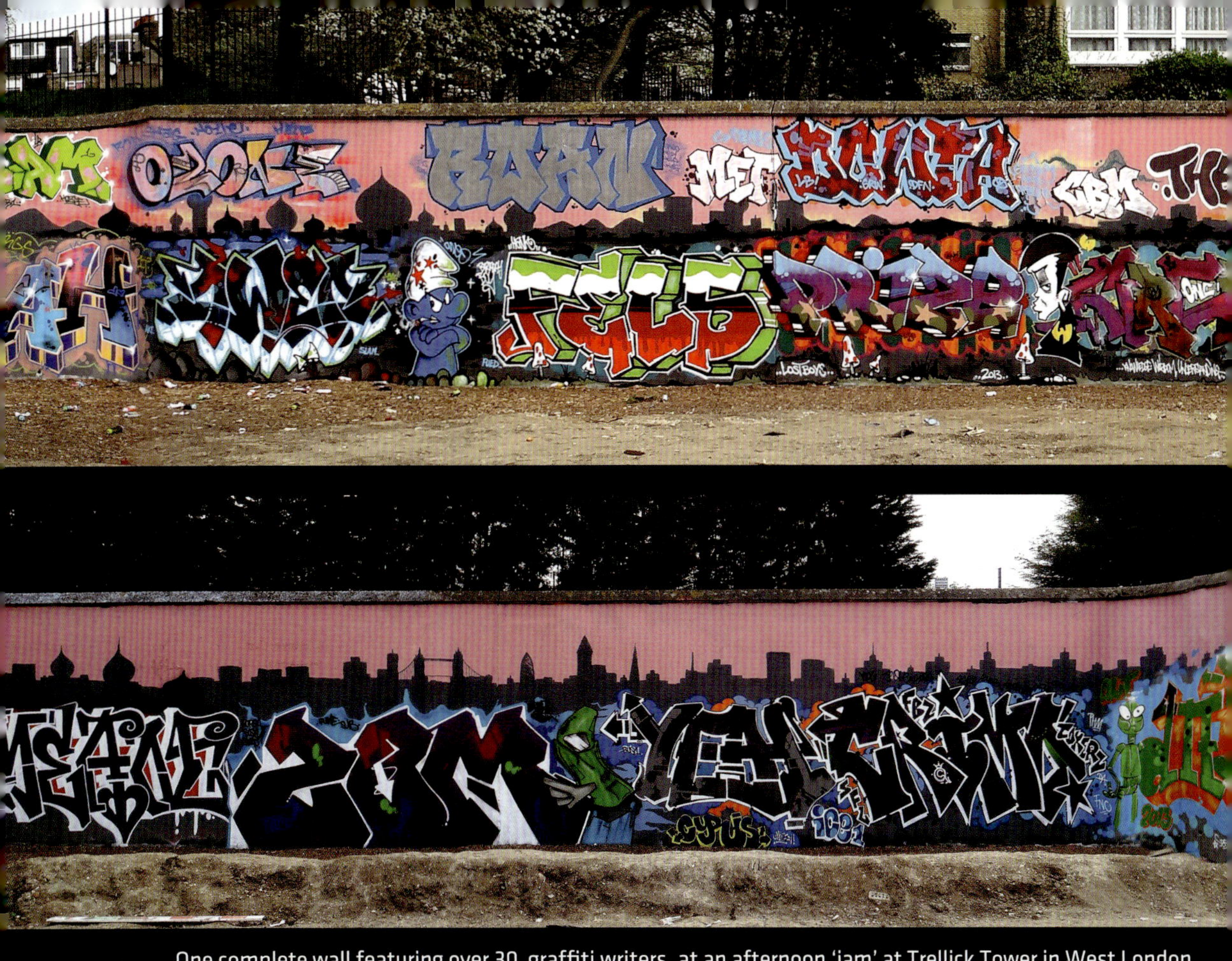

One complete wall featuring over 30 graffiti writers at an afternoon 'jam' at Trellick Tower in West London

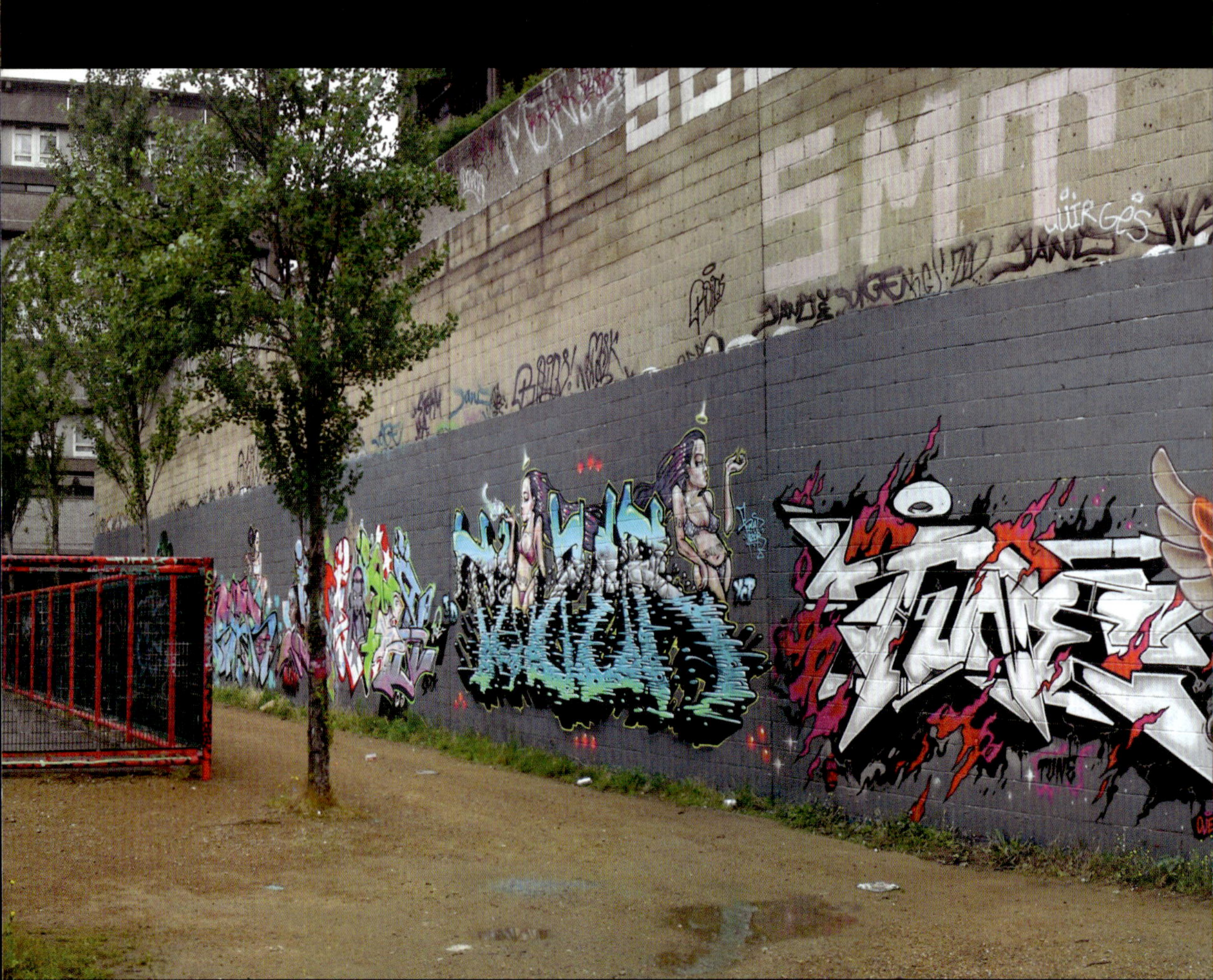

The walls of Trellick Tower are painted on a weekly basis by many local and international graffiti writers and artists.

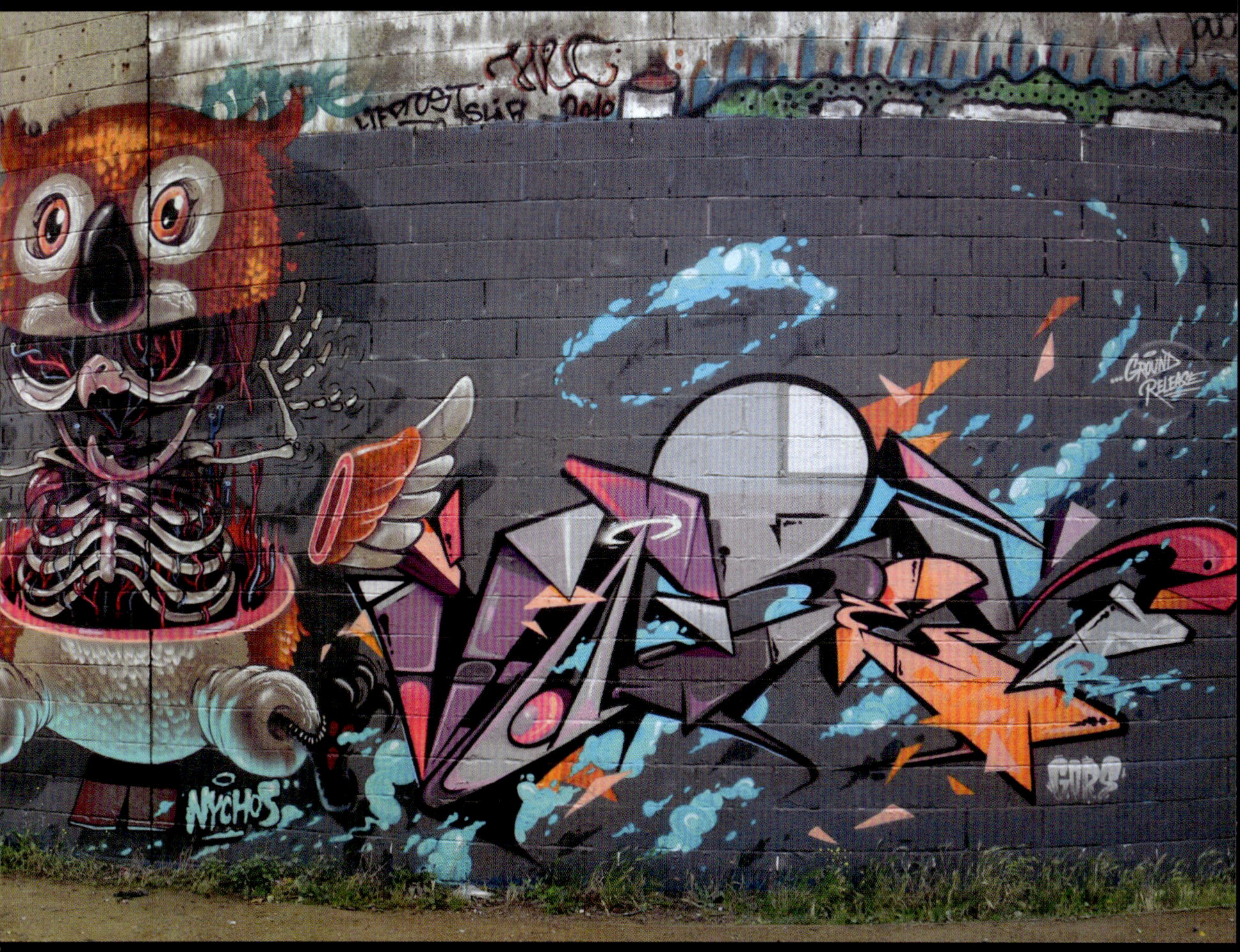

Tizer, Tune, Nychos, Vibes and more

LEAKE STREET, WATERLOO, SOUTH LONDON

Since Banksy and friends opened the Leake Street Tunnel in Waterloo, for the 'Cans Festival' in 2008, some of the best writers and artists in London frequent the walls, which are now painted almost every day. The tunnel hosts the annual 'Battle of Waterloo', organised by 'Chrome & Black' (the best place in London for graffiti art resources), and many other graffiti jams. It has become one of the last legal halls of fame in London, yet its future is uncertain.

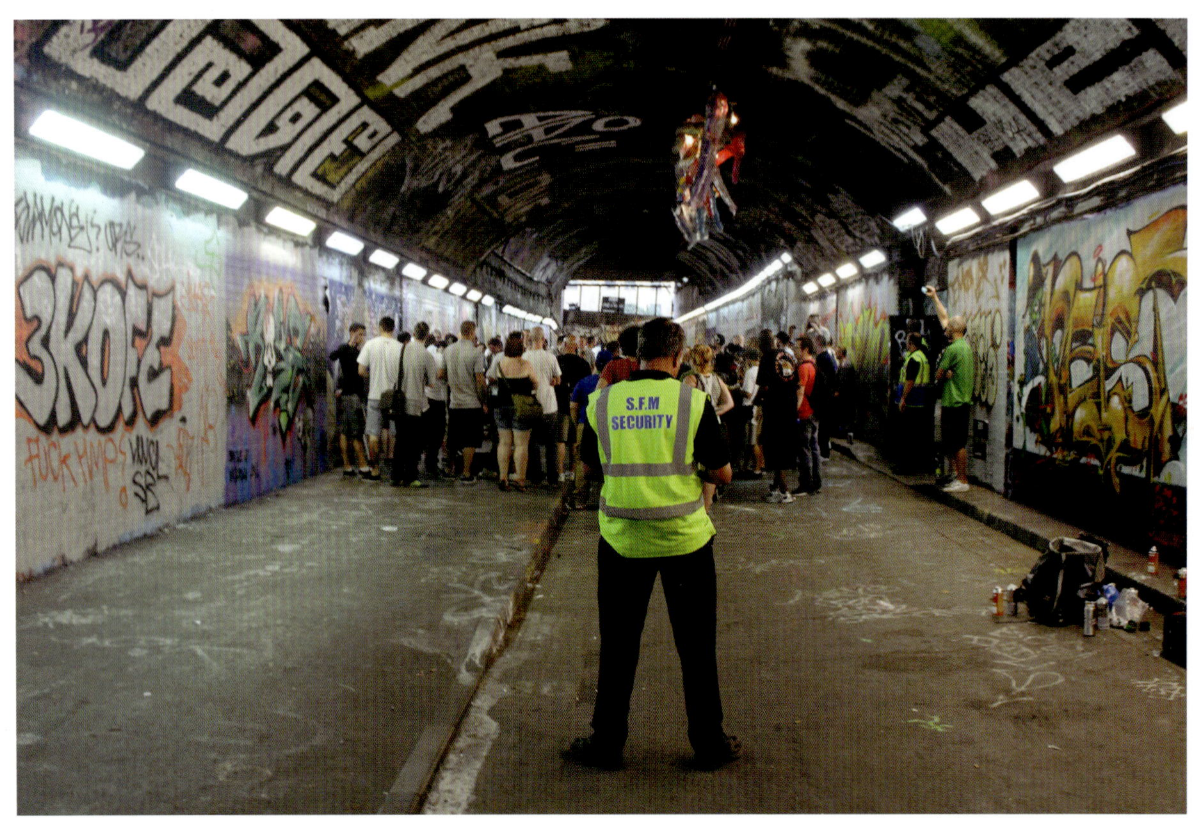

And the winner is... - The Battle of Waterloo 2011

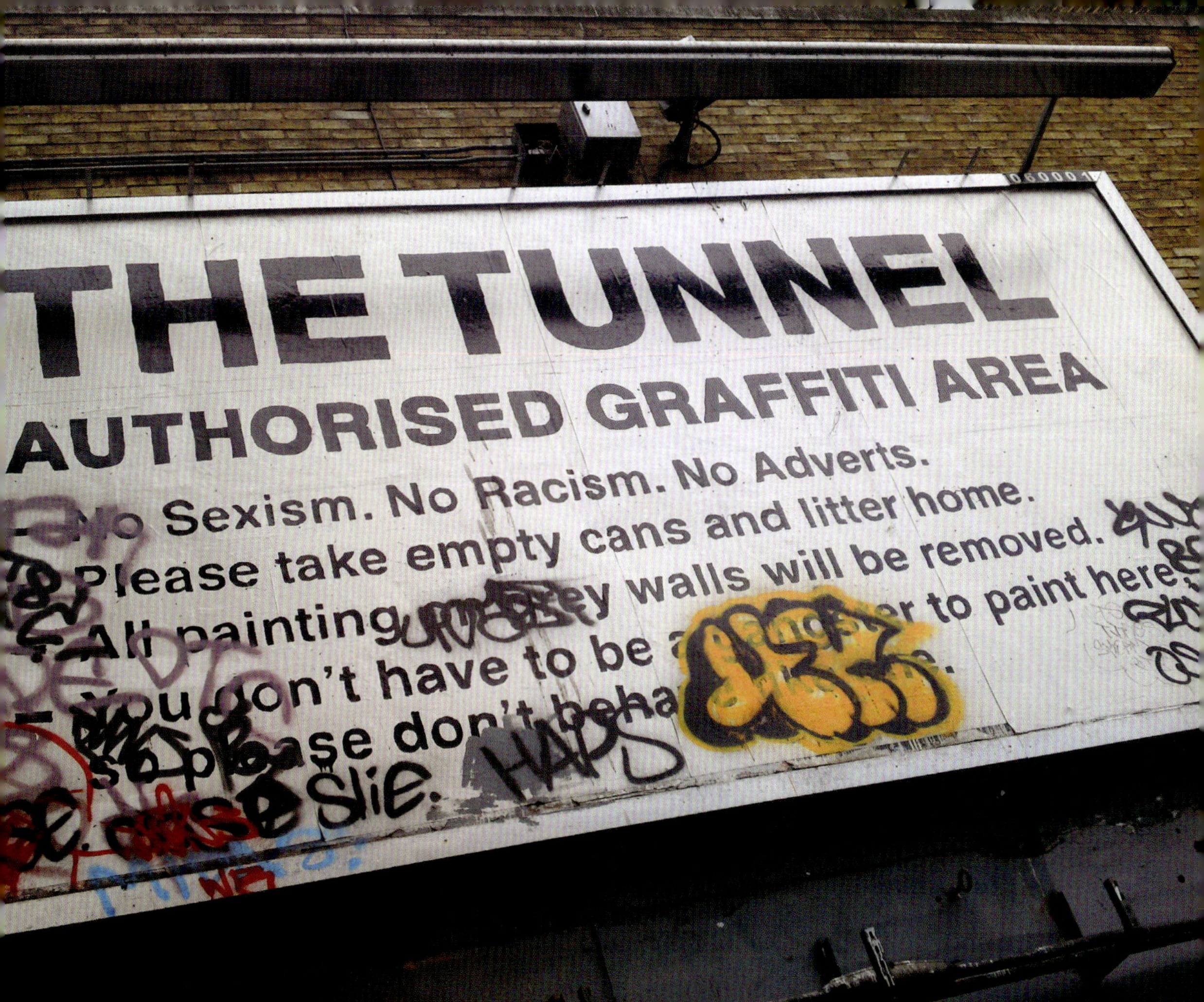

Leake Street, Waterloo, South London

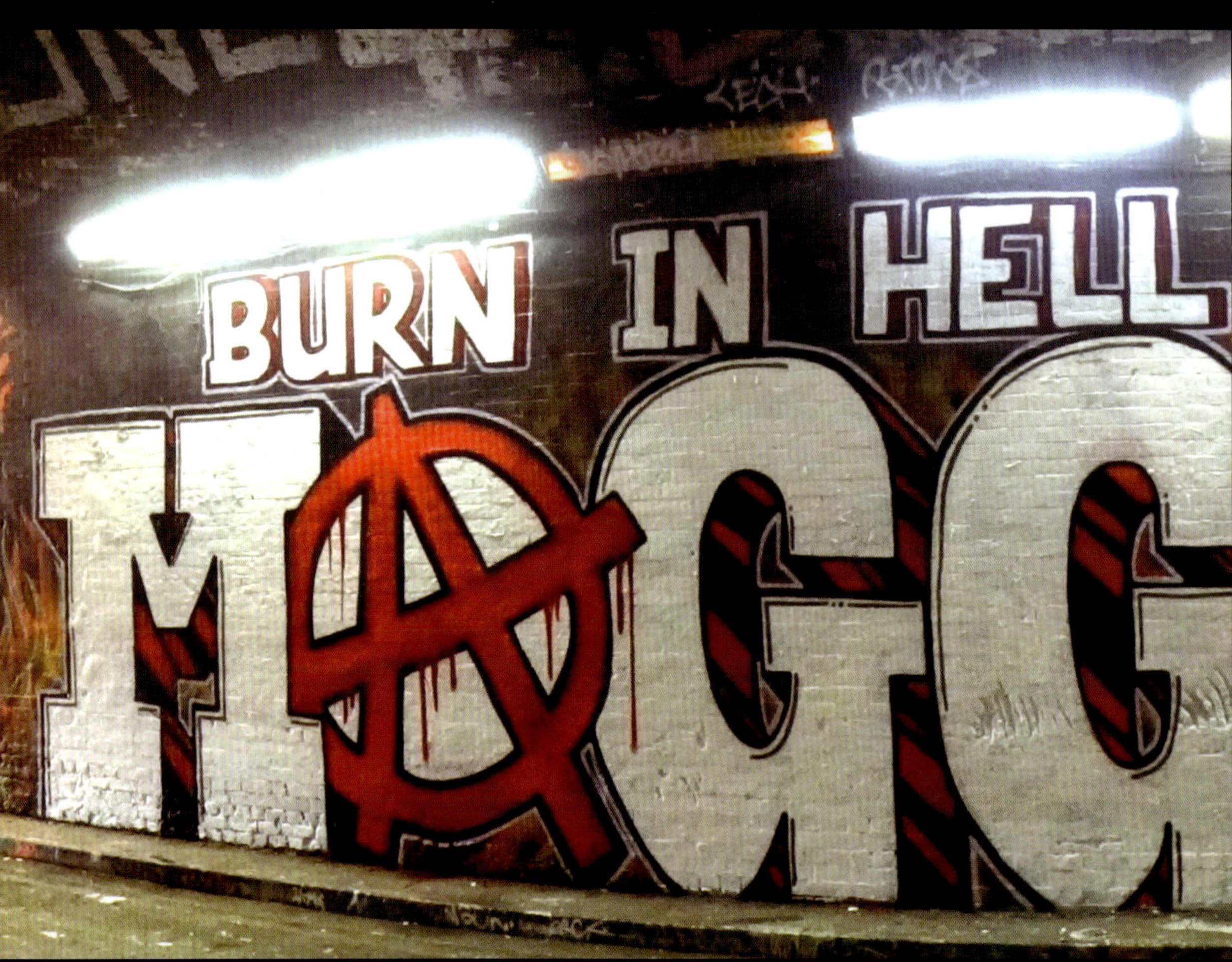

"What London means to me? Dreams, money and Stella Artois." - **Born**

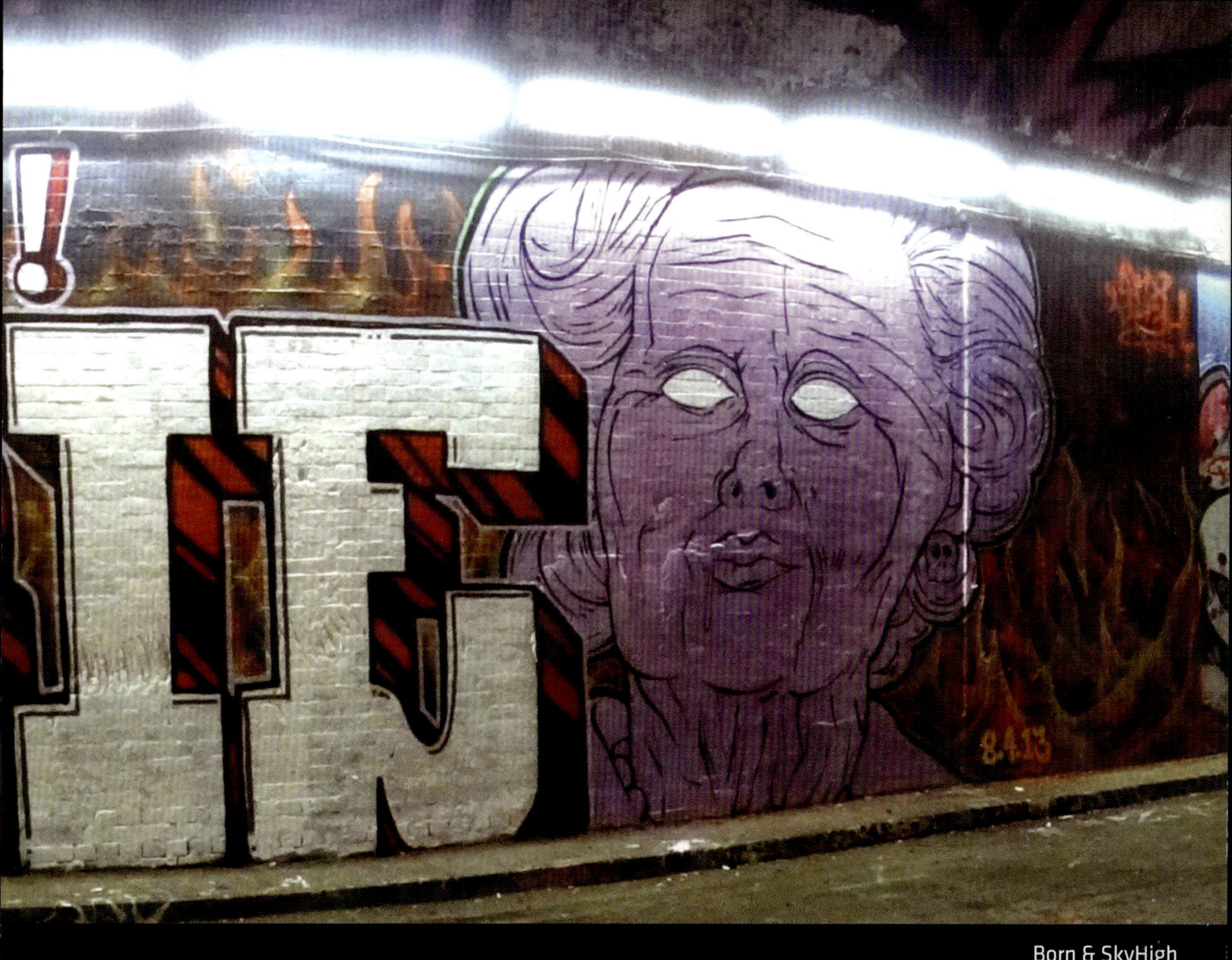

Born & SkyHigh

STOCKWELL, SOUTH LONDON

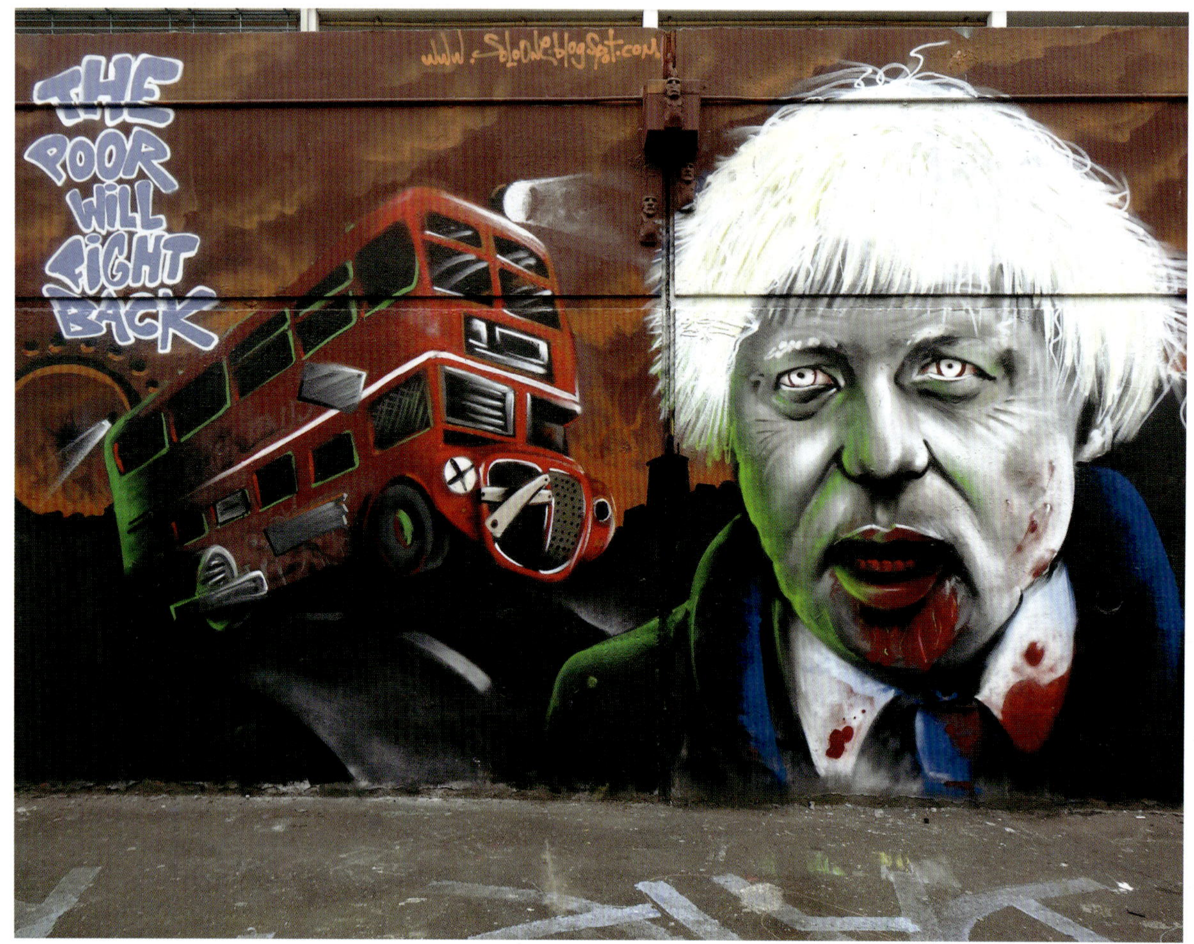

Irony

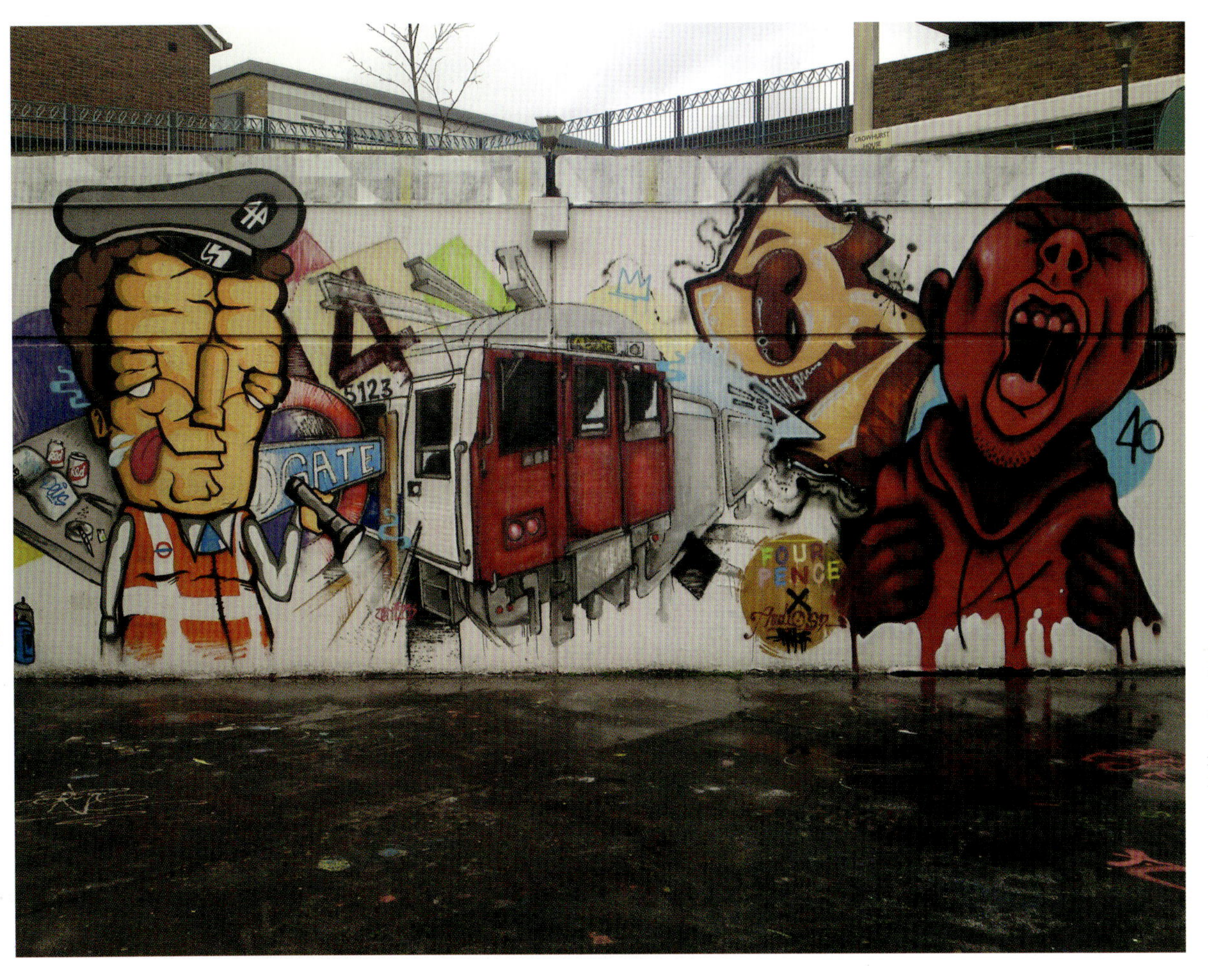

Deus, Vents137 TGB, Audio57 and InkFetish 40HK

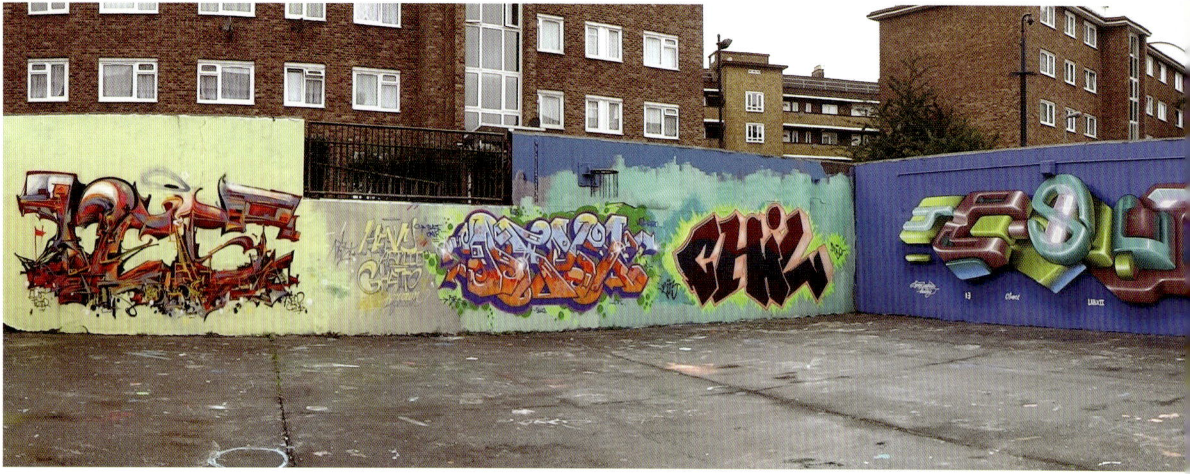

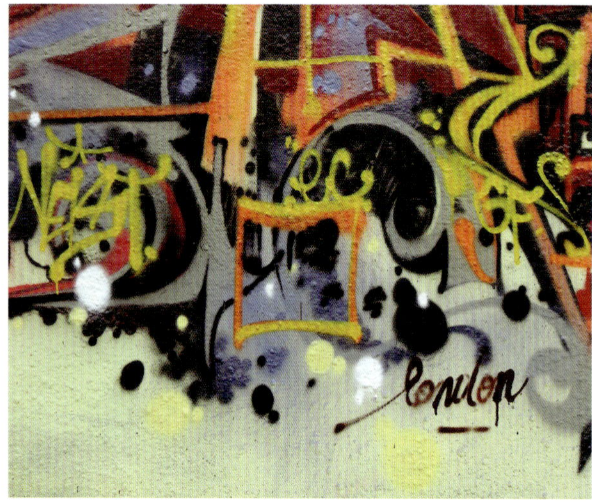
london

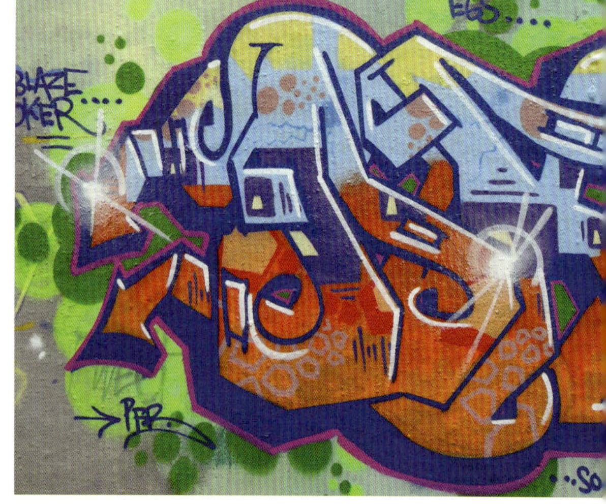
EGS....
BLAZE....

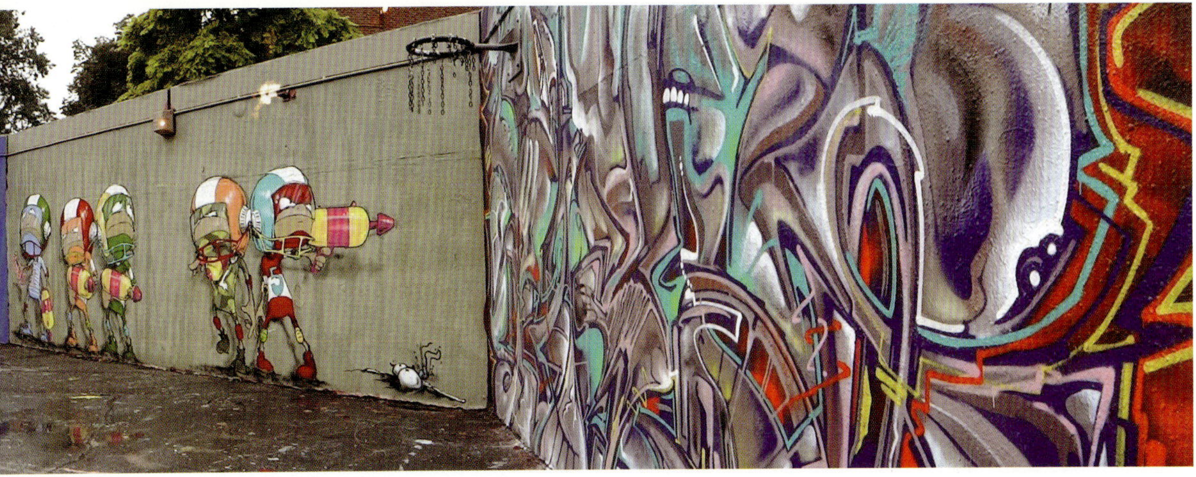

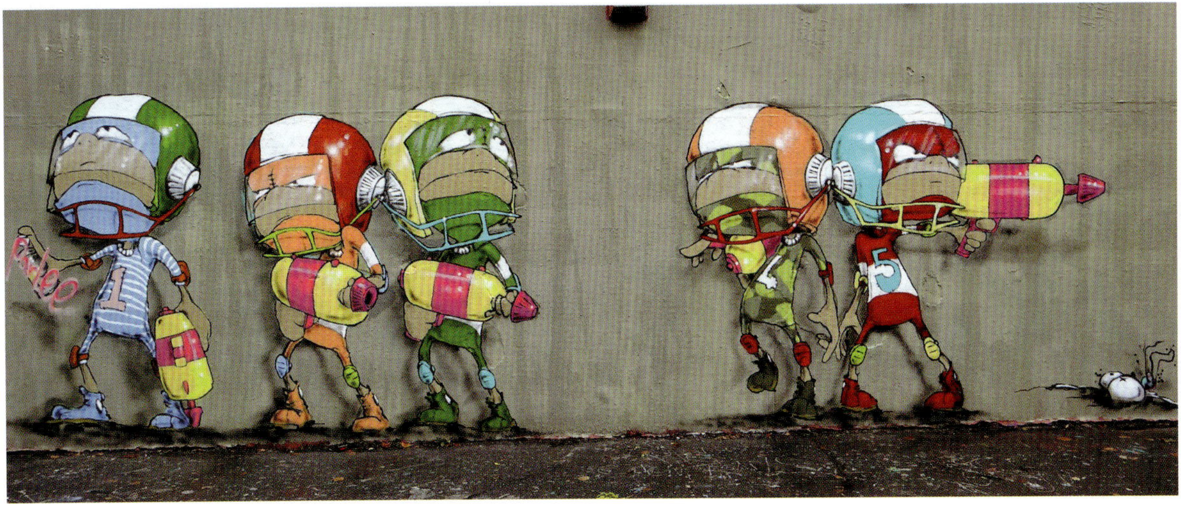

Neist, Drax, Chil, Lovepusher, Parlee and Solo One

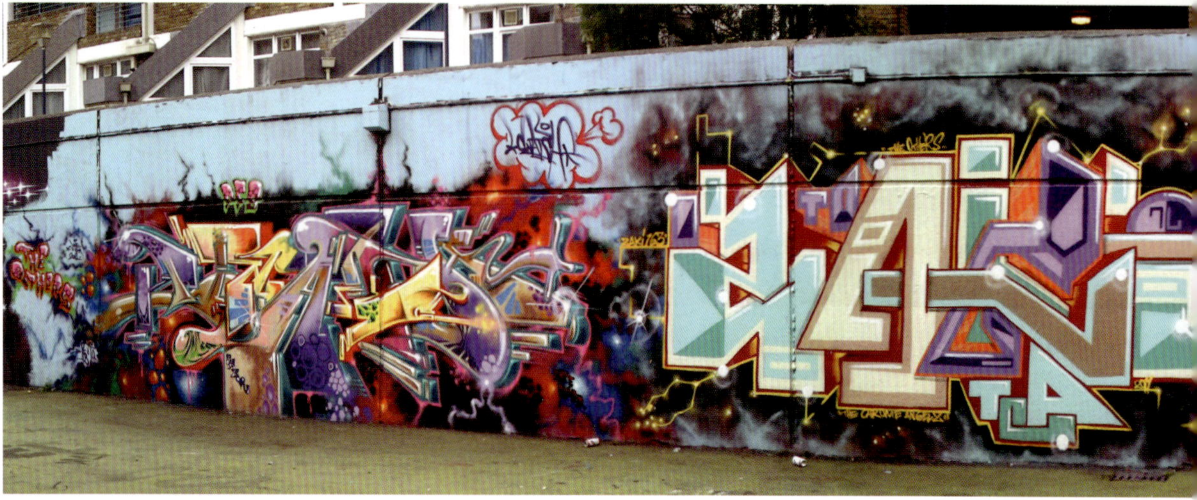

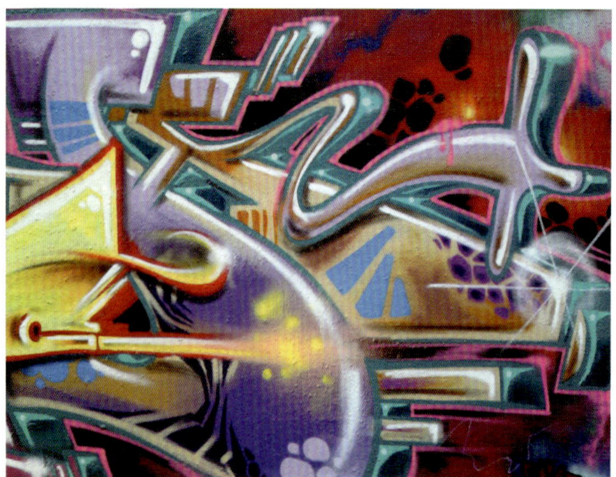

"Having been born in London, and grown up here in the 70s and 80s, through to the 90s, I was lucky enough to have been involved in, arguably, the three biggest movements of the last 40 or 50 years. From Punk and New Wave, into Hip Hop, through to the House/Rave scenes - and it's no coincidence that London was at the forefront of all these subcultures when they first exploded onto these shores. After all this time, the UK graff scene is still going strong, and in London you can see some of the best work this country has to offer." -
Zaki Dee 163 - The Chrome Angelz/The Others

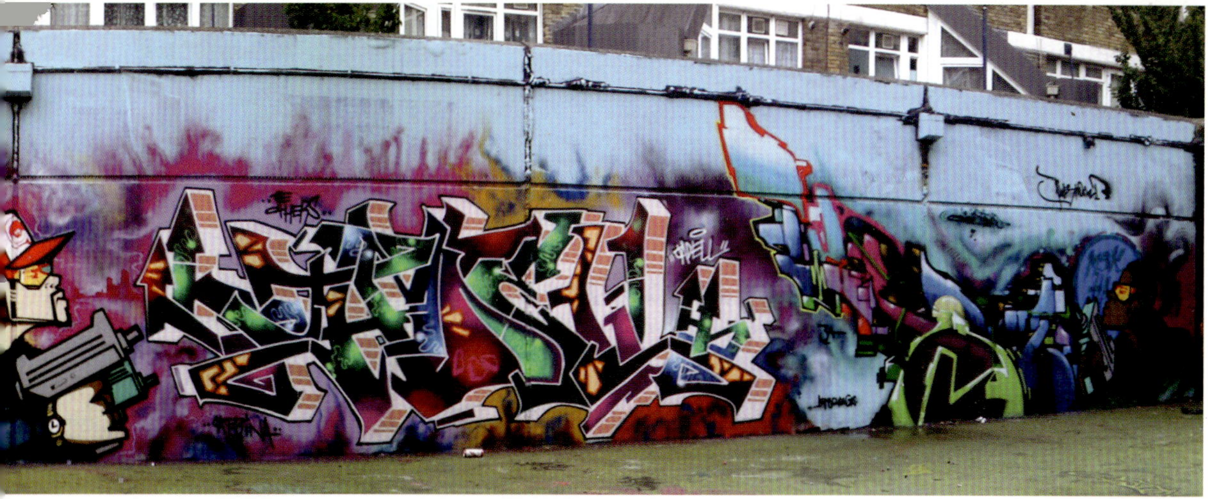

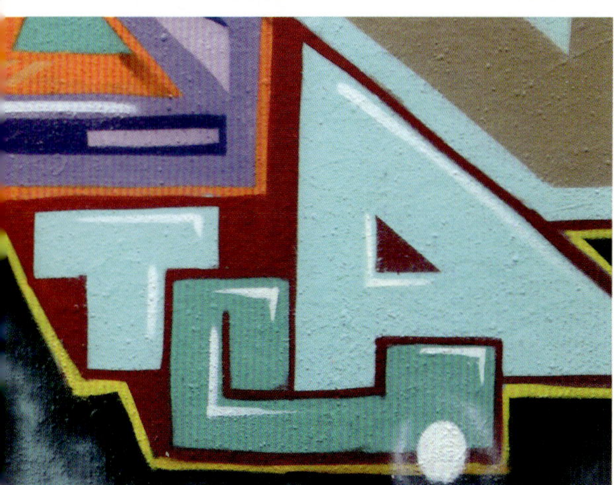

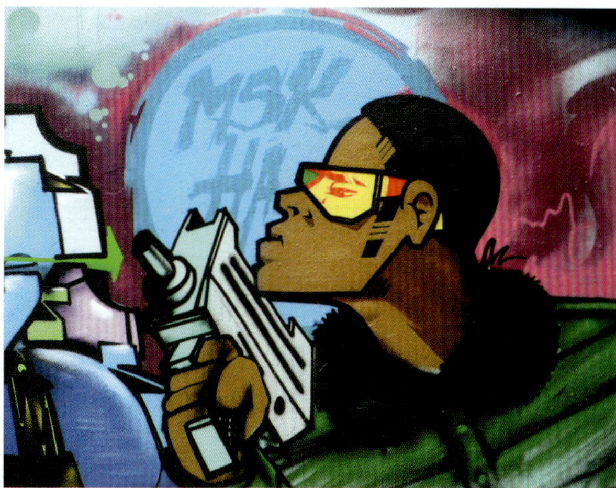

Snatch, Zaki Dee, Aroe, Jadell and Twesh

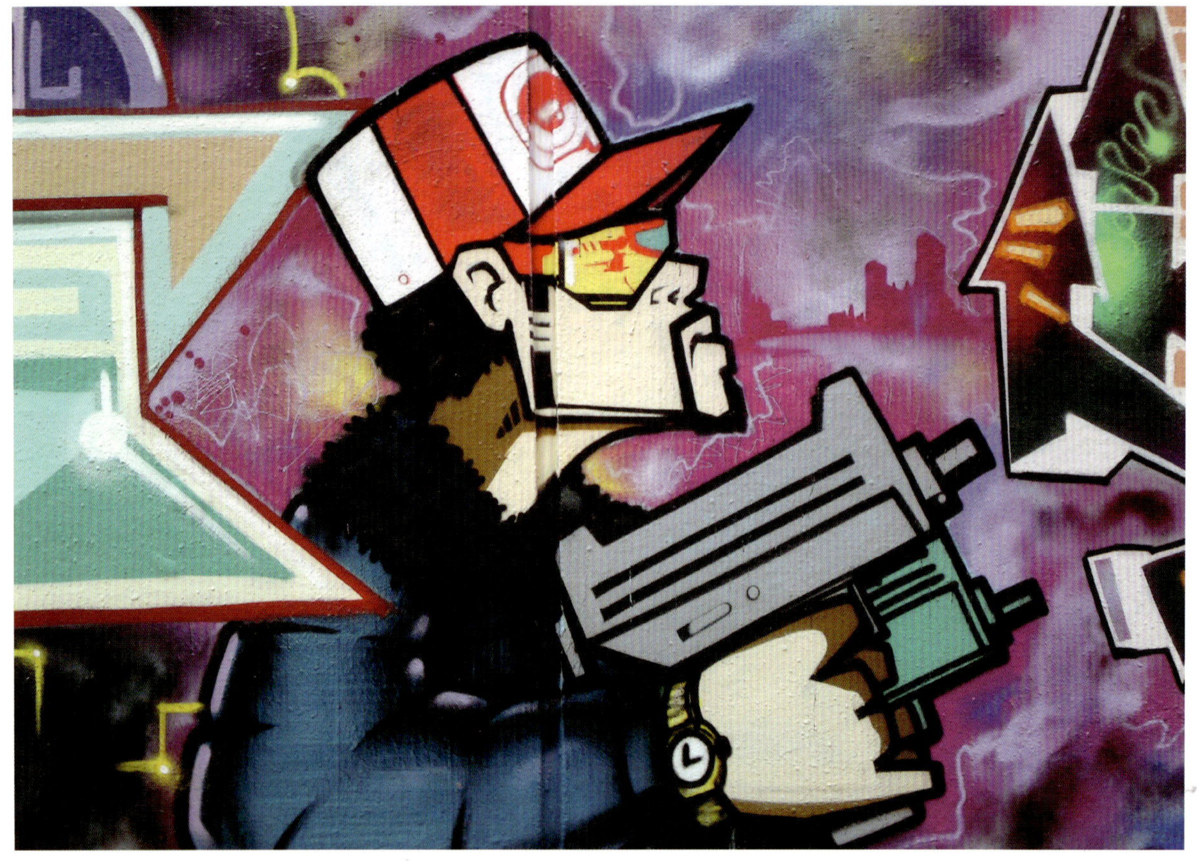

"I always look to London for influence and inspiration. Coming from the countryside means I am an outsider, but I think it makes me work harder and raise my game. I have deep respect for The Chrome Angelz, Zaki, Pride, Scribbla... and DDS in London; they are in the thick of it. Where I'm from, things have a different pace, we've been able to gain acceptance and recognition for our work, we've become part of the landscape. I will always look at London as one of the greatest graff cities in the world!" - **Aroe MSK HA**

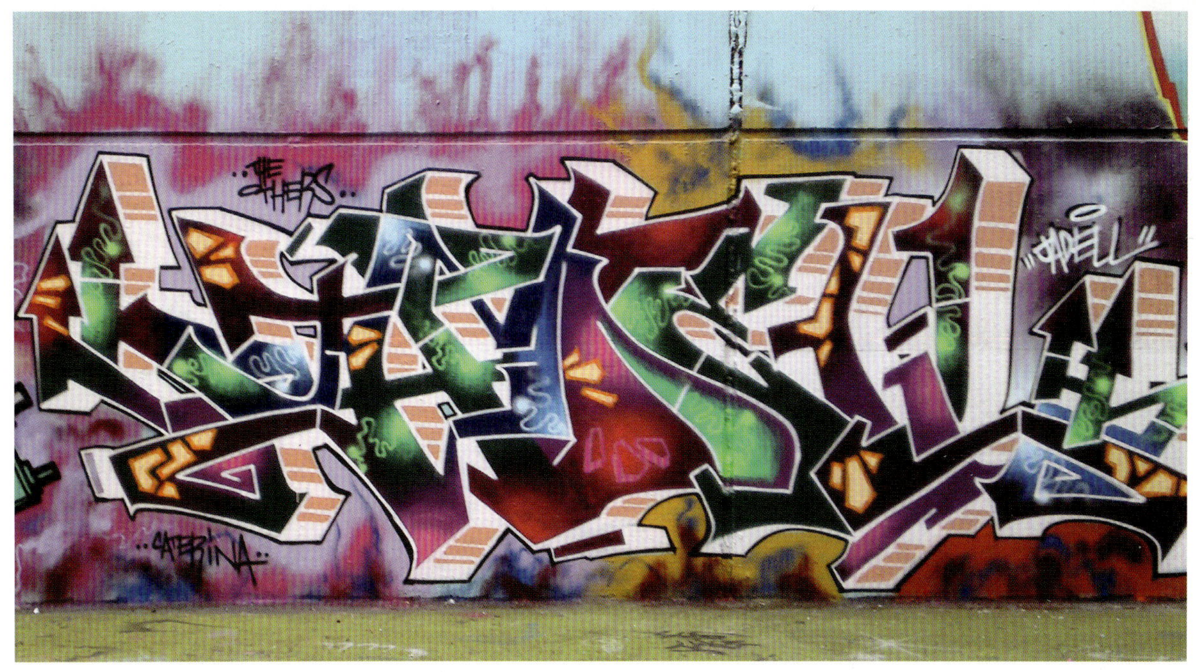

"Growing up in London, it felt for me like there was always something interesting happening somewhere. I was able to move more into the centre of London when I hit my early 20s, and it was one long succession of parties, music and craziness. Just being 'out' for as long as possible was a good enough excuse for me. During the day back then, if I wasn't making music or studying, then I was inside Soho's record shops. There was so much stuff coming in and out of there continuously, that it took a great deal of your time staying on top of it.

"It's similar now with London's graffiti scene, there is such a fast turnover of masterpieces being painted week to week. If you're not looking at new pieces, observing how style is continuously progressing and evolving and putting it into practice in your own pieces, then you're going to be stuck in the past and won't progress. I'm still nowhere near as good as I want to be and I'm still making loads of mistakes, but mistakes are a key to mastering your style. London has lots of mistakes, but lots of brilliance too." - **Jadell - The Others**

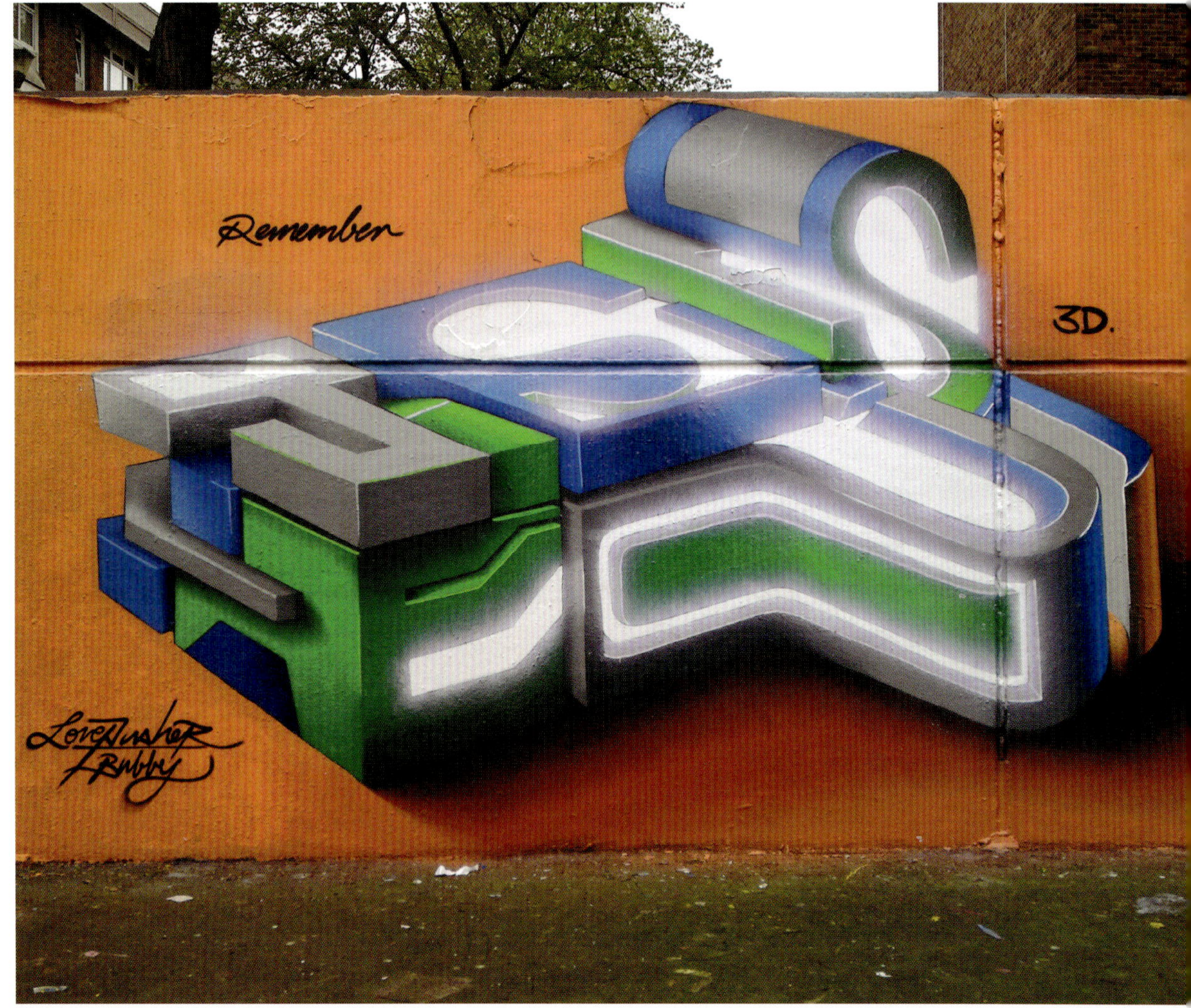
Remember
3D.

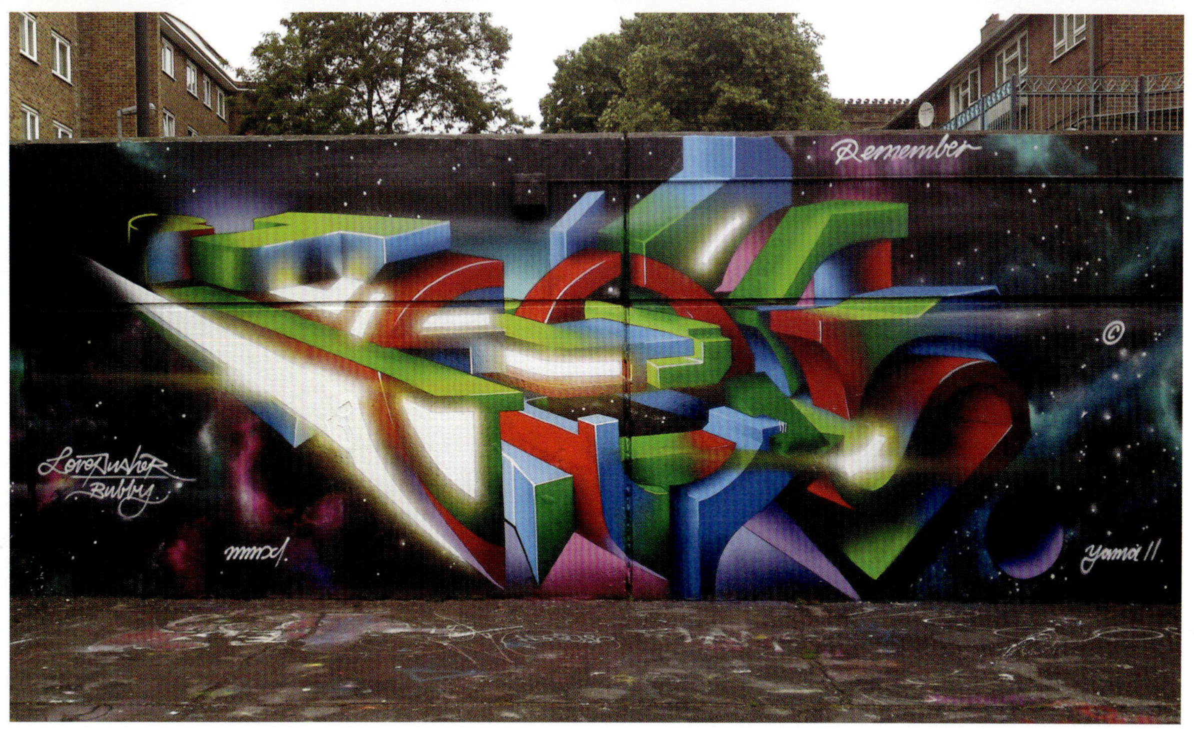

“As a Londoner, born and raised, this city means so much to me. London is the embodiment of a true multicultural society, acknowledging and embracing people from all over the world. With such a diversity of cultures thriving in London, it gives us all the educational opportunity to experience these international cultures right at our doorsteps.

“Visually, London is steeped in history and this can evidently be seen in the architecture of the city, with many great listed buildings dating as far back as the Victorian and Tudor eras.

“Personally, I've never really thought of London as just a city of bricks and mortar but rather a living entity, constantly evolving and changing with the times.” - **Lovepusher**

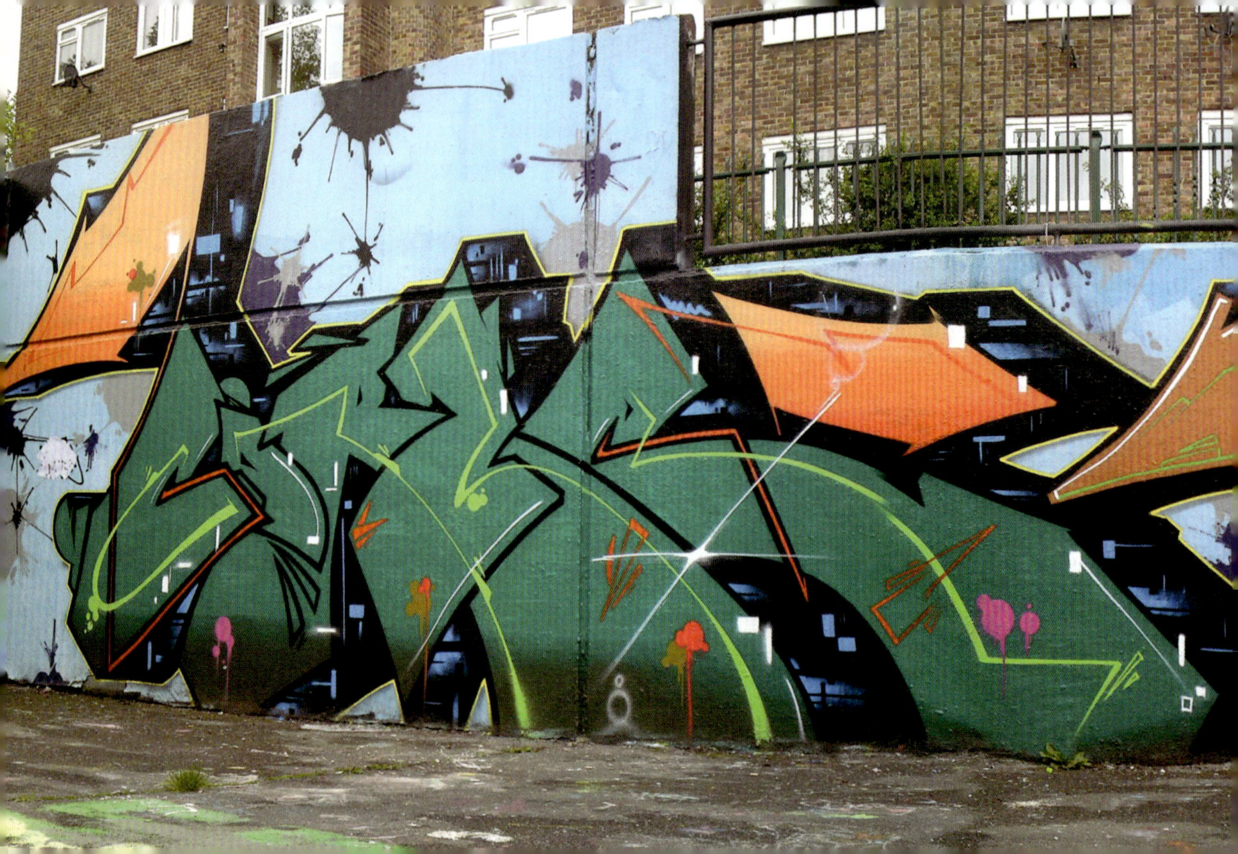

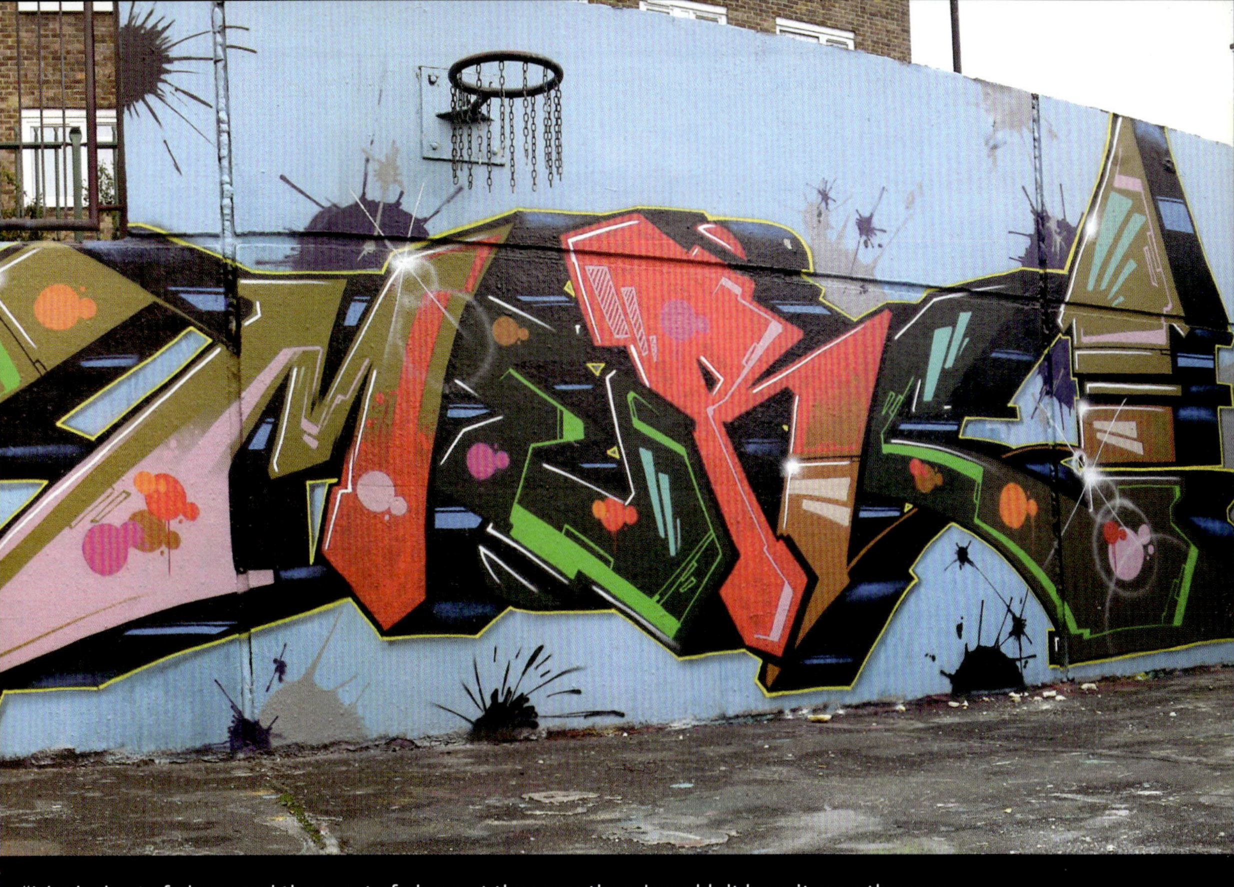

“It’s the best of places and the worst of places at the same time. I wouldn’t have it any other way, apart from pubs staying open longer...” - **Merc**

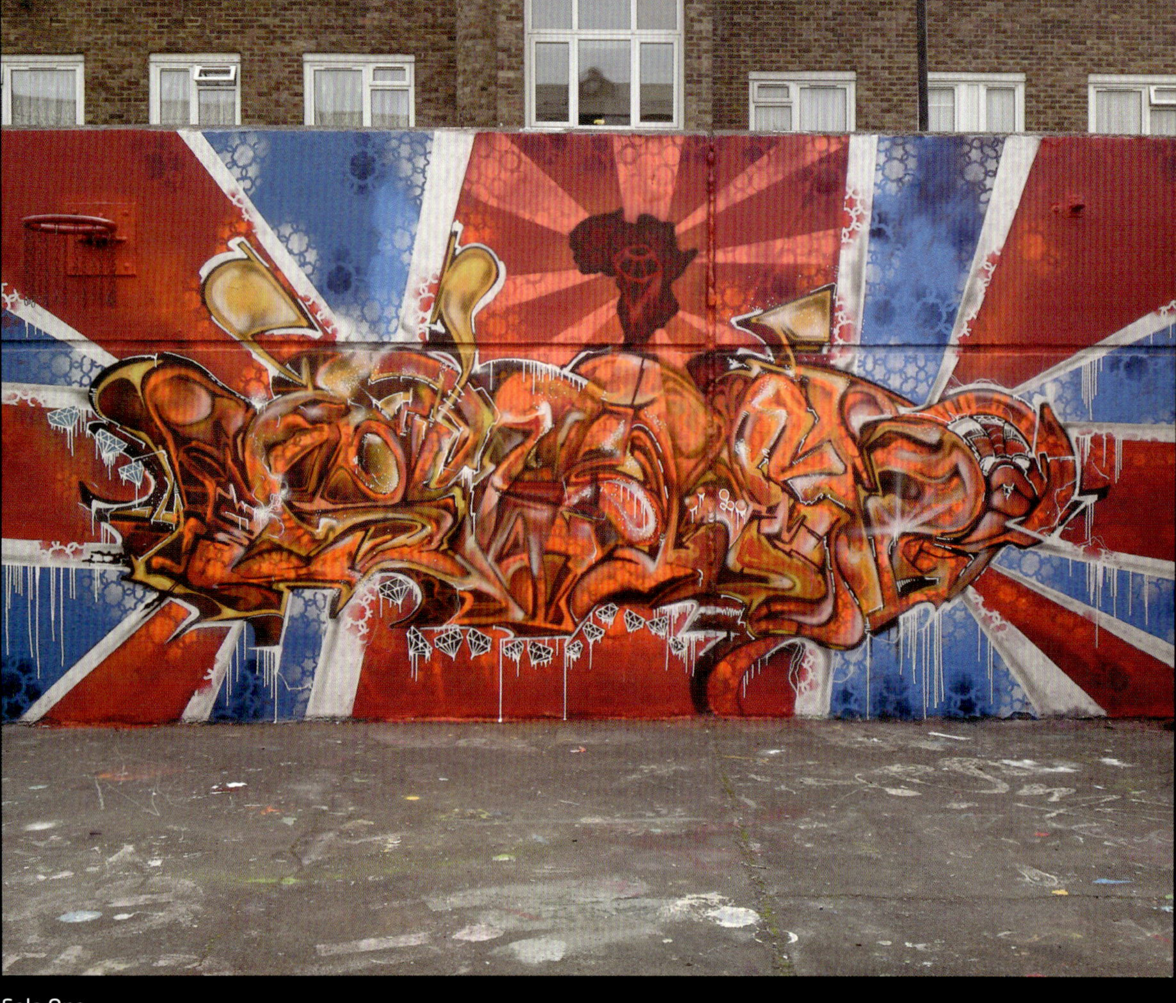

Solo One

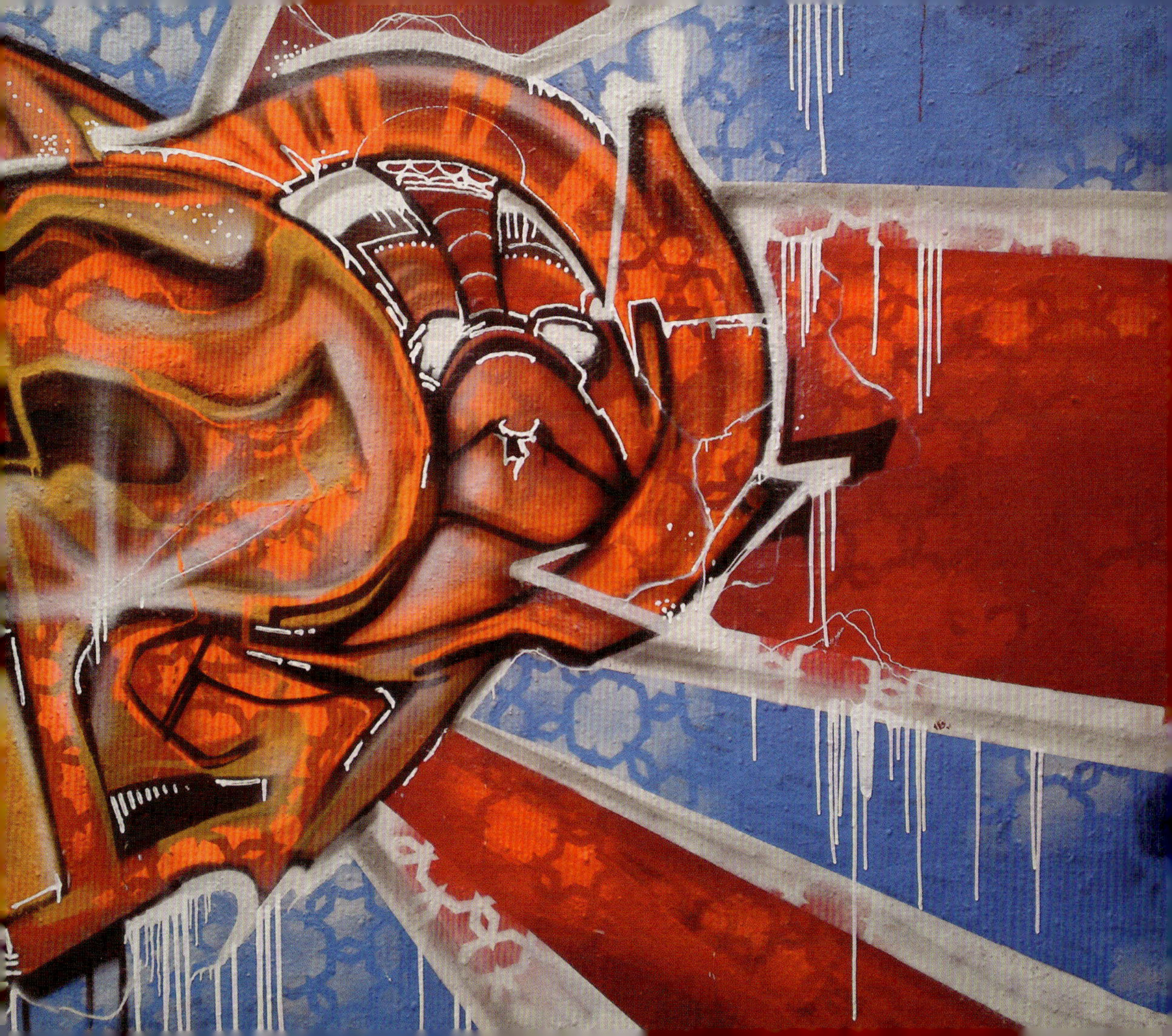

LONDON SITES

London's continual regeneration and ever-changing landscape provides a dynamic environment for writers and street artists to assess and interact with. The emptied spaces are a rich hive of graffiti and street art. 'Broken window theory' is certainly an aspect in society, but more often graffiti appears after the windows have been broken and the buildings left to decay.

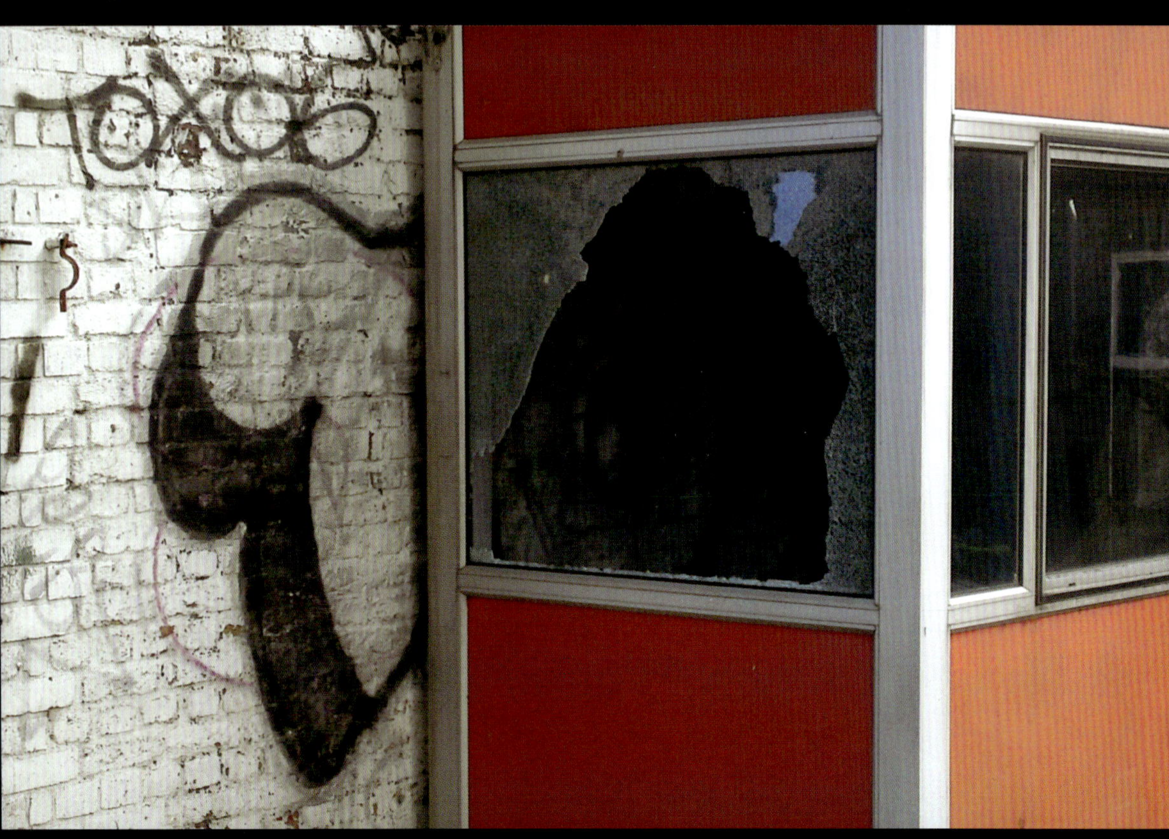

Tox06. North London

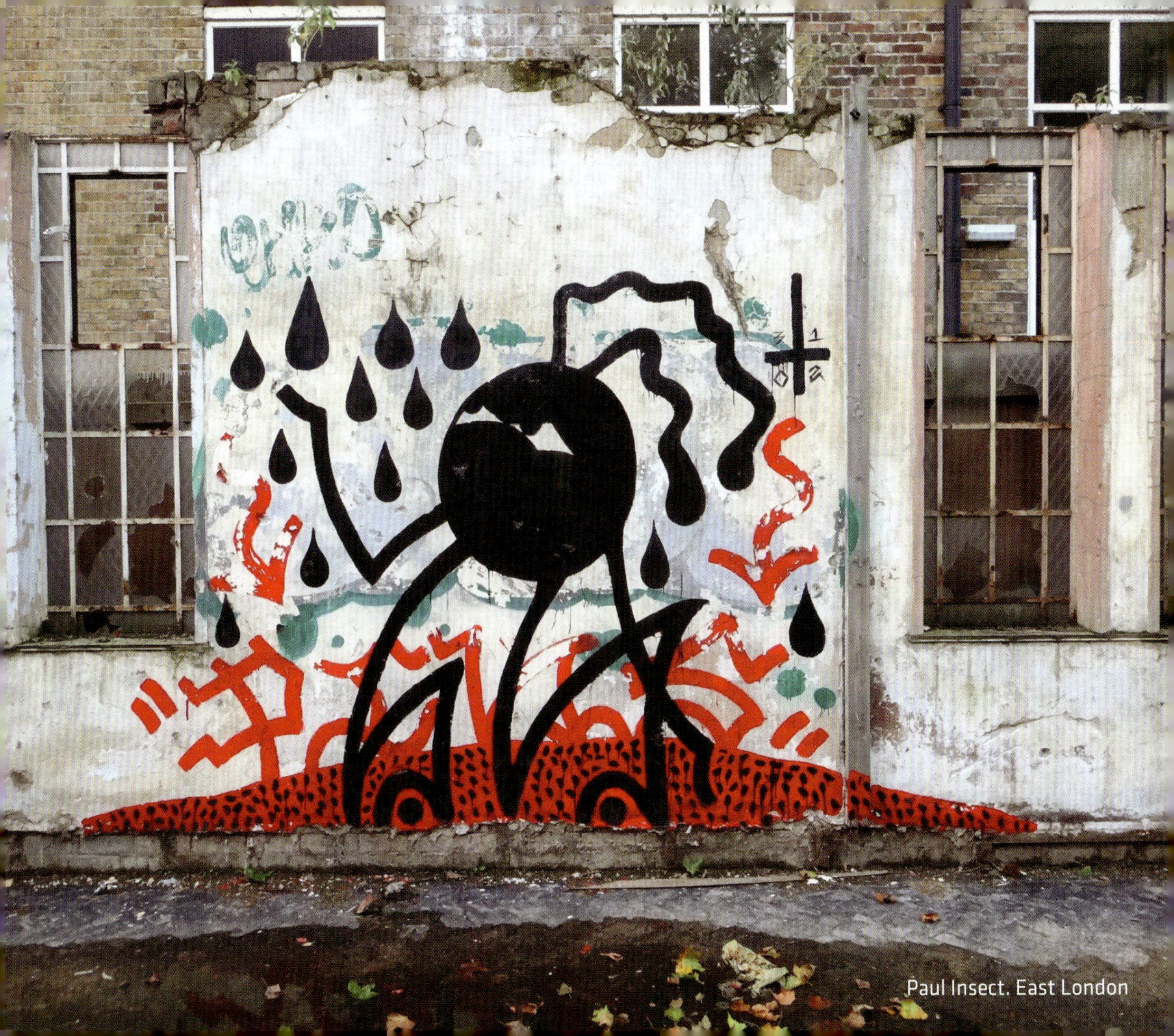

Paul Insect. East London

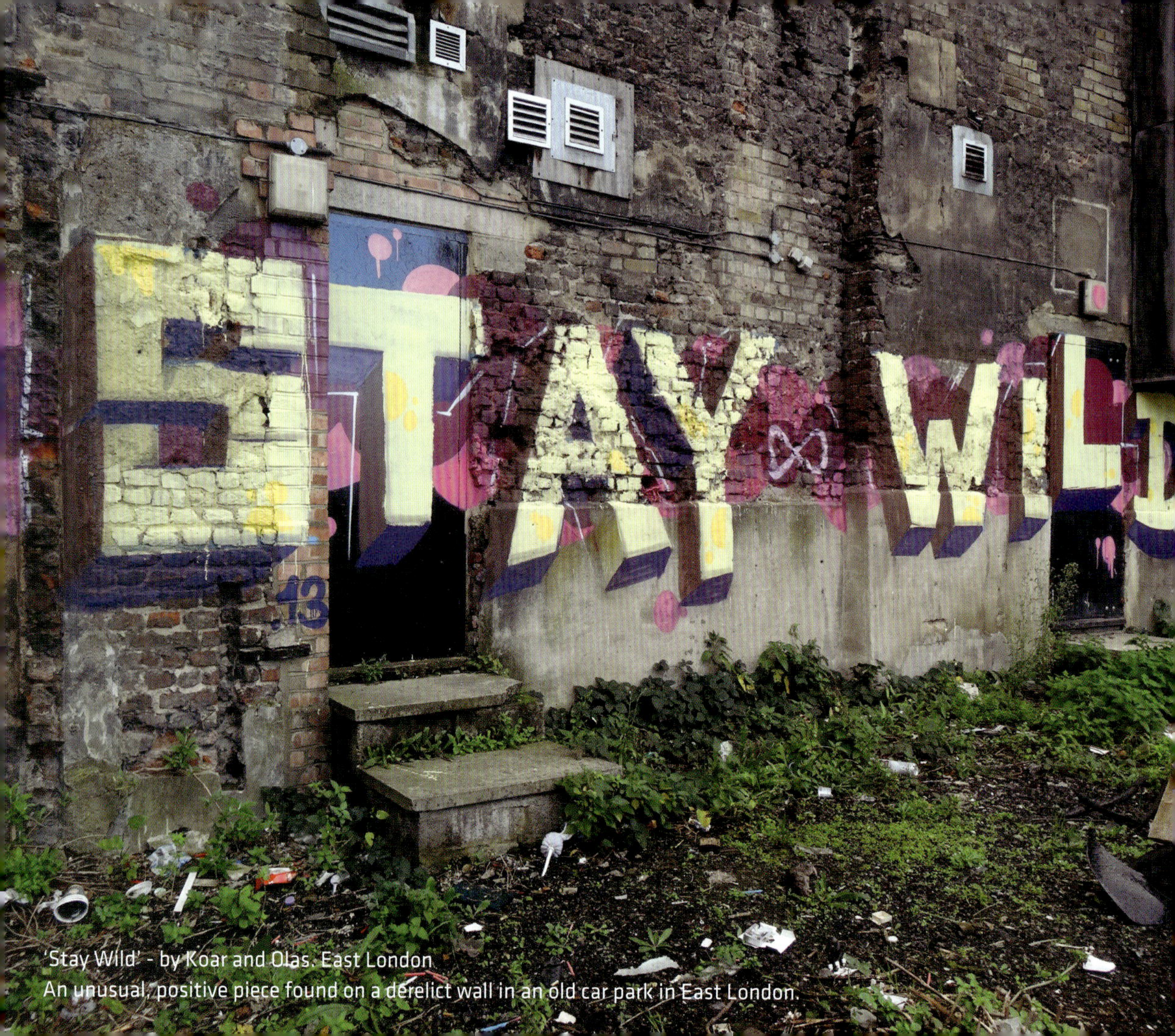

‘Stay Wild’ - by Koar and Olas. East London
An unusual, positive piece found on a derelict wall in an old car park in East London.

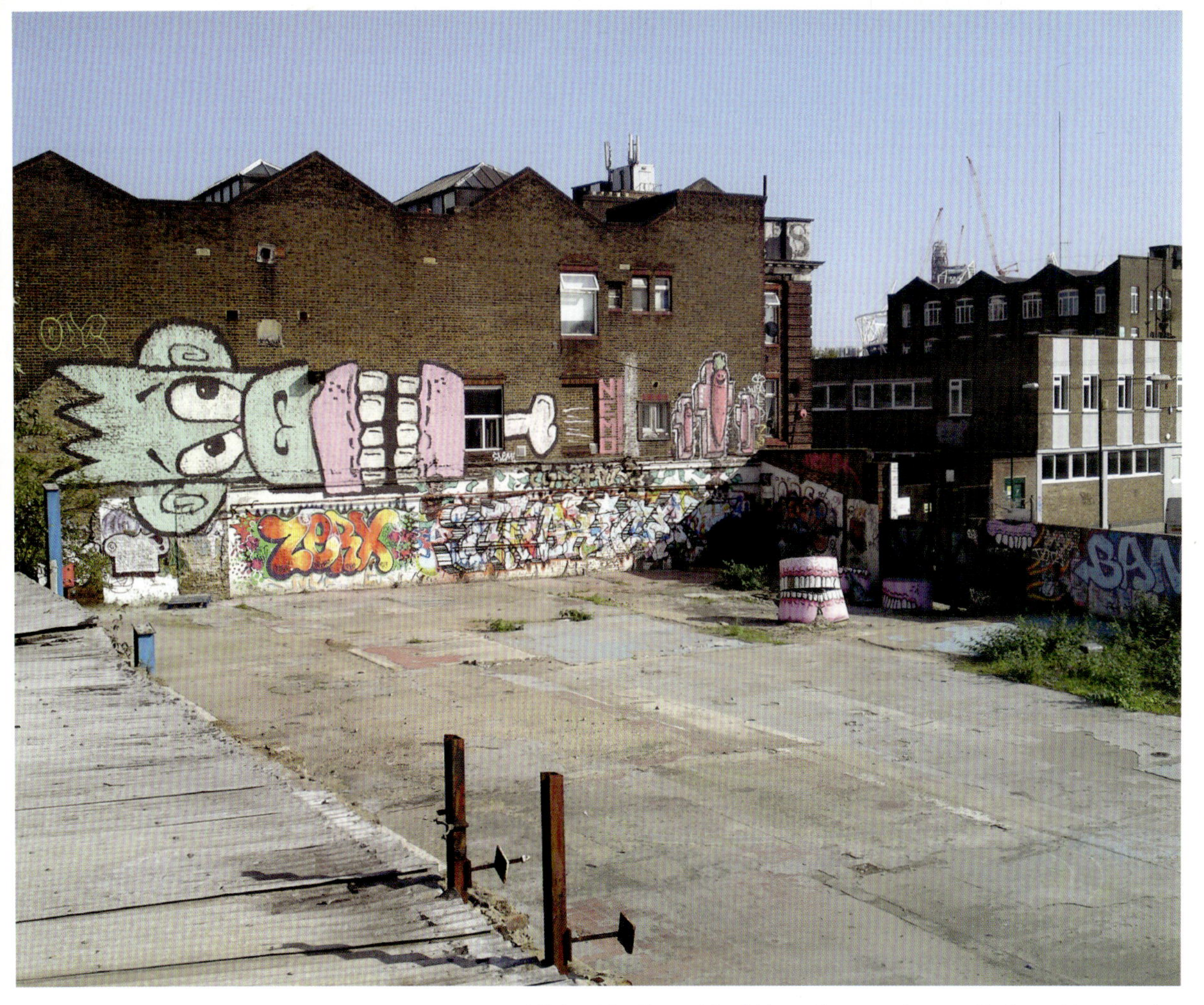

Mighty Mo, Sweet Toof, Zerx, Nemo and more. Hackney, East London

THE HEYGATE ESTATE, SOUTH LONDON (DEMOLISHED)

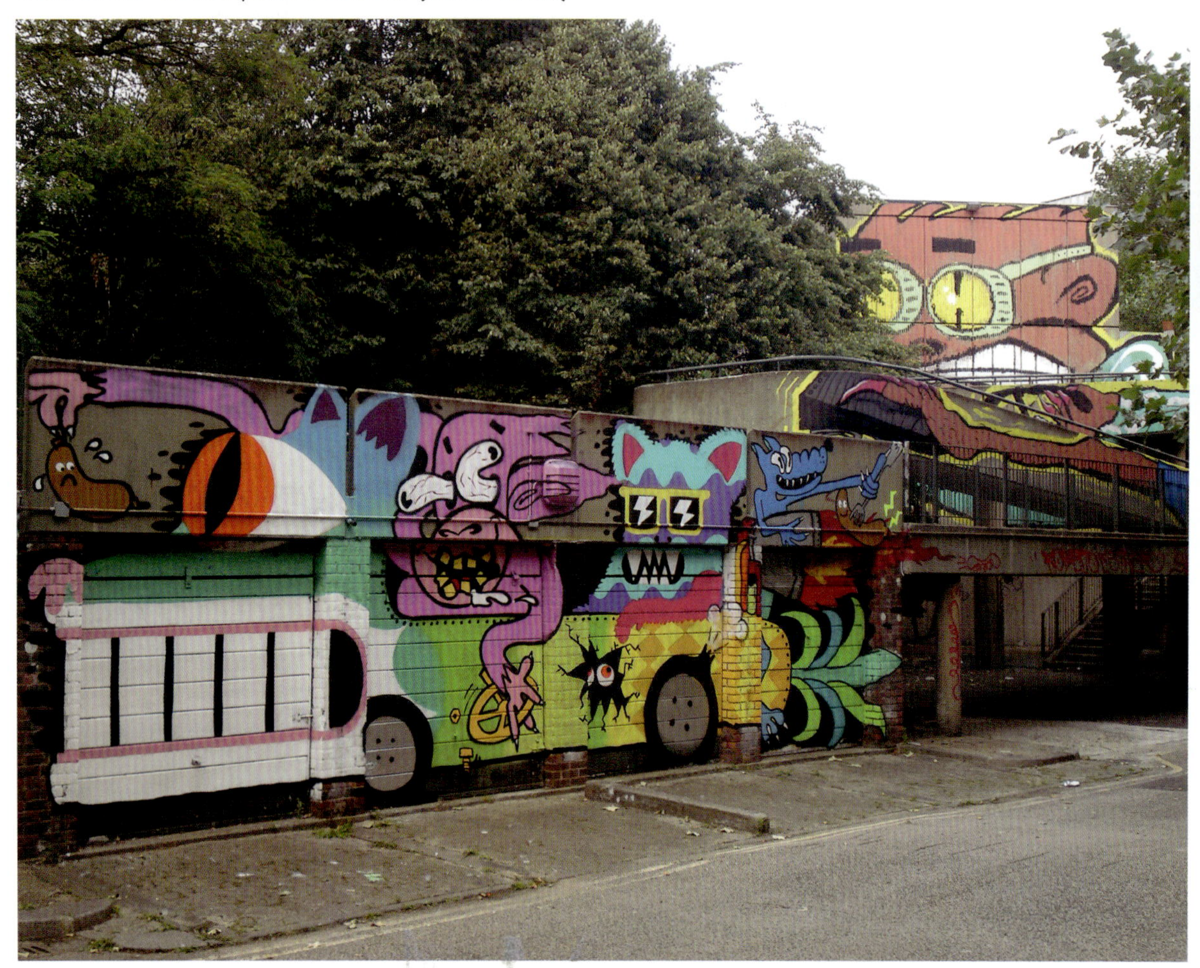

Malarky, Mighty Mo, Gold Peg and Rowdy

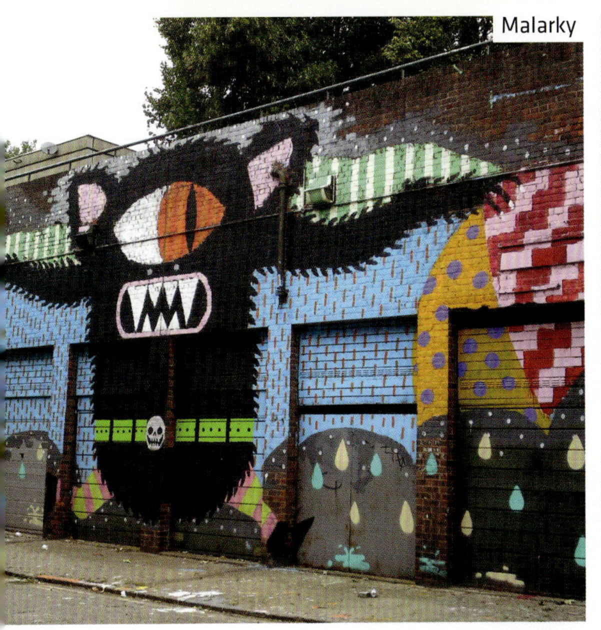
Malarky

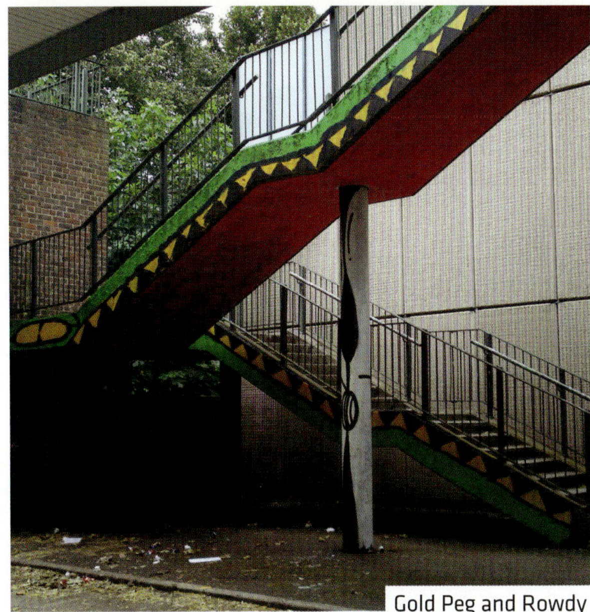
Gold Peg and Rowdy

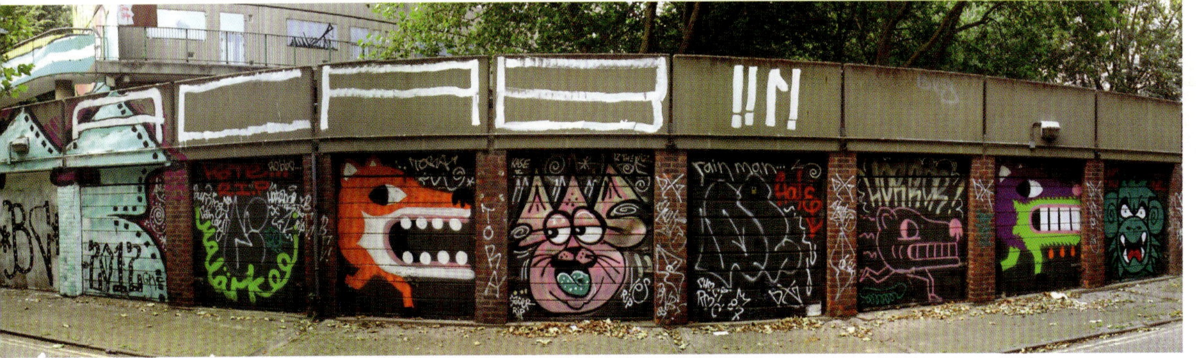
Tek33, Malarky, Mighty Mo and more

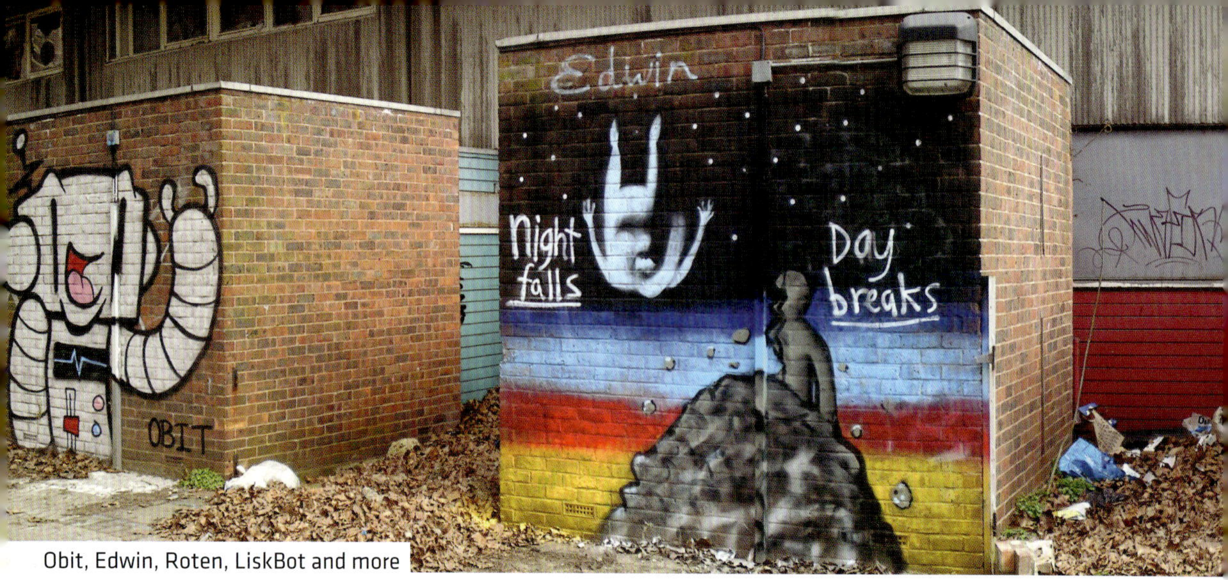

Obit, Edwin, Roten, LiskBot and more

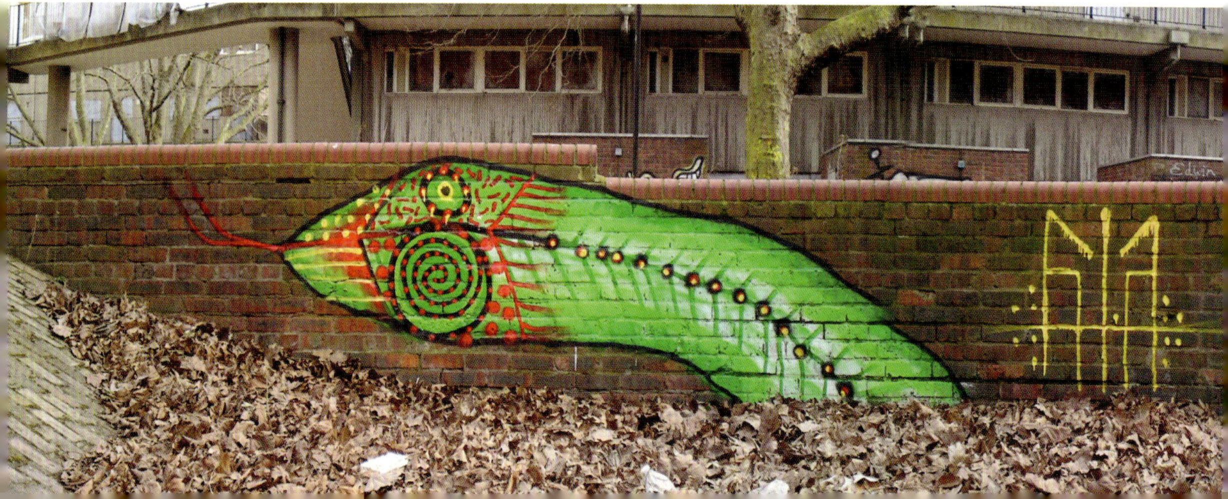

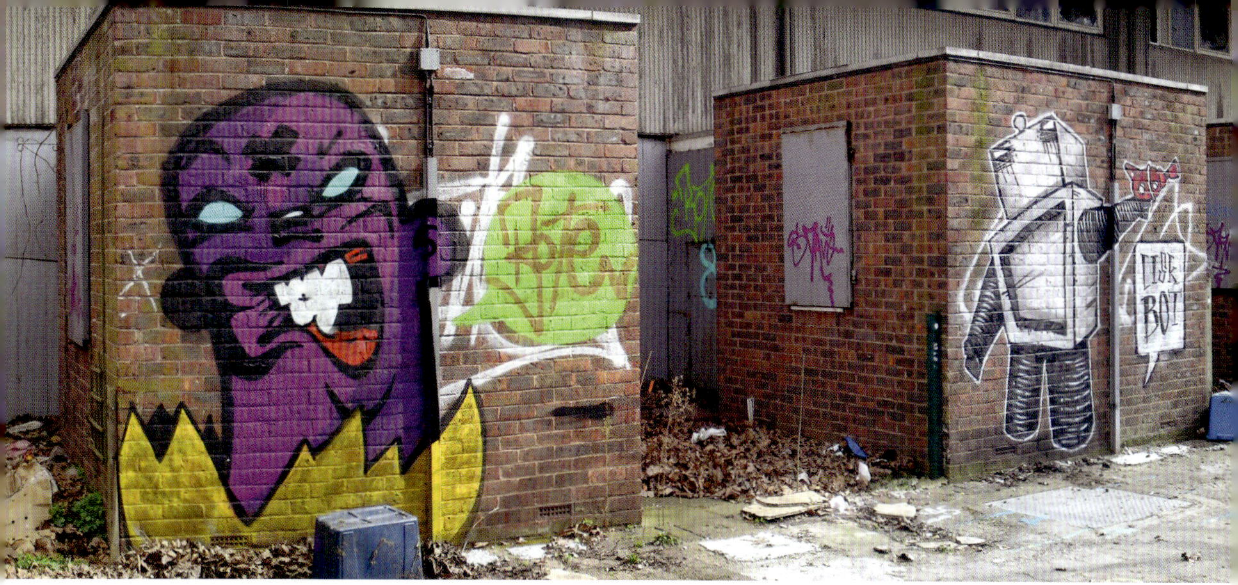

616

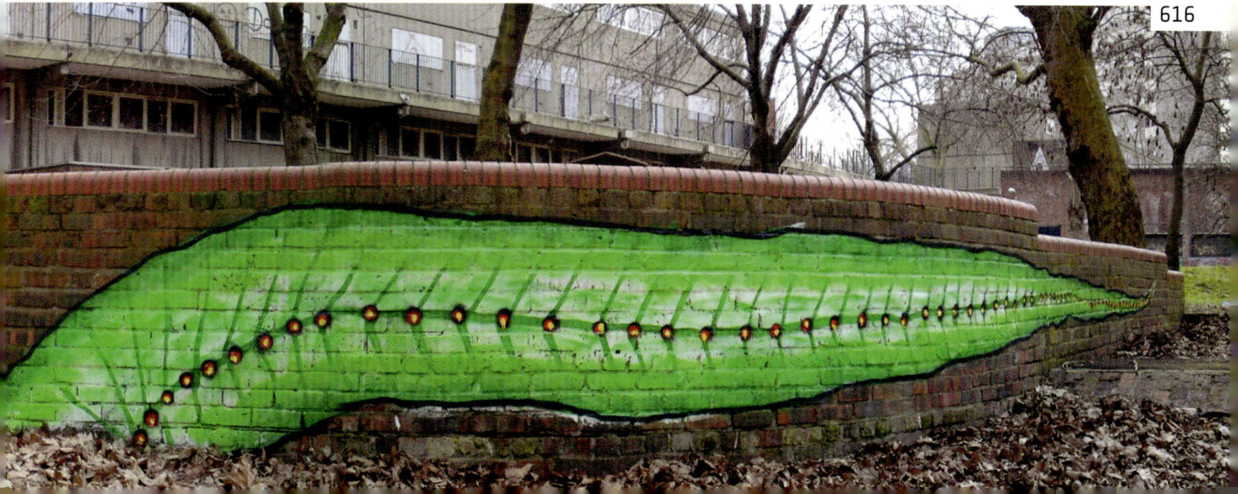

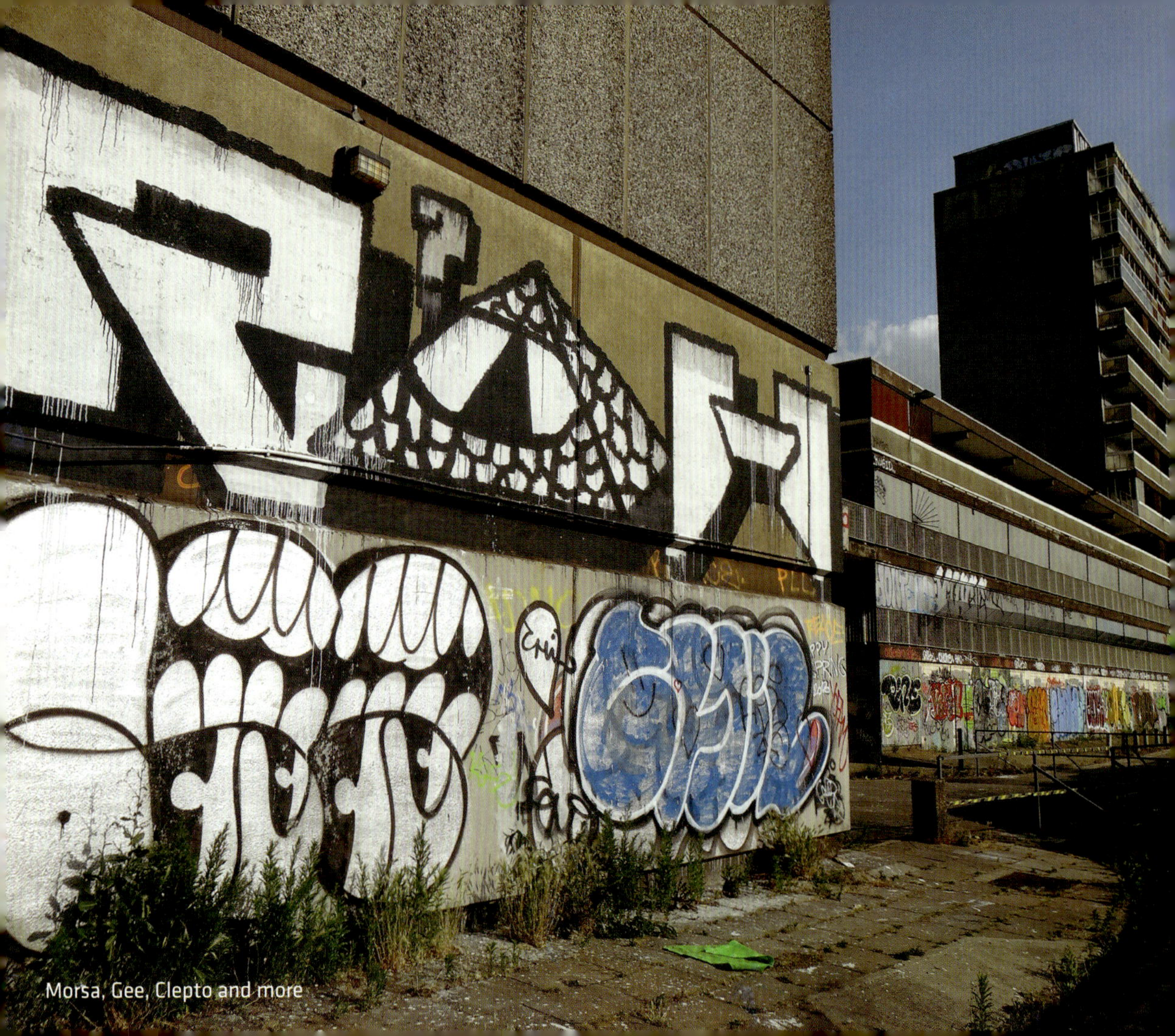

Morsa, Gee, Clepto and more

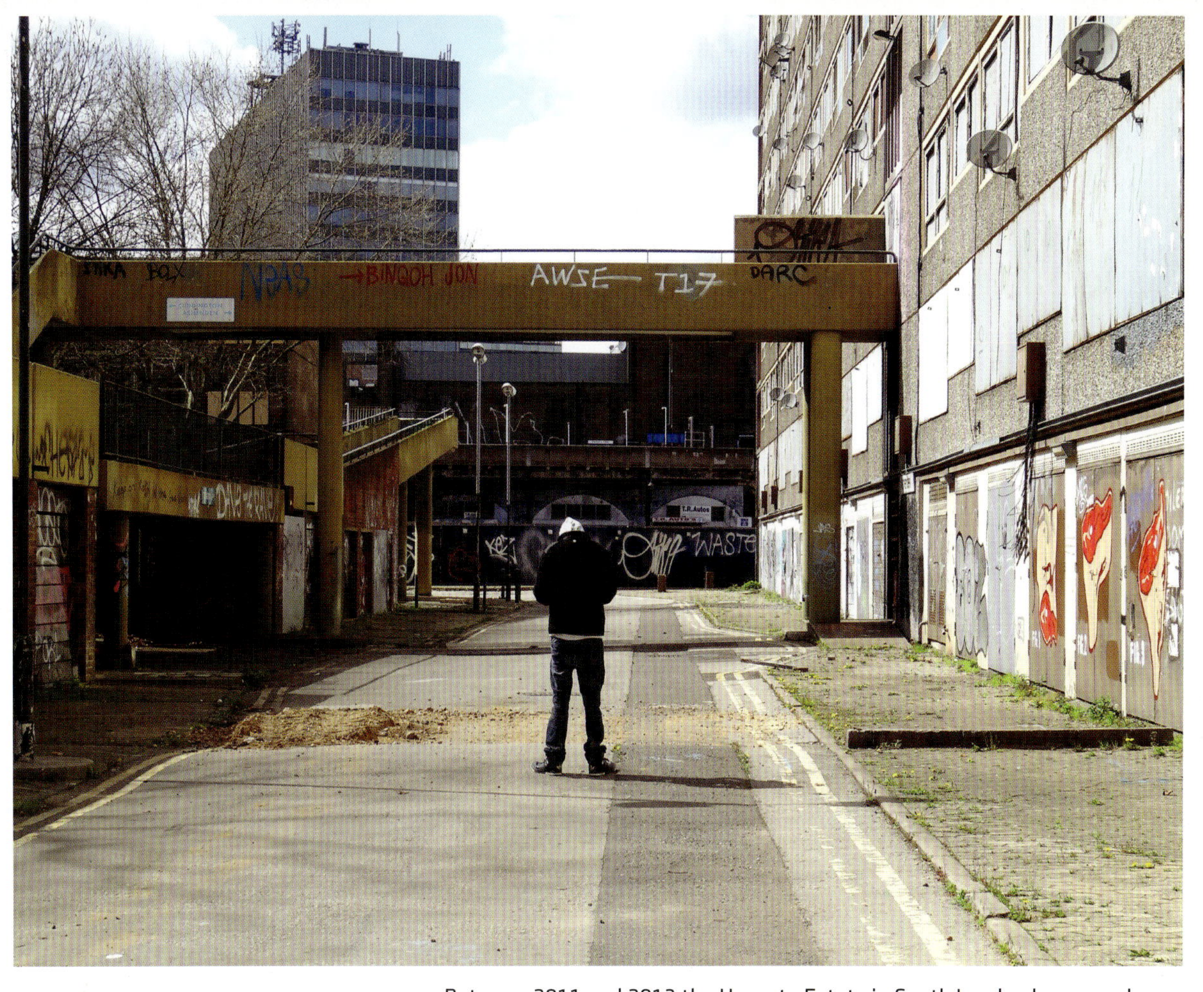

Between 2011 and 2013 the Heygate Estate in South London became a haven for many great artists, but sadly it has now closed for redevelopment.

LONDON STREETS

Regeneration and gentrification projects evolve the cityscape. The rooftops, building-ends, available walls and site hoardings become an ongoing canvas for many local and international artists, providing the local communities with a point of discussion and appreciation.

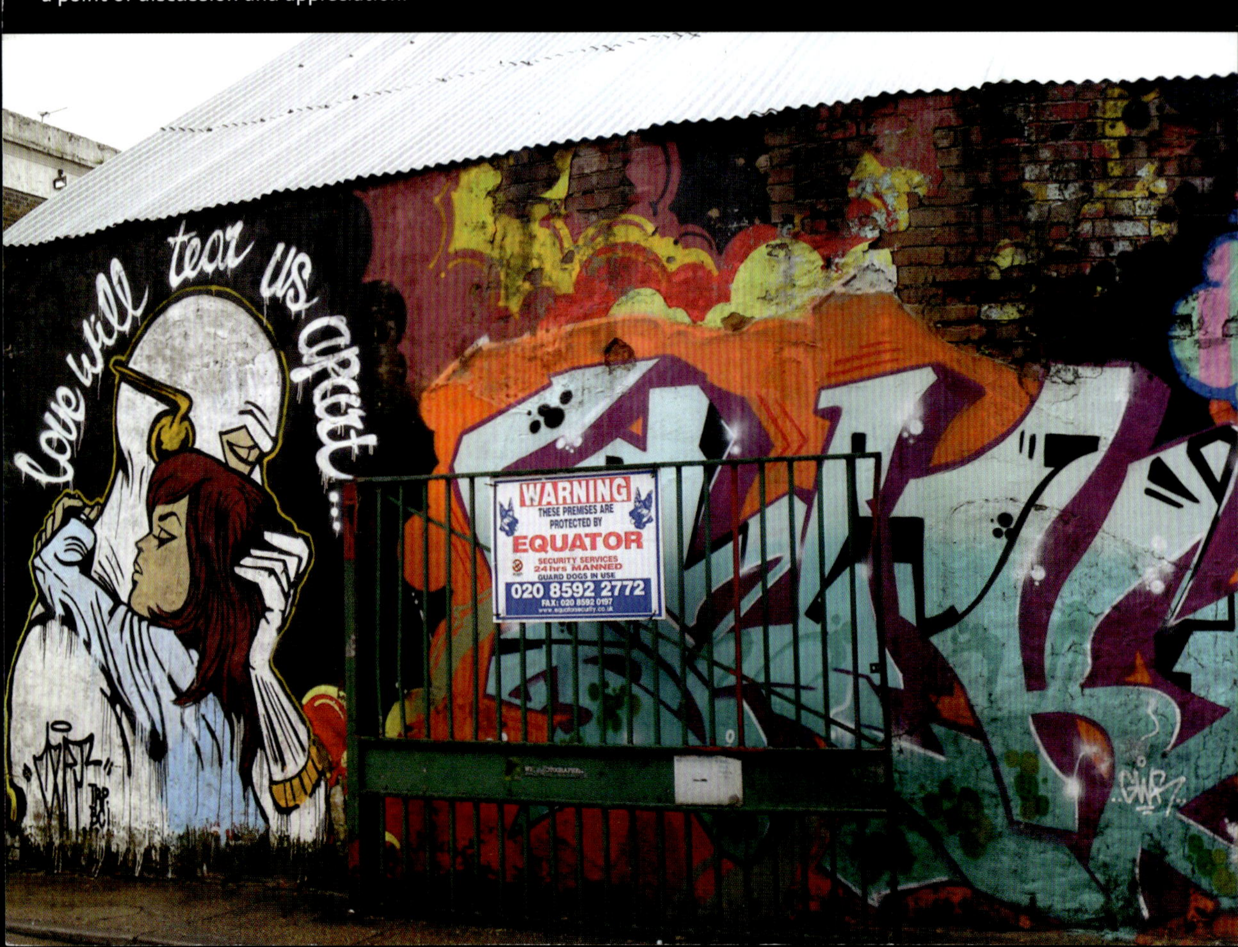

"London to me: An ancient city of infinite potential and endless fascination, which keeps moving forward so fast, it takes your breath away!" - **Snoe - The Rolling People**

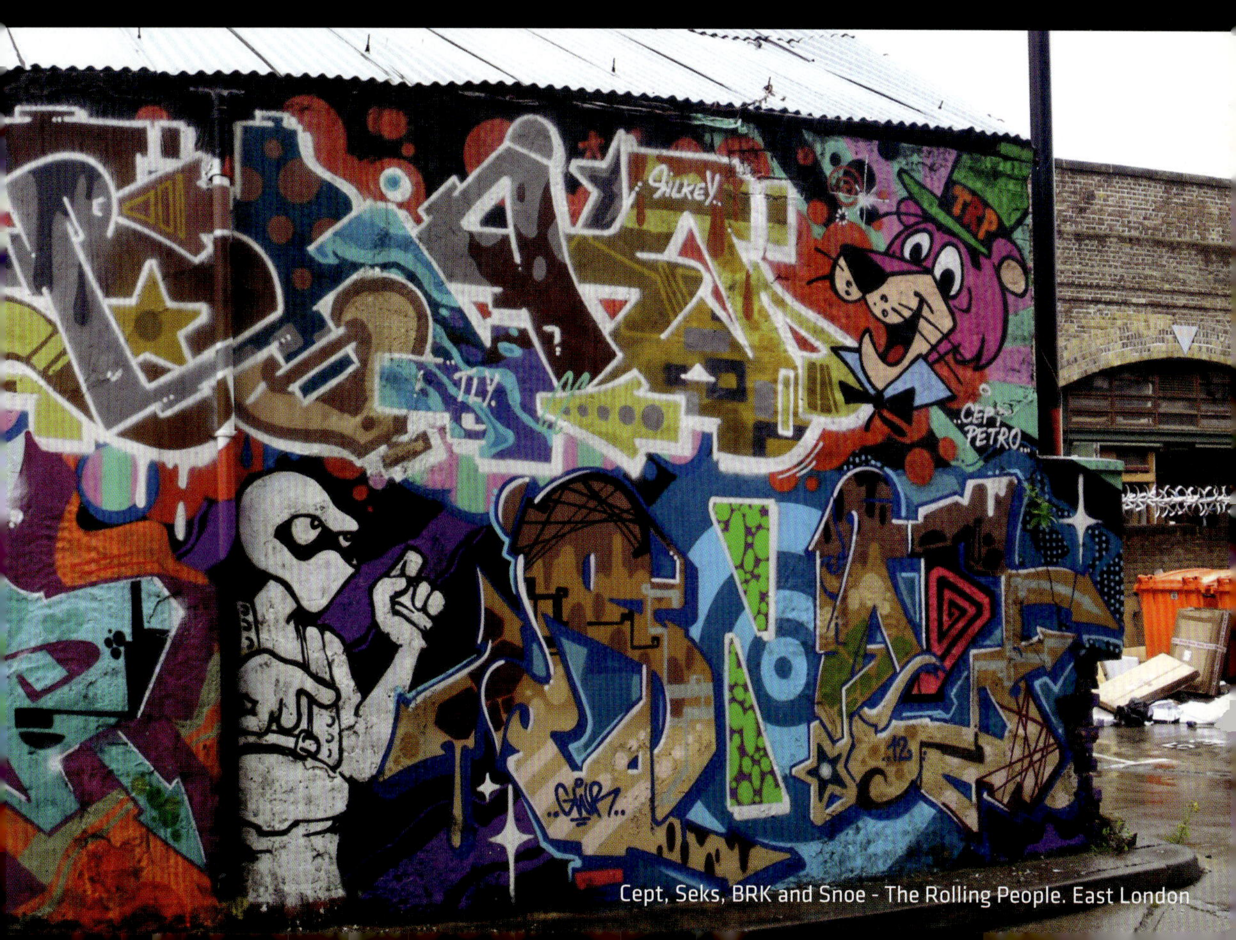

Cept, Seks, BRK and Snoe - The Rolling People. East London

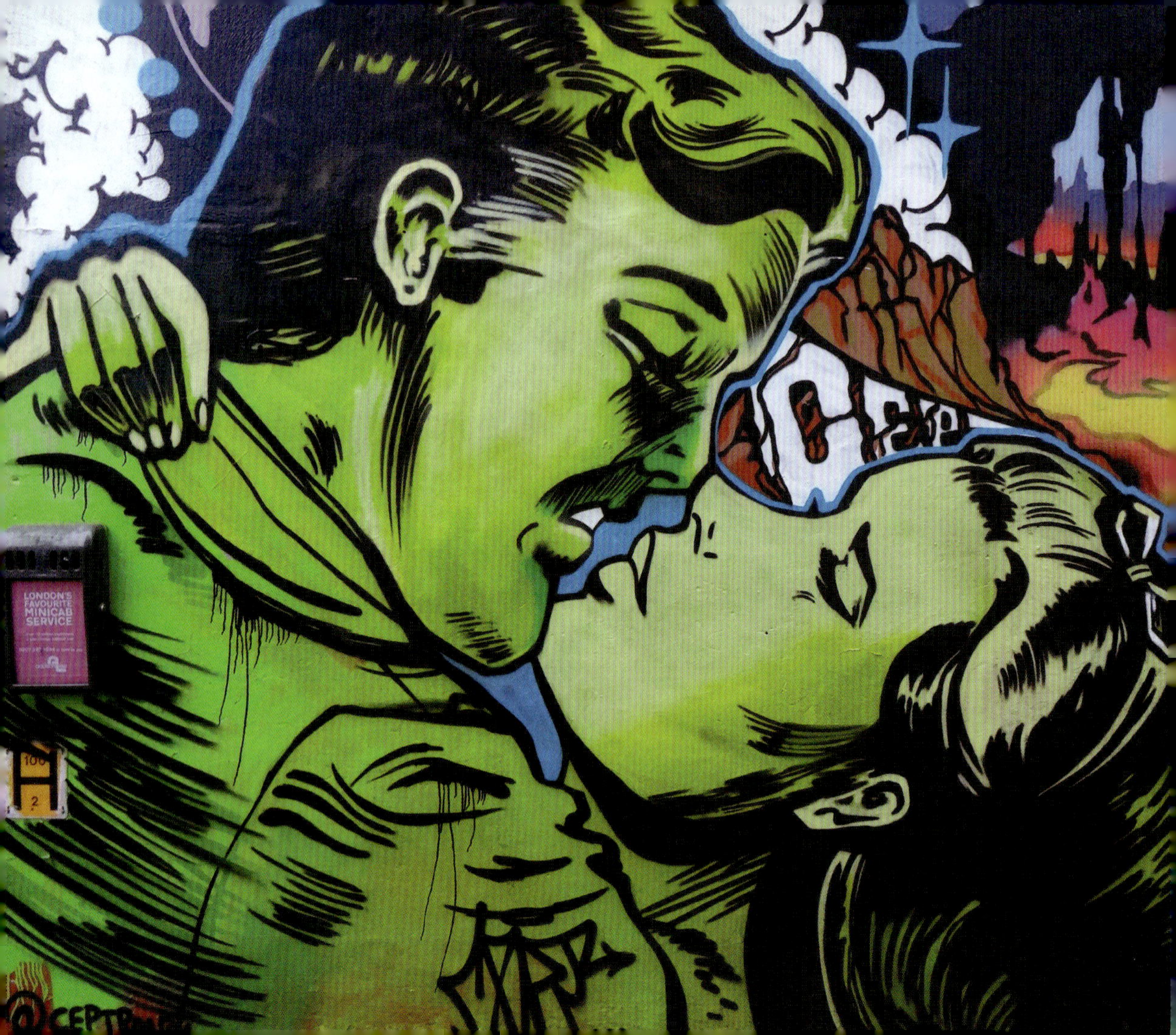
LONDON'S
FAVOURITE
MINICAB
SERVICE
H
100
2

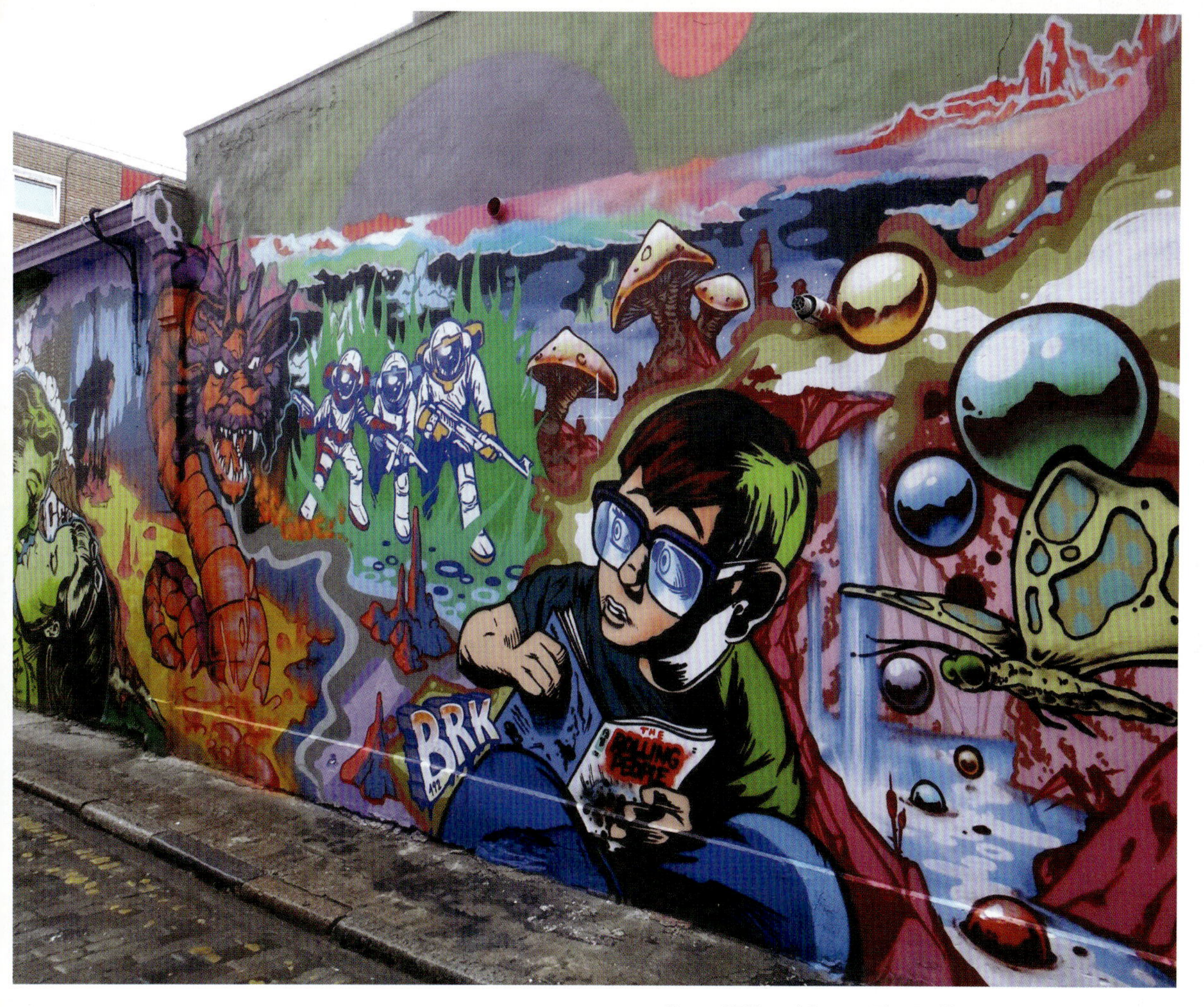

Cept, BRK and Snoe - The Rolling People. East London

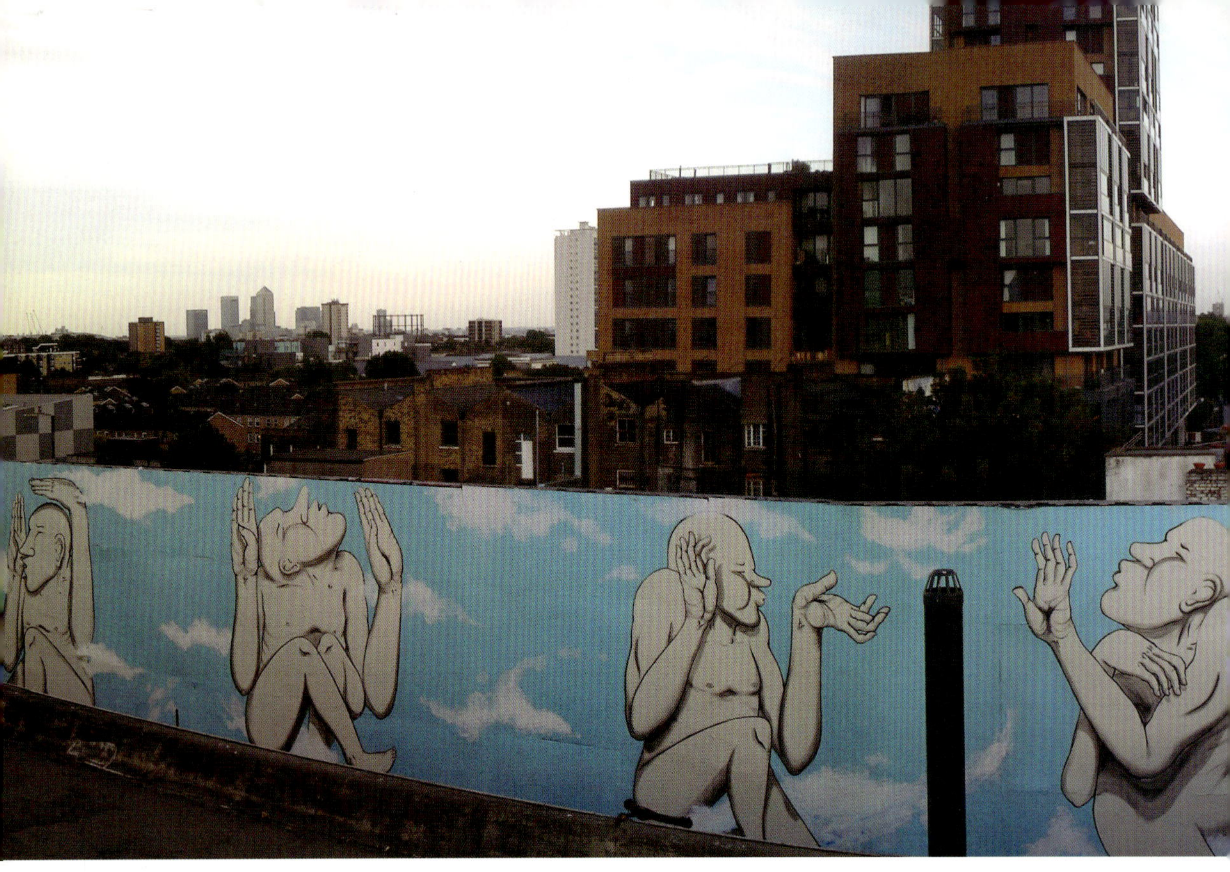

“Living in London for me is an ongoing fight to legitimise what I do. I almost didn’t choose to be here, but now I call it home... I love it and I hate it! I suppose it depends on how you feel, how much satisfaction you achieve, and how many doors you open. London is a cosmopolitan animal with 8.3 million people, the largest city in Europe. The epicentre of culture, avant-garde fashion, art, music, politics and cultural diversity.

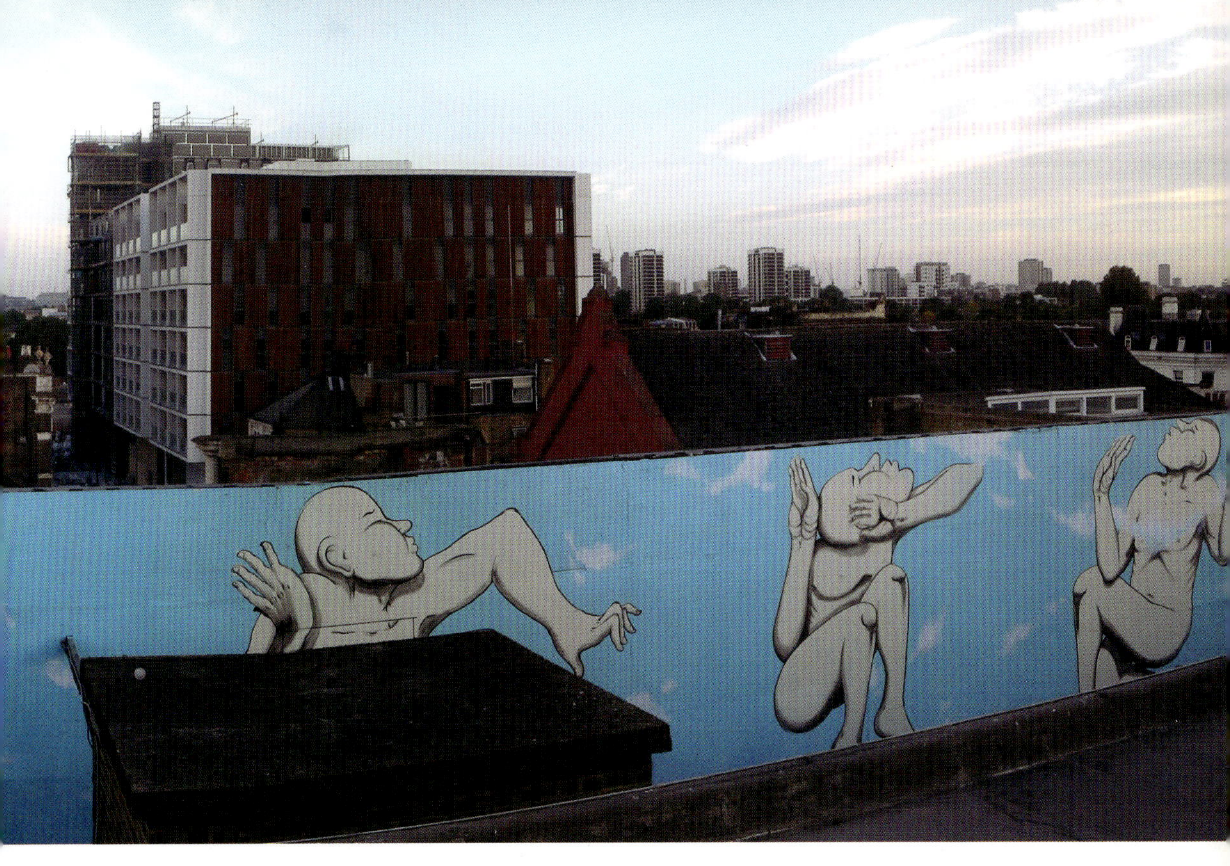

"My art is in the right place here, but I want it to be public... I want public art to be the substitute to the masses of advertisements, and I am empowering myself to choose the place and the time where the paintings are going to appear to the public, it's fair and it's right like that." - **Run**

Dalston, East London

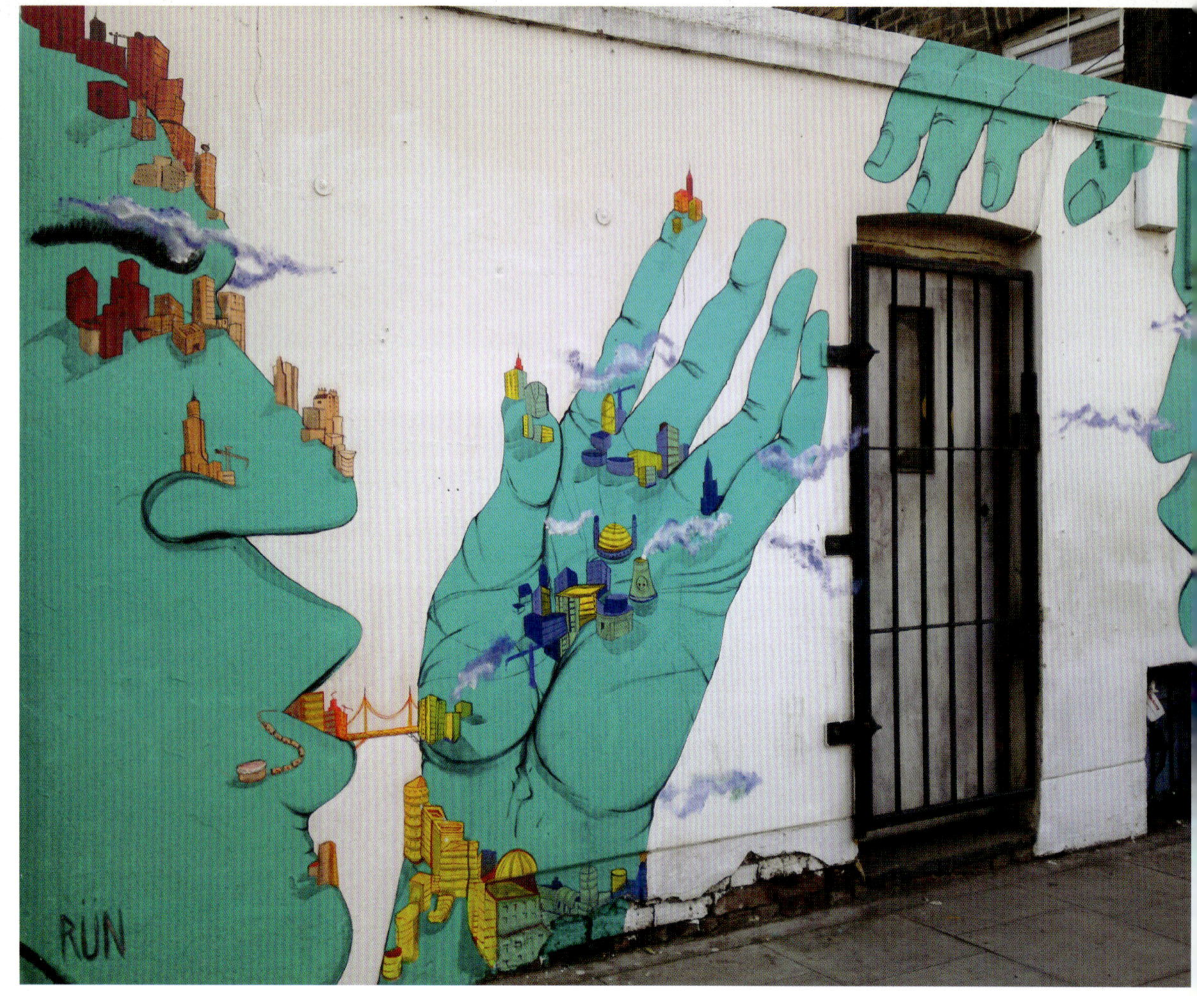

Run. East London

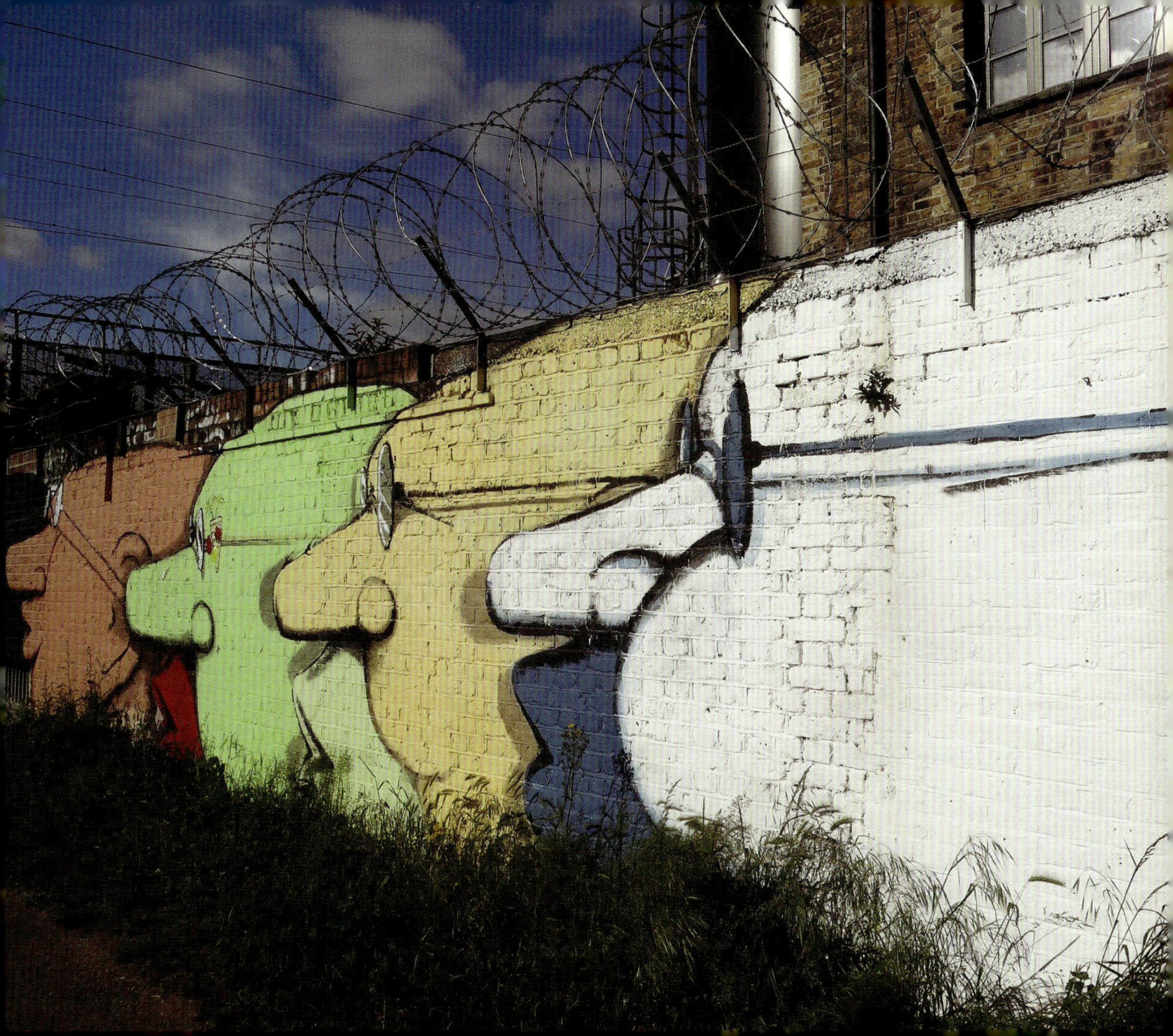

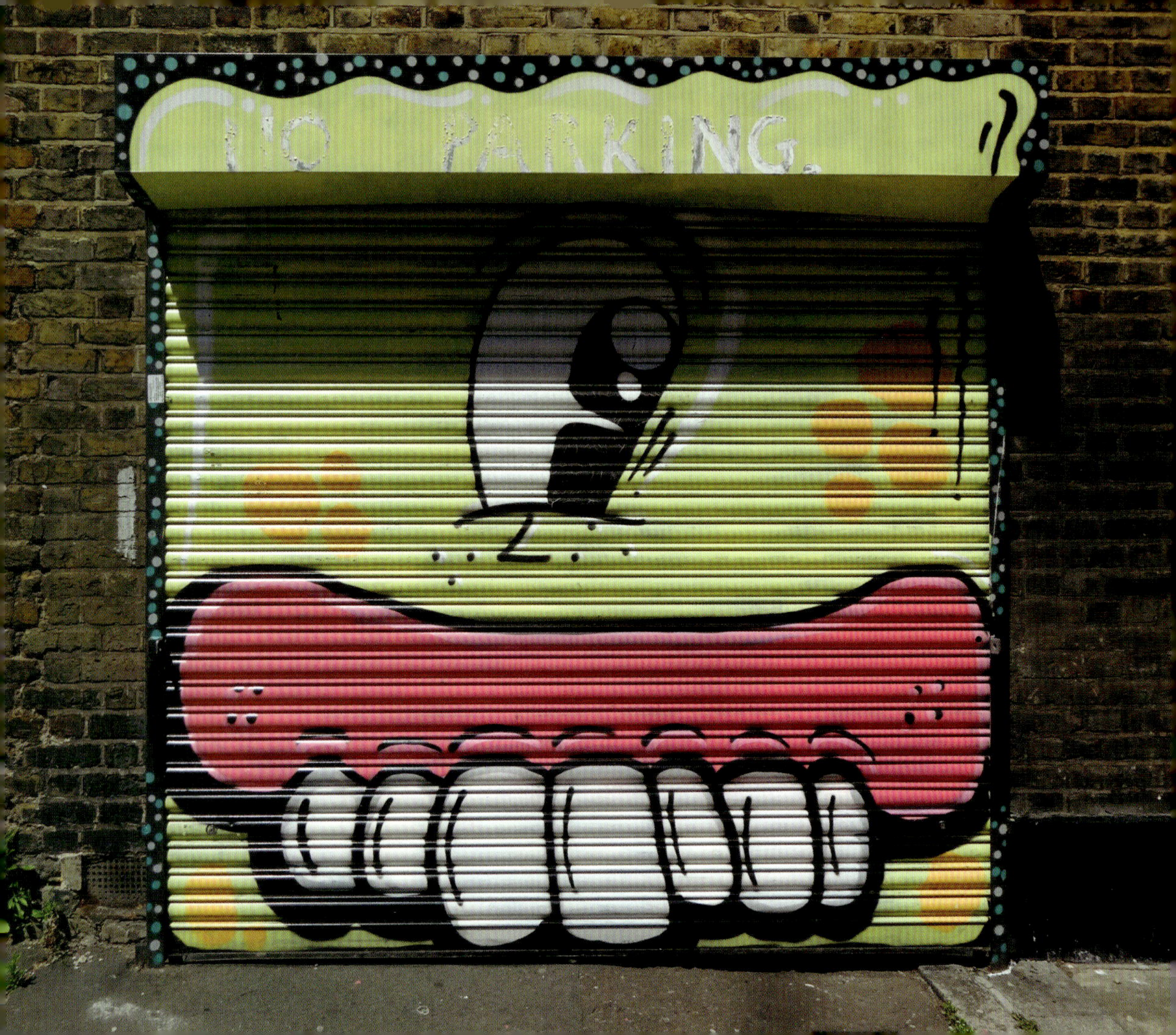
PARKING.

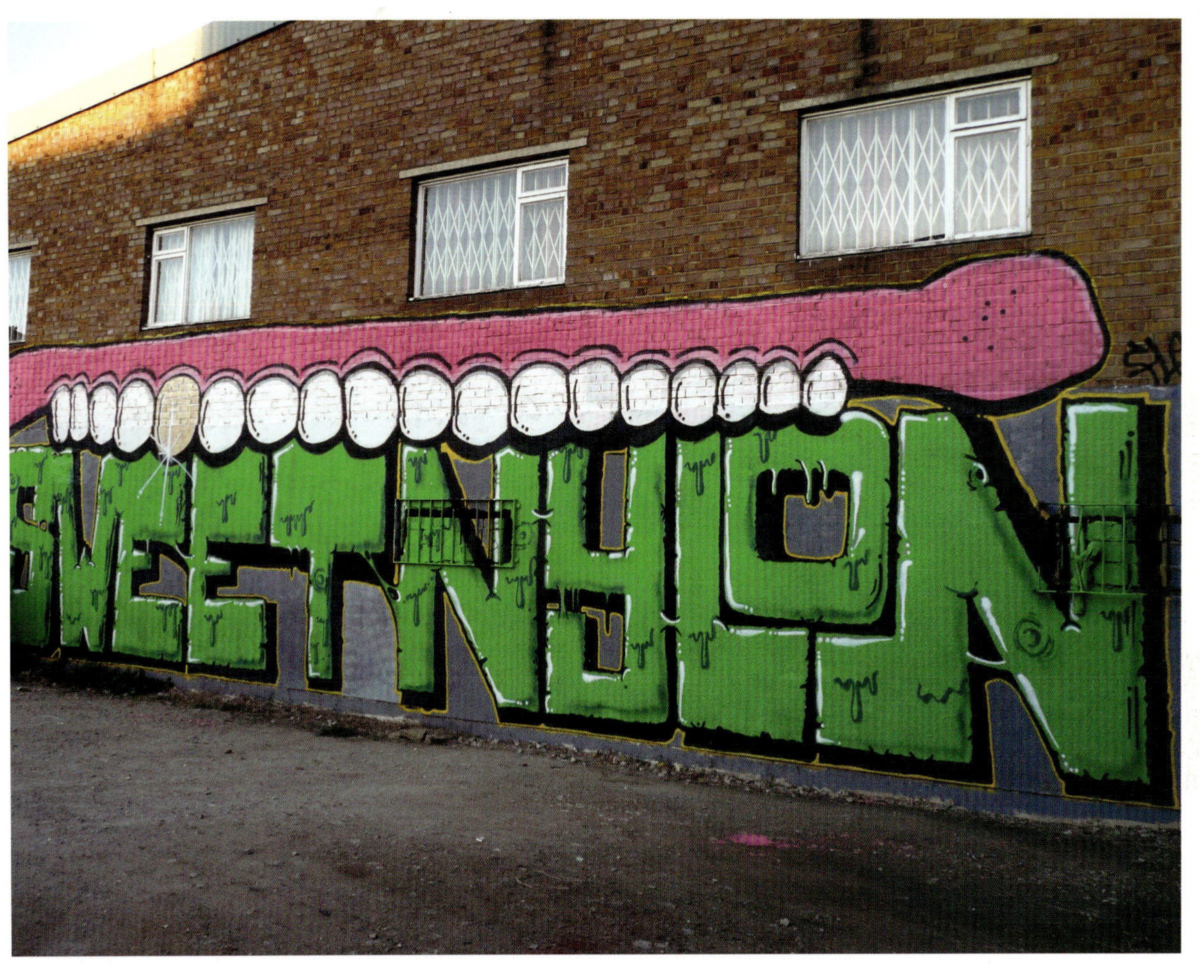

Vinnie Nylon & Sweet Toof. Hackney, East London

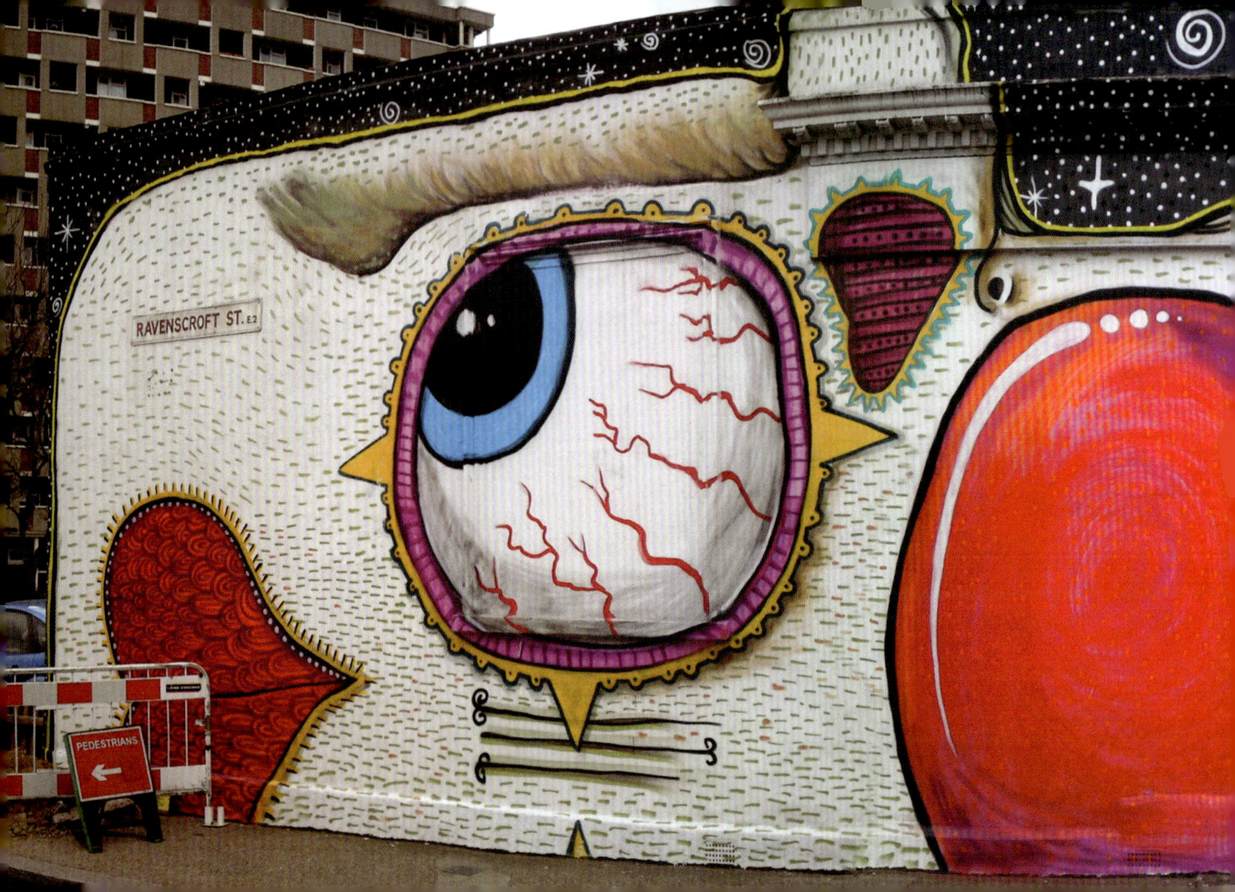
RAVENSCROFT ST. E.2
PEDESTRIANS

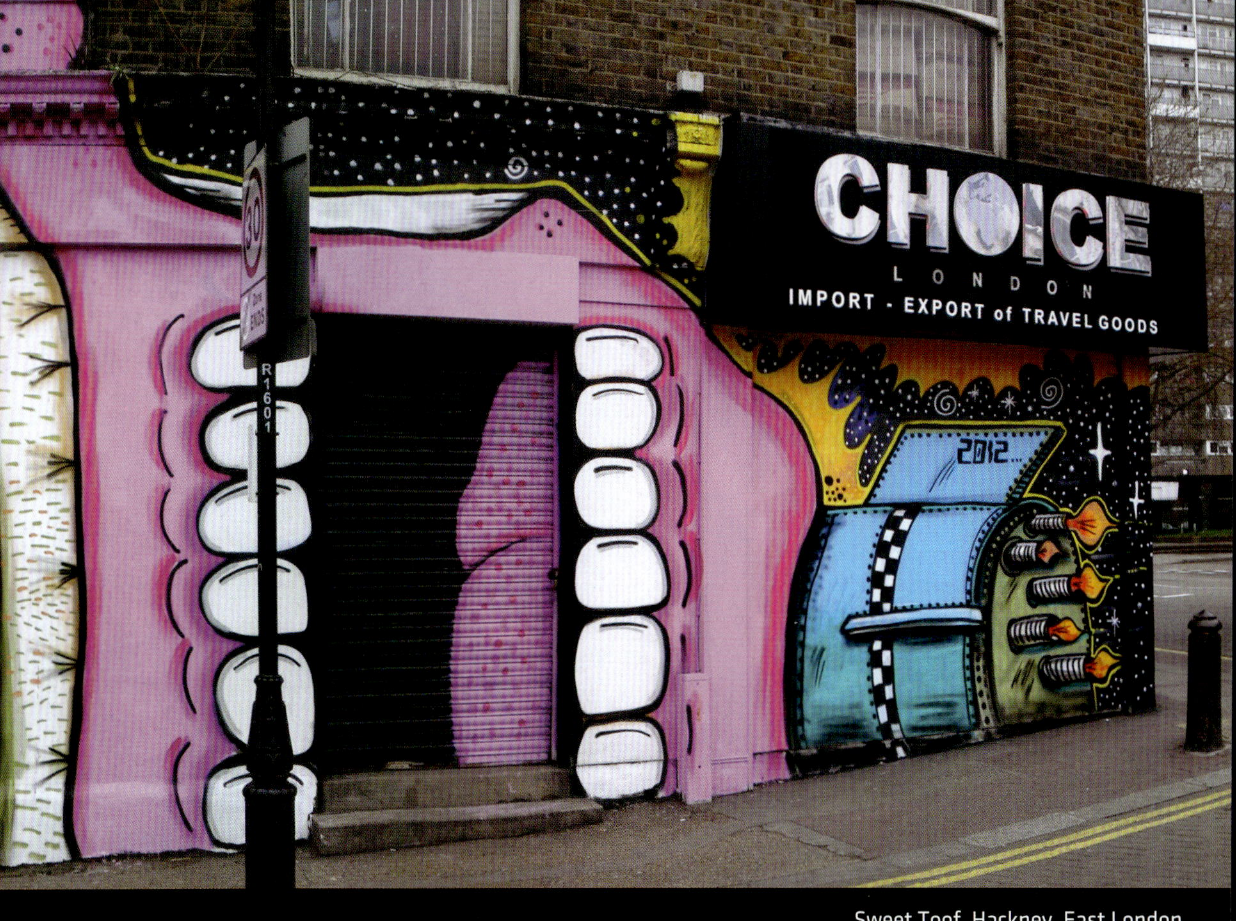

Sweet Toof. Hackney, East London

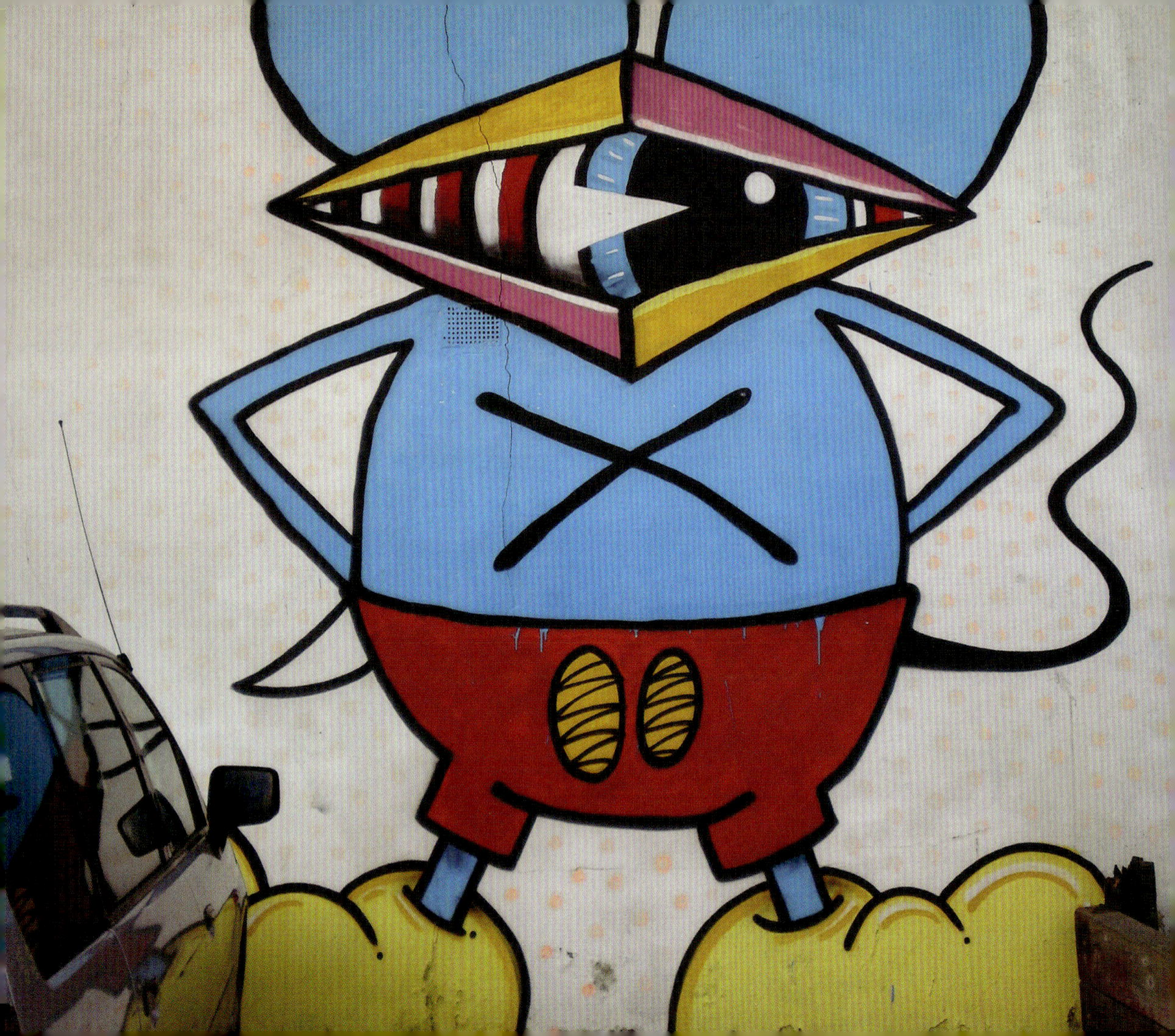

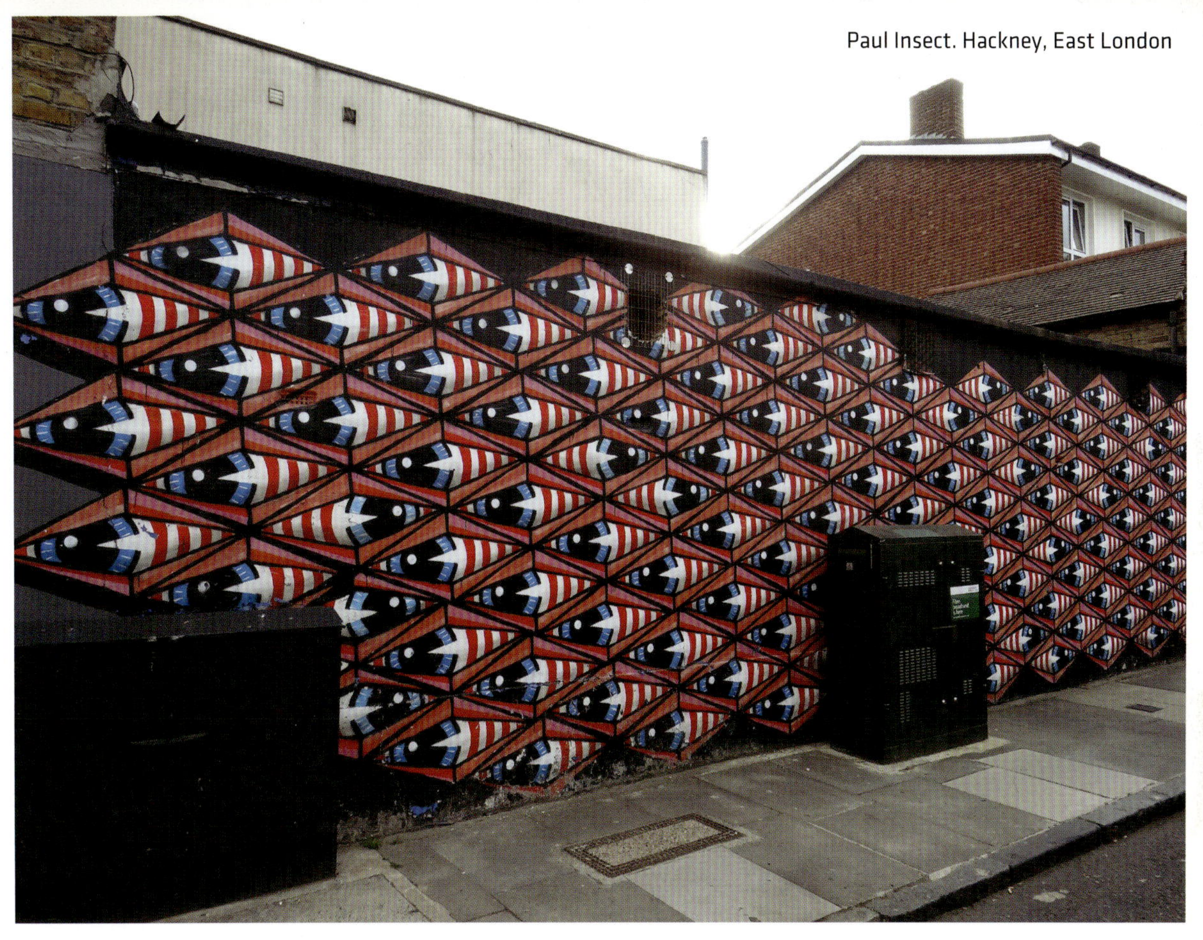

Paul Insect. Hackney, East London

"London stinks of piss, especially the places I seem to paint in. CCTV cameras sitting on every street corner like magpies waiting to dive down and snatch your every movement. Do I hate London? No, I love it. So you love London? No, I hate it." - **Paul Insect**

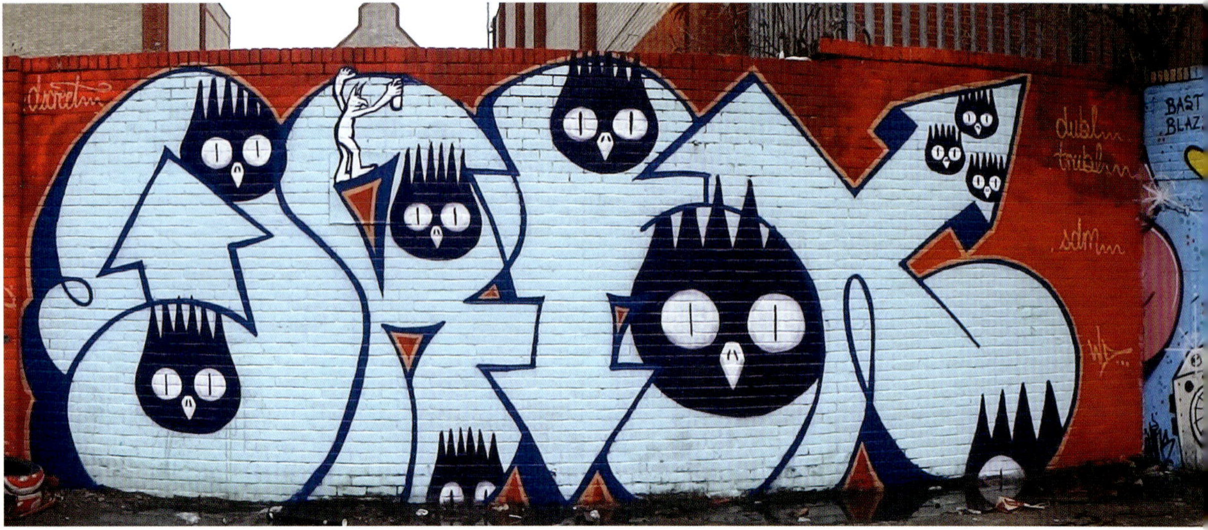

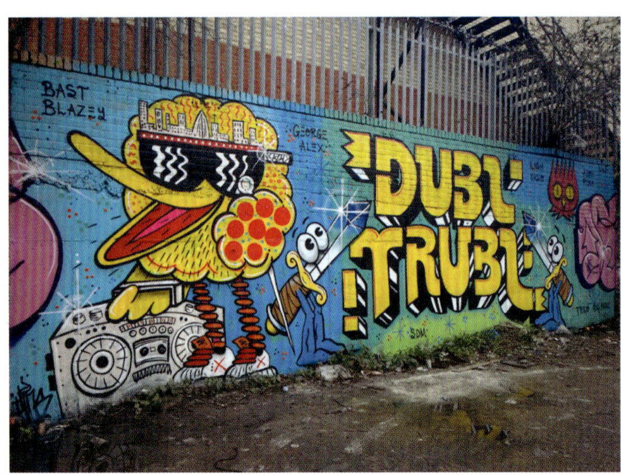
BAST
BLAZEY
GEORGE
ALEX
DUBL
TRUBL
SDM

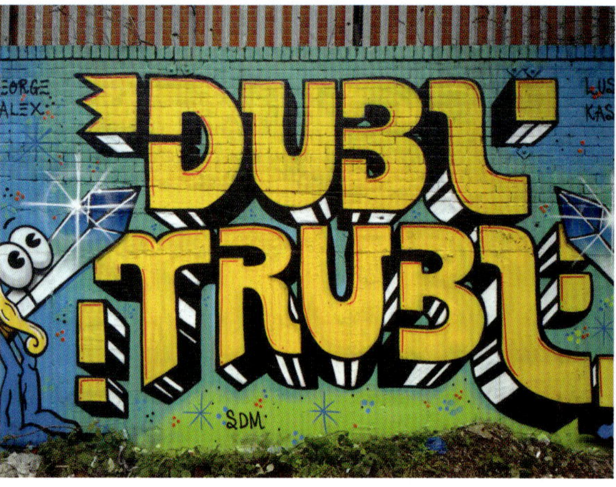
GEORGE
ALEX
DUBL
TRUBL
SDM

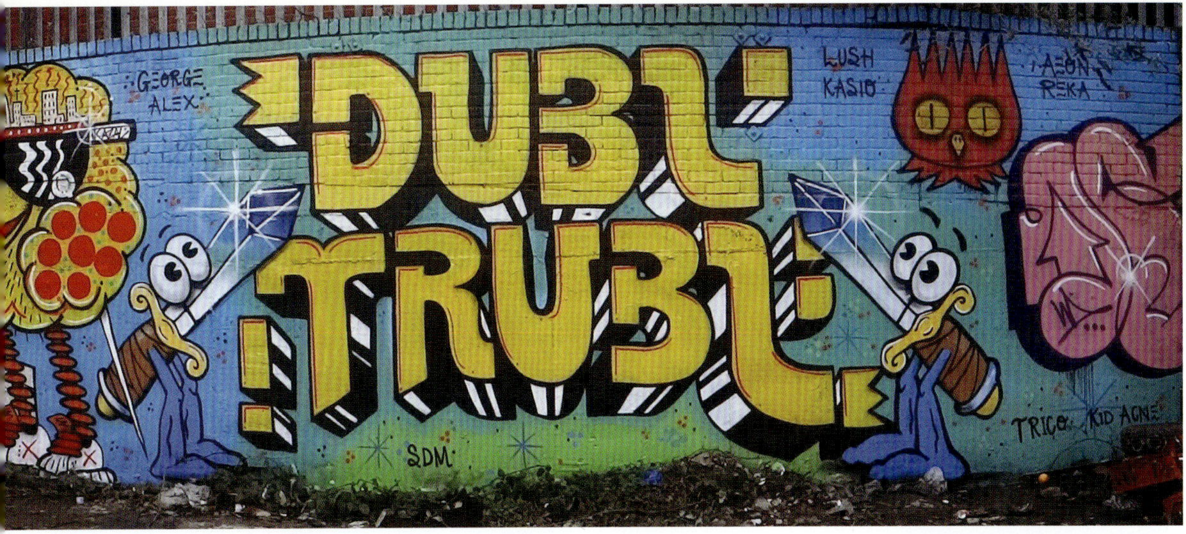

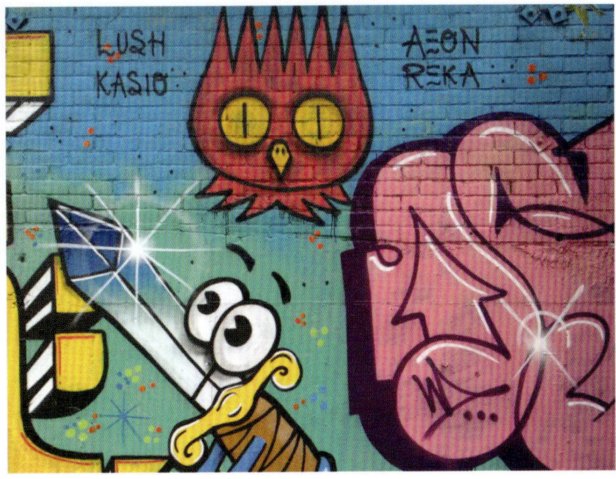

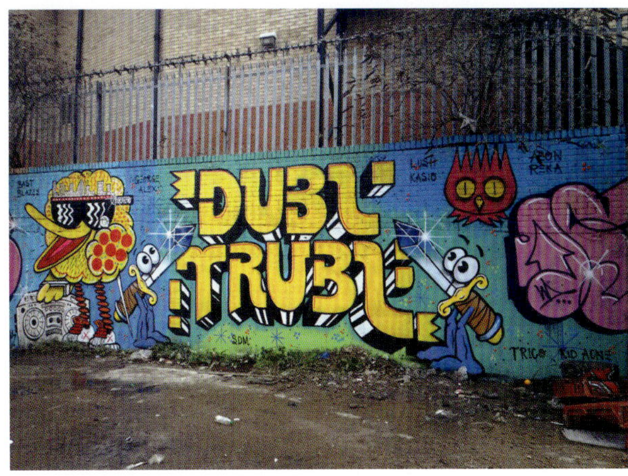

Drax, DSCREET and Paul Insect. East London

“London means many things to me. Some good, some bad and some just downright ‘different’. For example: Police with no guns - apart from when they shoot people; Taxi drivers that speak virtually no English and don’t know an address that’s 100 yards from the office they’re based at; Soggy fish’n’chips, drowned in vinegar; Standing on the platform at Finchley Road - watching the trains go by; Black people with Irish accents; Chinese schoolgirls that speak a cockney/ yardie hybrid - until they answer the phone in Cantonese. Pie’n’mash - even though I hate mash; Rhyming slang that hardly anyone understands; Arsenal Football Club; The PFB crew; Writing my name on the same wall - that I wrote it on nearly 30 years ago!

“London! When I’ve been away for a month, I can’t wait to get home. London! When I’ve been there for a month, I can’t wait to fuck off! London! I wear its stench with pride!” - **Drax PFB**

“Good times, great people, shit weather.” - **DSCREET**

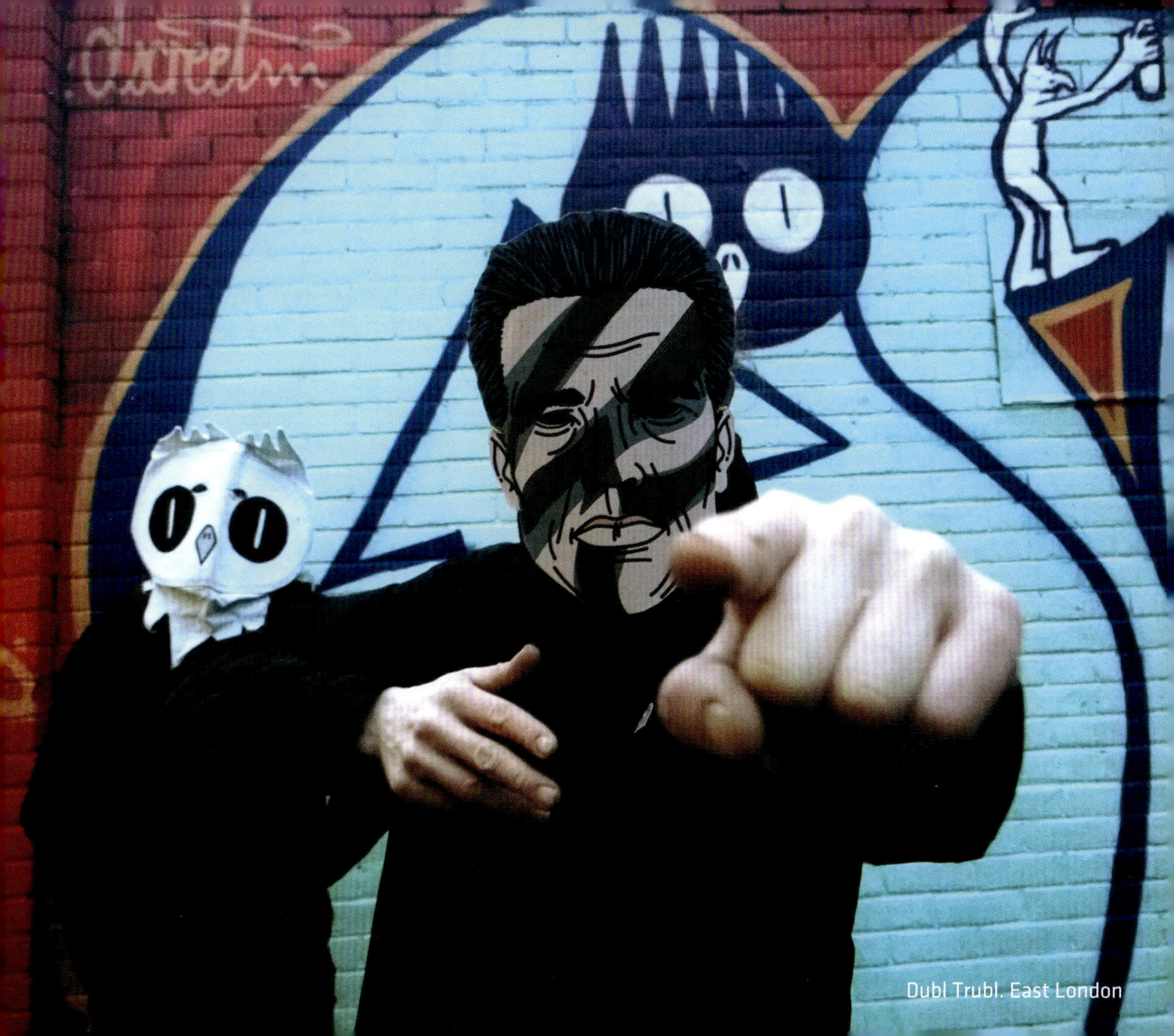

Dubl Trubl. East London

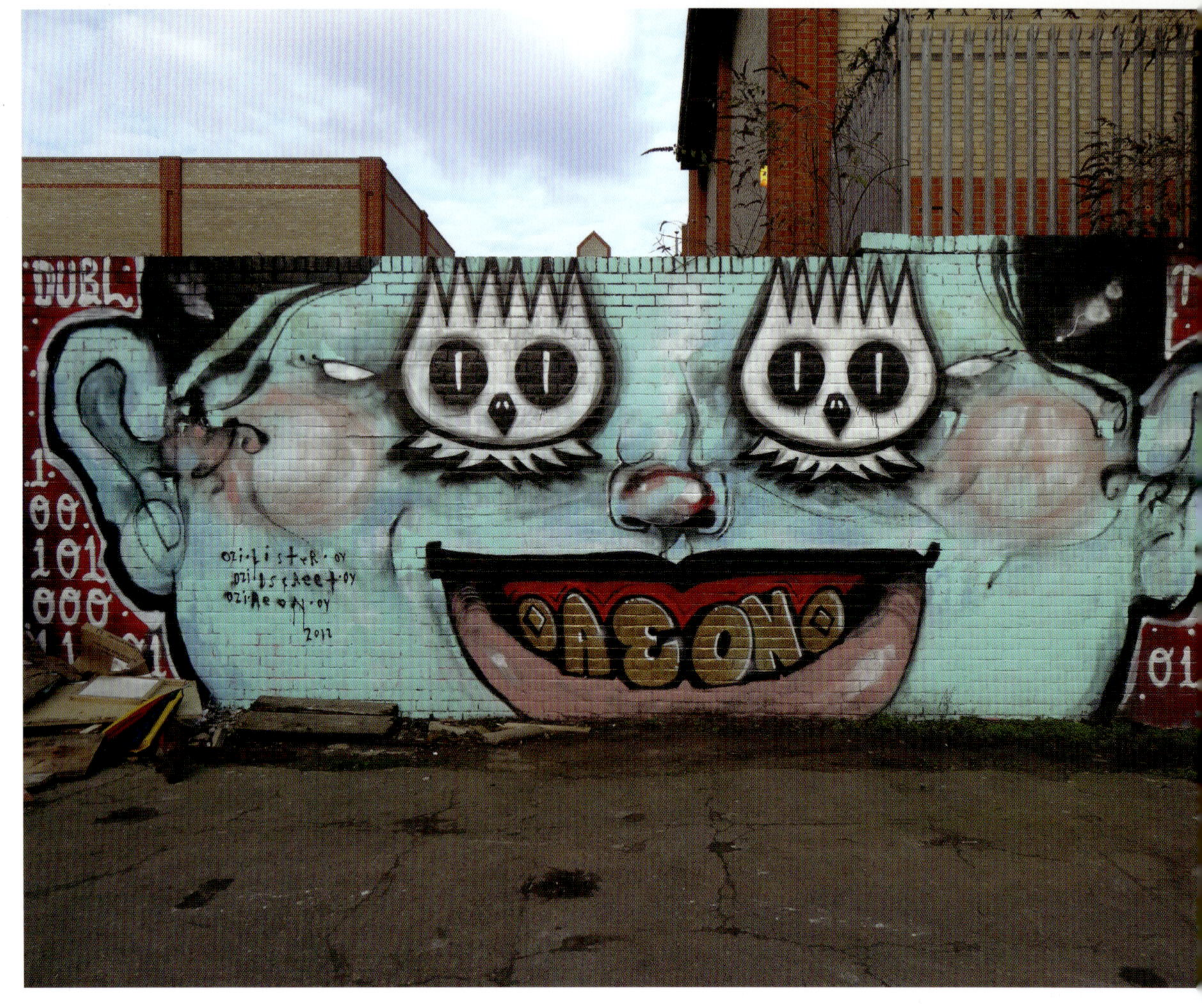

Anthony Lister, DSCREET and Aeon Fly. East London

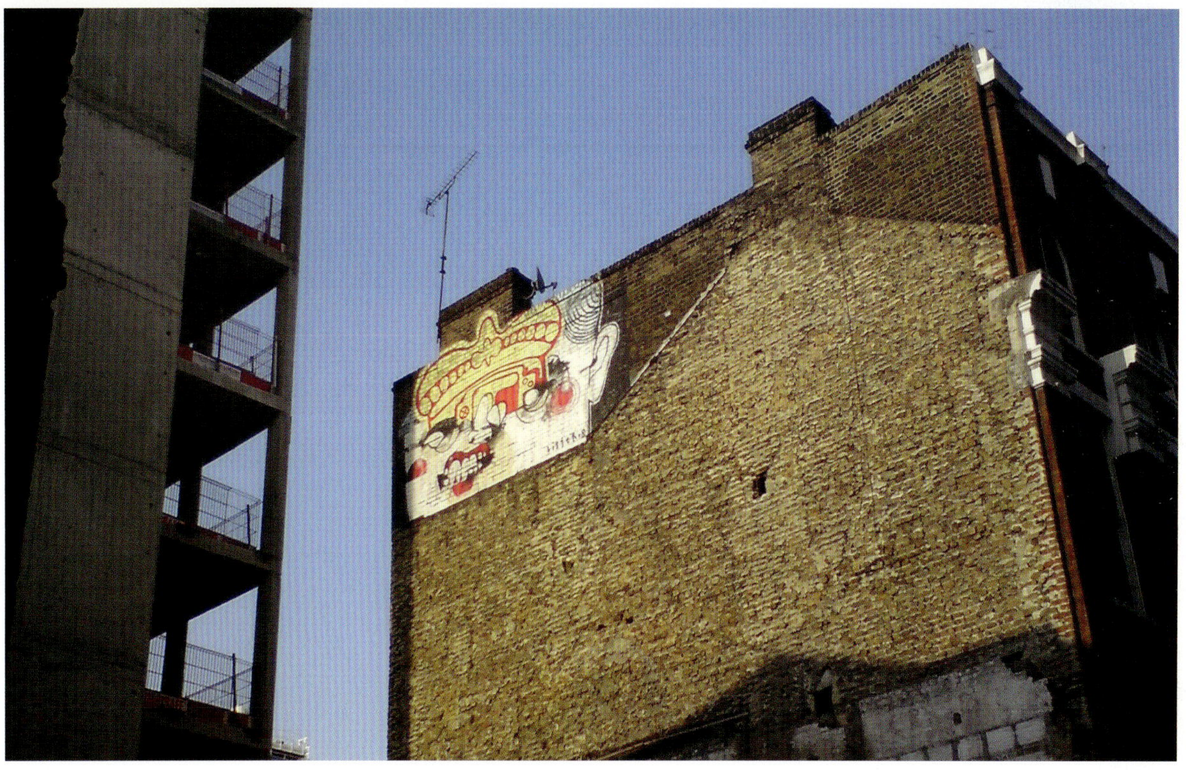

The collaboration above by Sickboy and Anthony Lister was originally painted on the roof of an old bar, before the building was demolished in 2009, leaving the ‘floating’ artwork exposed.

“London means about as much to me as I could pack into mum’s lunch for Christmas. Thinking of this question, I have flashing memories of the Dragon bar before it burnt down, and the glimmer from Chewie’s eye as I snuck on the roof with Sickboy for that last paint that eventually made a floater. Nothing tickles my crumpets, and few more, than getting back into London town and seeing one of my drunk street crawl ramblings active and at large, in the possum pocket of my mother country.” - **Anthony Lister**

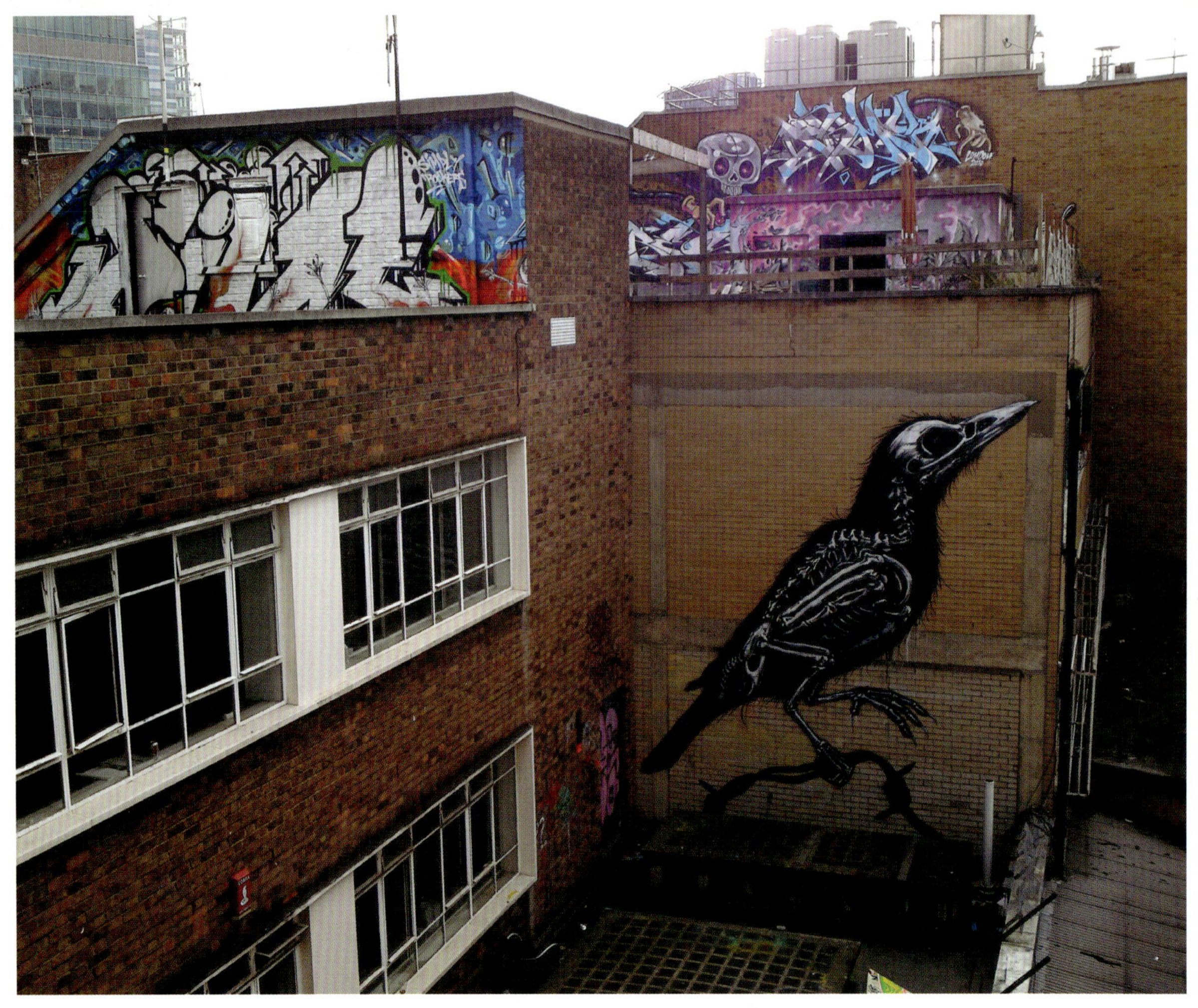

Jive, Nychos, Crome, Roa and more. East London

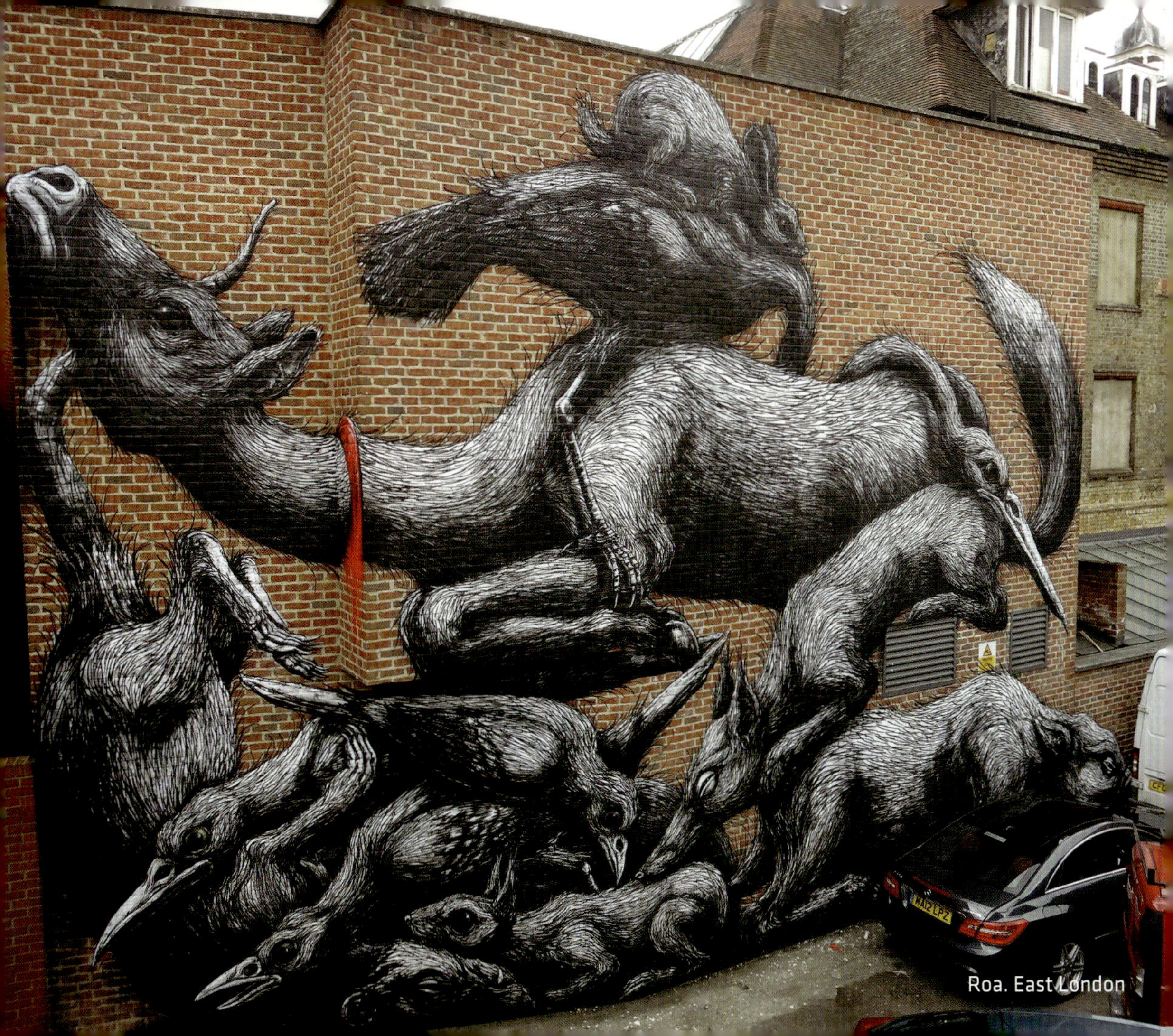

Roa. East London

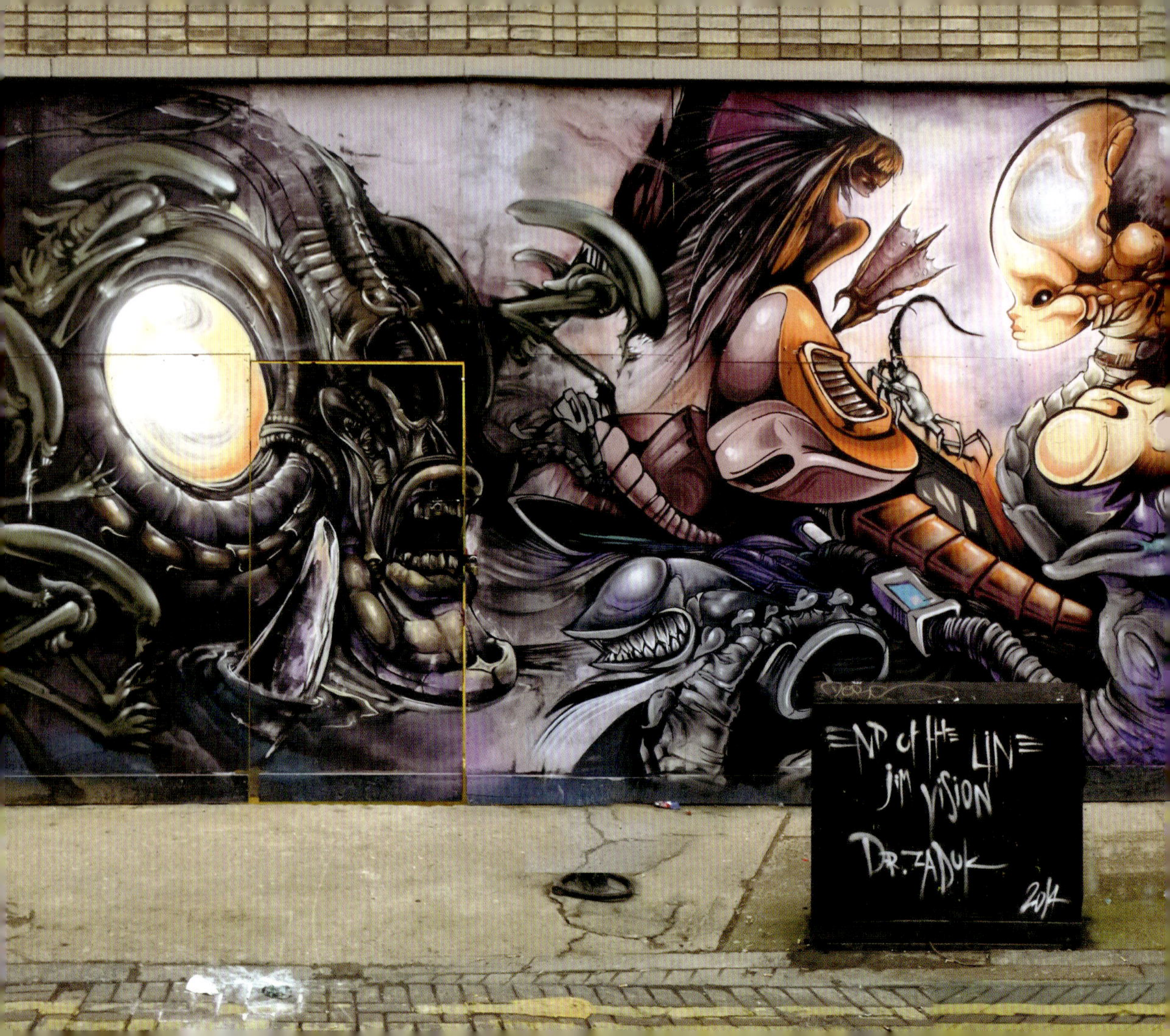
END OF THE LINE
Jim Vision
DR. ZADOK
2014

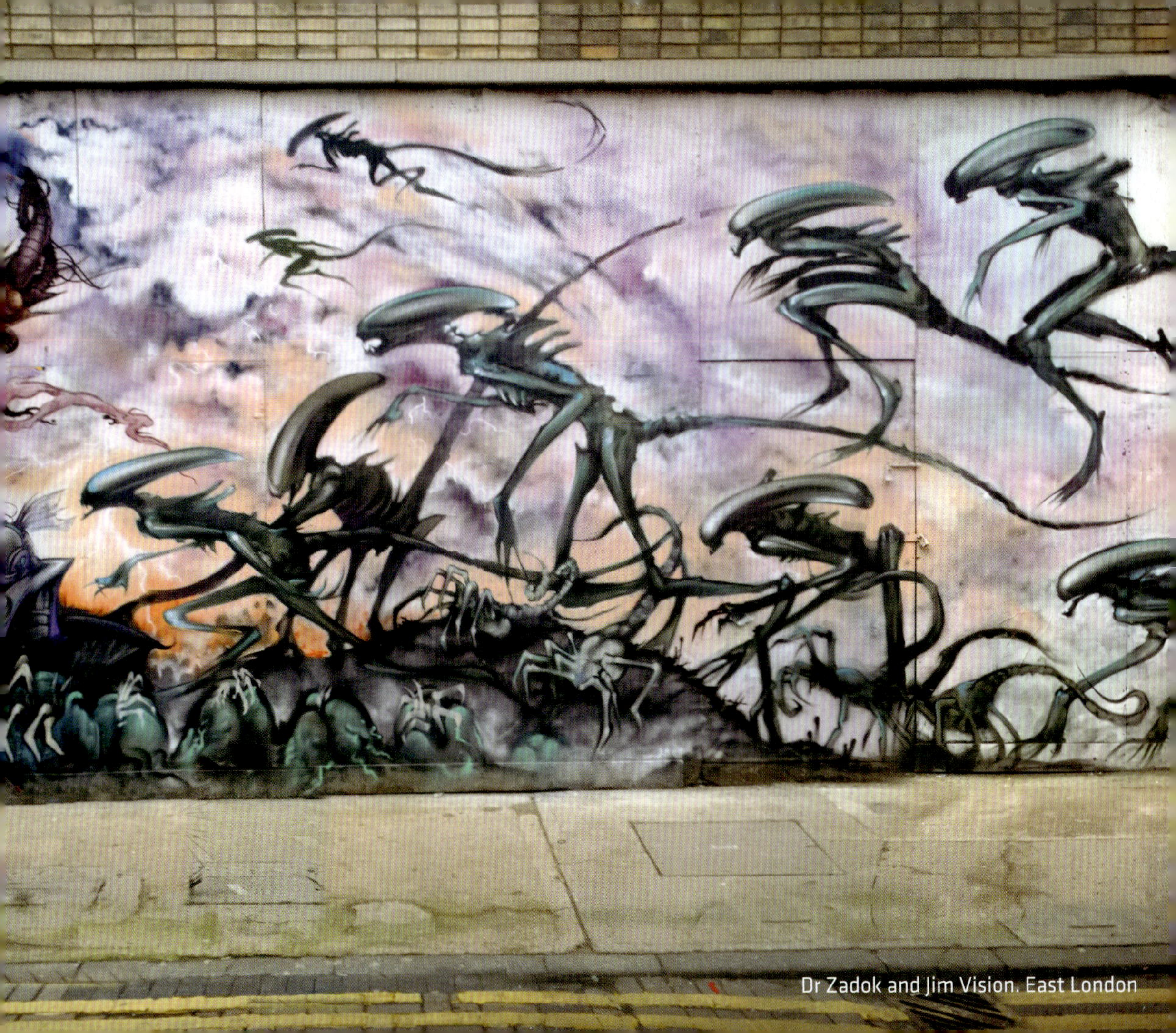

Dr Zadok and Jim Vision. East London

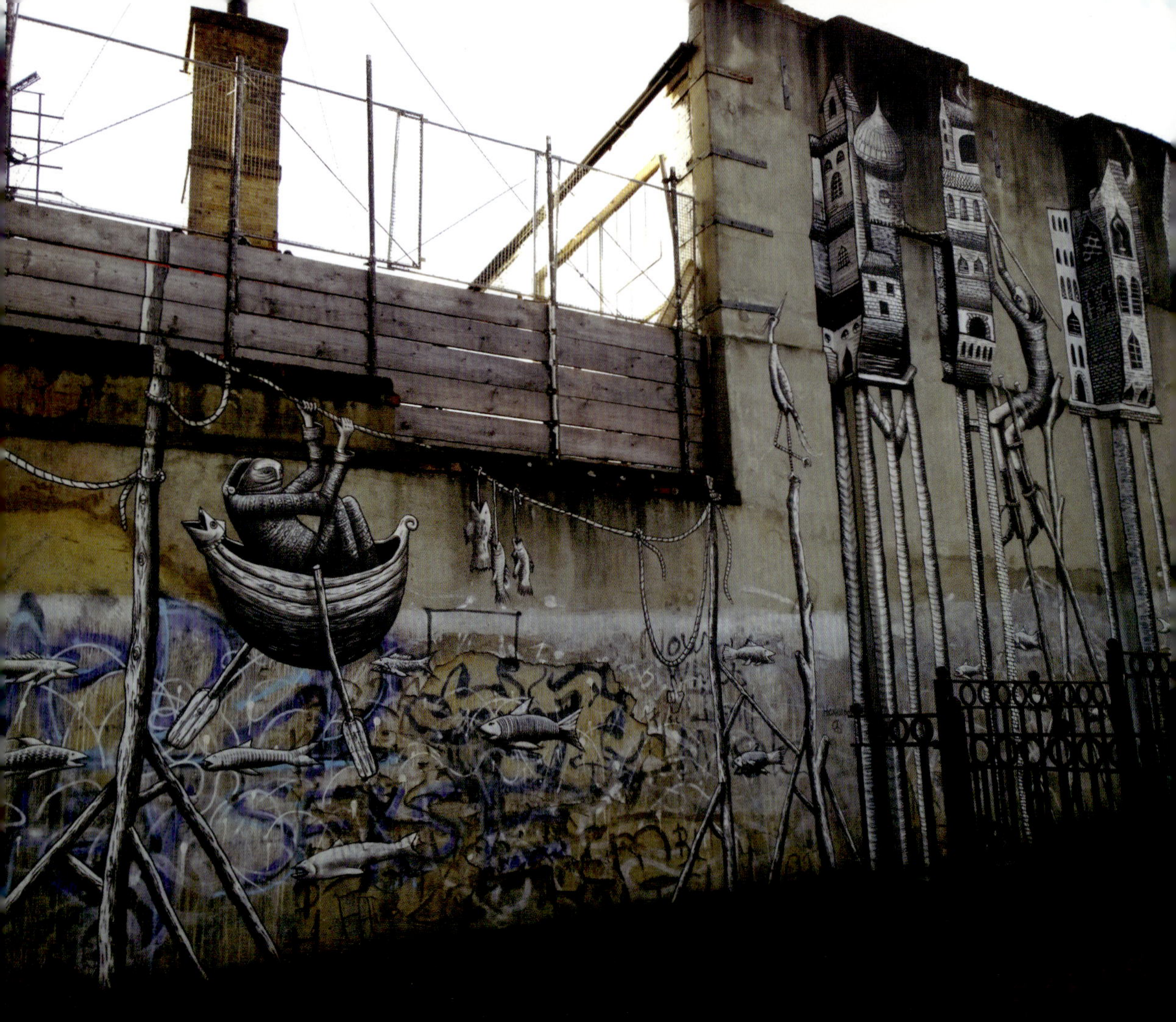

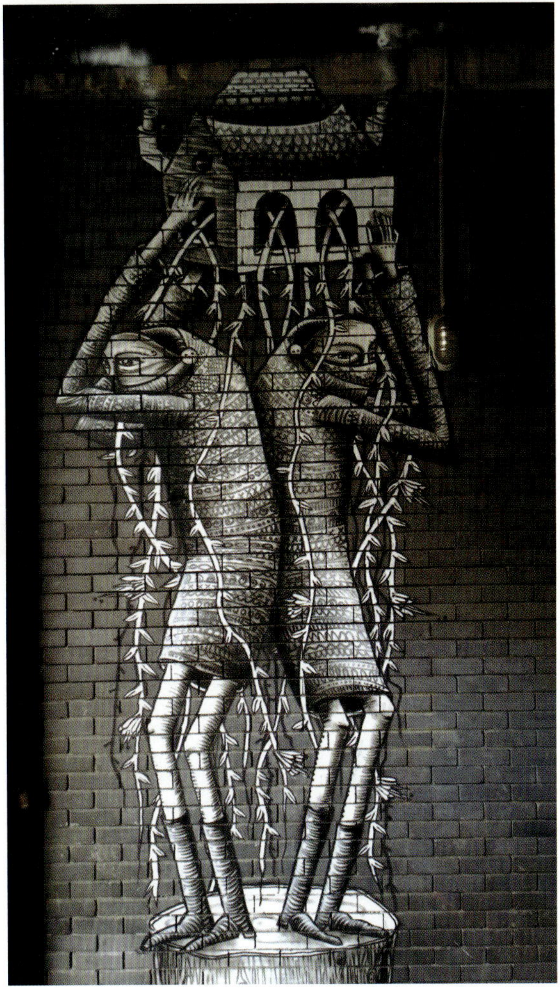

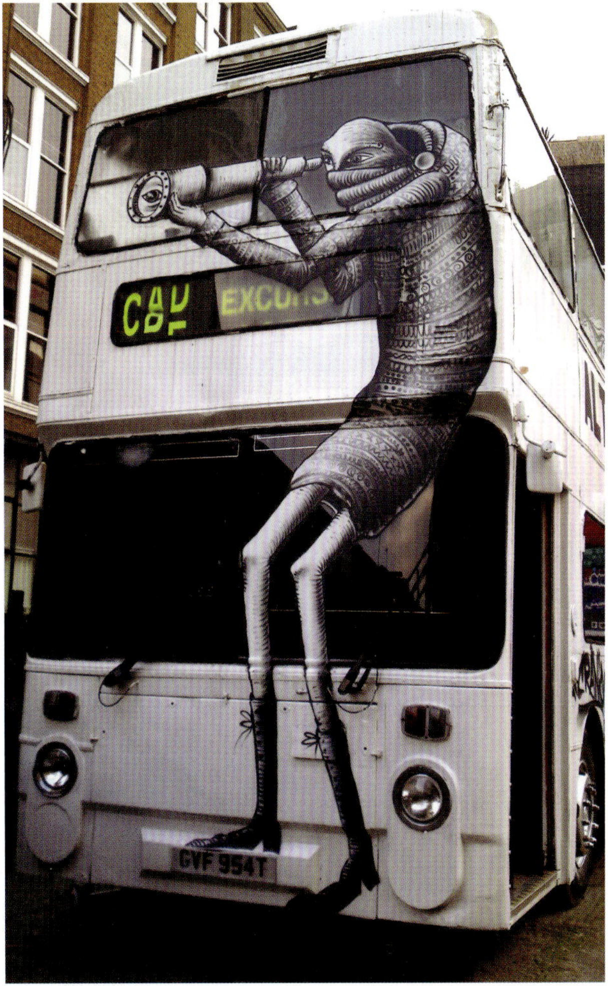

Phlegm. East London

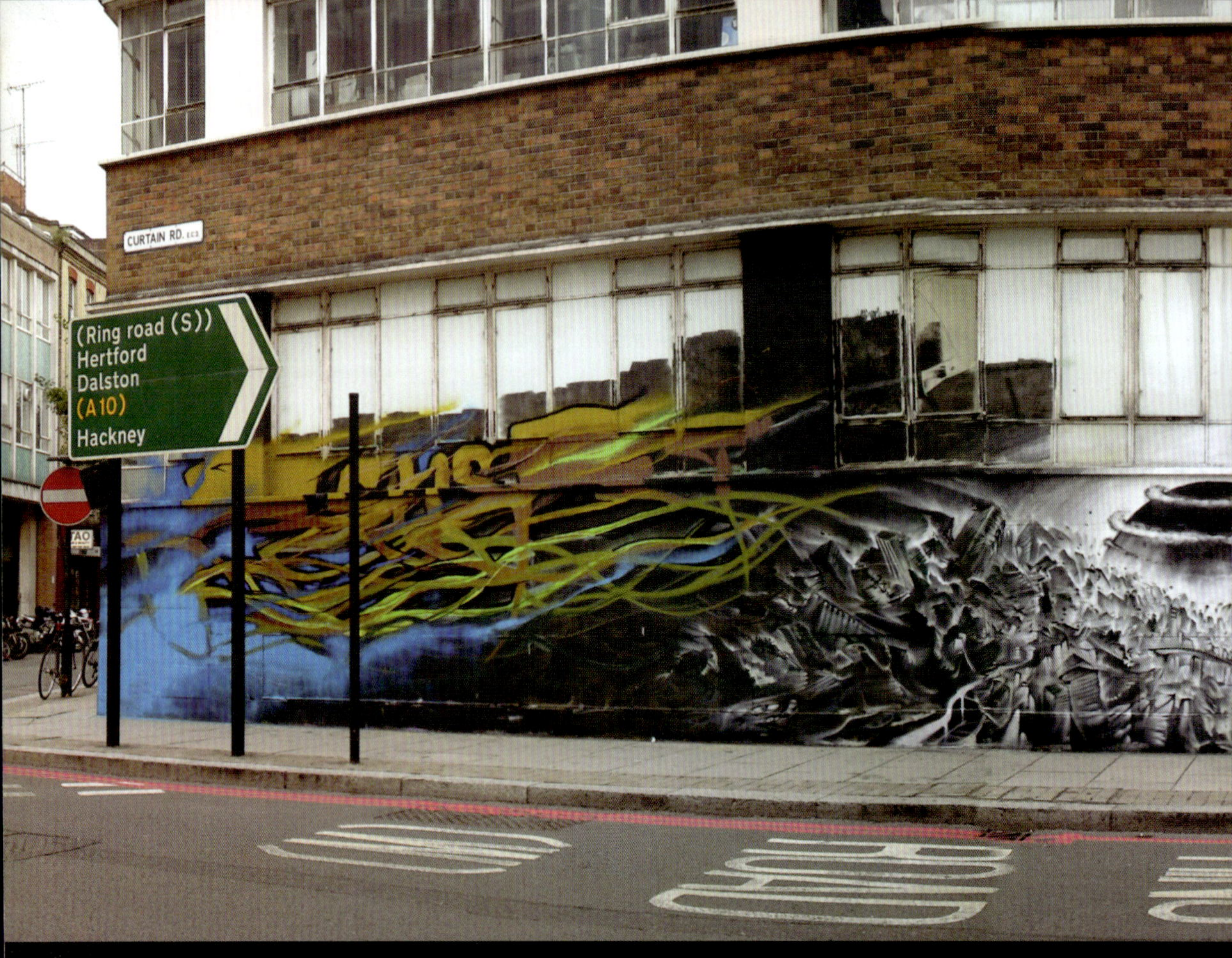
CURTAIN RD. E.C.2
(Ring road (S))
Hertford
Dalston
(A10)
Hackney

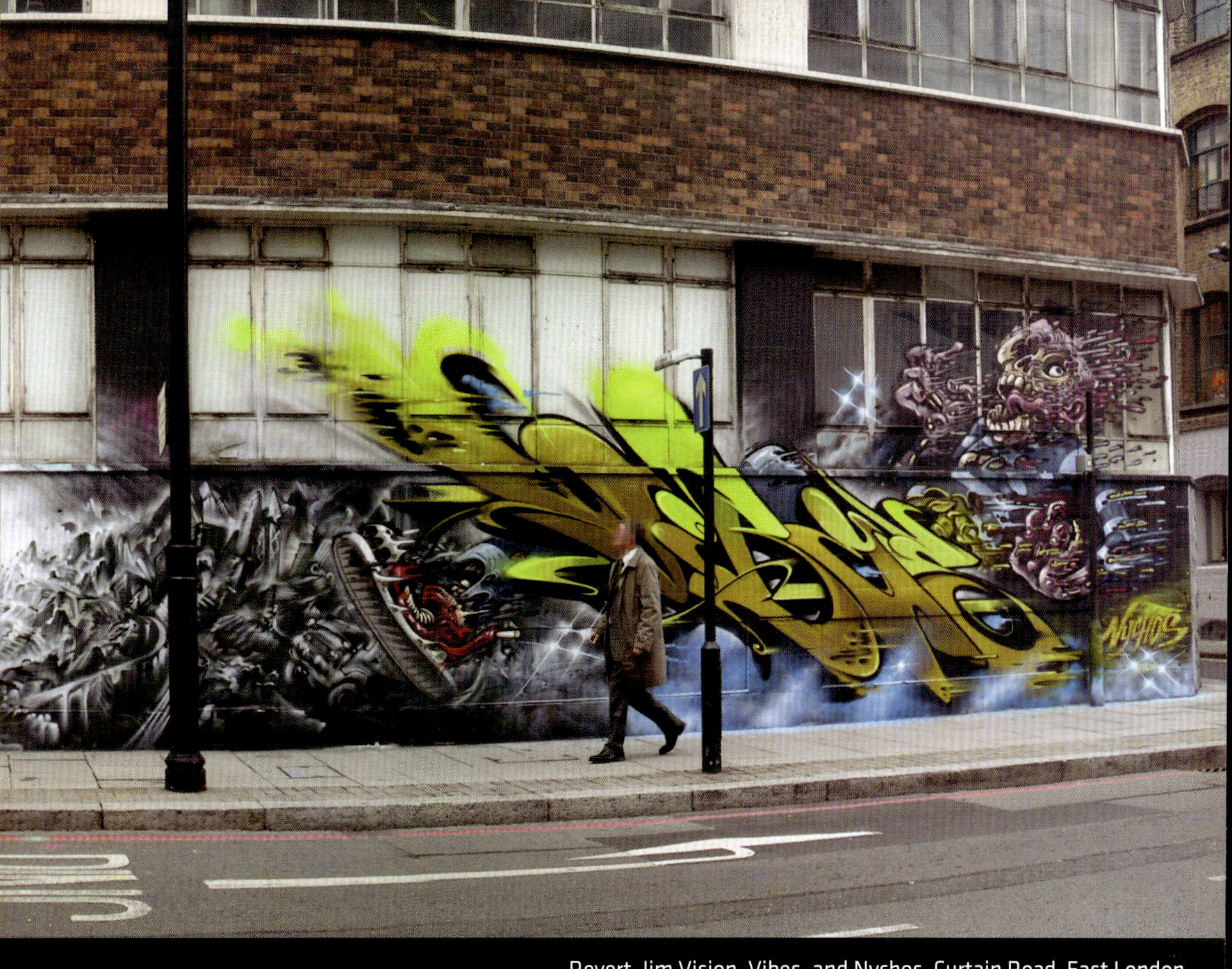

Revert, Jim Vision, Vibes, and Nychos. Curtain Road, East London

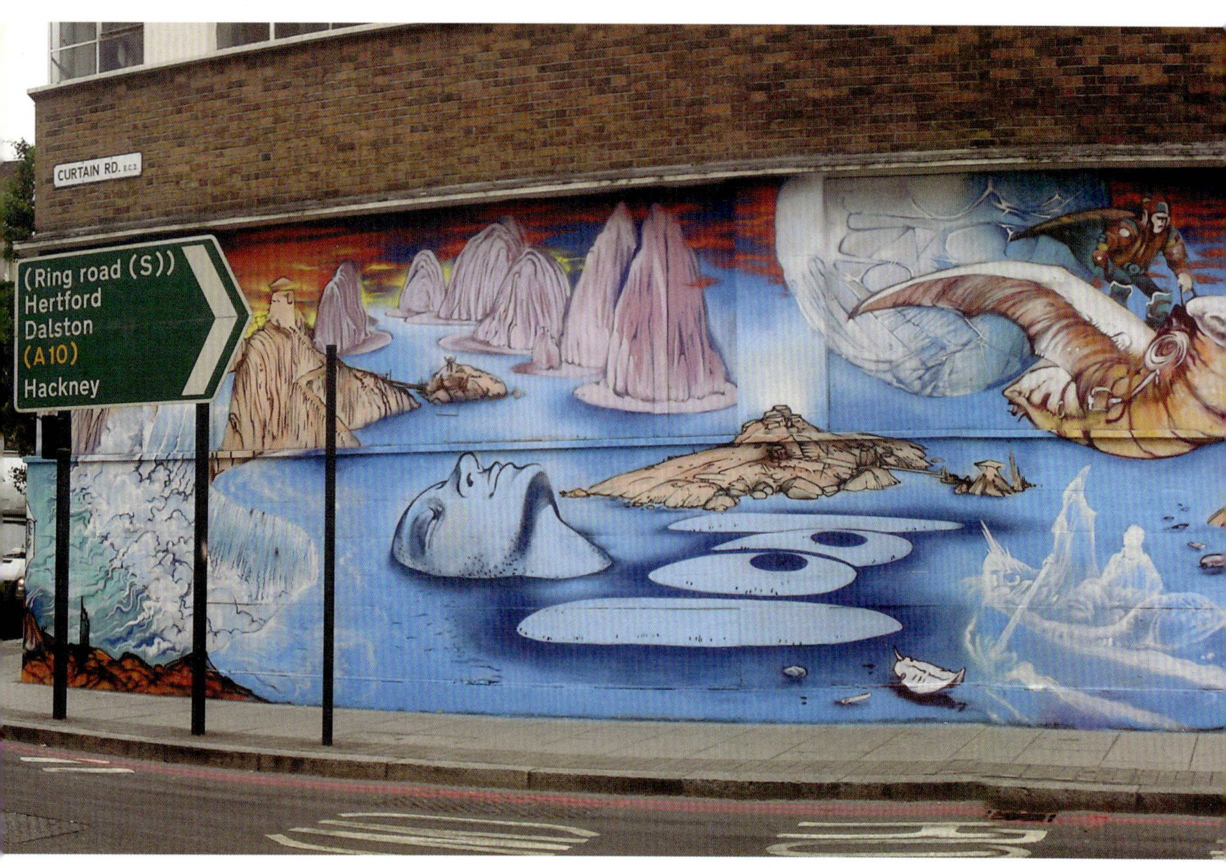
CURTAIN RD. E.C.2.
(Ring road (S))
Hertford
Dalston
(A10)
Hackney

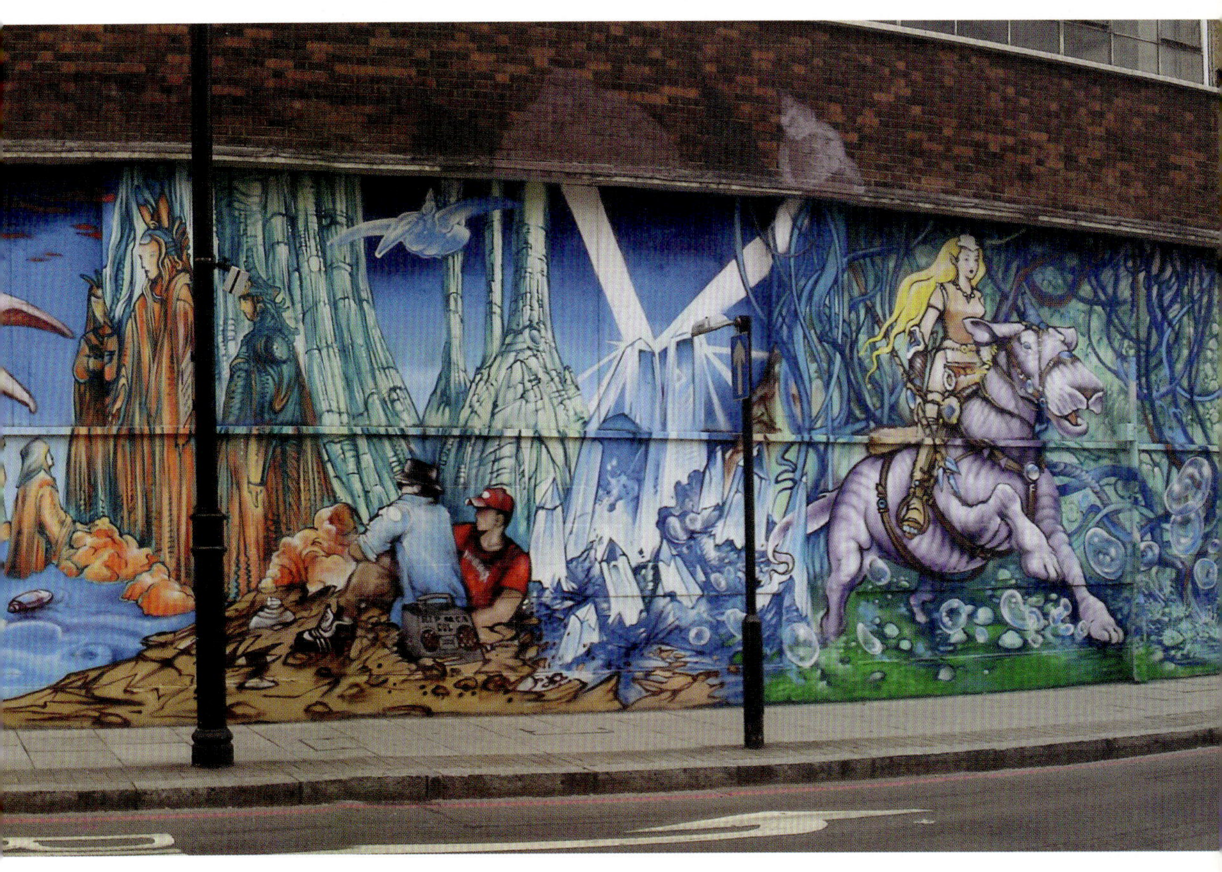

'Tribute to Mœbius and MCA' by Jim Vision. Curtain Road, East London

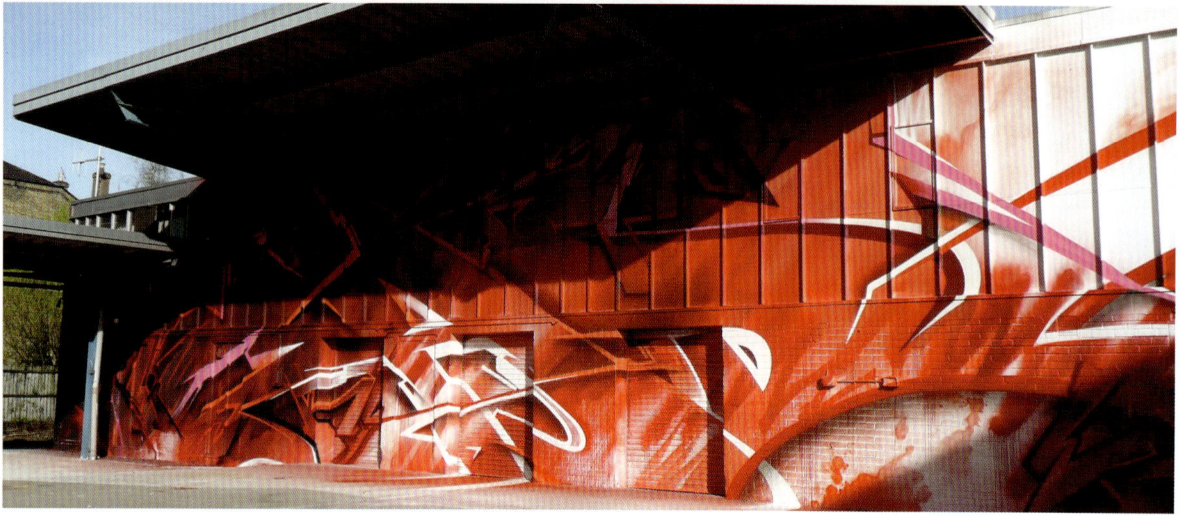

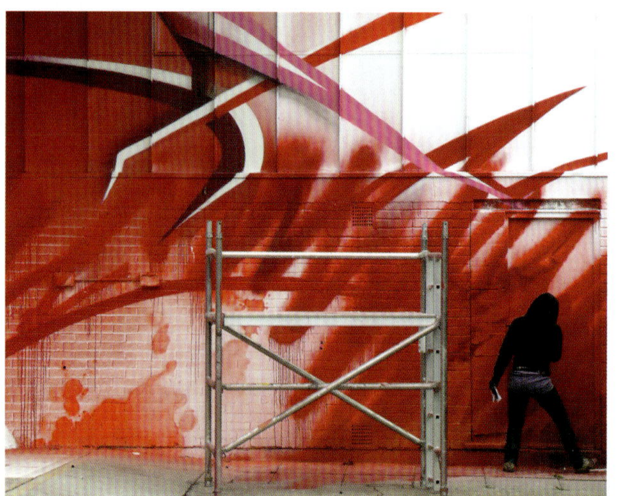

"First of all, London is my second home and the place where some of my closest friends live. It also is a source of inspiration and energy. On every corner you find creativity and diversity, not just in graffiti and street art. I don't like super clean cities where all the past and present life is wiped away from walls and streets. In London you can feel the past, the history and the buzzing life. And that makes it so much fun adding a little more life to the walls of the city." - **MadC**

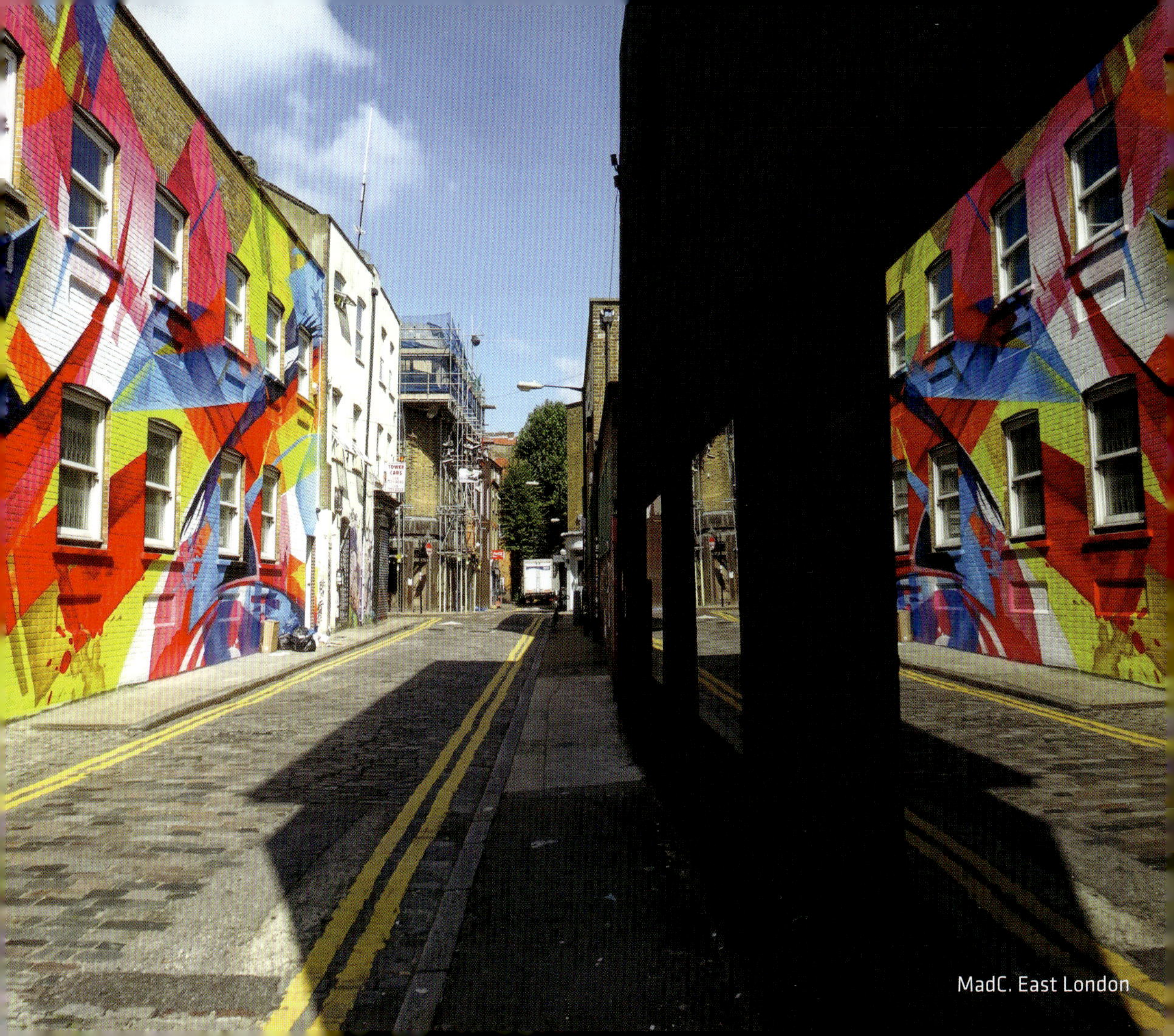

MadC. East London

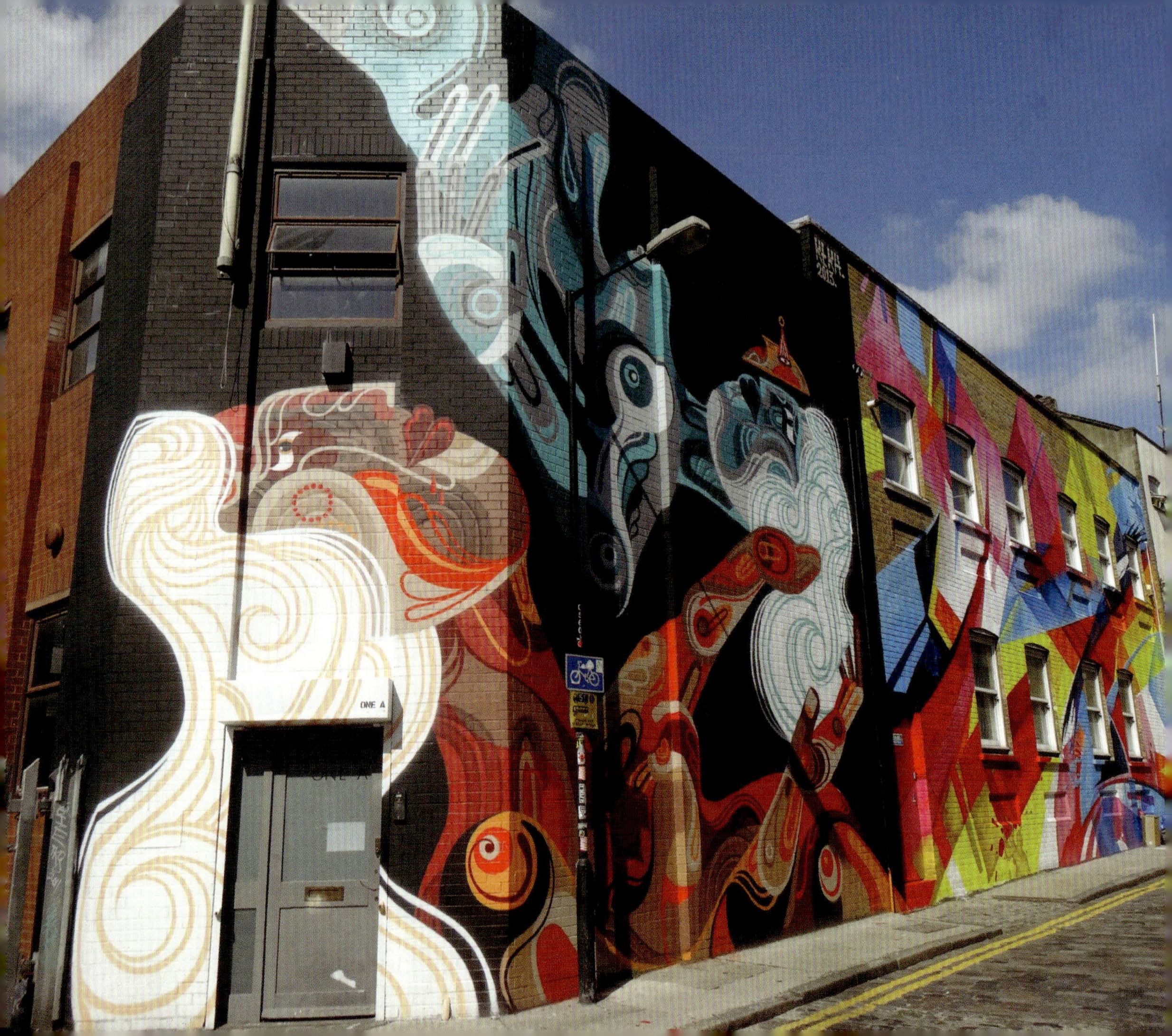
ONE A

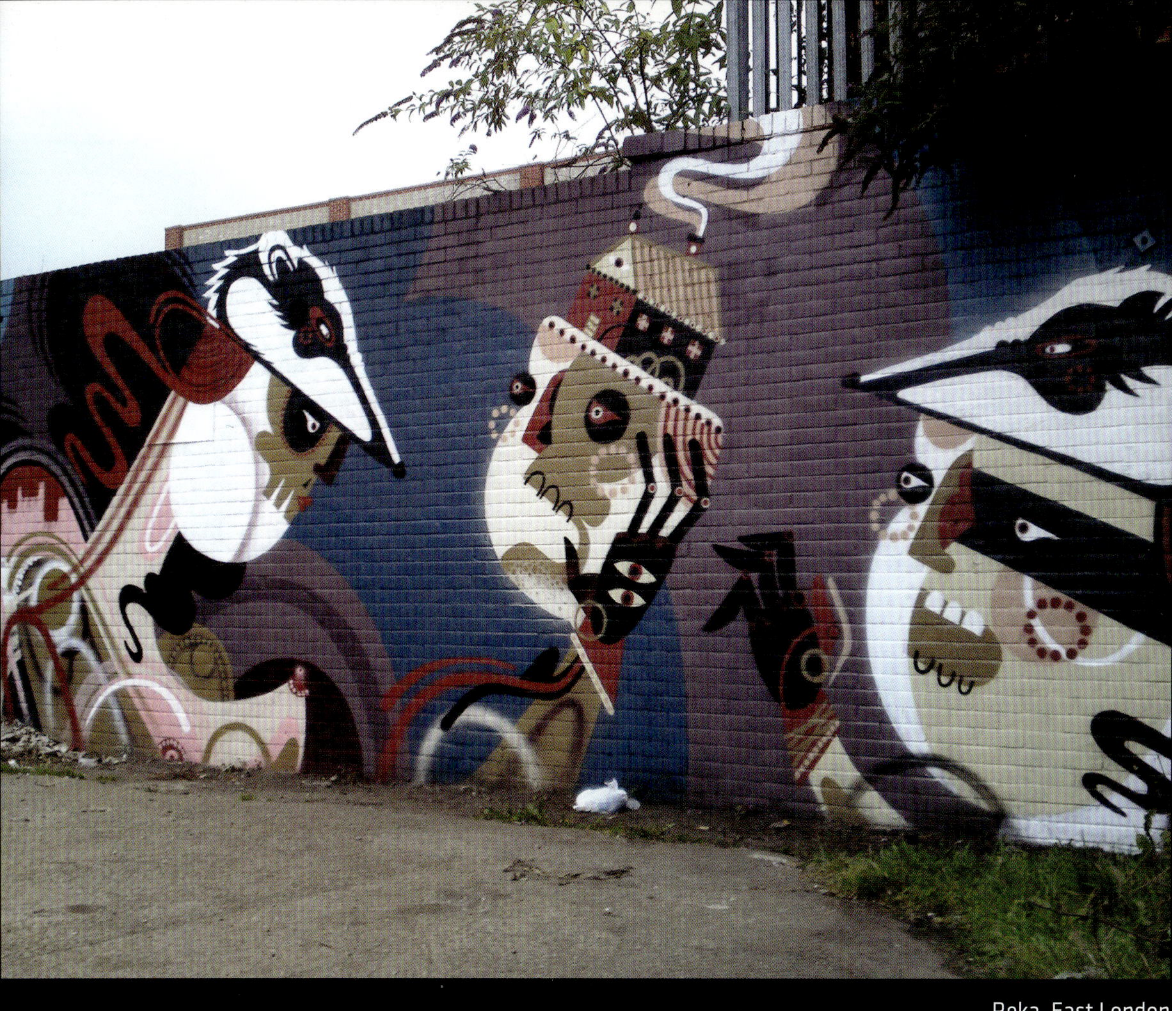

Reka, East London

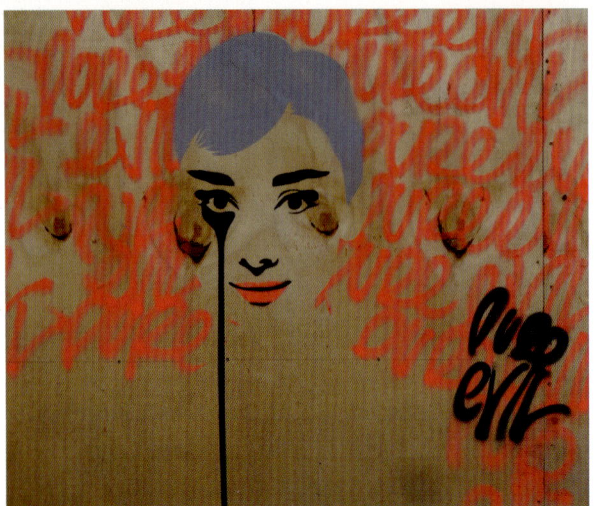

RATS + PIGEONS

IT'S A DIRTY CITY
BUT YOU NEED DIRT
TO MAKE THINGS GROW...

~~VIOLIN MAKERS GET THE BEST SOUNDS FROM WOOD FROM THE SIDE OF THE TREE THAT IS BATTERED BY THE WIND.~~

THAT'S WHY LONDON HAS
ONE OF THE BEST CULTURAL
SCENES IN THE WORLD...
CULTURES NEED DIRT TO SURVIVE.

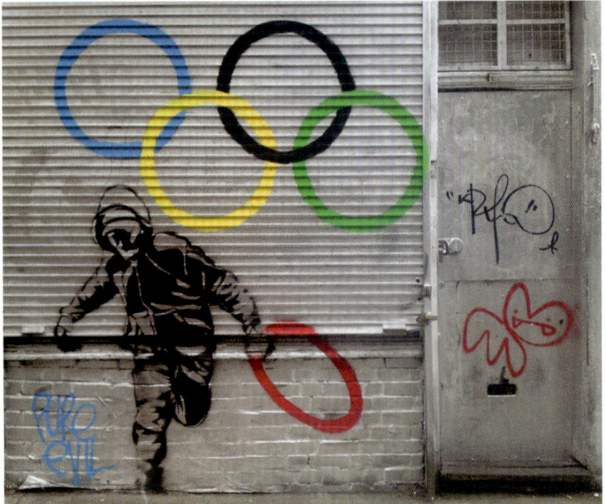

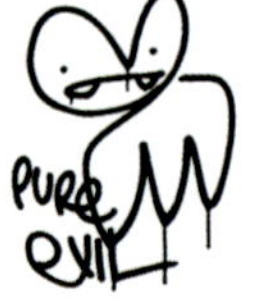

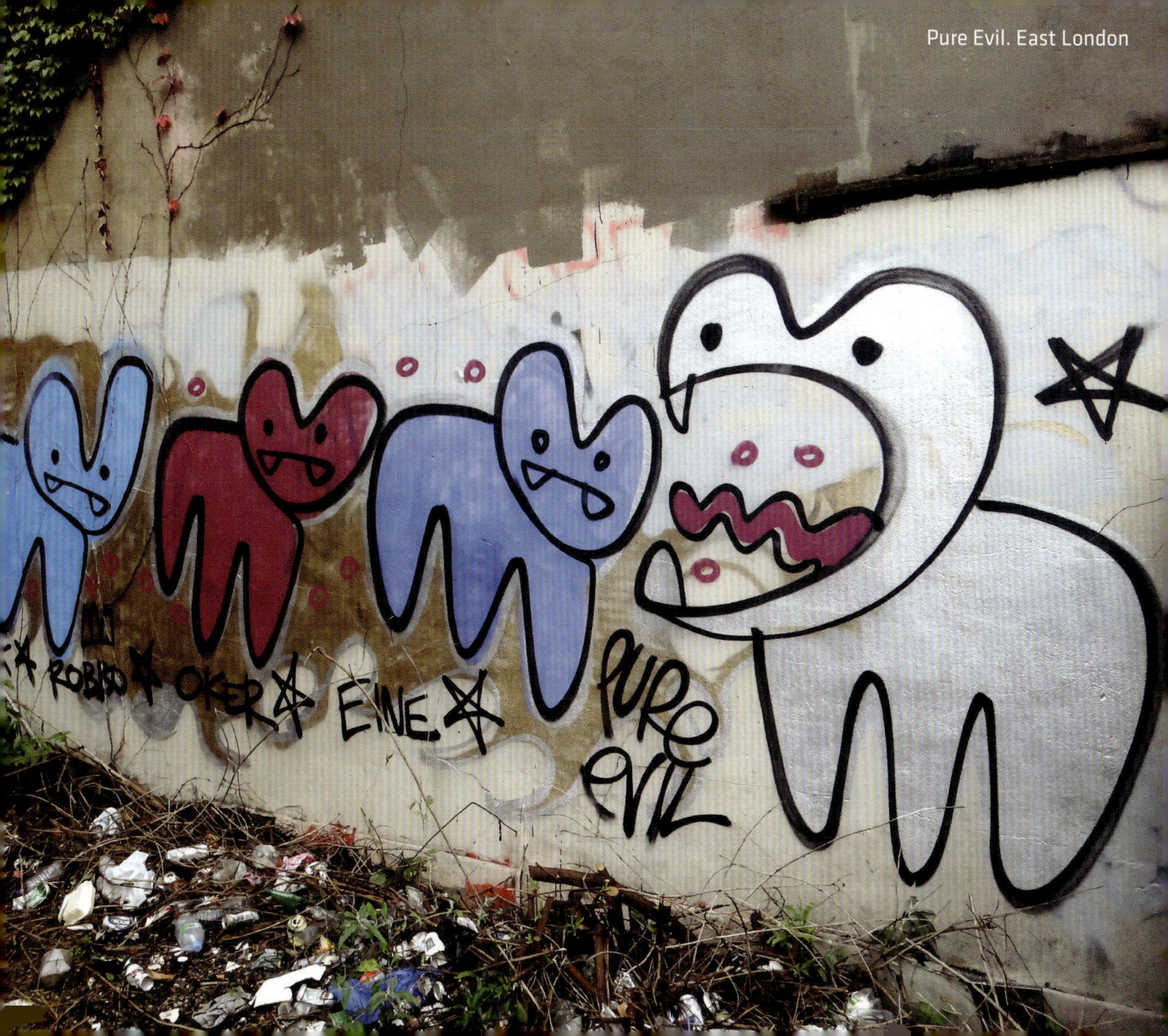

Pure Evil. East London

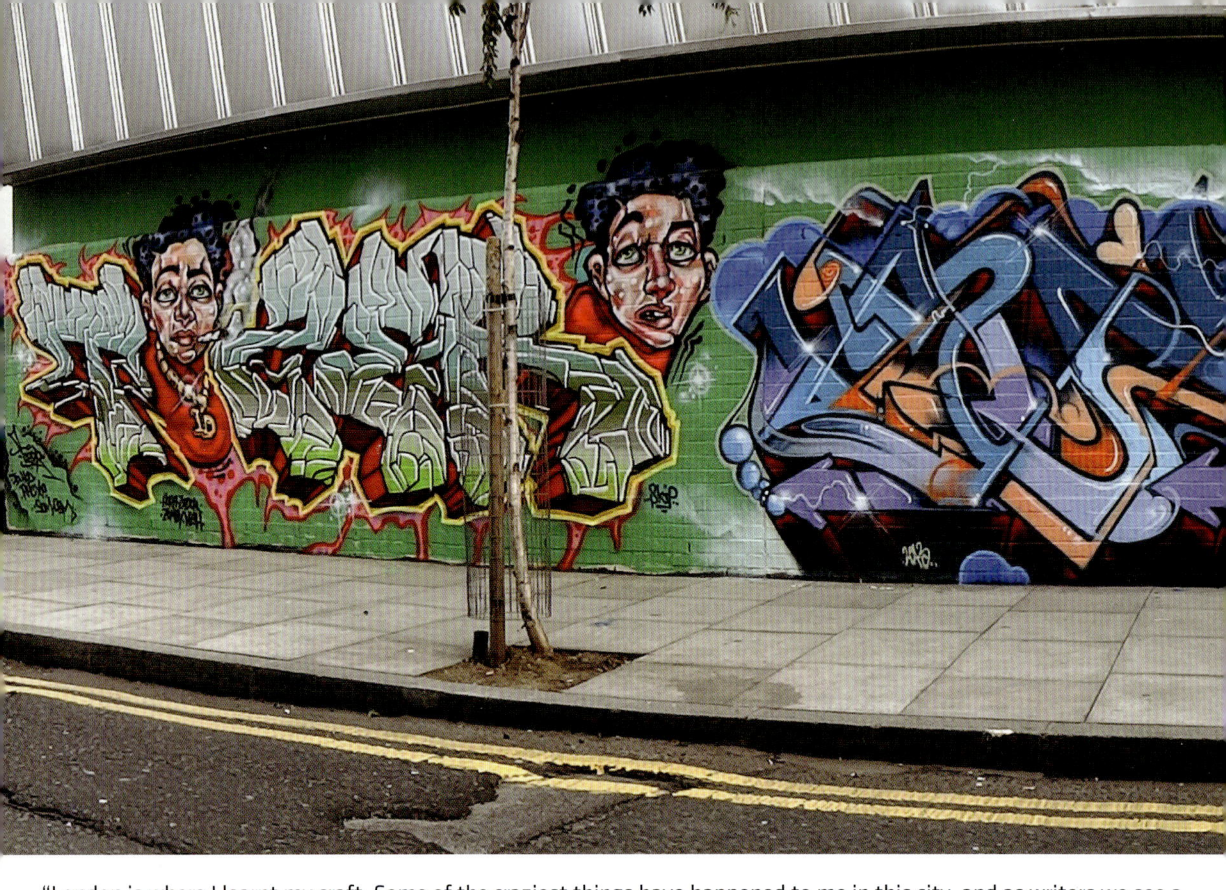

"London is where I learnt my craft. Some of the craziest things have happened to me in this city, and as writers we see a version of London that many others don't know exists. Walking home through this metropolis in the early hours following an all night mission, through the empty streets, we've seen the dirty underbelly, but it only makes me love the place more.

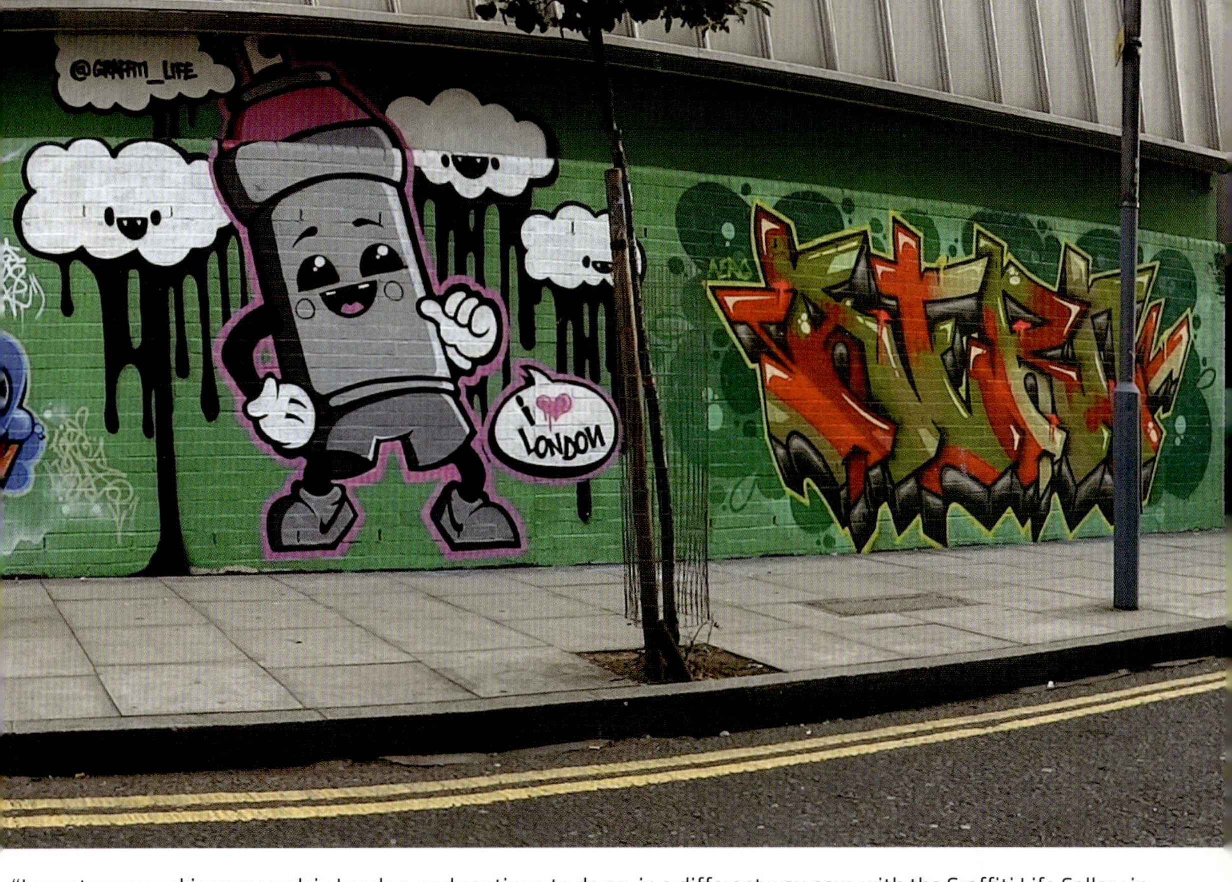

"I spent years making my mark in London, and continue to do so, in a different way now, with the Graffiti Life Gallery in East London. London means everything to me; it made me who I am, both as a person and as an artist. I've painted in New York, Amsterdam, Paris and many other cities but none of them compare. Ya get me?" - **Benjamin Badbones - Graffiti Life**

Tizer, Mr Cenz, Graffiti Life and Aero. Redchurch Street, East London

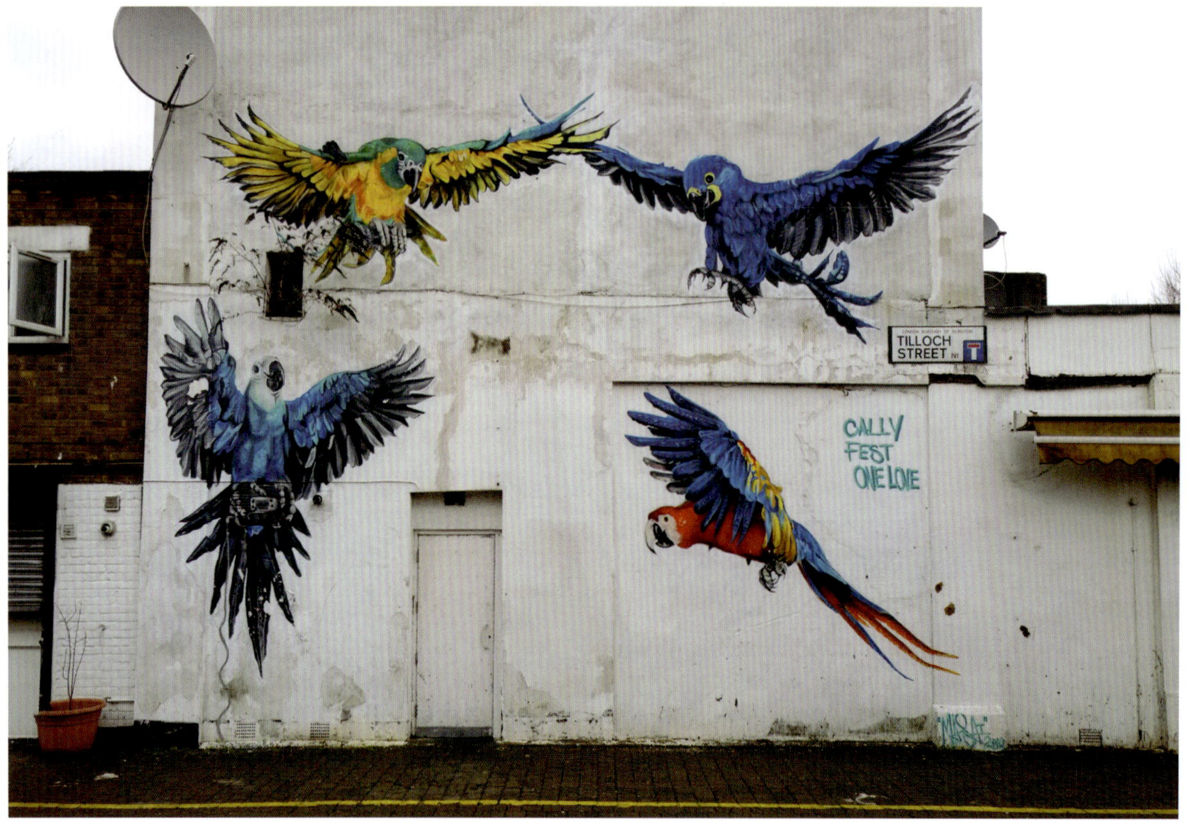

"London is a melting pot, within this city is someone from everywhere in the world, and someone doing something different from the next, I find that fascinating. London is also immensely competitive, whether that be a negative or a positive thing, I'm unsure, but it certainly encourages me as an artist to work harder. I moved to this city not far from four years ago and before that time I was living on the coast in a beach house, I loved that life but I was not being true to myself and using any creative energy. So above all London has allowed me to be what I need to be as a person... London presents opportunity, but it's only received by those that work for it..." - **Louis Masai**

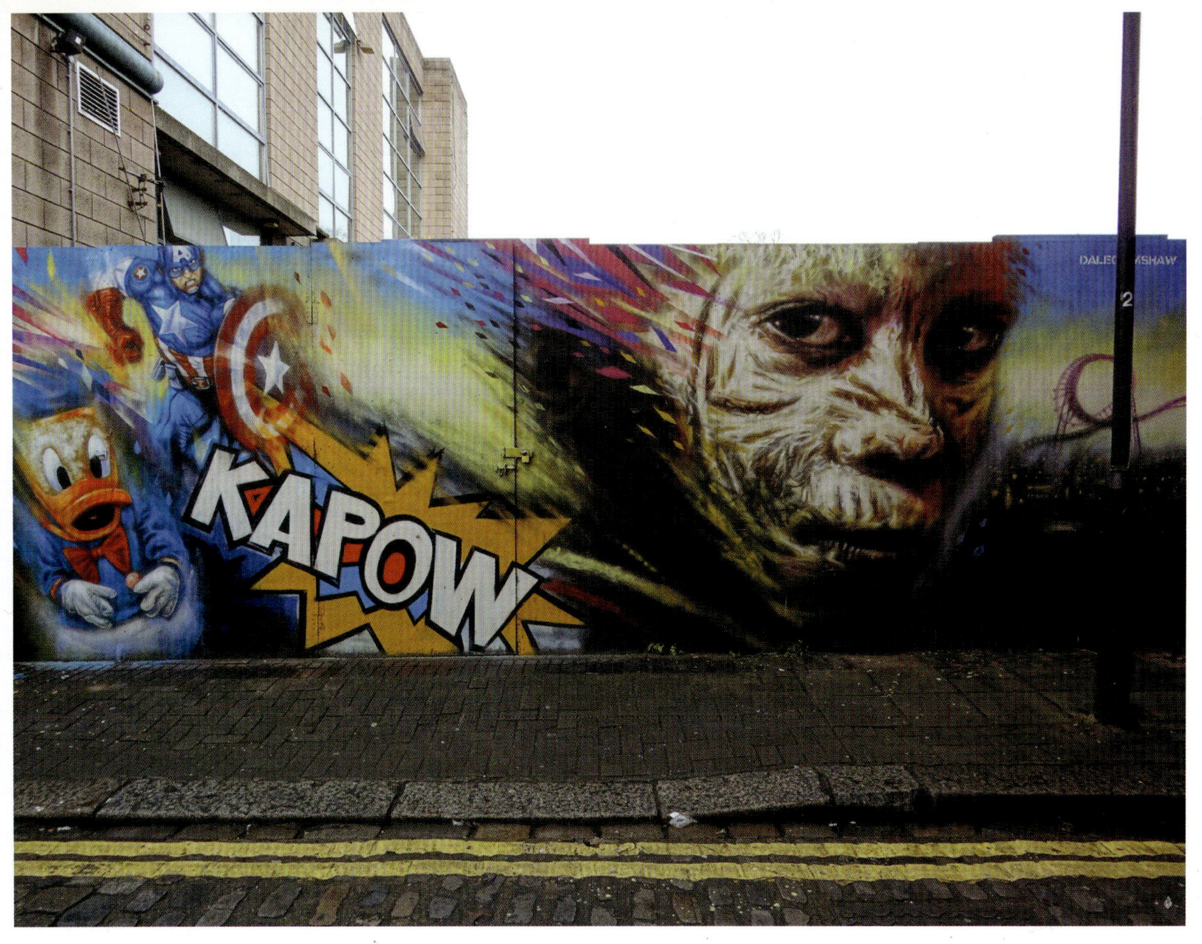

"London reminds me of an overflowing bucket under a running tap. Always renewing itself - whether that's people, events, ideas, and of course, street art. I've found that at worst, it can be a lonely and cold place. On the other hand I still get excited about the city - it's such a hive of activity with so many possibilities and opportunities to tap into." - **Dale Grimshaw**

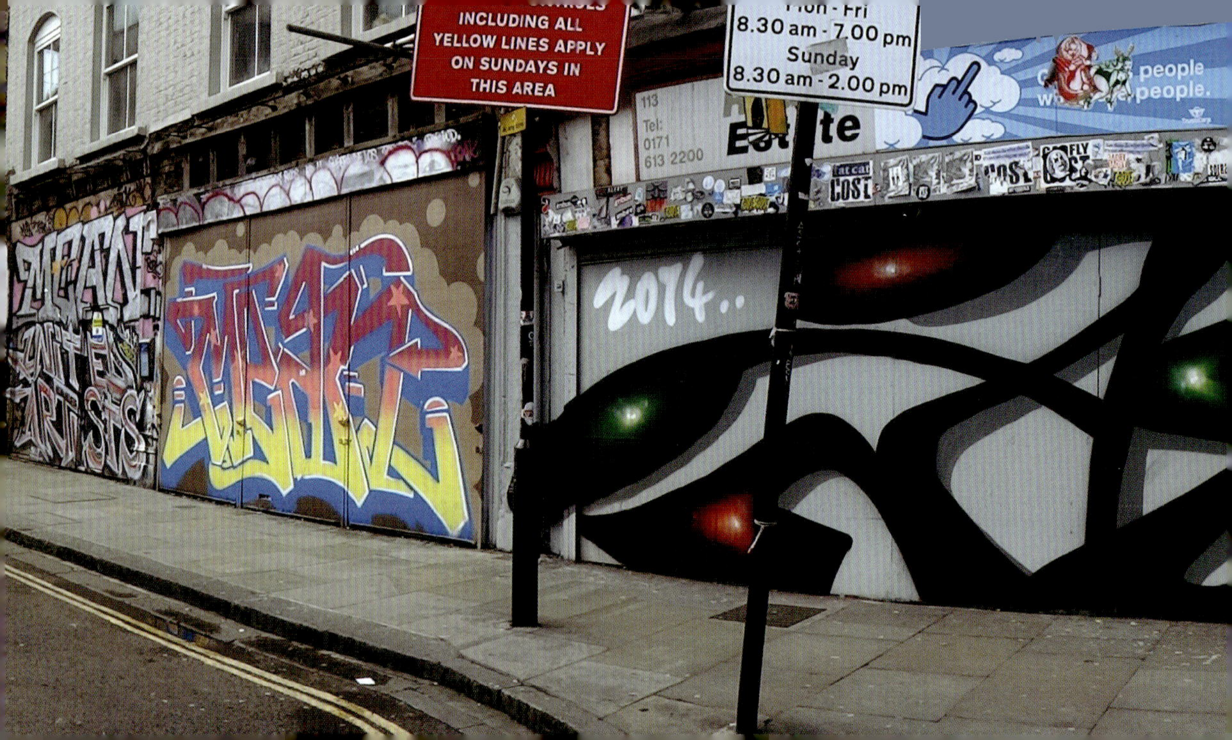
INCLUDING ALL
YELLOW LINES APPLY
ON SUNDAYS IN
THIS AREA
8.30 am - 7.00 pm
Sunday
8.30 am - 2.00 pm
113
Tel:
0171
613 2200

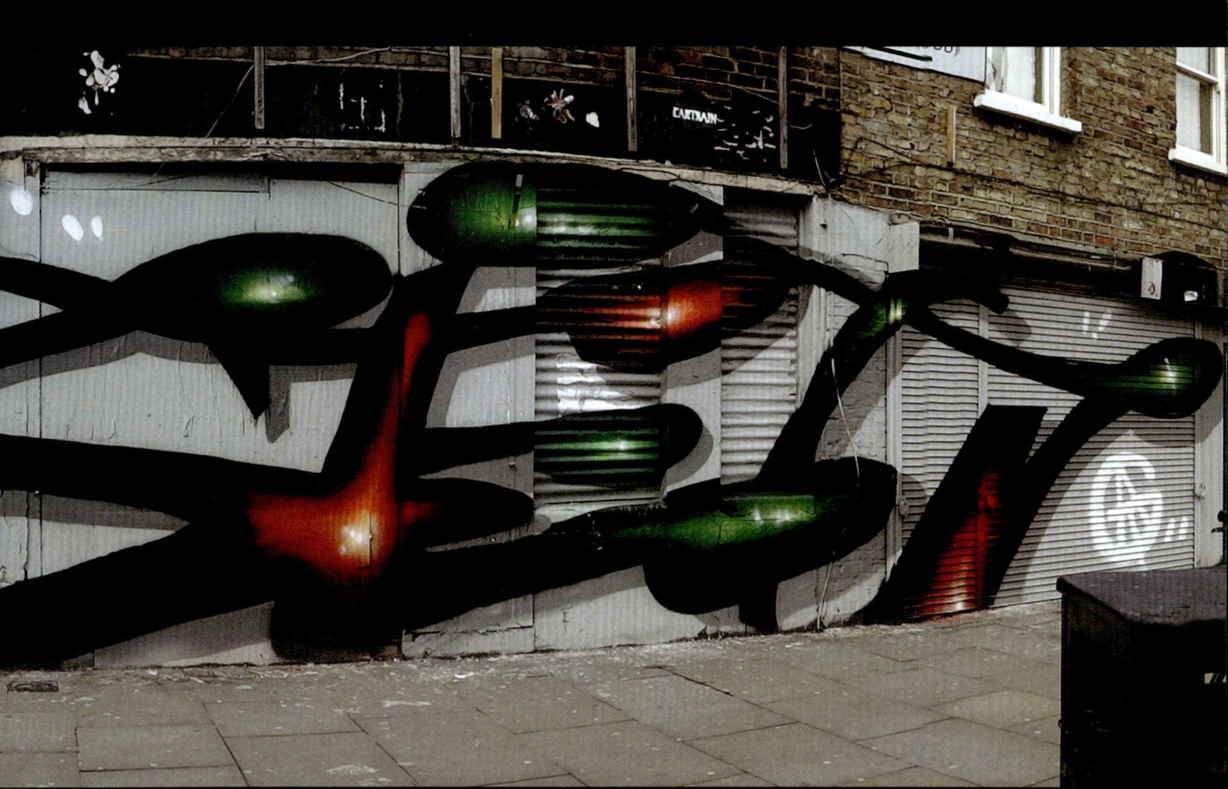

'United Artists' by Don, Mean, Aset ATG and more. Redchurch Street, East London

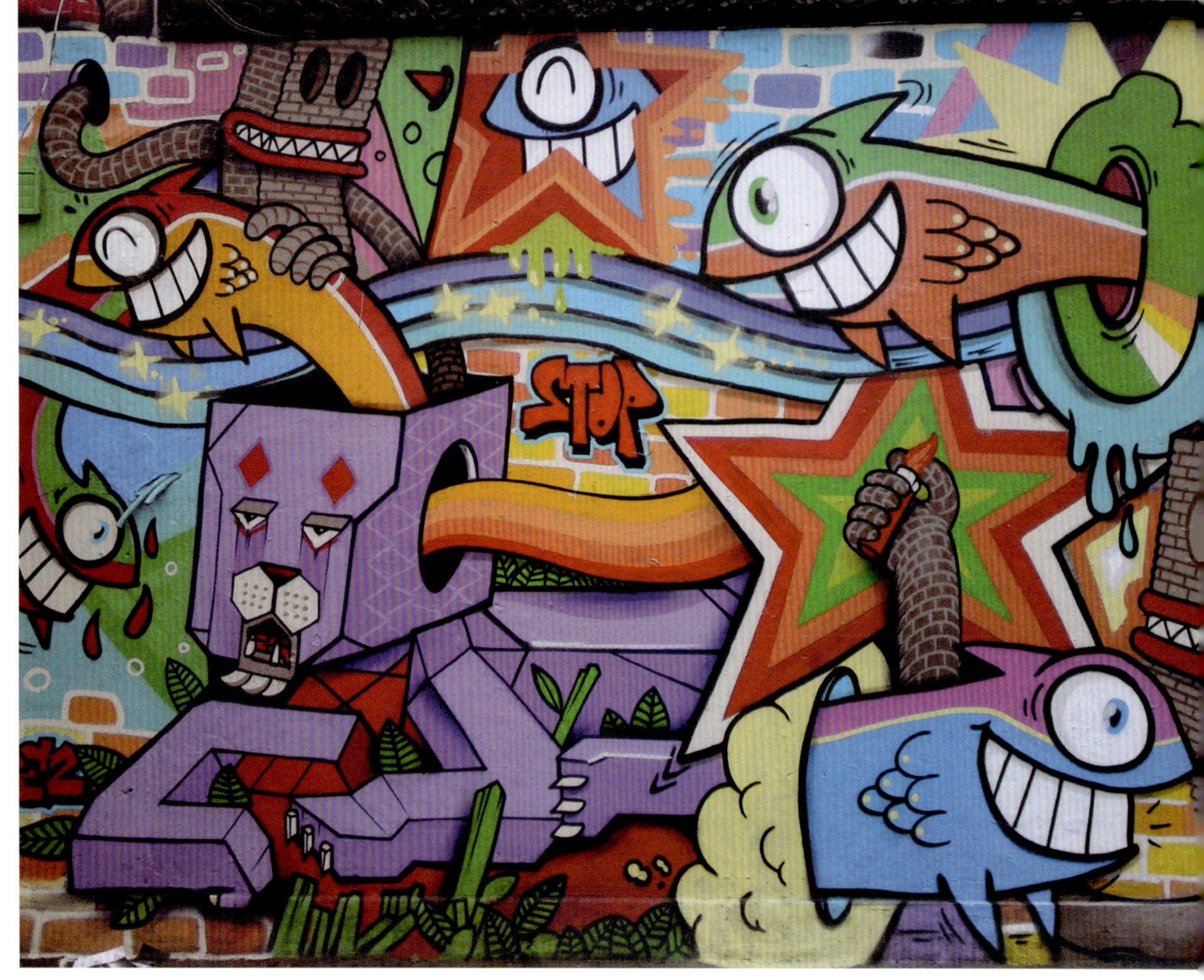

"London means to me acid techno party." - **Pez**

Pez & Dibo. Pedley Street, East London

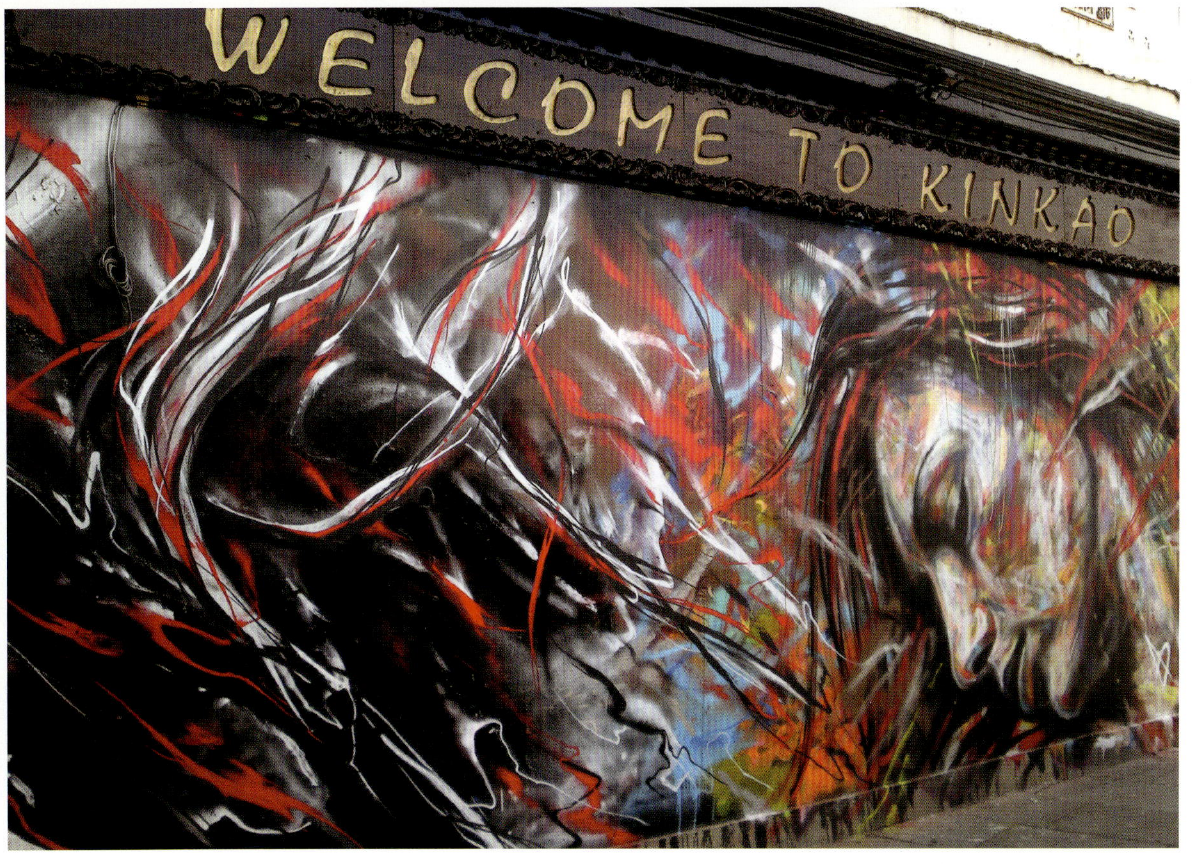

"I guess I feel like many people do, I have a love/hate relationship with the city. Sometimes I want to kick it in the face and take all its money and other times I just want to buy it flowers and say thank you. Good or bad, to me London means home, if it wasn't for the people I've met and opportunities that have arisen there, my life would not be the same fantastic mess it is now." - **David Walker**

She One and David Walker. Pedley Street, East London

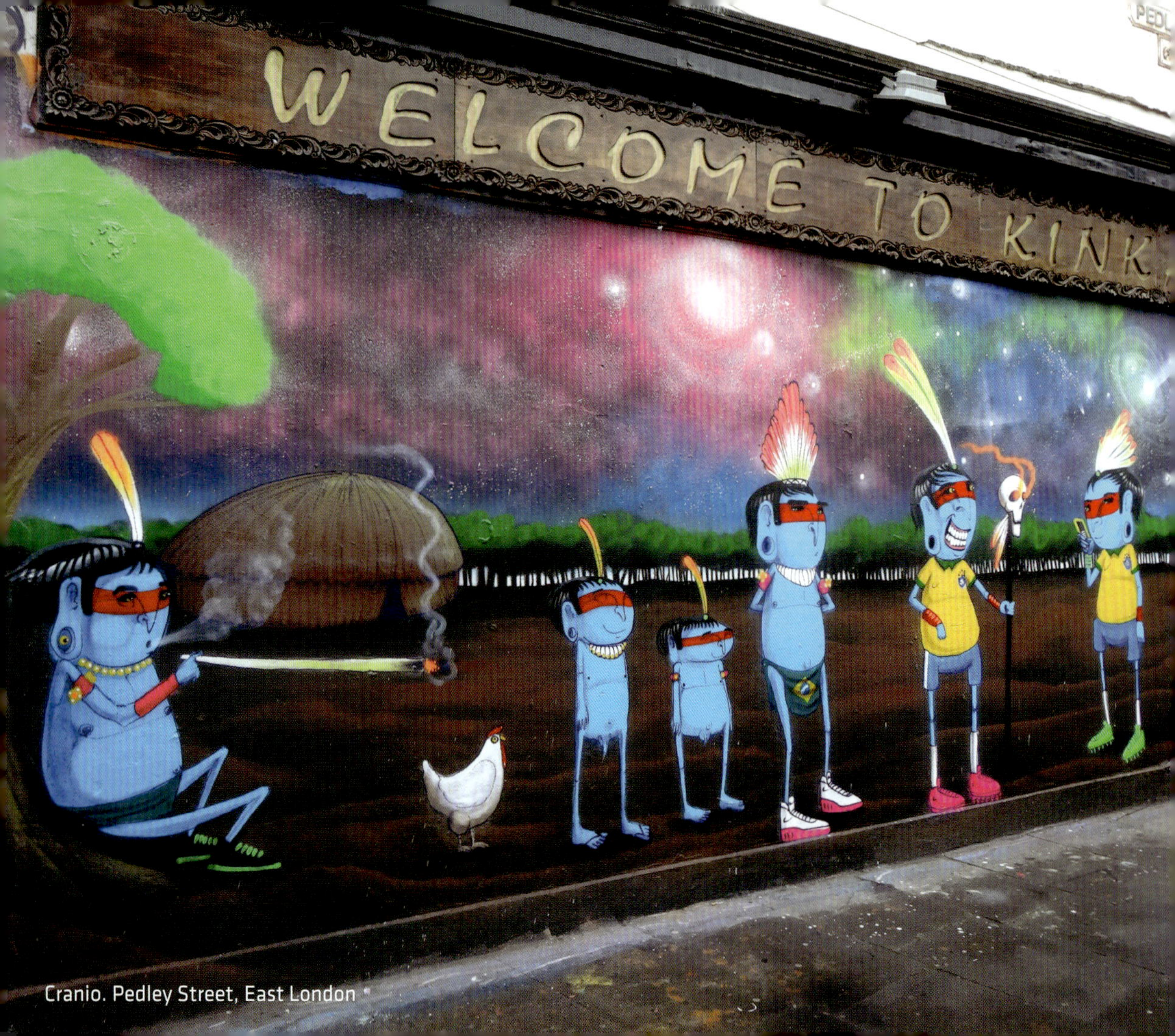

Cranio. Pedley Street, East London

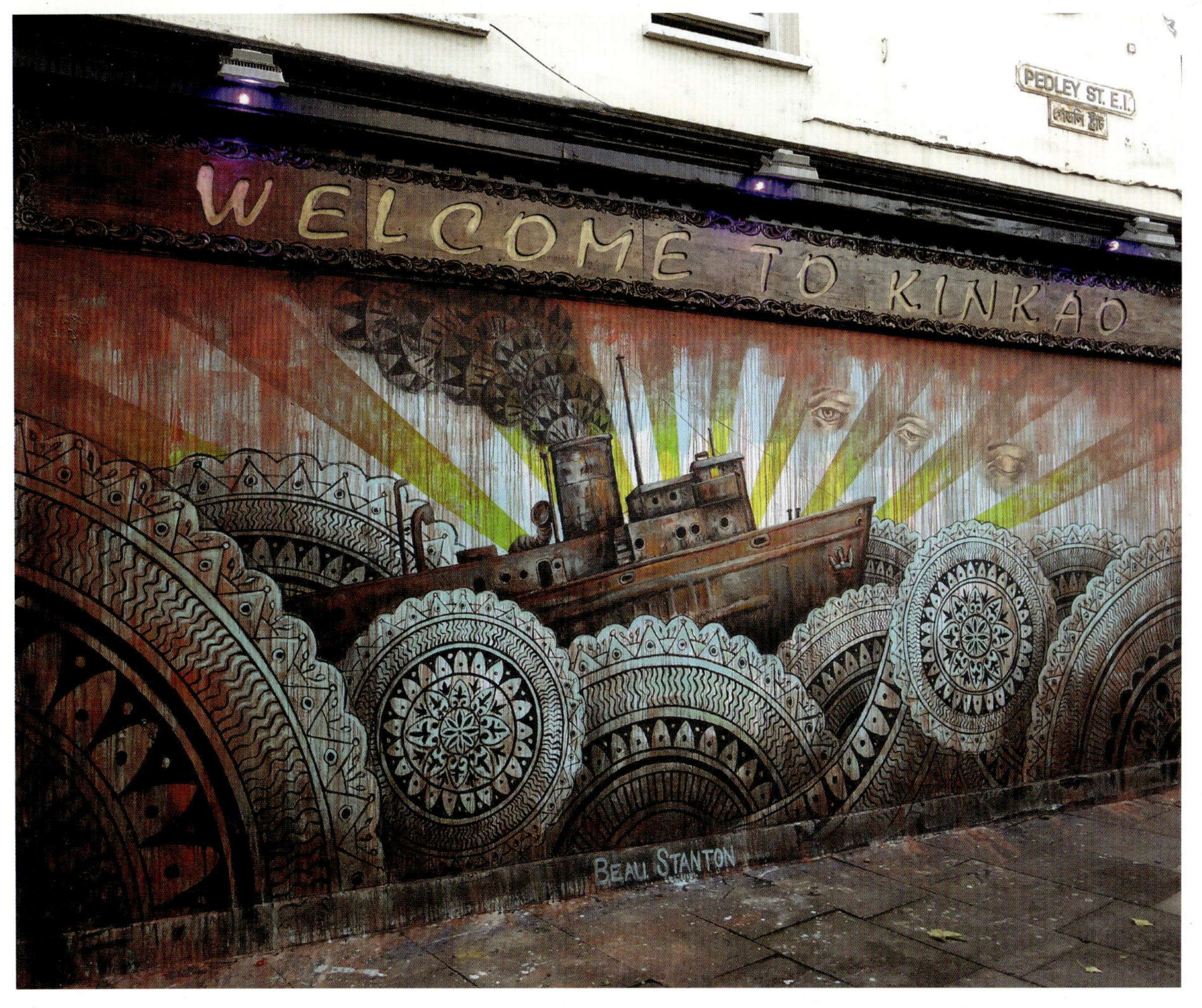

Beau Stanton. Pedley Street, East London

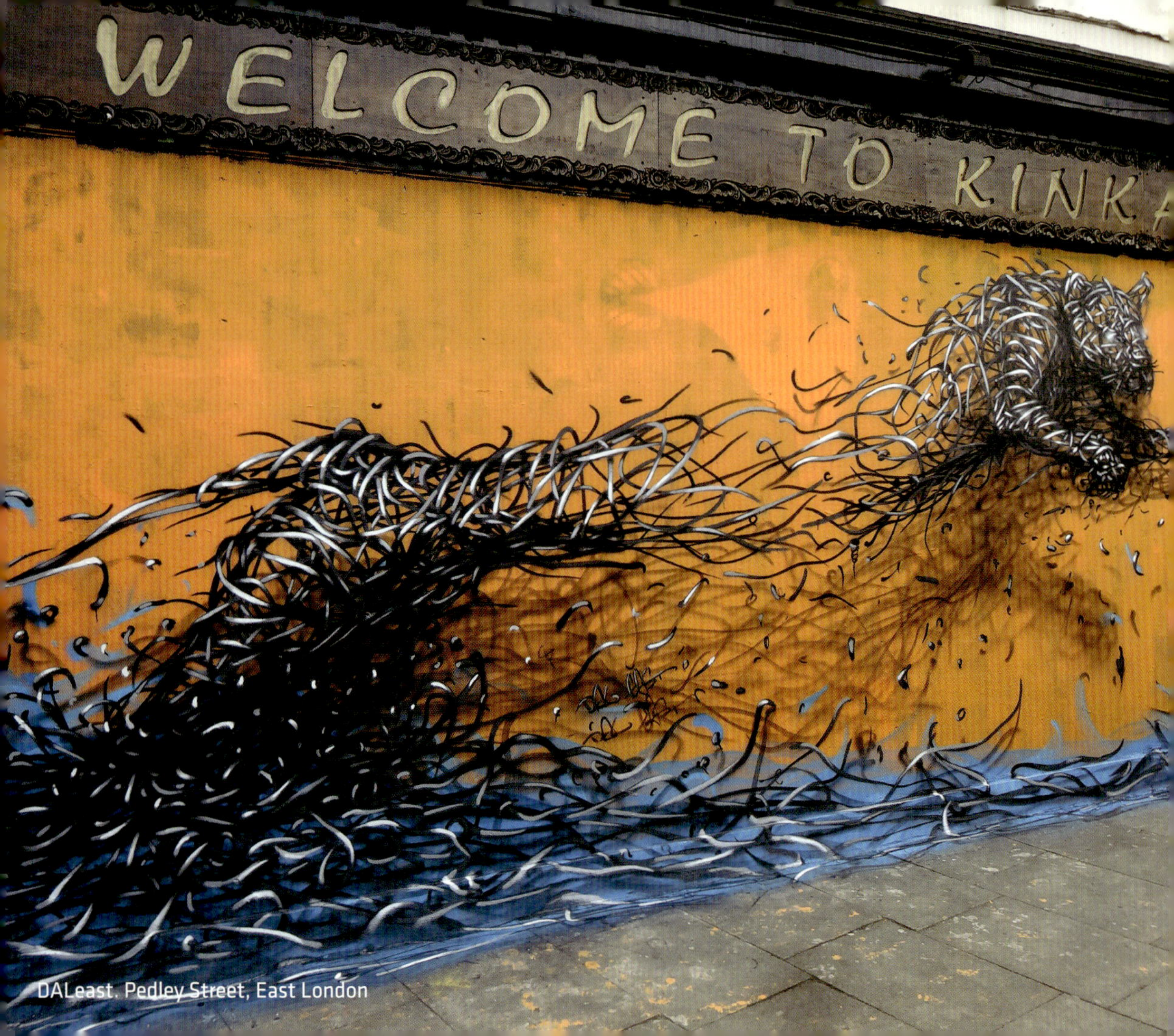

DALeast, Pedley Street, East London

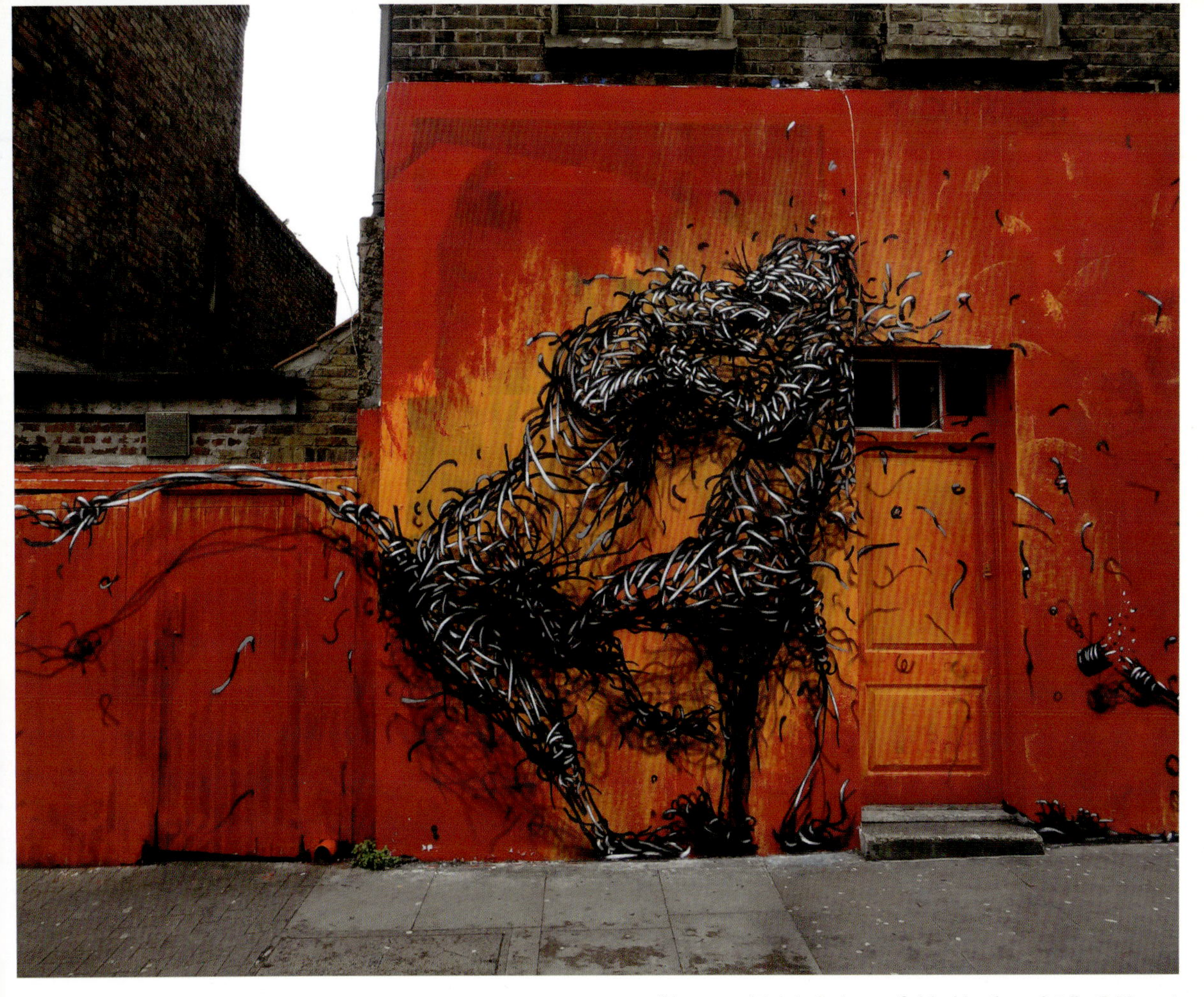

"A map which is being unfolded in the mist." - **DALeast**

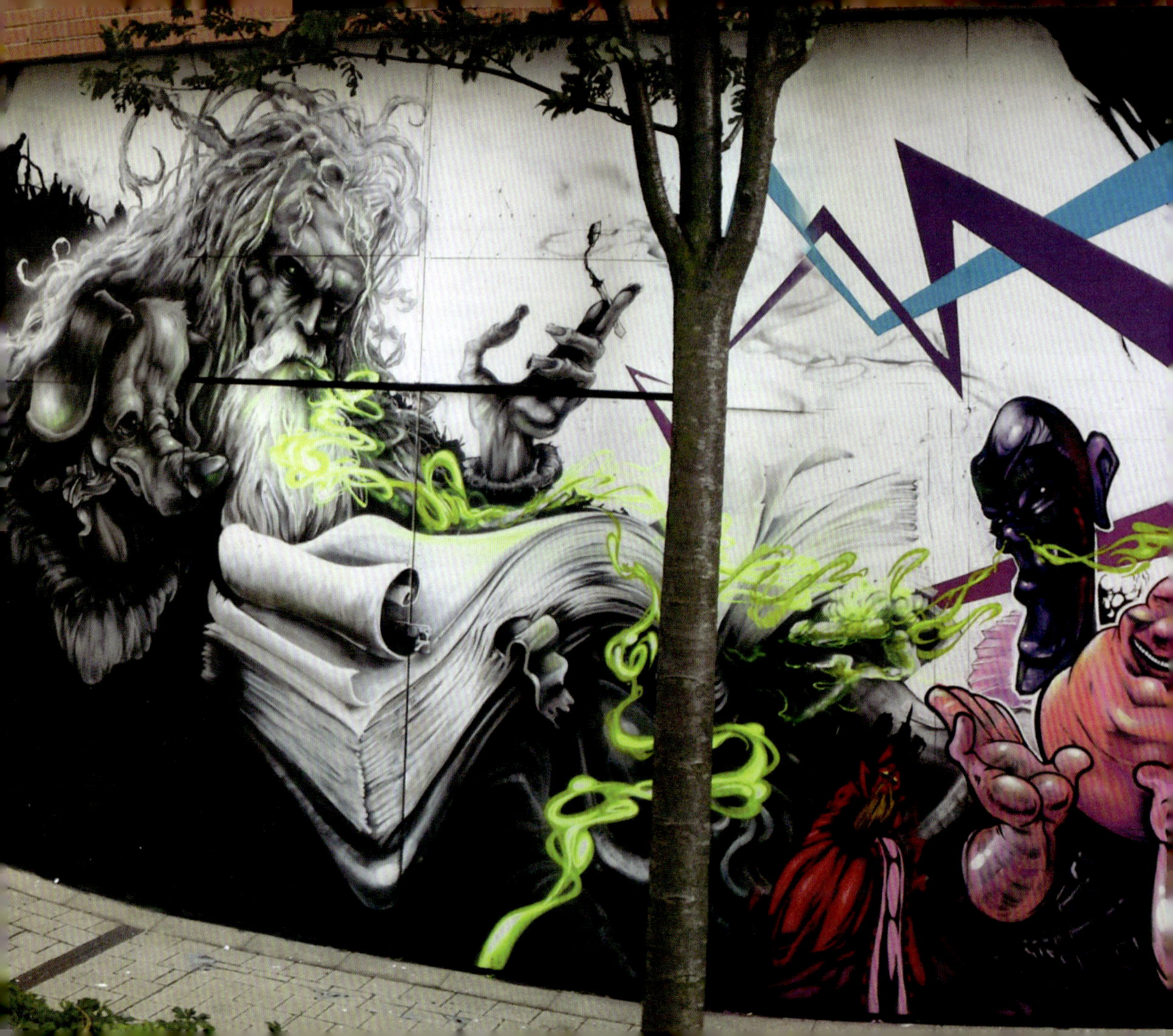

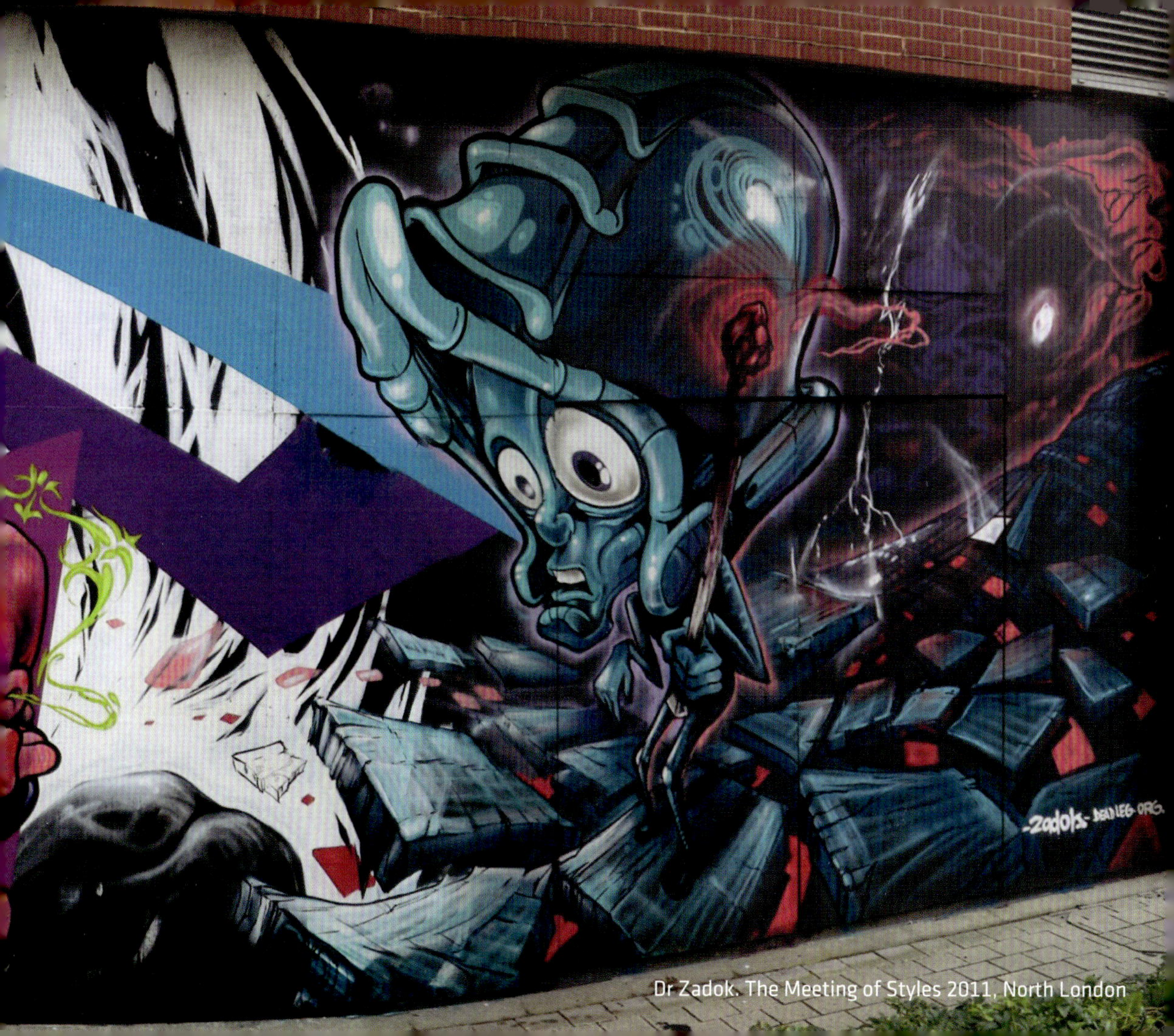

Dr Zadok. The Meeting of Styles 2011, North London

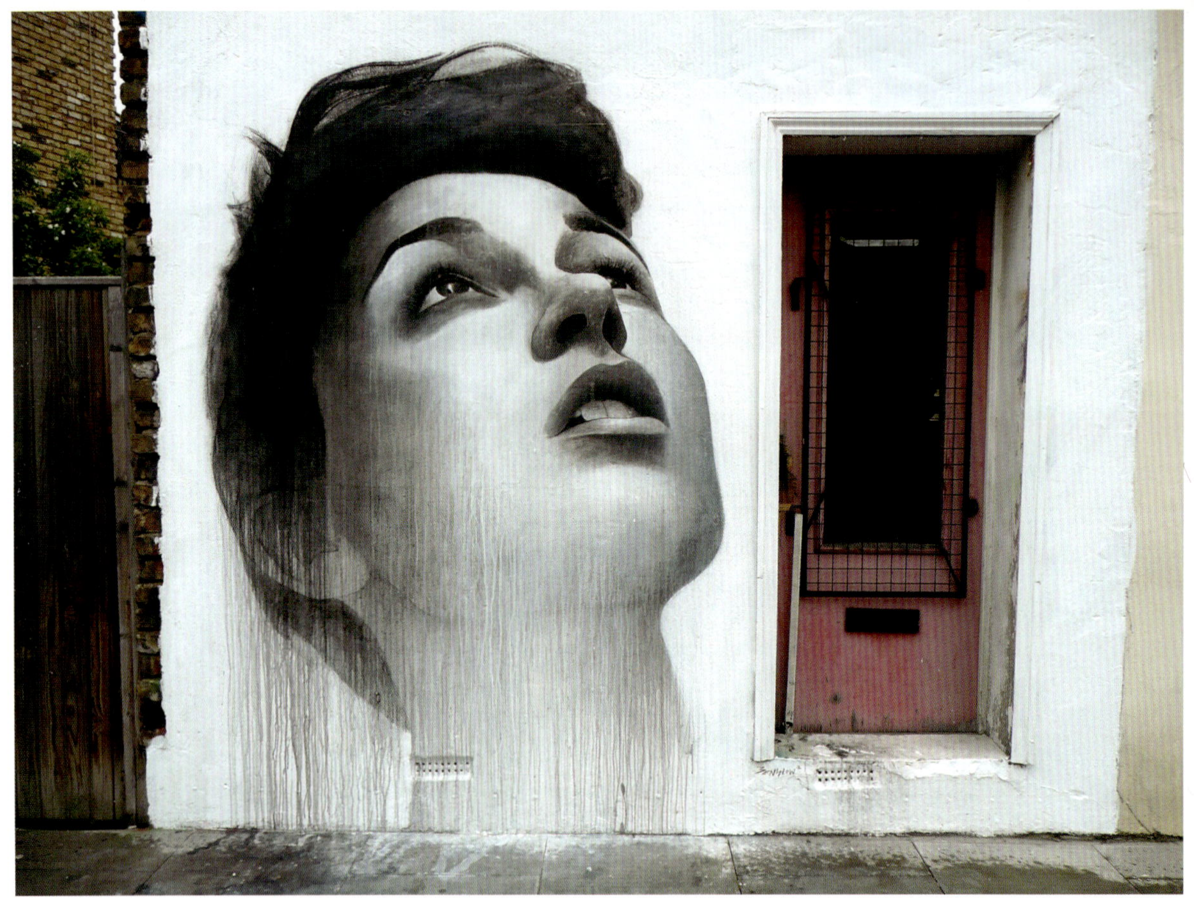

"To me, London means the centre of so much, from its incredible, rich history that continues to amaze and inspire me every day, to the characters I see getting on and being themselves. I am surrounded by so many inspirational people on a daily basis. People flock to London, it has so much potential, but I fear for its future. As much as it has for a long time allowed alternative cultures, communities and individuals to prosper, I fear that may not be for much longer.

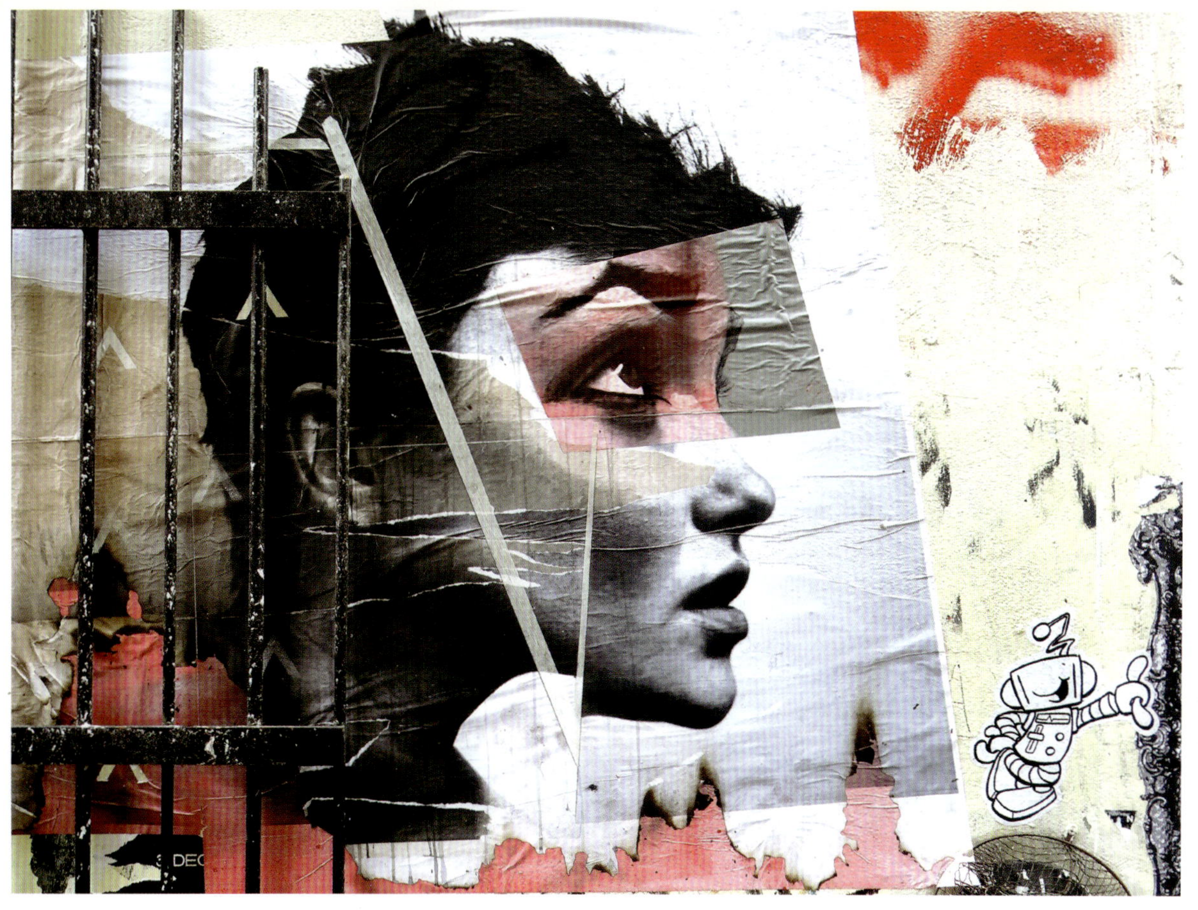

"In a world ruled by power and greed, London is at the centre of that, as I'm sure it always will be. Its leaders place so much emphasis on that world, but London has so much to offer outside the square mile. I fear that those things that make London so unique and interesting, may soon be but a distant memory." - **Ben Slow**

Ben Slow/Obit. East London

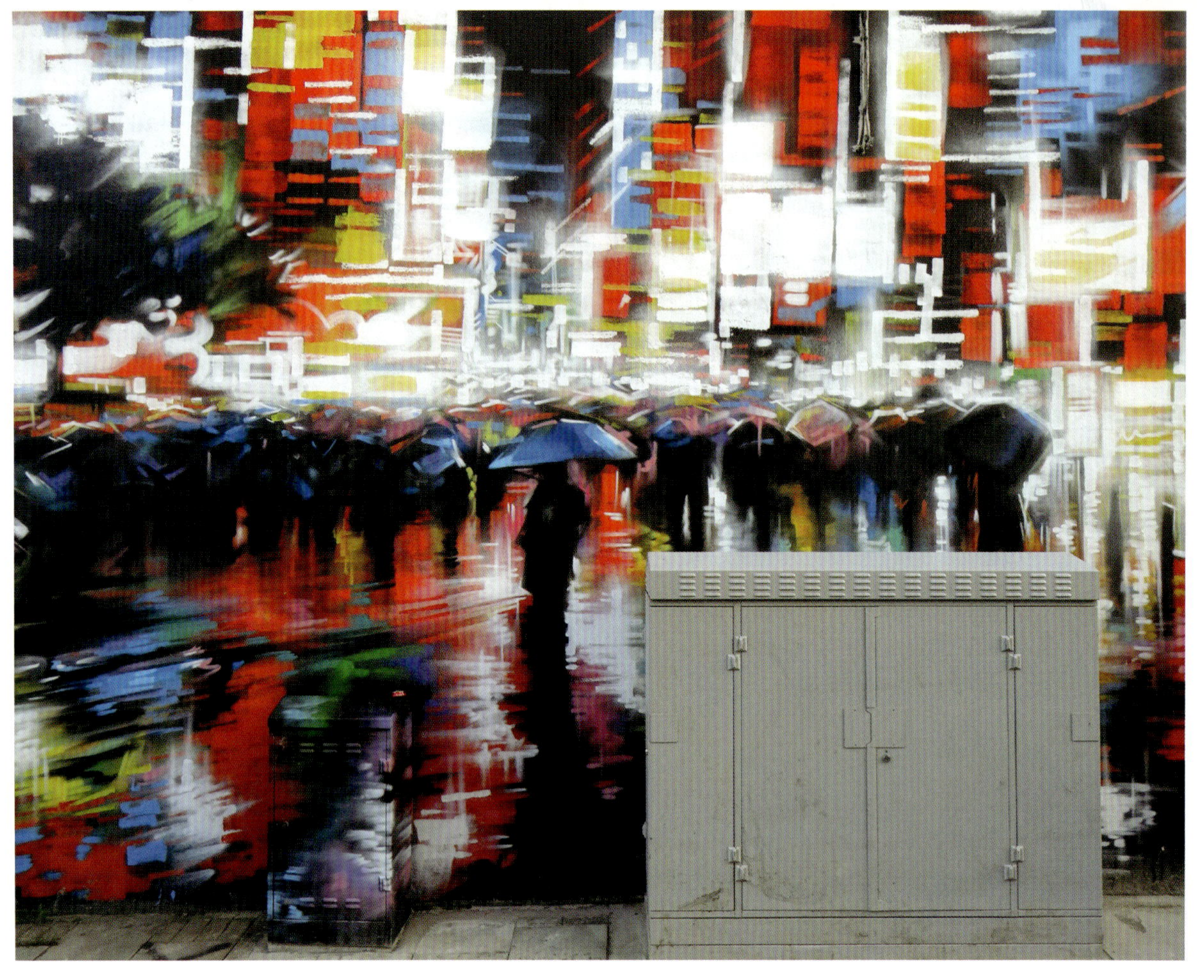

"London to me means history, diversity and vibrancy, twisting alleys, cobbled streets, hidden places, tunnels running all over the city. It's a secret world, full of subcultures, strange people, magic!" - **Dan Kitchener**

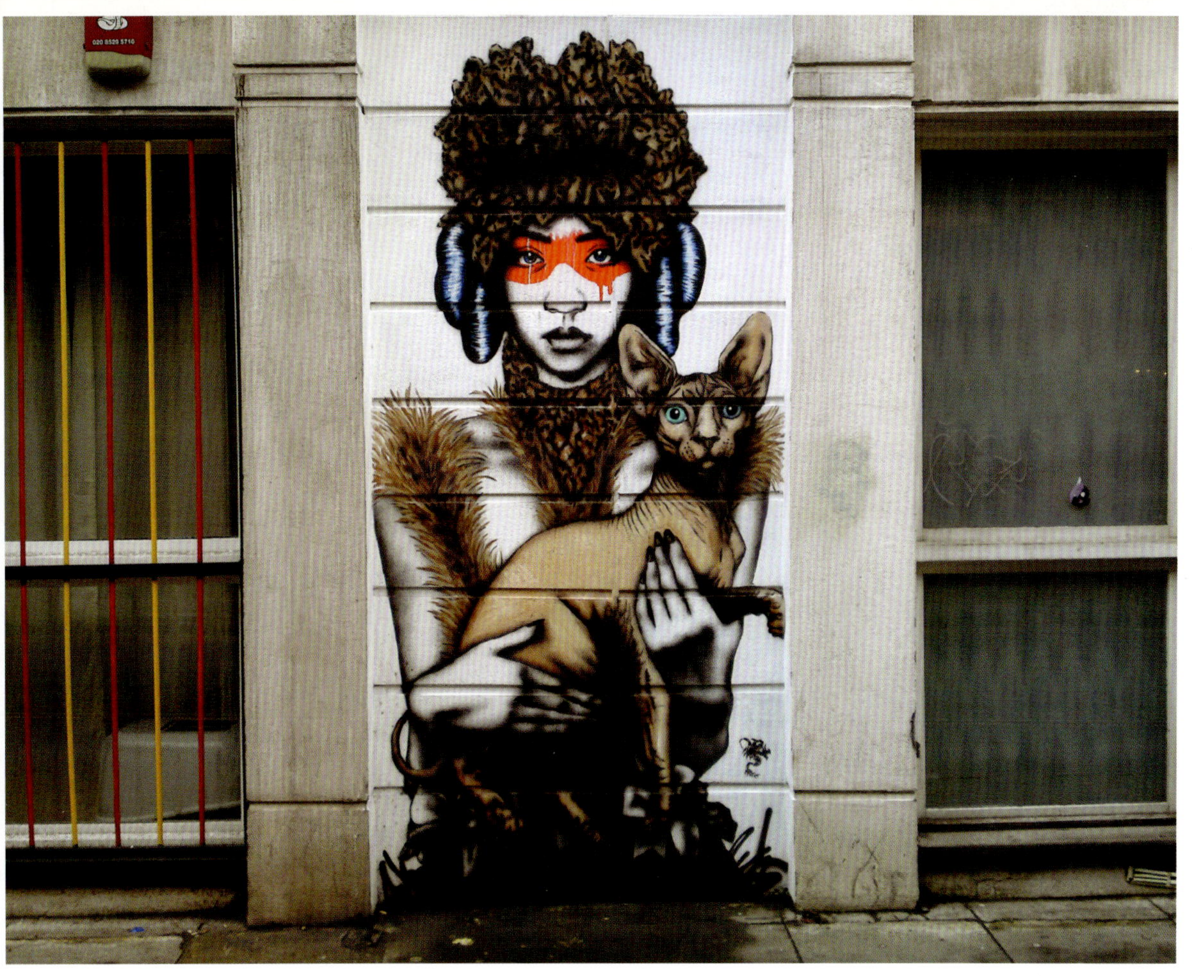

“London is a genuine hub of ingenuity and a hive of alternative creative thinking that can provide the impetus and the inspiration for any type of creative person.” - **Fin DAC**

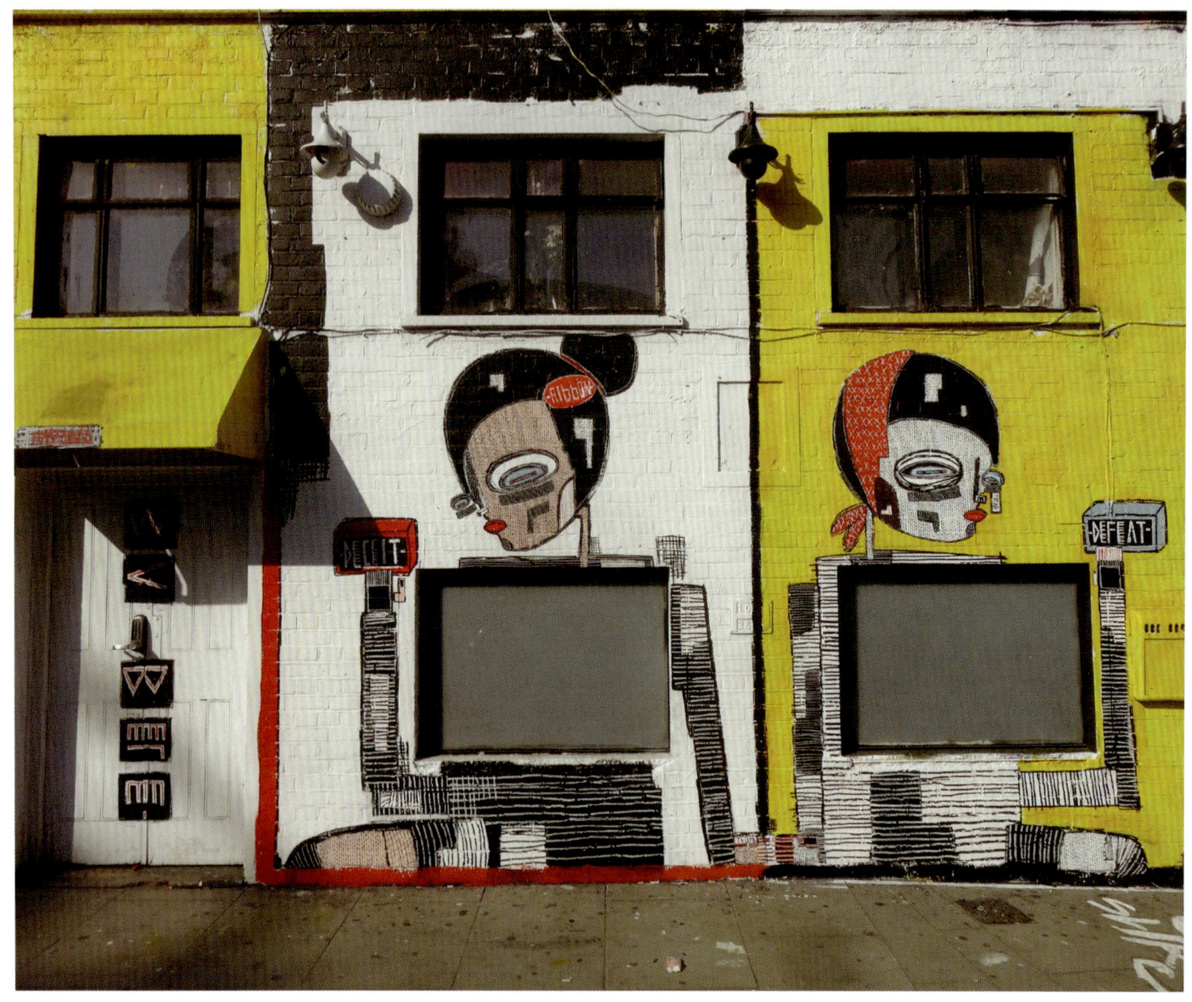

"To me, London simply means EAST London." - **Alo**

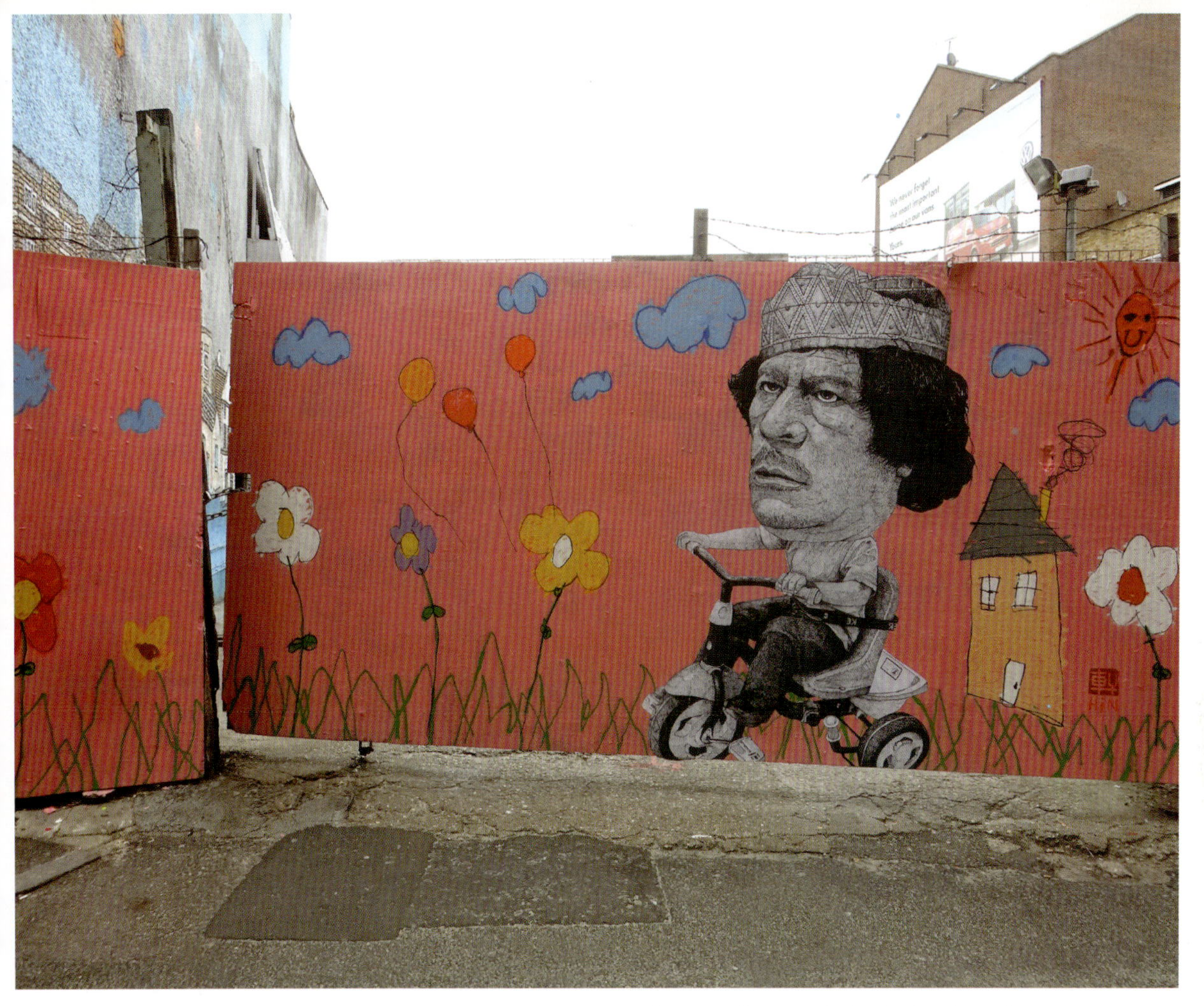

"Everyone from outside, dreams to come to London, the ones who live here dream to be in Thailand." - **Hin**

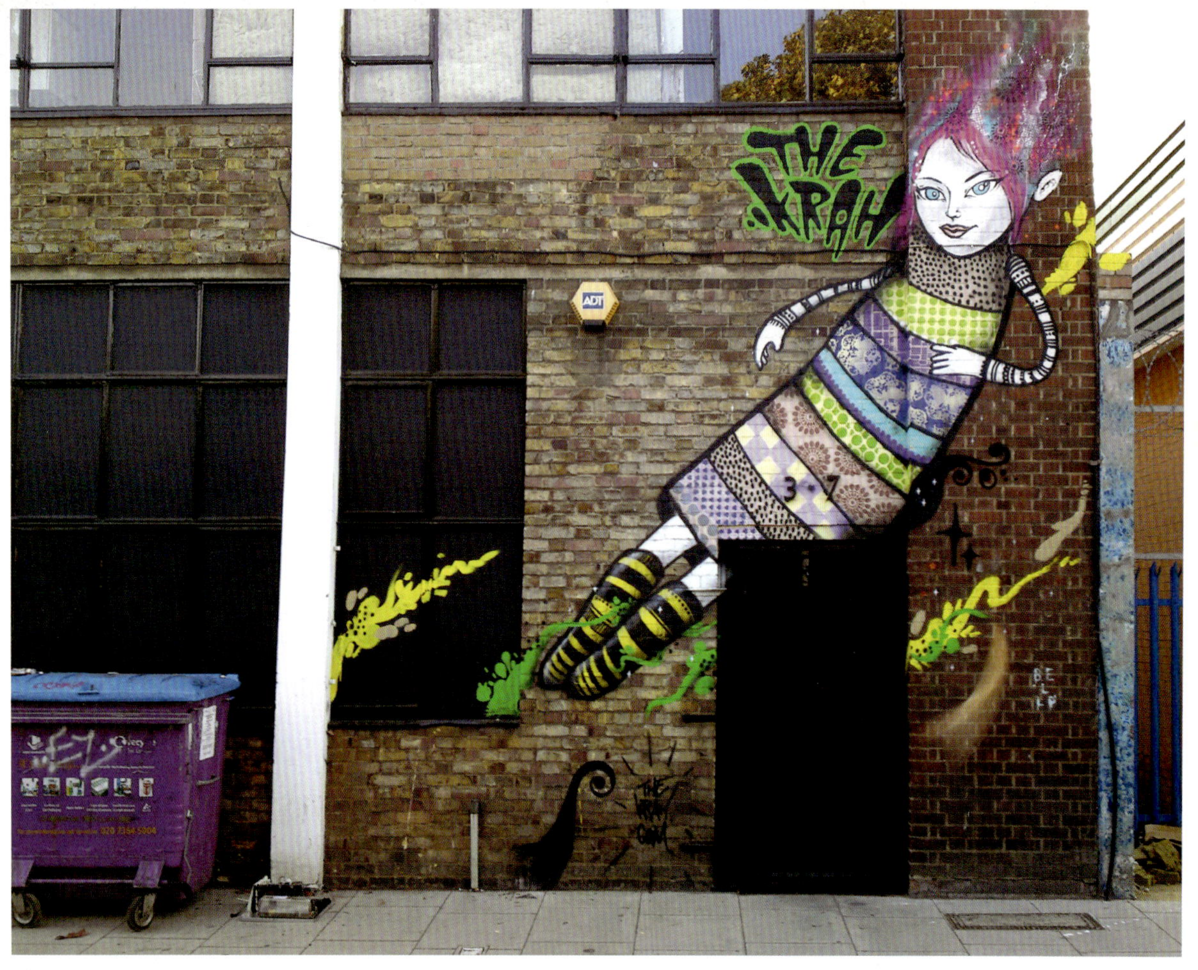

"A place that never sleeps, full of lights, imagination, opportunities, excitement and a magnet for interesting people from all over the world. But blink twice and you can easily fall into the trap, waking up into a rat race." - **The Krah**

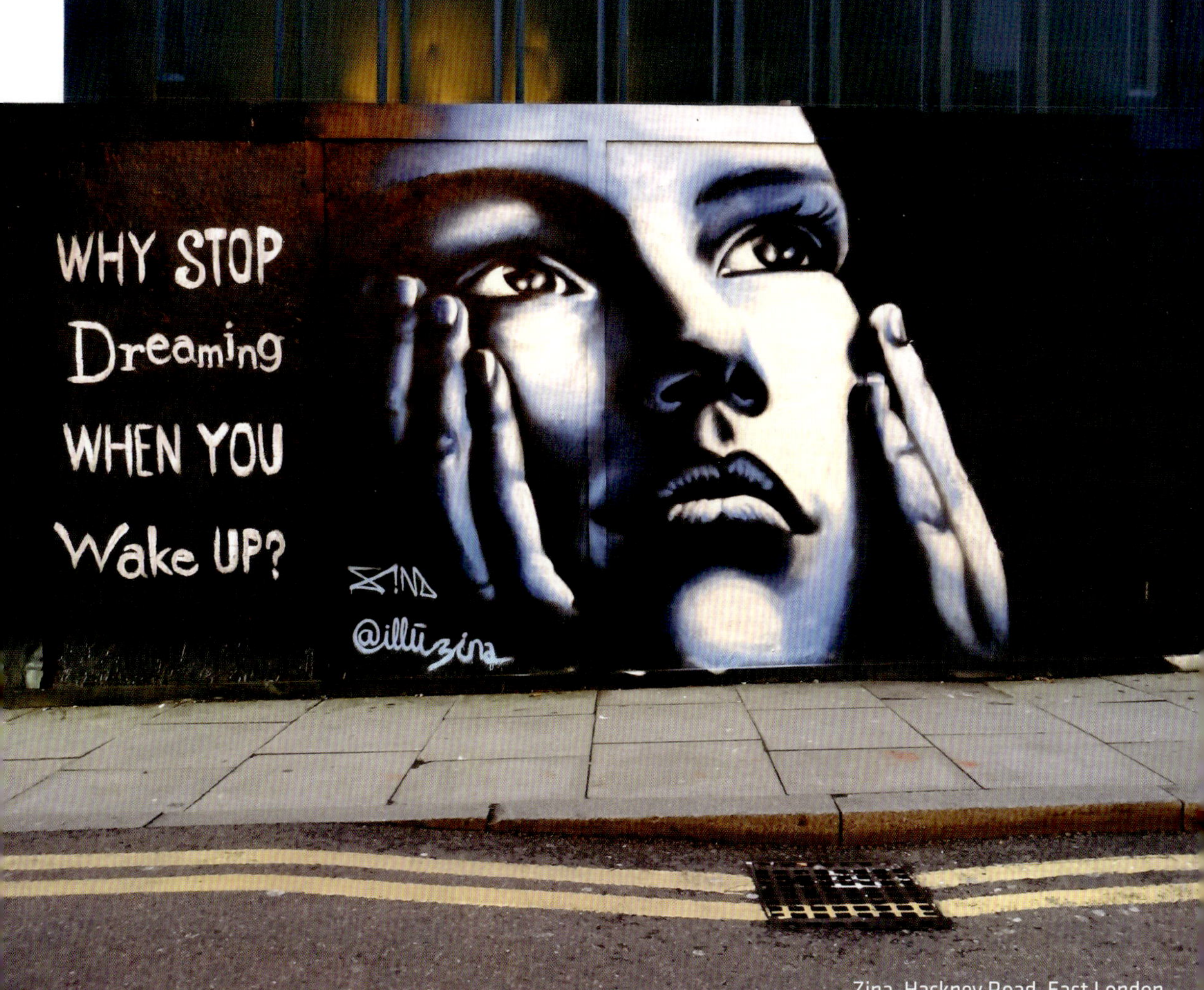

Zina. Hackney Road, East London

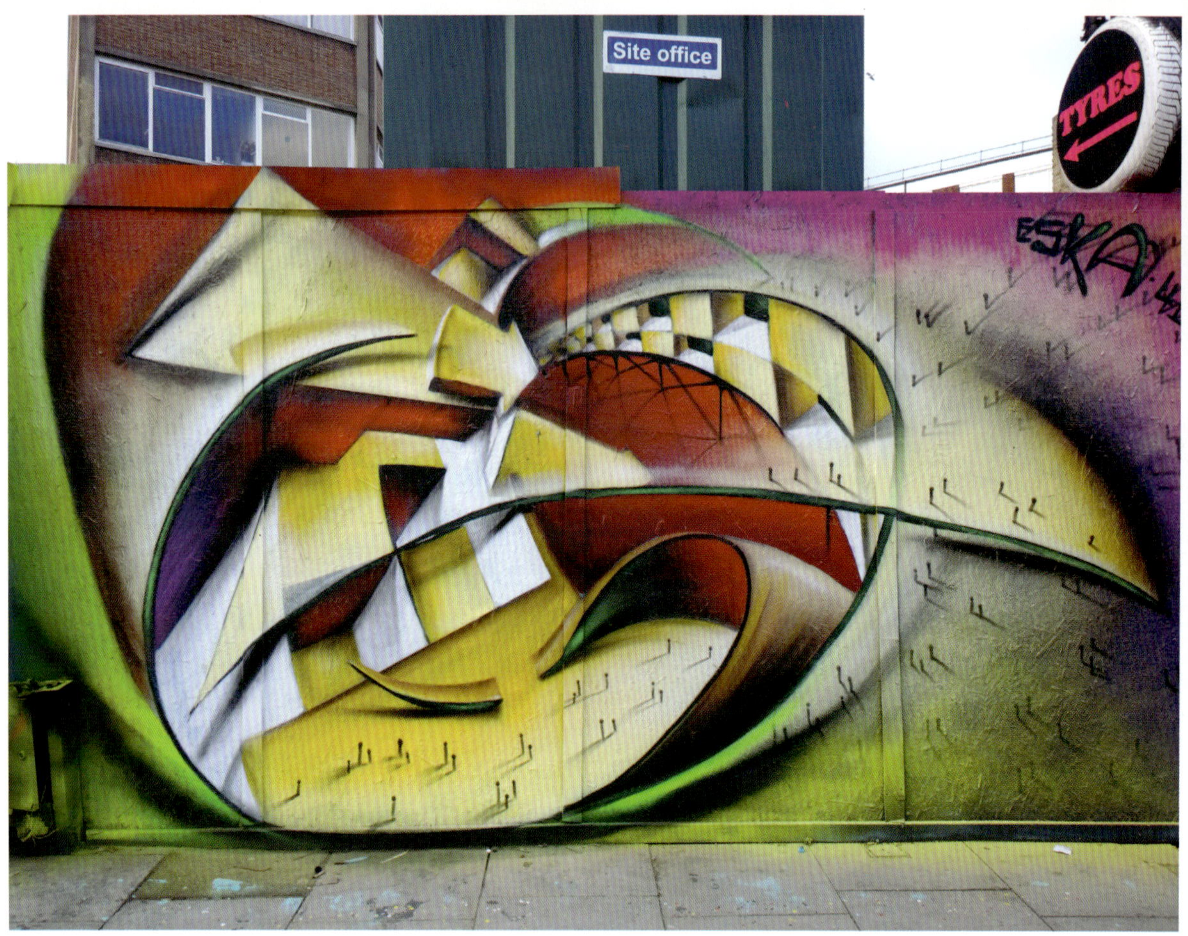

"London is my second home, as I'm originally from Poland. I've been living here for the last 11 years. Graffiti was the reason I came to London. To me, London means open gates, opportunities and possibilities. Never-ending discoveries and progress. This town doesn't sleep..." - **Eska**

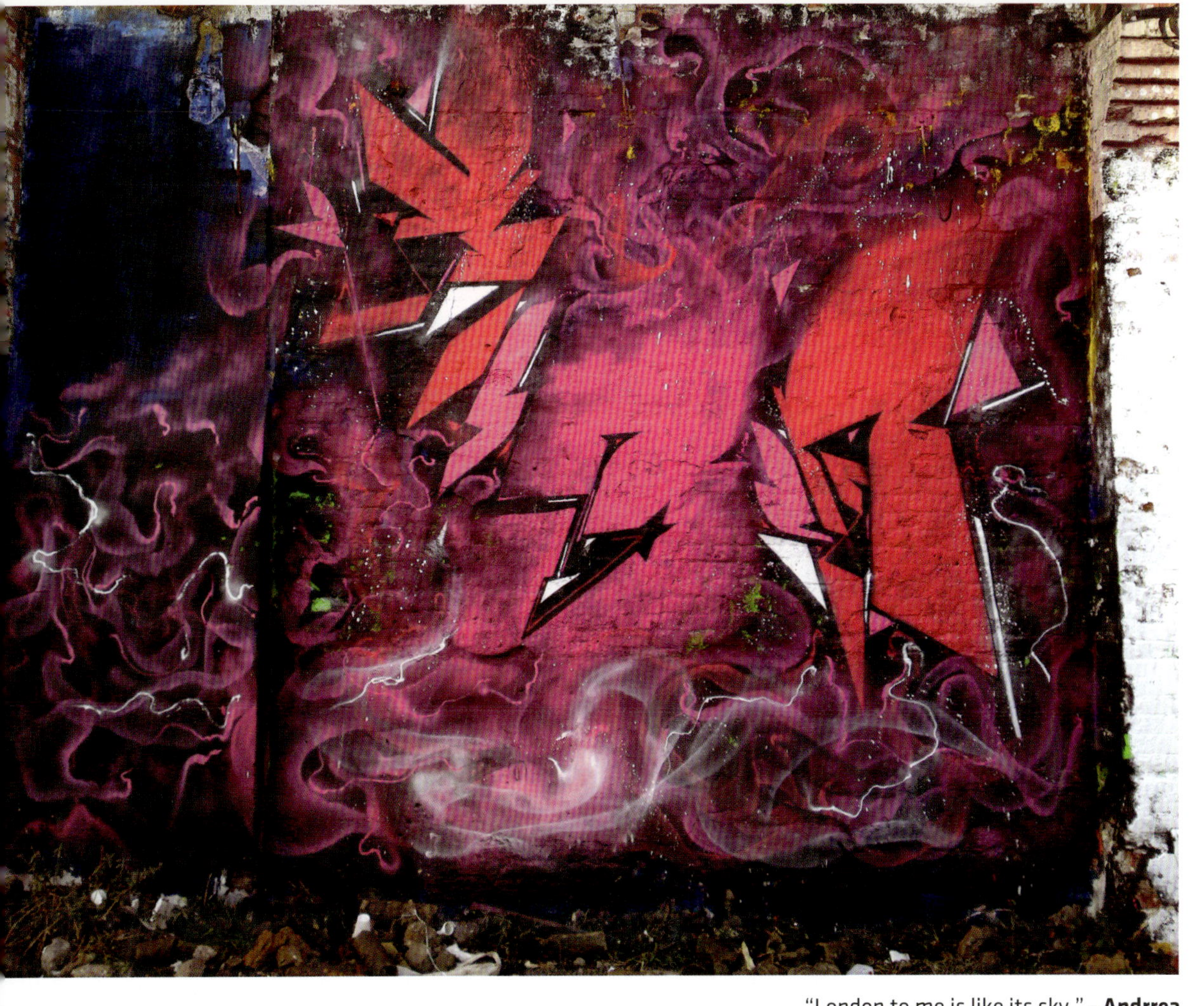

"London to me is like its sky." - **Andrrea**

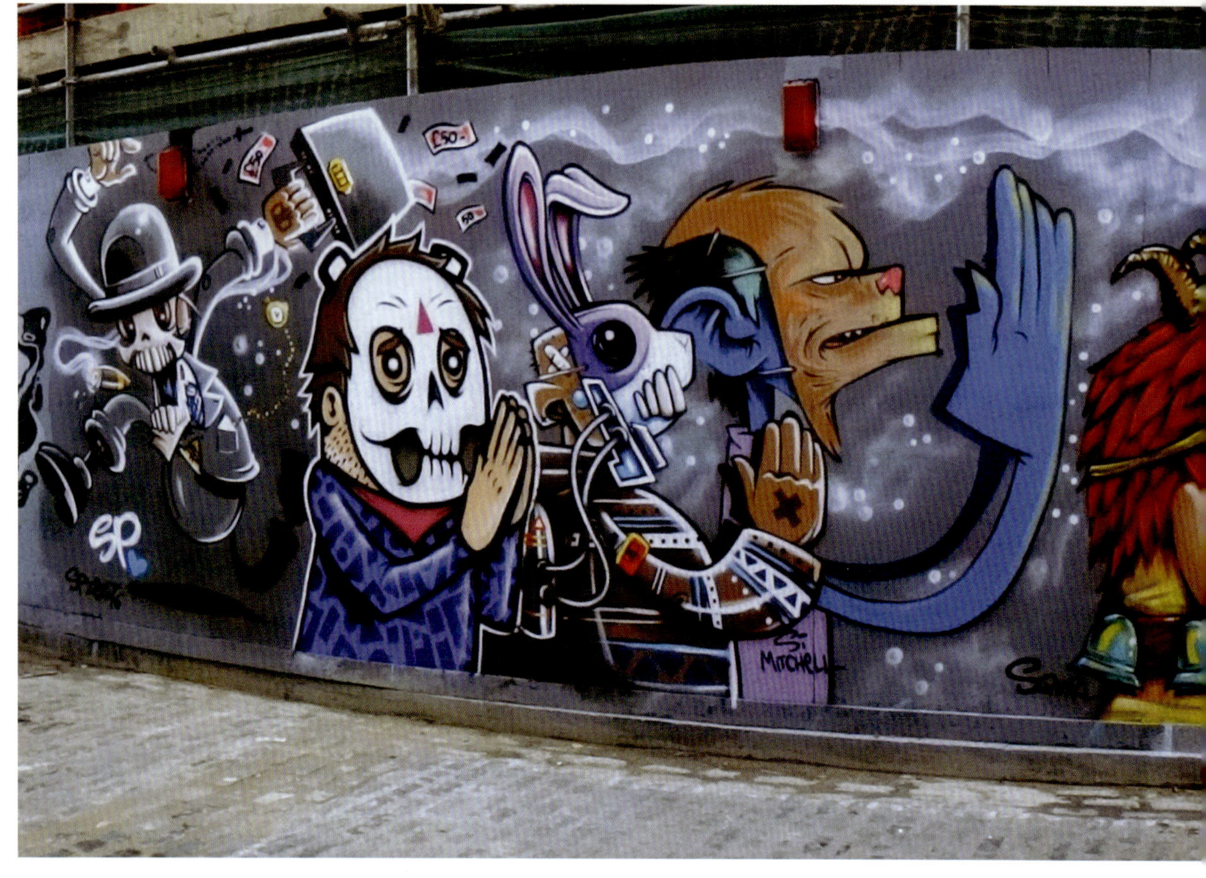

"London means fun and painting! I live in Bristol but every time I'm heading to London it's to paint or for an exhibition and a few beers. Usually we are painting with the Lost Souls guys and, if we are lucky, alongside other awesome artists. It's always hard work as we cram as much into our London time as possible, but it's loads of fun!" - **SPZero76**

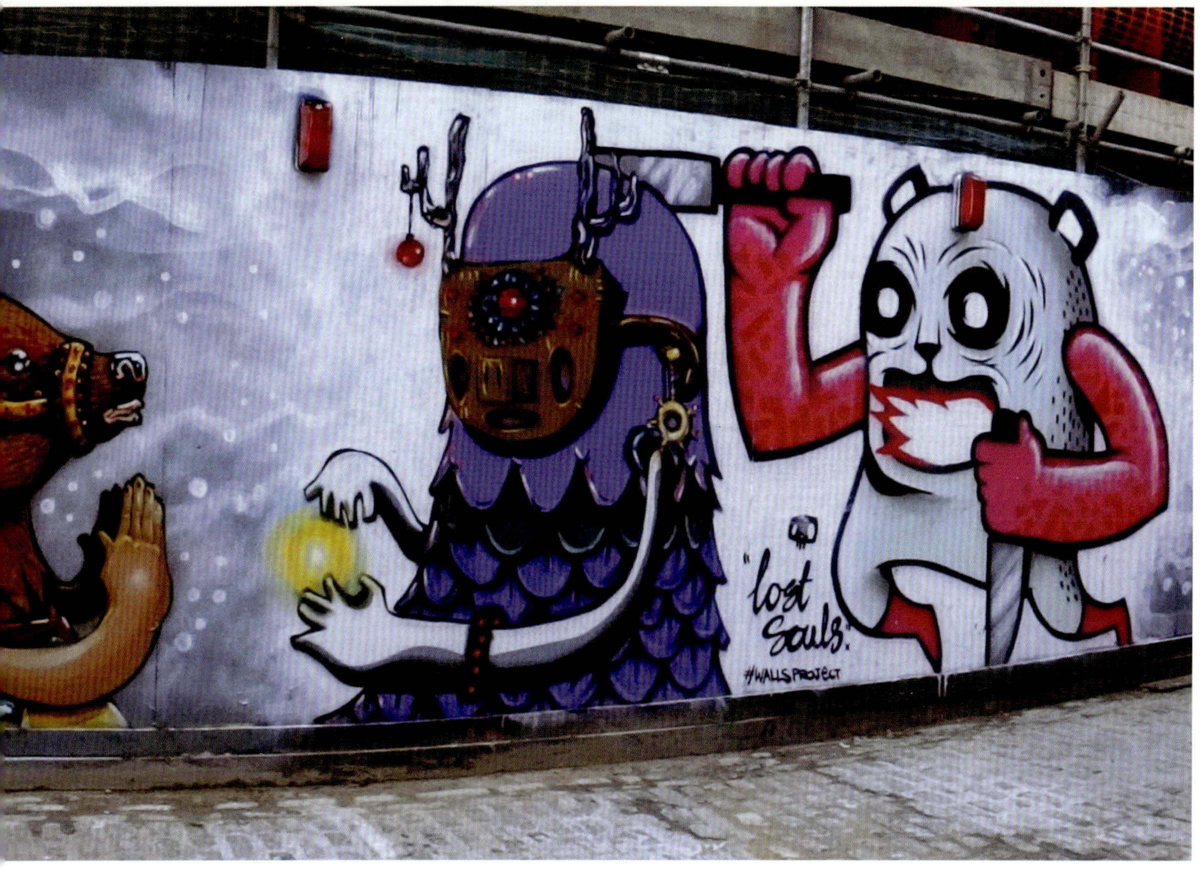

"London has meant that I've been able to meet and work with great people and artists all the time. It's given me the chance to connect and experience things that don't happen in other places, and the ability to enjoy what I'm doing here even if I'm soaking wet with a massive hangover, crammed into a tube train with five hundred other people." - **Captain Kris**

SPZero76, Si Mitchell, Squirl and Captain Kris - The Lost Souls. East London

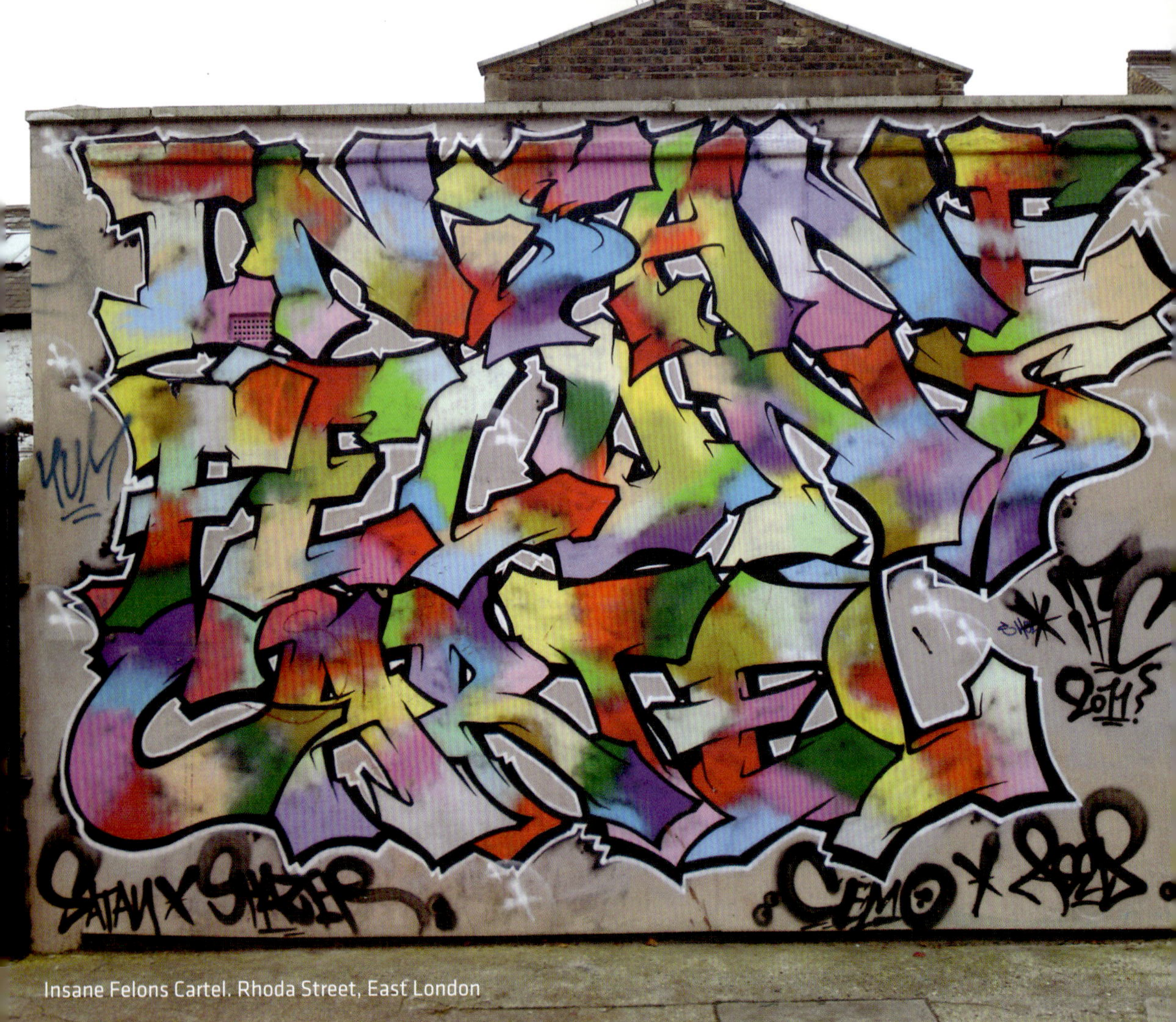

Insane Felons Cartel. Rhoda Street, East London

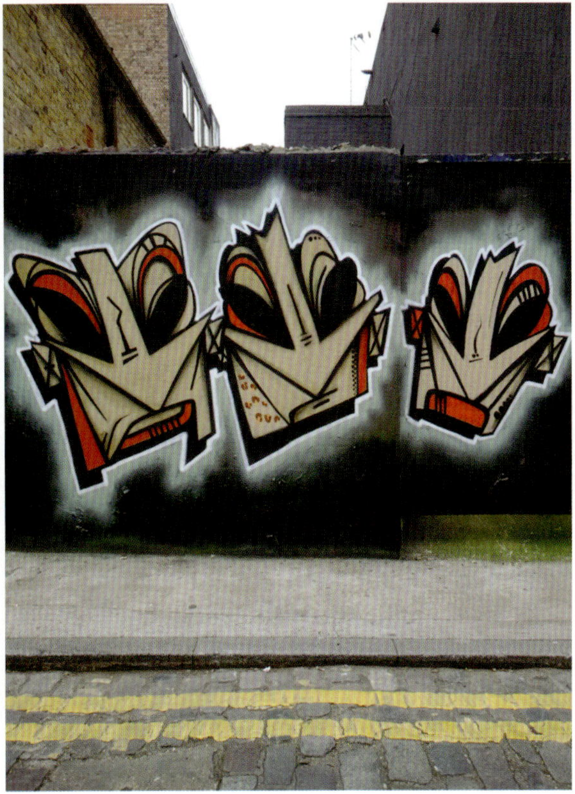

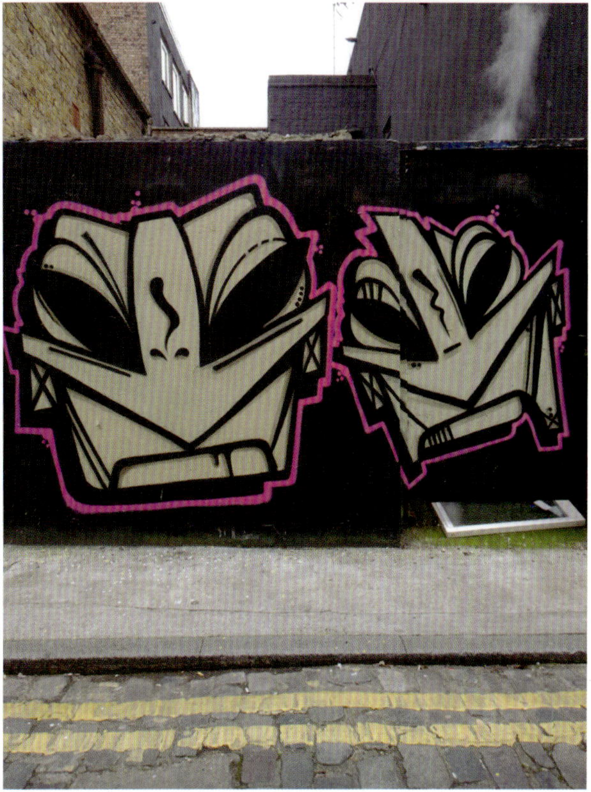

"London is everything and nothing. It's been the best and worst place to be. It seems to always be ahead of the rest of the world, but at times it can be insular and blinkered. It's generally grey (due to the weather) but for artists, graffiti or otherwise, London's sprawling boroughs have pockets of light that open for just the right amount of time, then close the door as the corporates cotton on and move in. When thinking about London and Graffiti, the early/mid nineties come to mind, as that was the time when everyone seemed to have a killer style and colour schemes. There seemed to be a train with a piece on it at every station. It was a time that formed our collective mind and was a great influence for us... Or maybe it's just rose-tinted spectacles talking..." - **TML Stars**

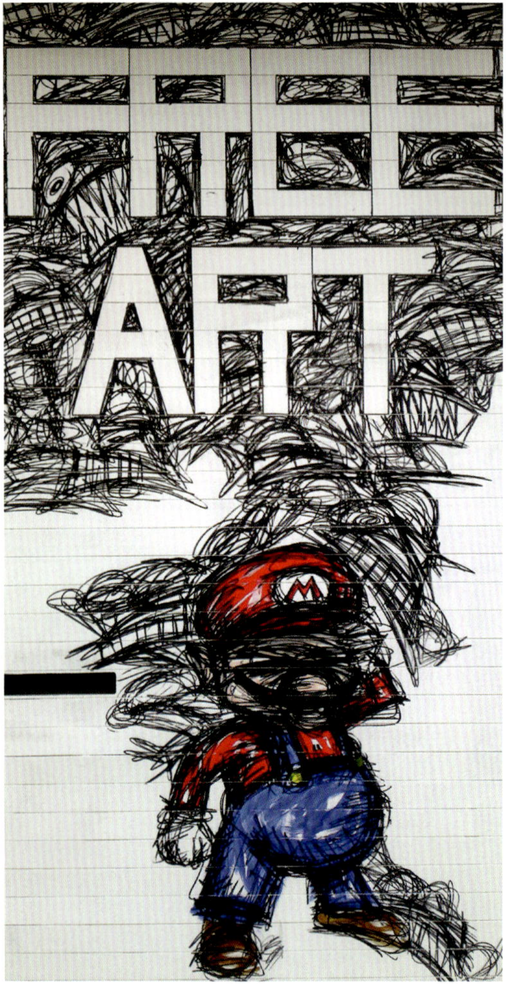

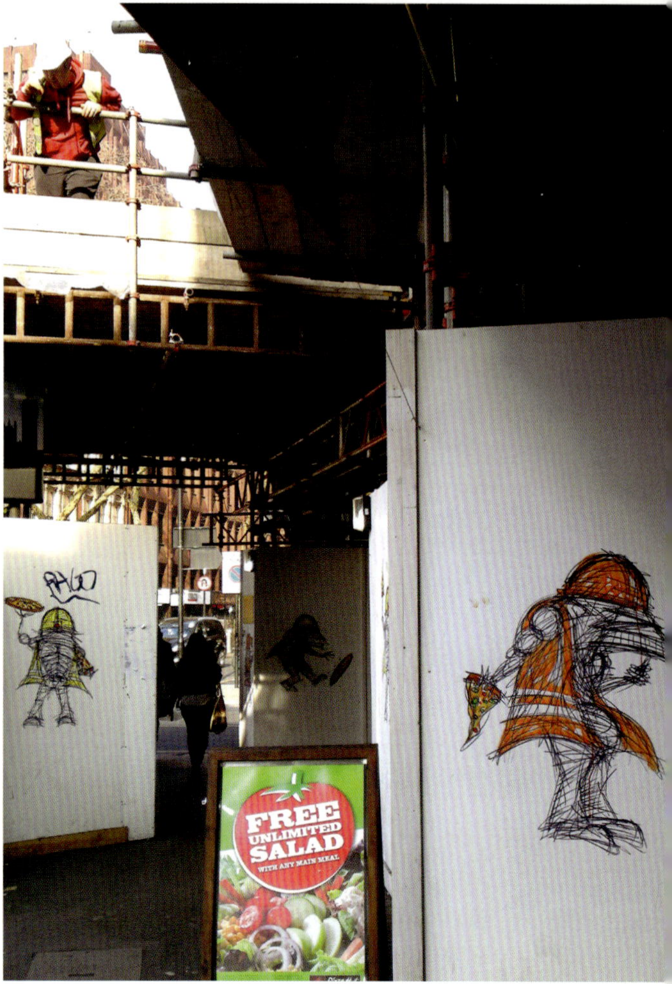

Nathan Bowen. East/Central London

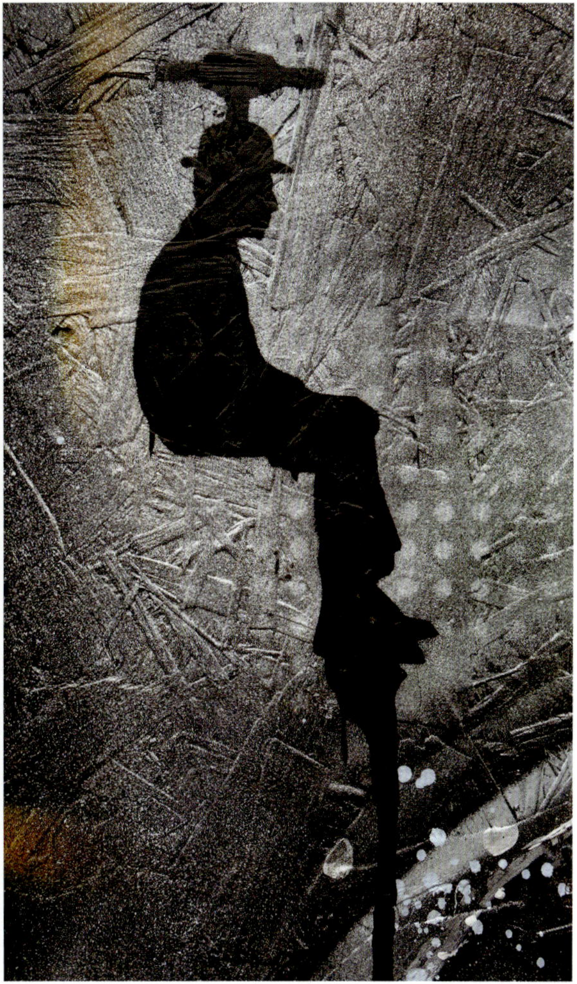

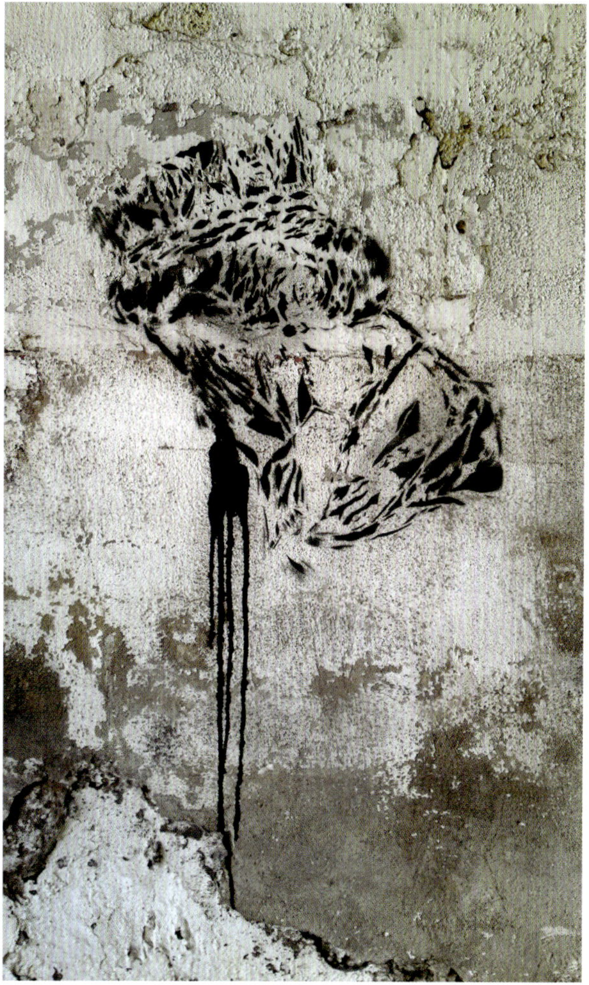

Don. East London

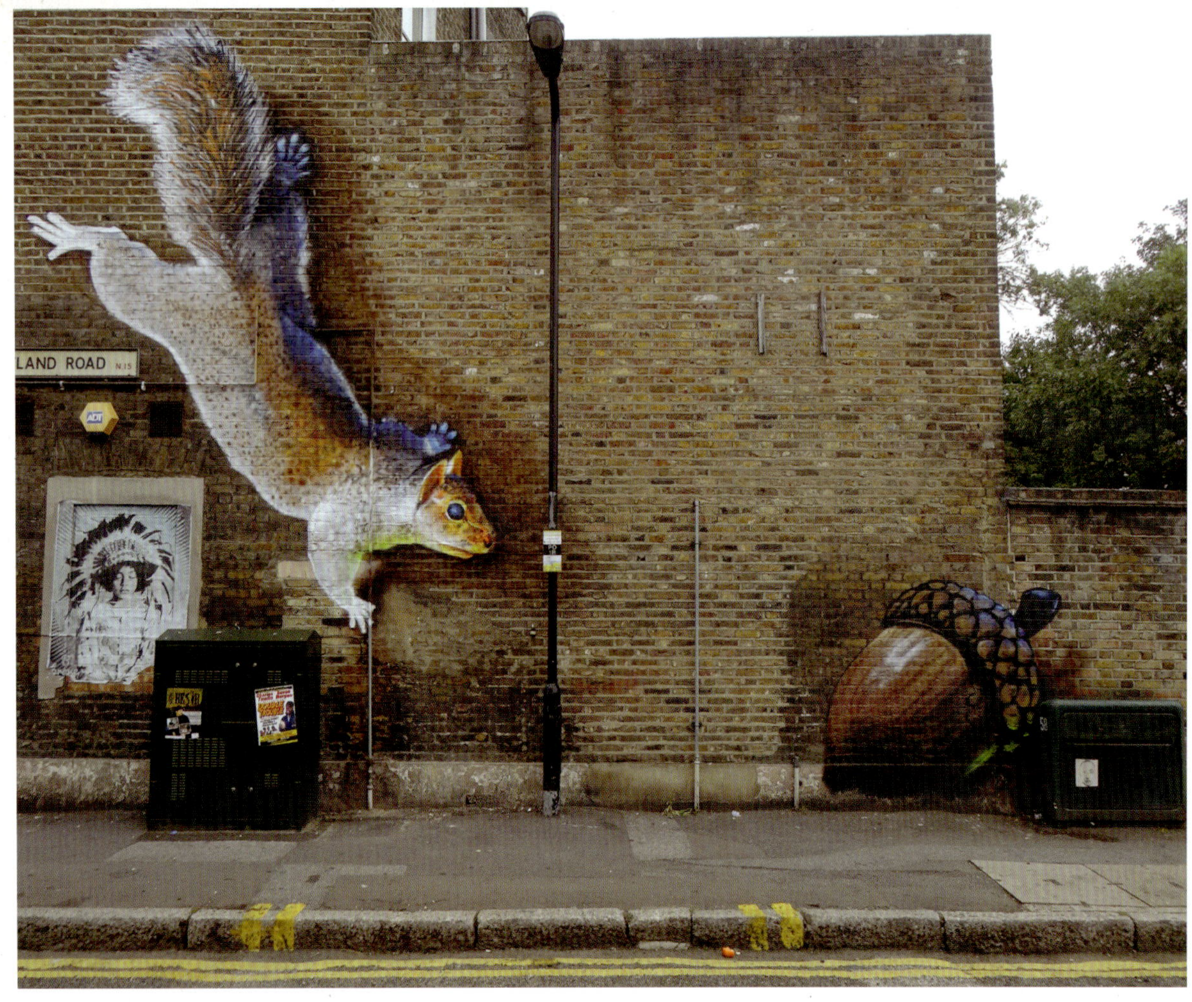

Boe & Irony, Donk and more. North London

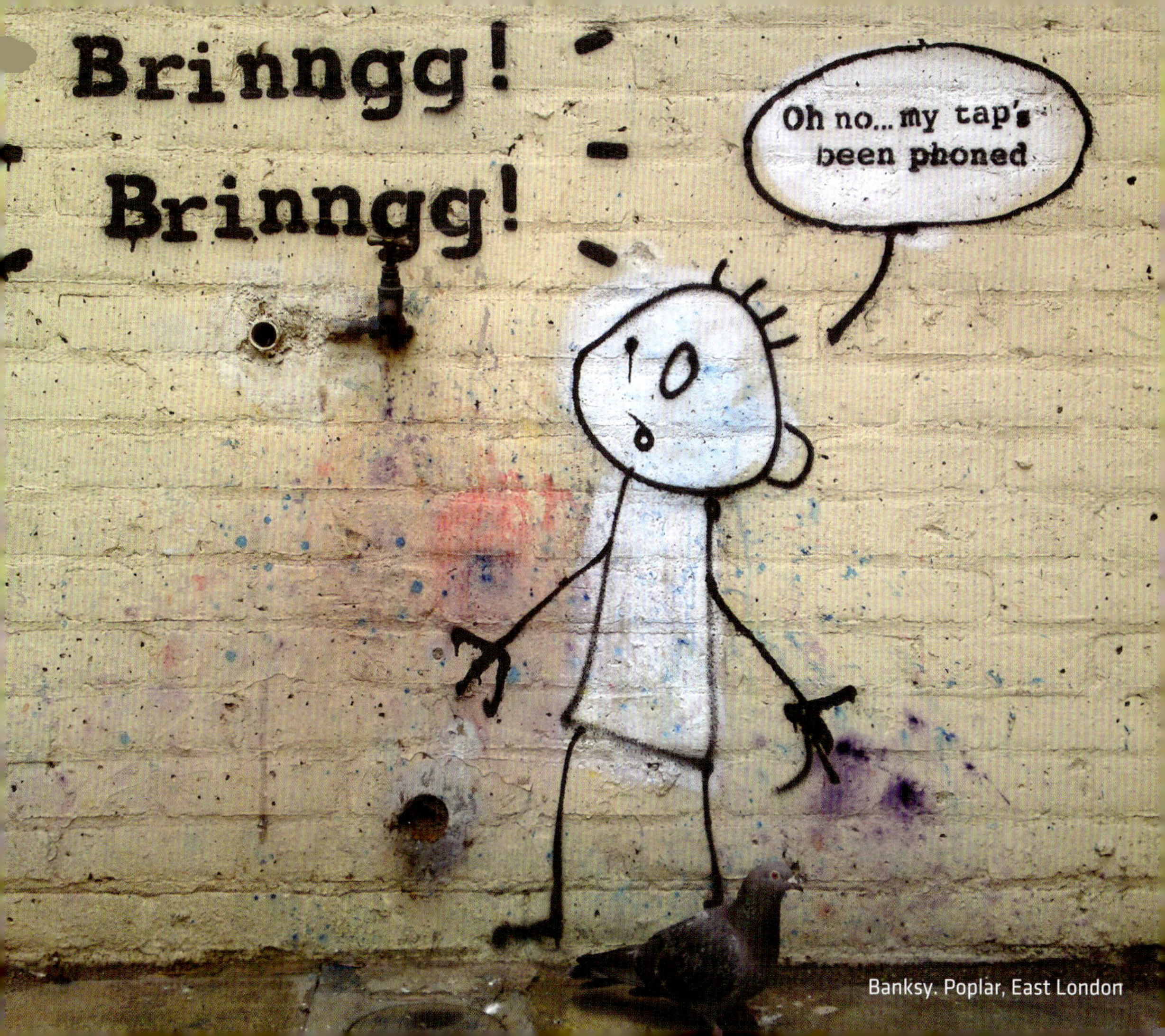

Banksy. Poplar, East London

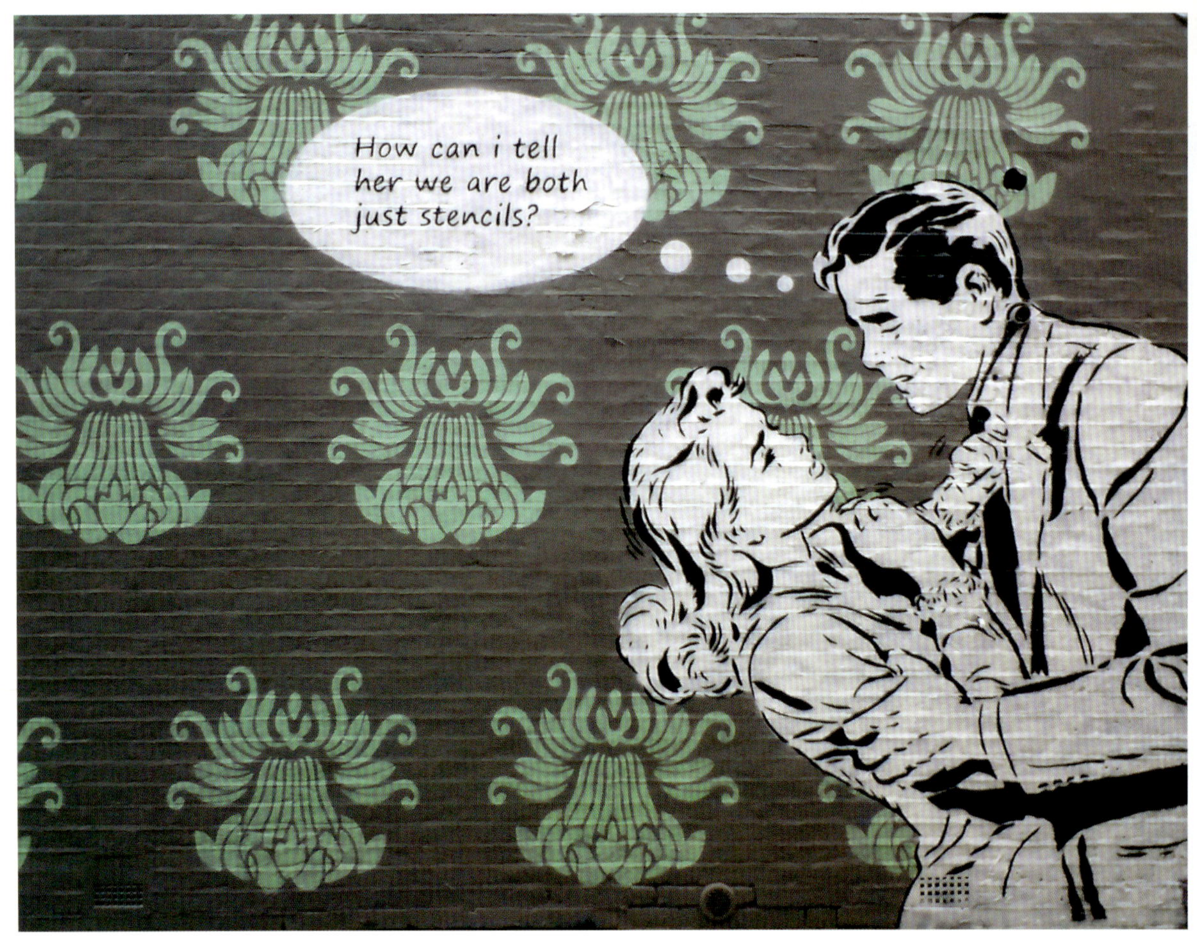

"London means a great many things to the both of us. It's currently an enjoyable home, work and playground. It can, however, also be quite foreboding and troublesome but we think that's one of the reasons we like it. You never quite know what's going to happen next..." - **Id-iom**

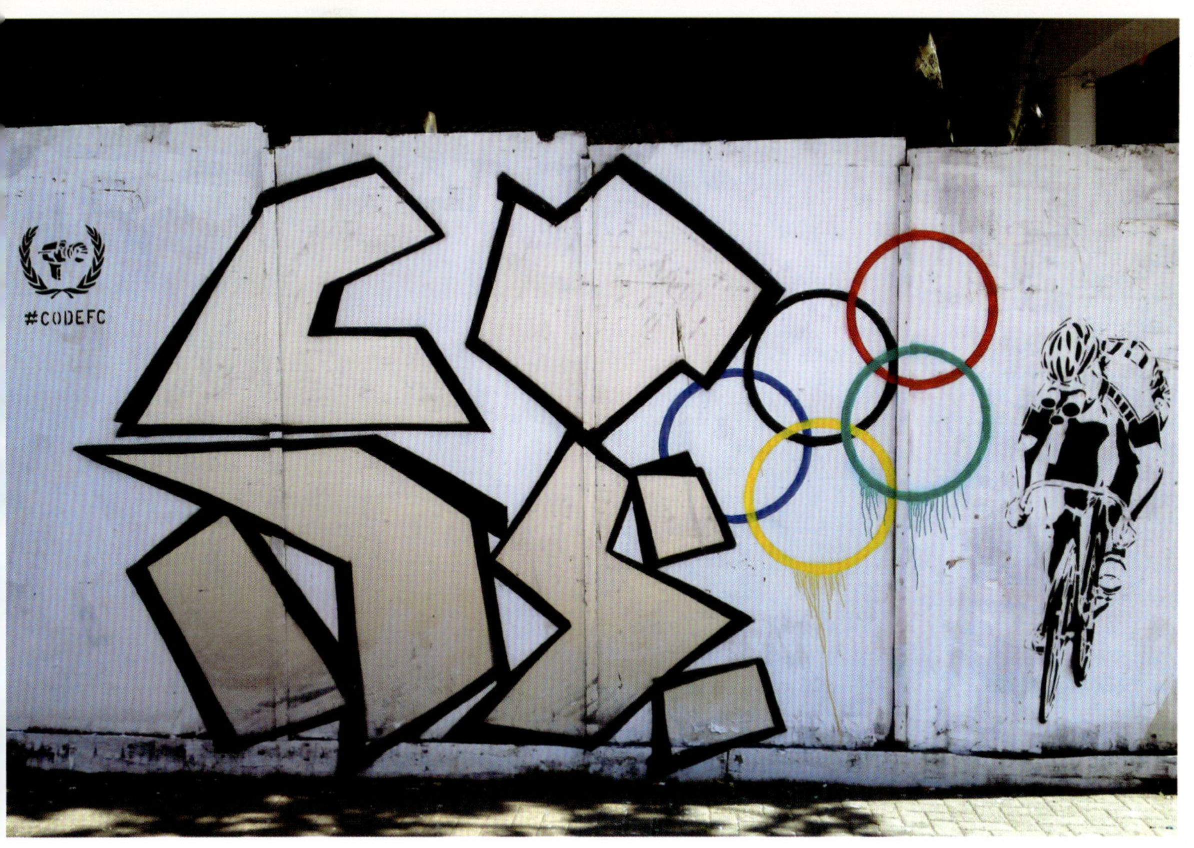

"London is where I first saw graffiti (lettering) when I was a kid and since then, I've always felt attracted to it. It's where my home and studio are. I now have some sort of love/hate relationship with it, and need to escape from it every now and then. I call it my other half, as I spend half of the year in London and the other half travelling around the world for my painting projects. But the amount and quality of artistic input I get in London makes it worth coming back every time. It's definitely one of the major hubs in the world. It's the best place to live if you can afford not having to spend the whole year there." - **CodeFC**

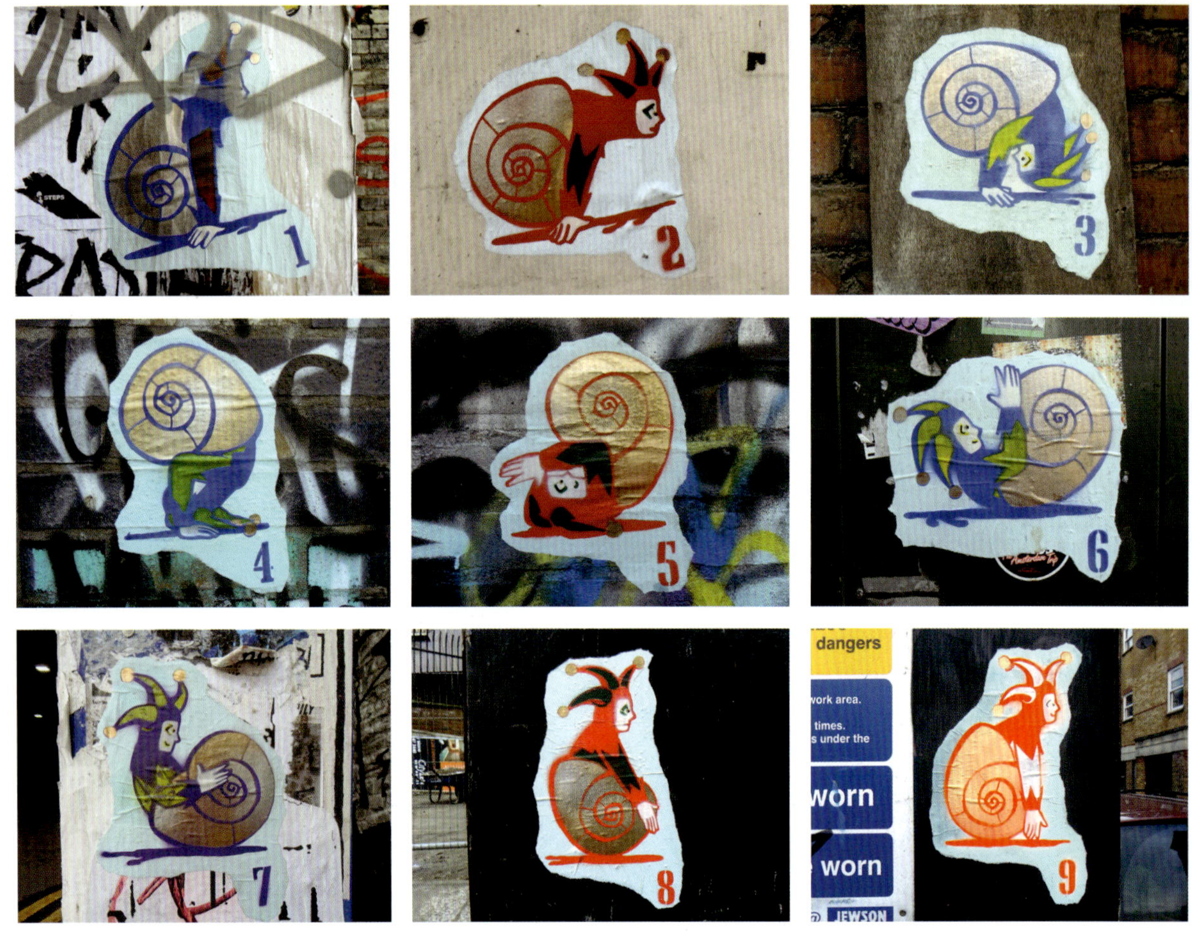

"Even though there has been an attempt to sterilise the most interesting parts of London through redevelopment, stainless steel and glass, the city streets still represent a fantastic arena for artists of all styles and persuasions to share their creativity with the world." - **Dr Cream**

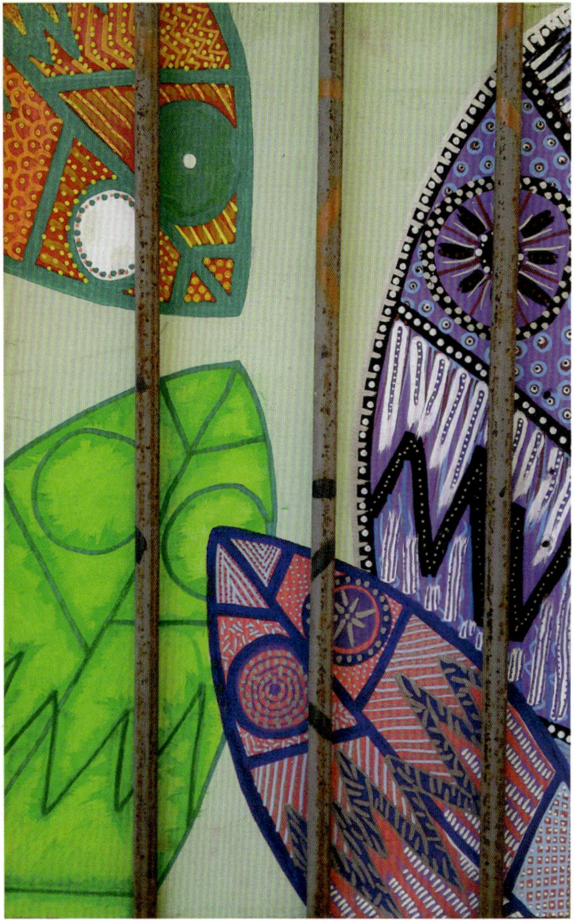

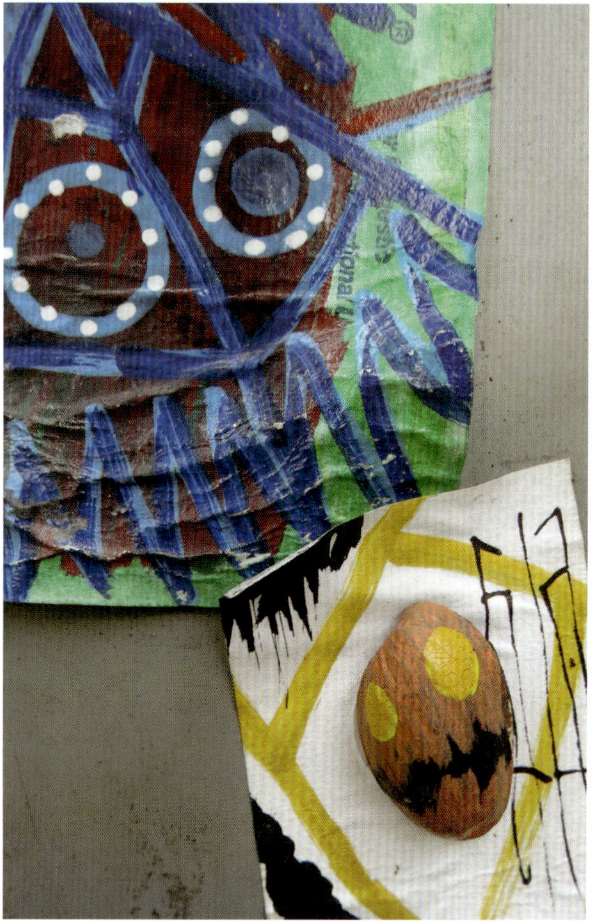

"London has so many faces, whether they be buildings or people. I love the dirt and history, and being part of it all. London, the eye opener. Get out and get up." - **616**

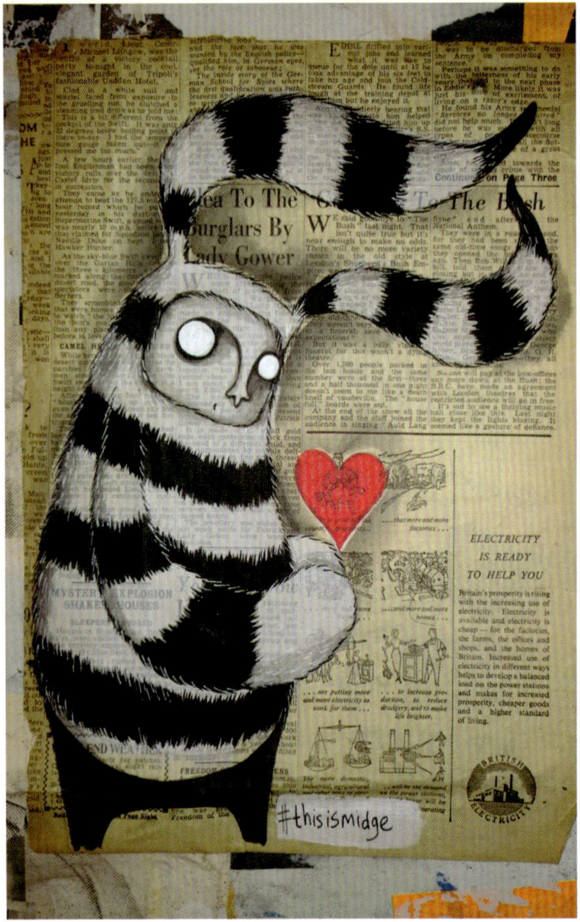

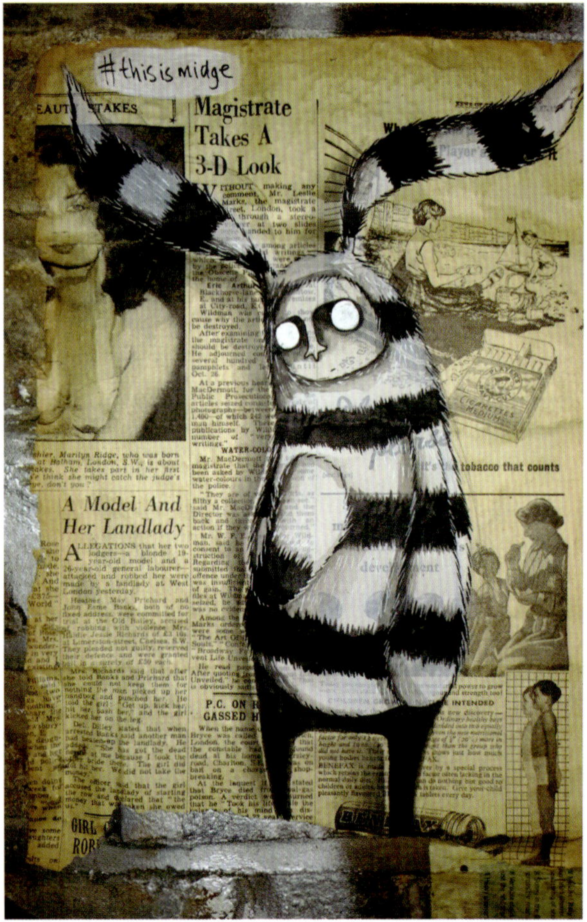

"London means waking up early, a long train journey, the build up of another potential adventure, a day to create another memory inside a world I barely know. It's full of strange people, strange colours, strange smells and strange sights. It's dangerous, scary, exhausting, exhilarating. And I love every minute of it." - **Midge**

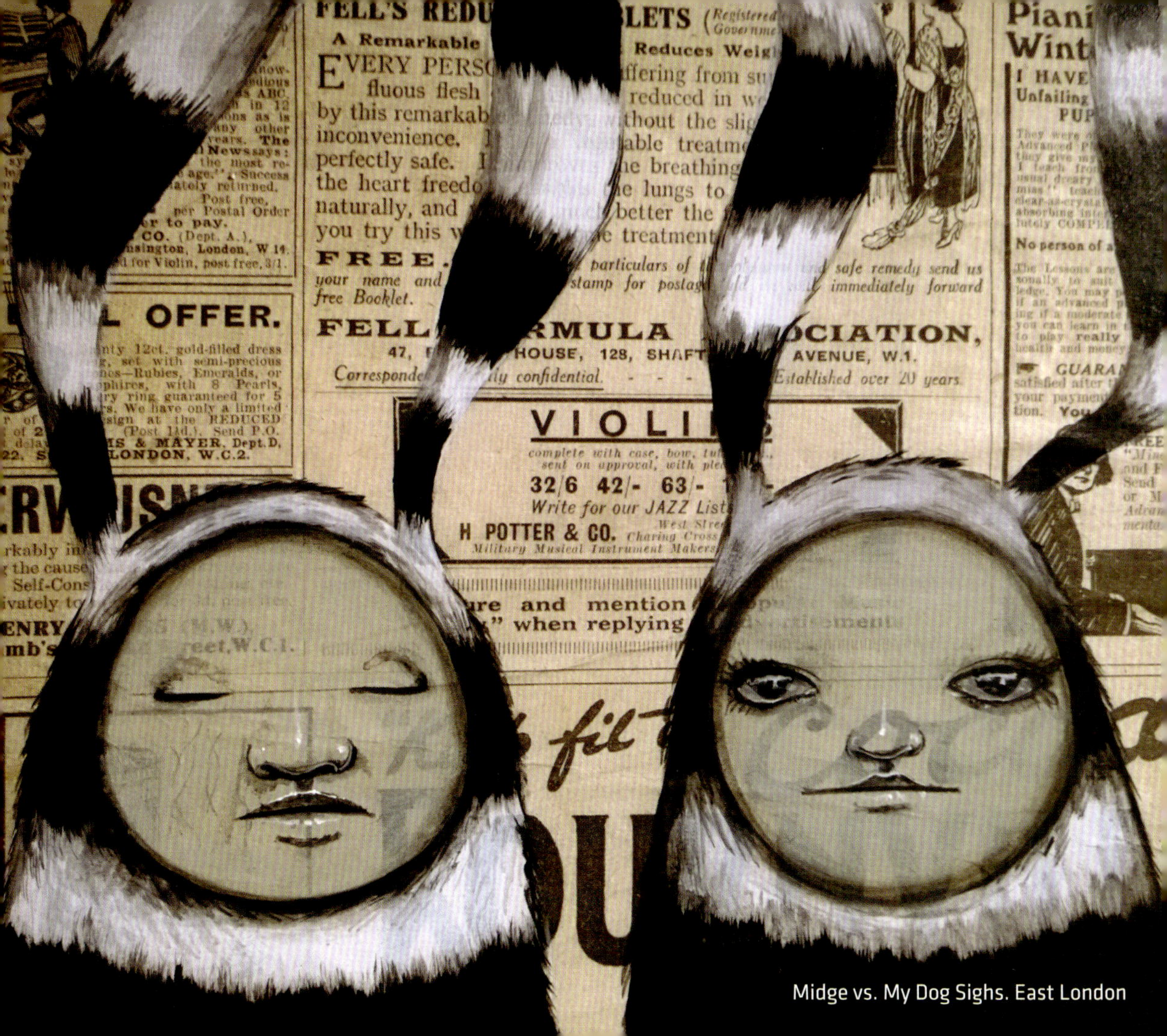

Midge vs. My Dog Sighs. East London

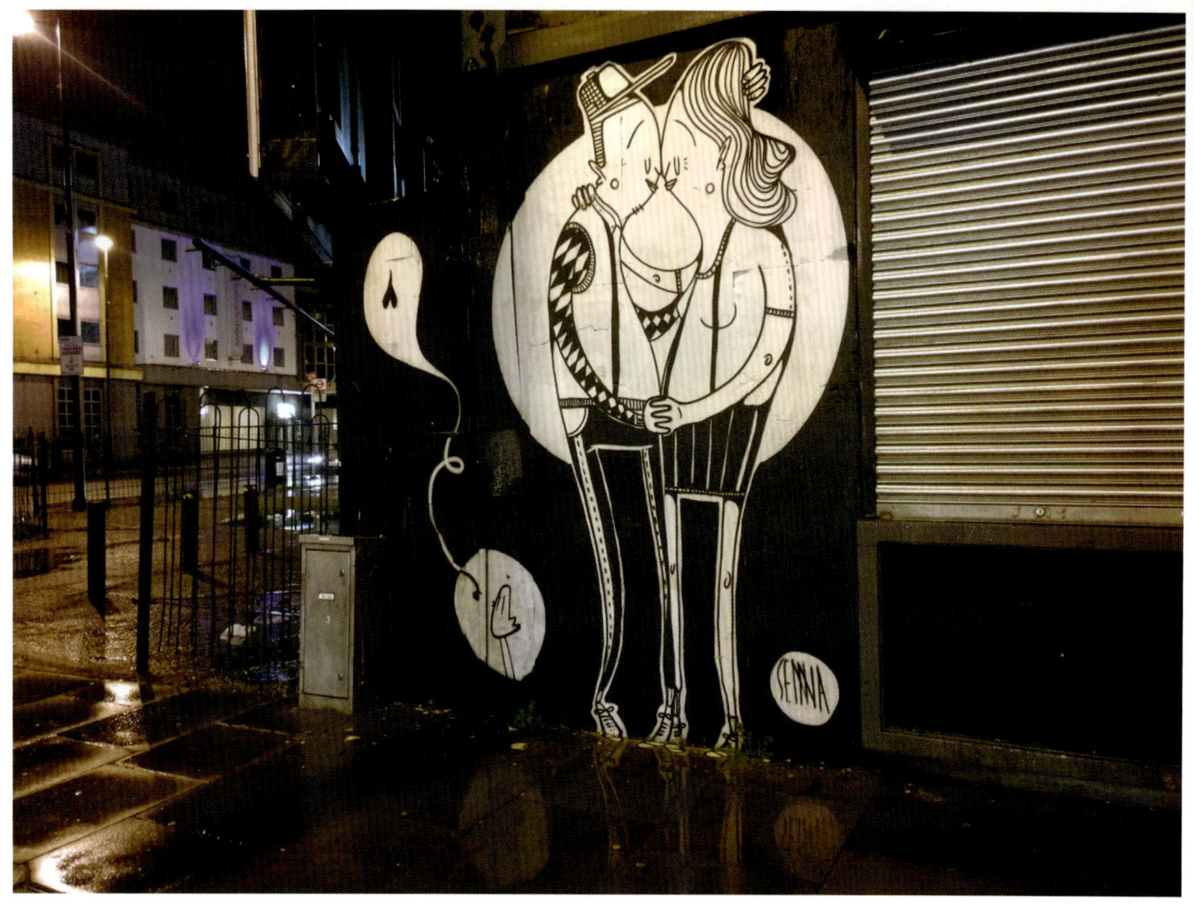

"London to me is one of the best cities I ever visit. Great atmosphere and great people. As a street artist, I love the scenario that London brings, something really old and new. The mix of cultures makes the experience richer and richer, and it never stops! I have the feeling that everything is happening in London, like, it is the place to be. I've made a lot of friends there, and I hope to always return to London! Cheers mate!" - **Alex Senna**

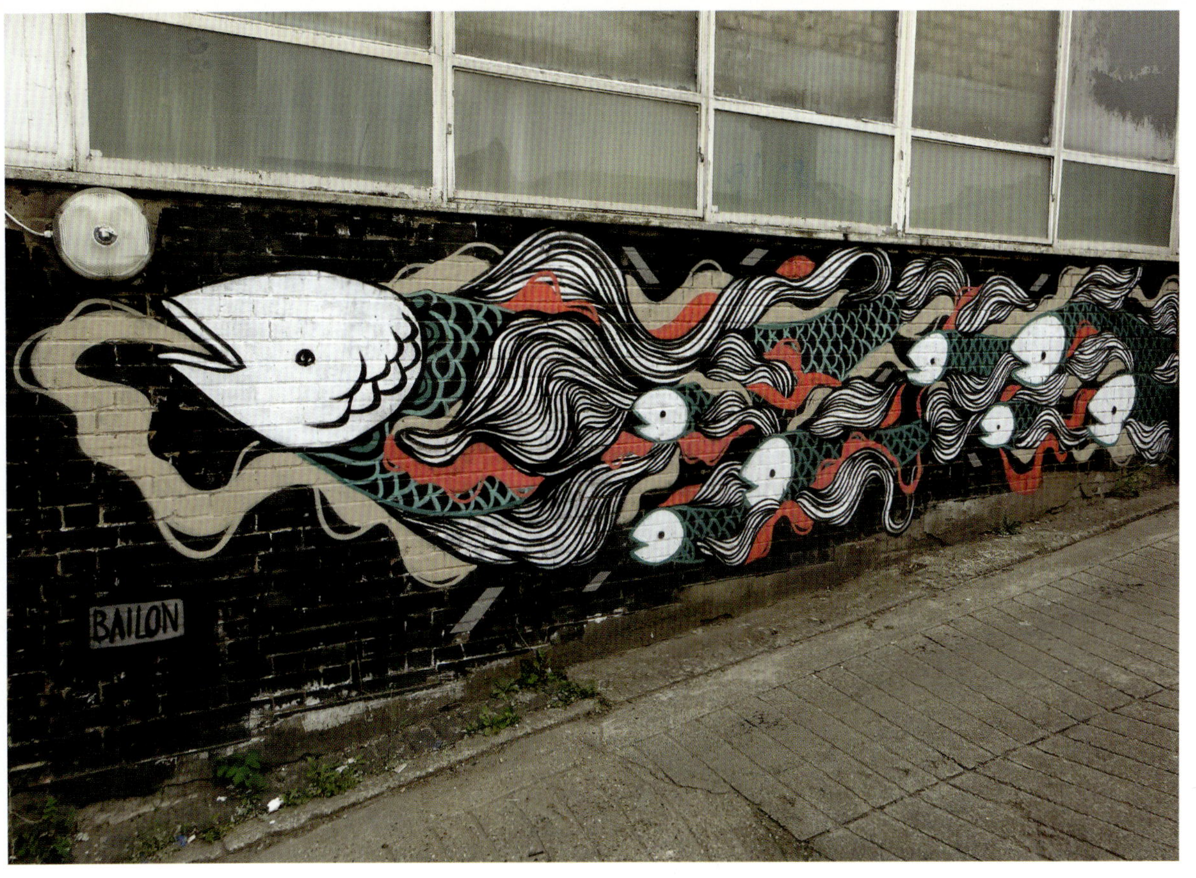

"I think what I love the most about London is all the diversity you find there. You just bump into interesting people from every single country you can imagine, all the time and suddenly, you have new good friends all over the world. The graffiti scene is impressive, quite active and diverse, but besides that, you can also find a whole range of artistic and cultural options, like great exhibitions, festivals and music concerts. For me, London means diversity, intensity and, although CCTV is always watching you, freedom as well." - **Bailon**

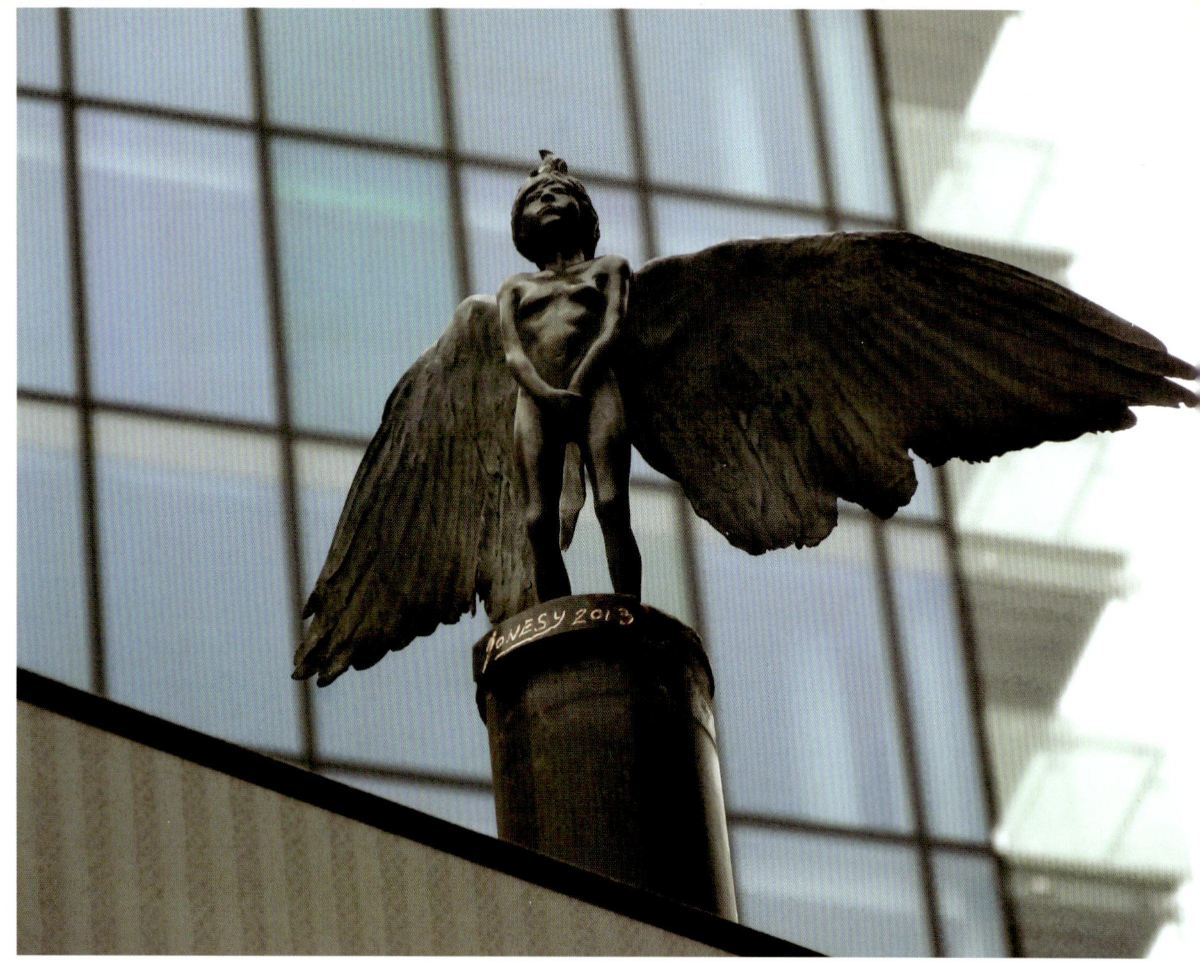

"London, it's like Paris was for artists just after the turn of the last century, the East End being here, it's hard not to be inspired." - **Jonesy**

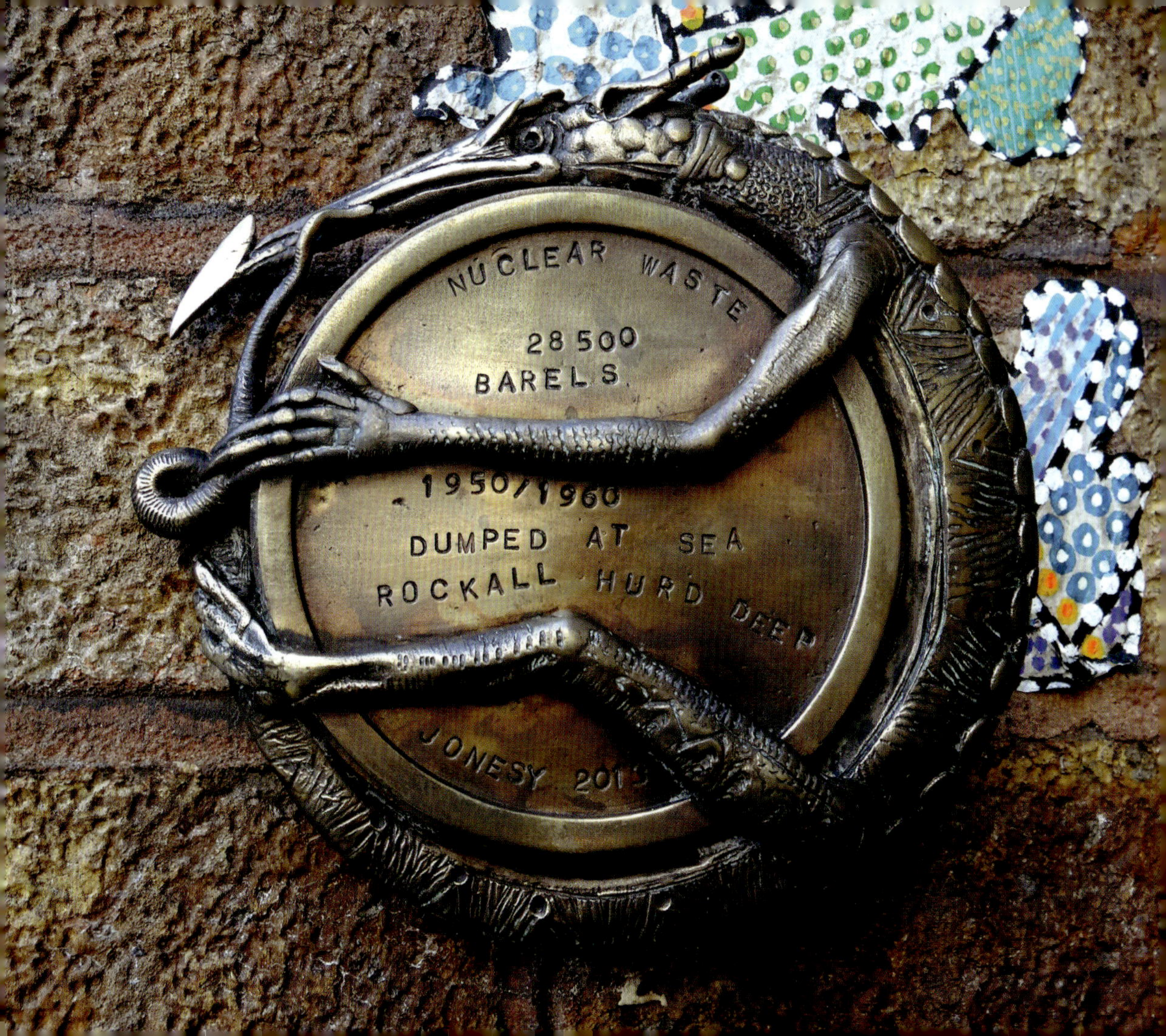

NUCLEAR WASTE
28 500
BARELS
1950/1960
DUMPED AT SEA
ROCKALL HURD DEEP
JONESY 201

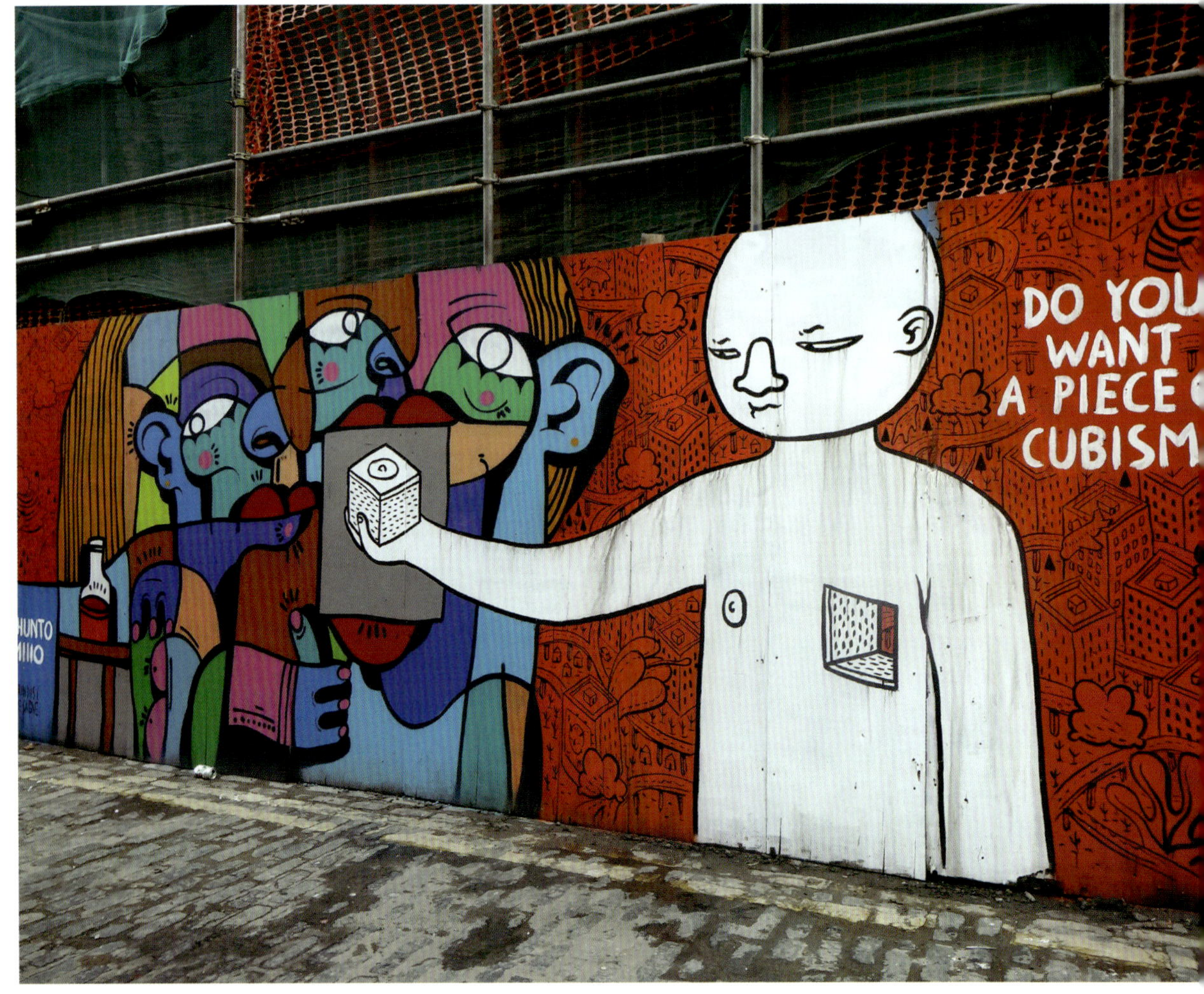

Hunto and Millo. Brick Lane, East London

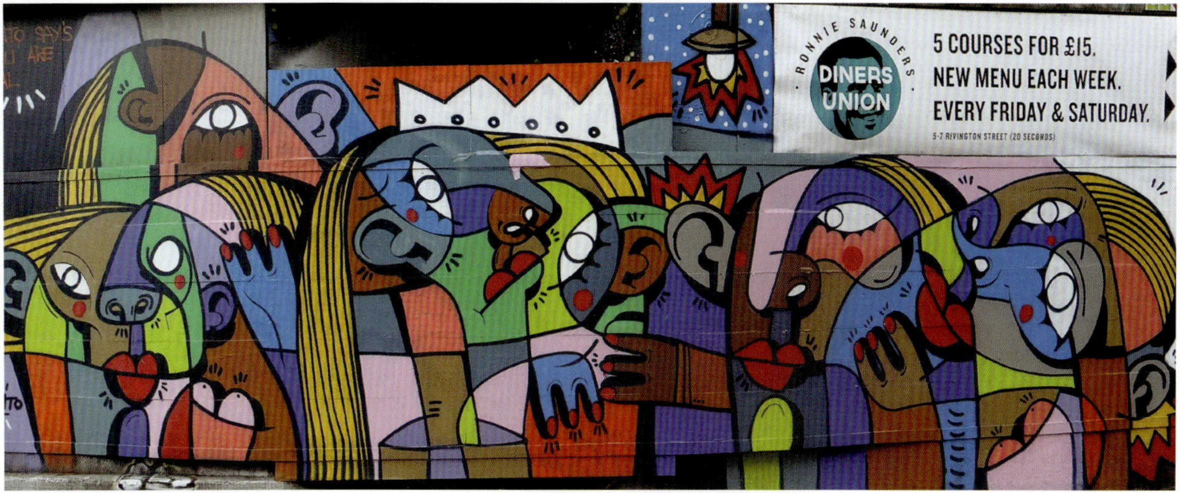

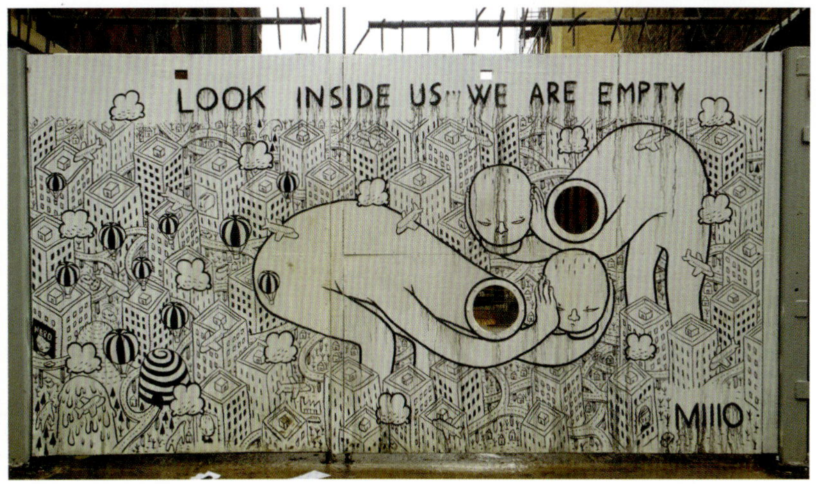

Millo. East London

"What I love about it is not the design of the city, but the people from different cultures and different personalities. Different women's colours inspire my works." [Hunto, expressing his 'miss of Italy' when he stays in London, and he takes the energy from his roots to the London city.] "London for me, means one place where the people wait for somebody to create something somewhere... and then the mass of public is happy to go and discover it." - **Hunto**

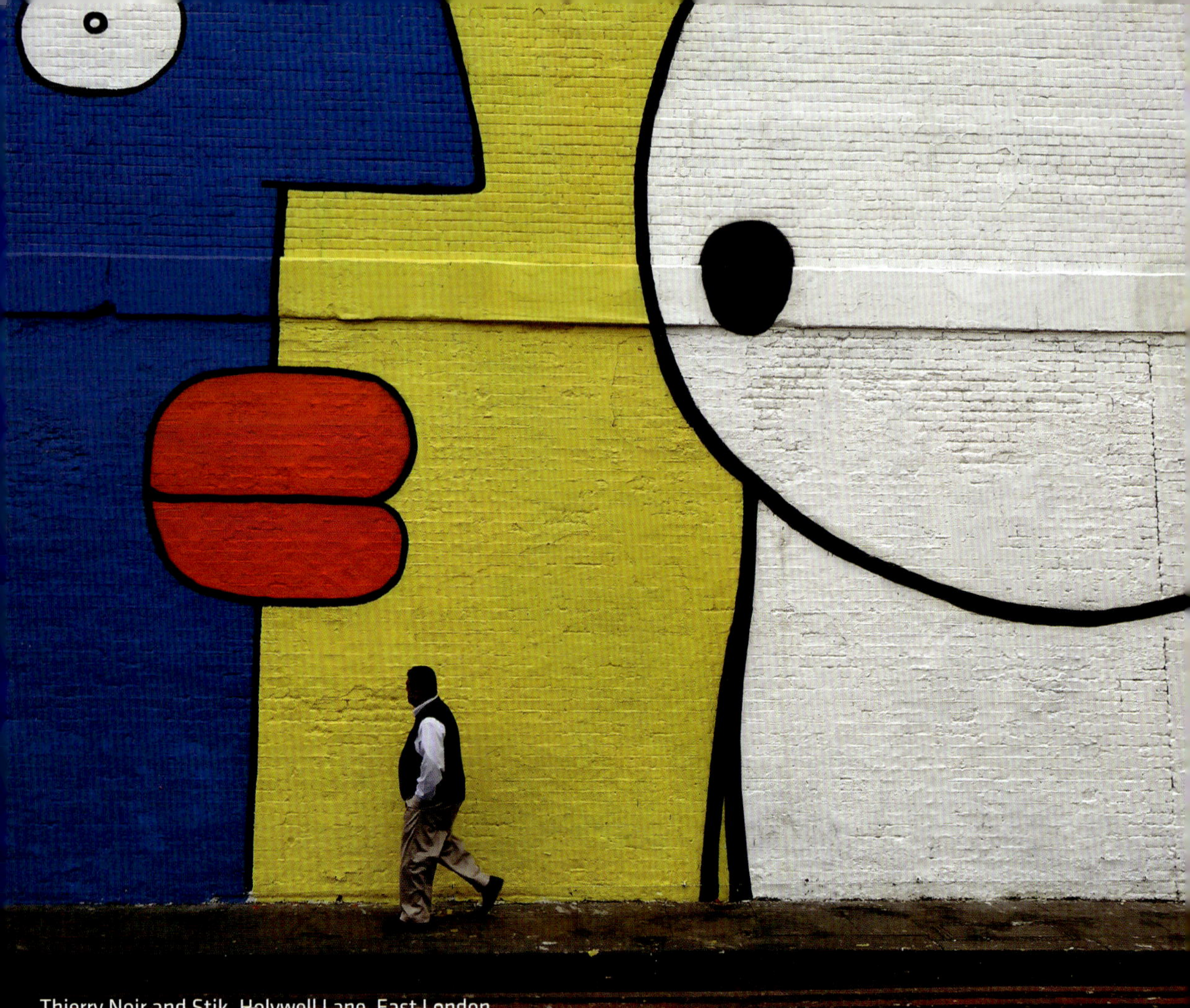

Thierry Noir and Stik, Holywell Lane, East London

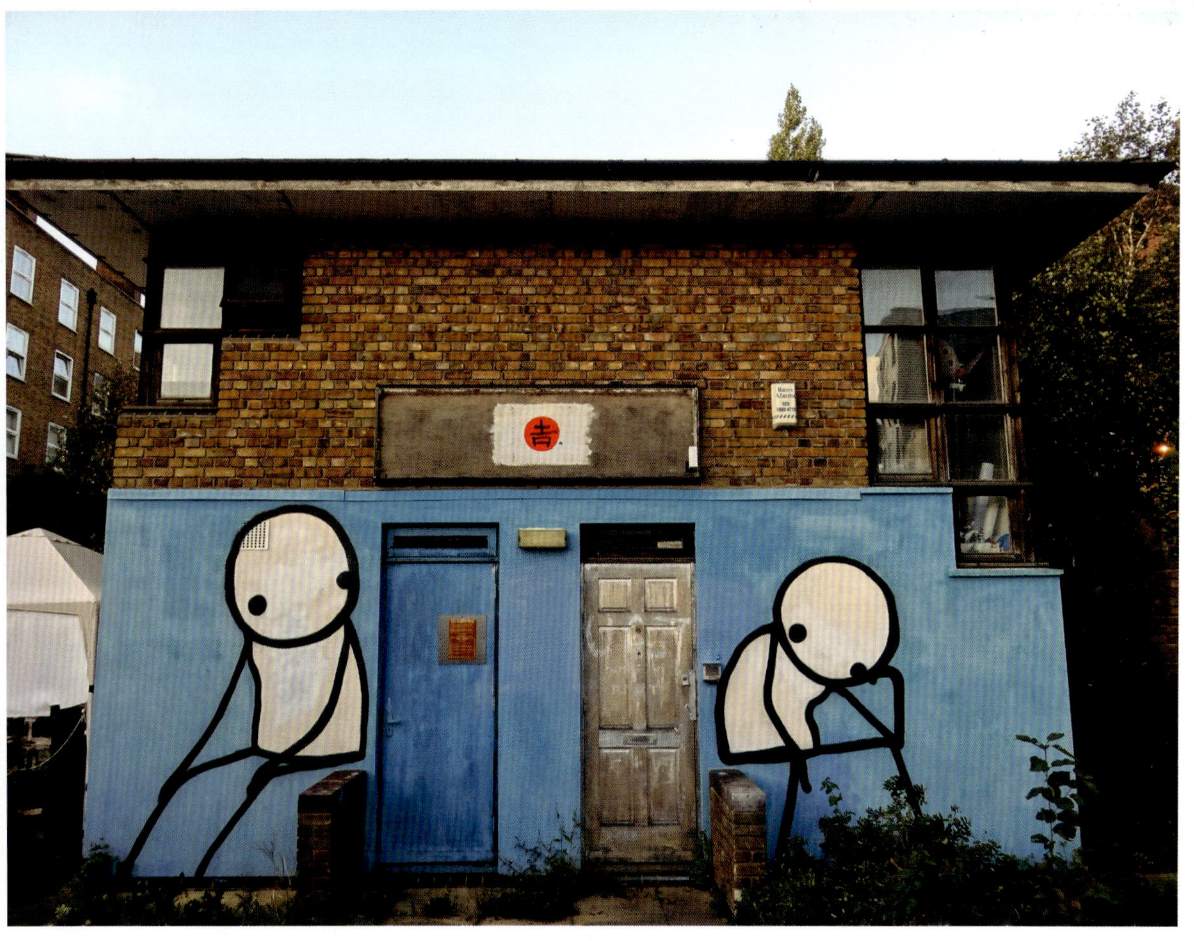

"London is a big city and can feel quite lonely. The paintings on the walls make it more familiar somehow, and it is exciting to see when someone new is in town. I try to make my characters react to the space they are painted in. It's all about context for me. I got to know London by painting it, and that is how London got to know me too!" - **Stik**

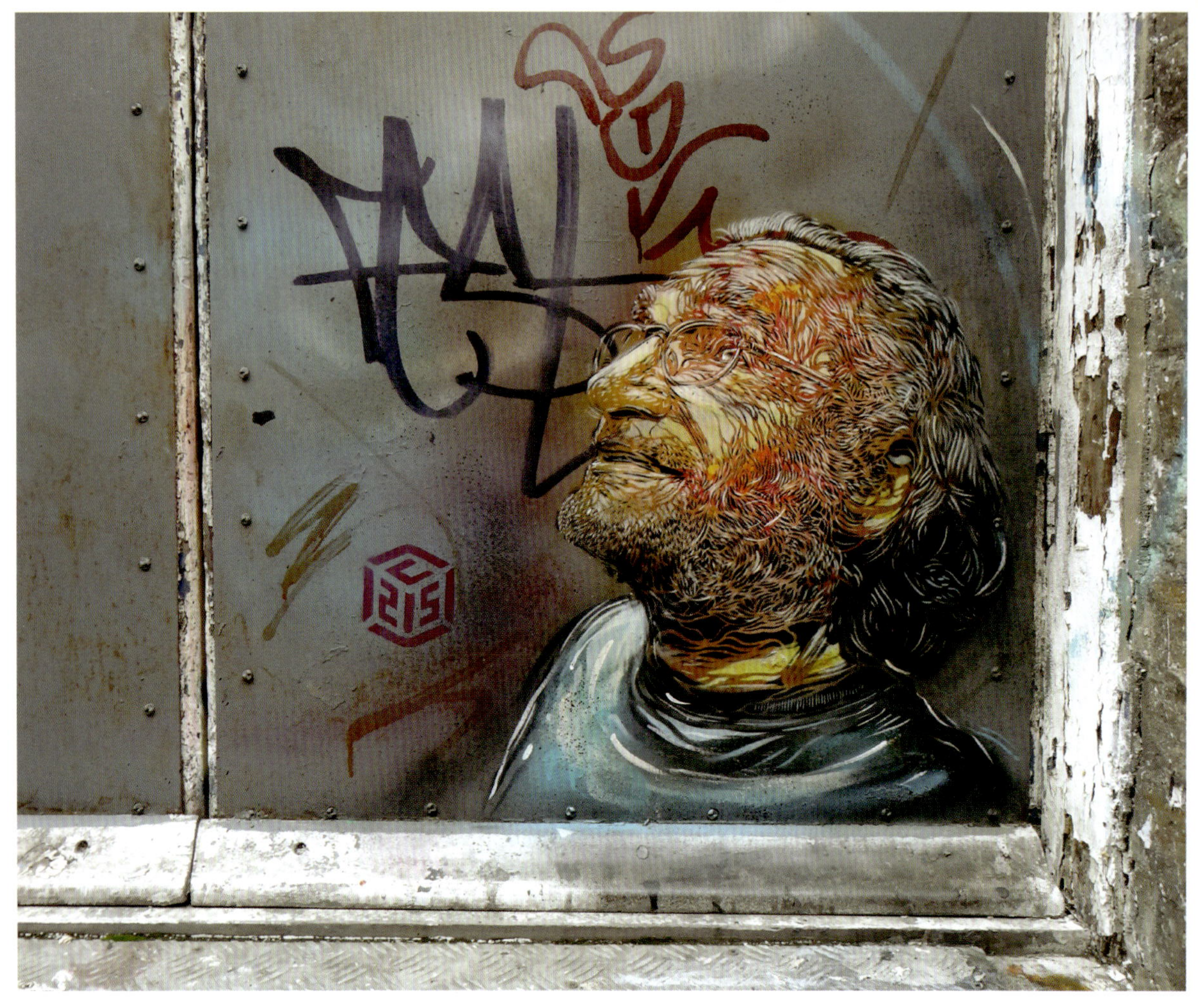

C215 and more. Blackall Street. East London

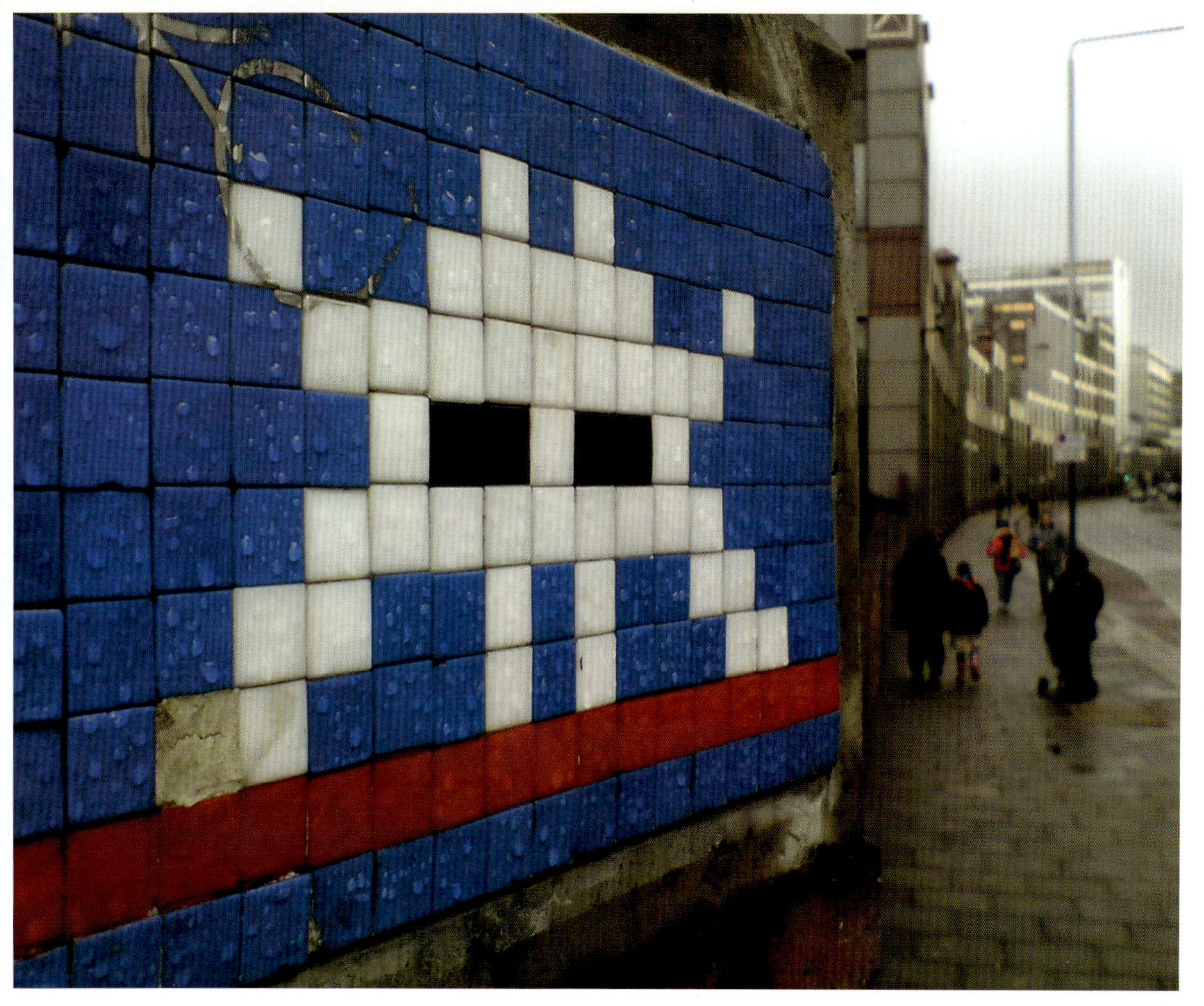

Space Invader. Clerkenwell Road, East London

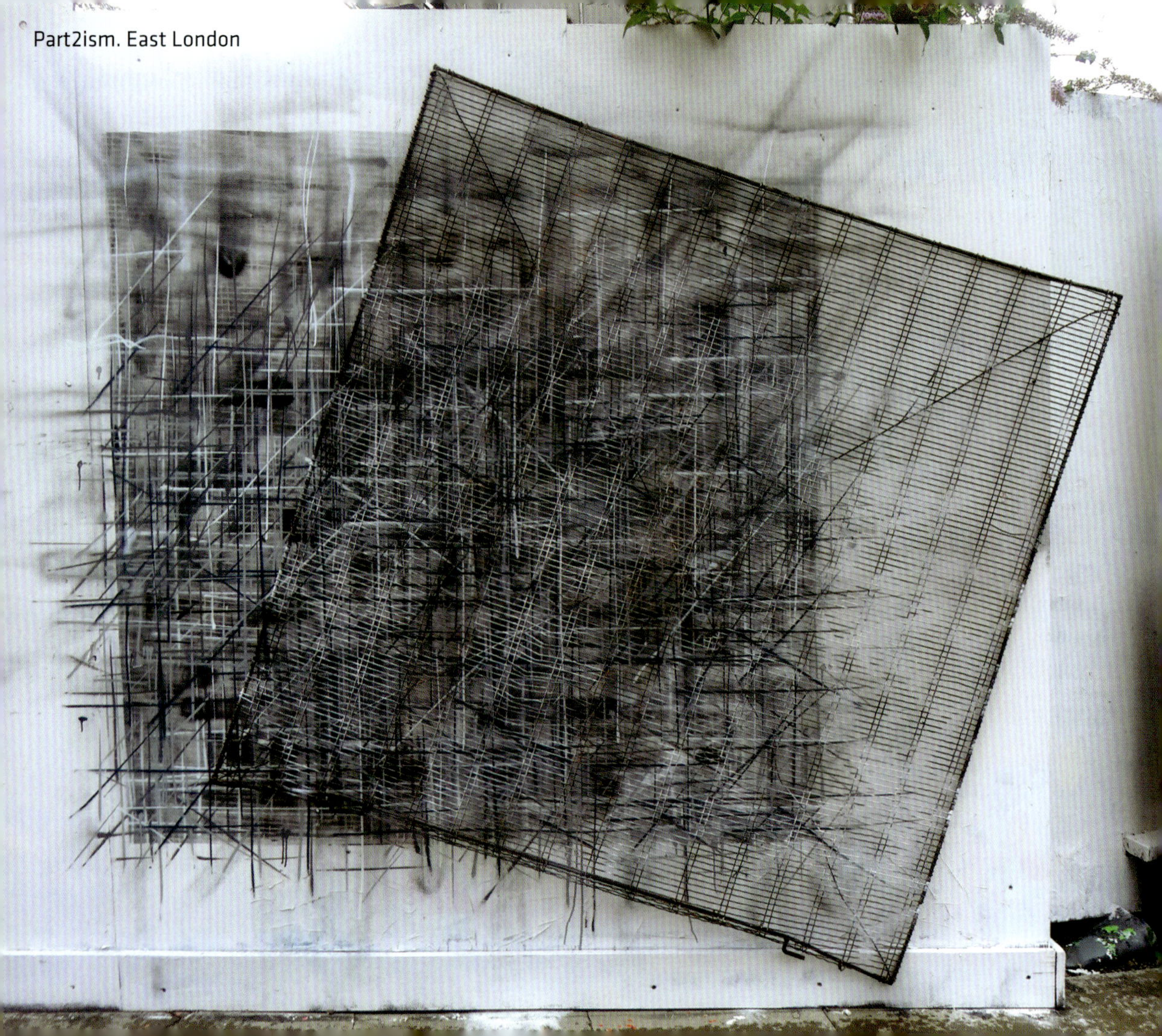
Part2ism. East London

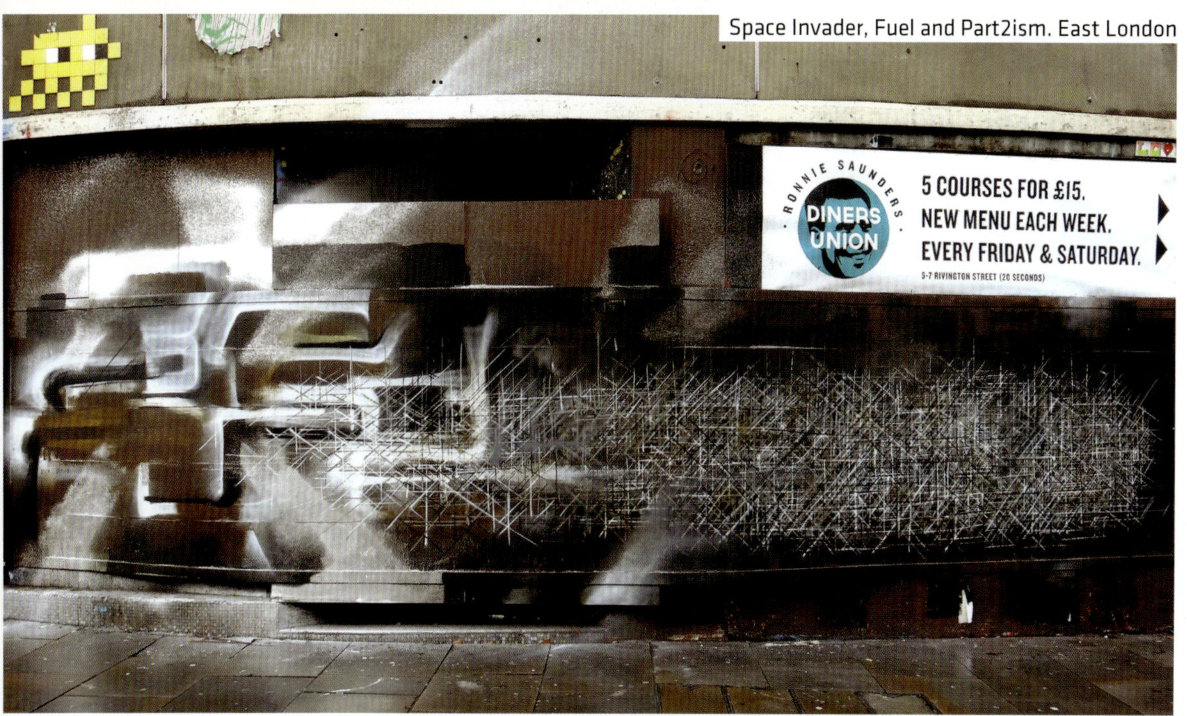

Space Invader, Fuel and Part2ism. East London

Re-Drawing The Map - "In an age where 'meaning' itself appears to have been extracted from culture in an everyday sense, London's landscape becomes a map of temporality and disappearance. East London in particular has become an institution in terms of the appropriation or re-appropriation of a once unorthodox sub-cultural 'art' executed in the capital's public sphere.

"However, true beauty is found in the locations and coordinates that sit on the threshold and edges of all this activity. To arrive at a 'pirate utopia', if only for an afternoon, to leave clandestine traces on the dense surfaces of London's pockets, is the true purpose of those possessed with the will and necessity to spray down autonomous symbolic orders. A holistic re-rendering of the map, as an 'open source' universe, where ideas ubiquitously appear, and then disappear into the fabric of the city." - **Part2ism**

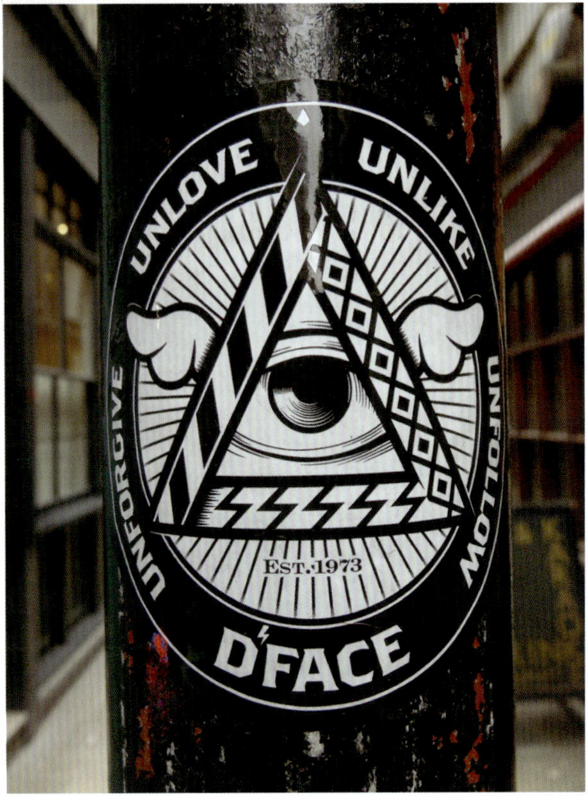

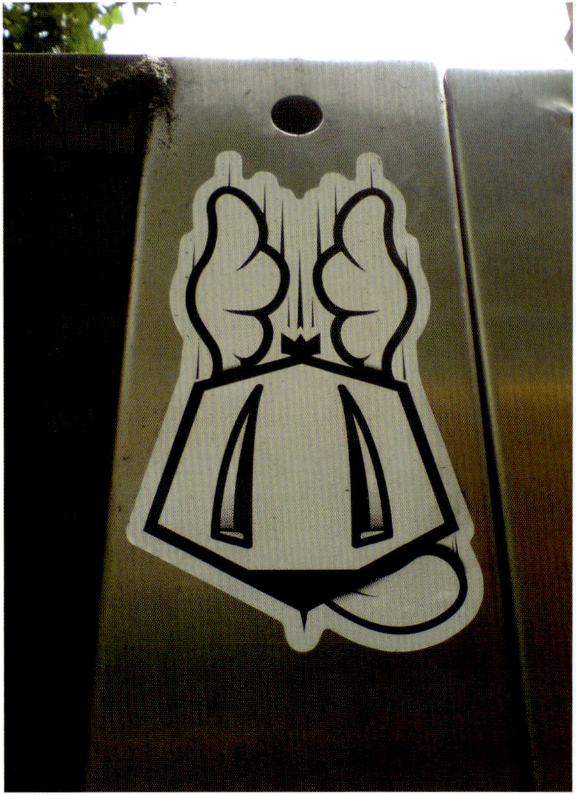

"London is a constant hustle, the grind, the battle, it's the hum in the back of your mind, the stone in your shoe that won't go away, the moody, sultry mistress that somehow you can't let go, as much as it's damaging your health, it's the see-saw, the tick tock pendulum, the love and loathe; on some days the most miserable grey place on Earth, and on others, the most amazing city in the world. Londoners are a breed amongst our own, we get shit done, we make shit happen, and all the while being able to laugh at our own stupidity... For living in that grey battleground called London." - **D*Face**

"When a man is tired of London, he is tired of life." - **Samuel Johnson**

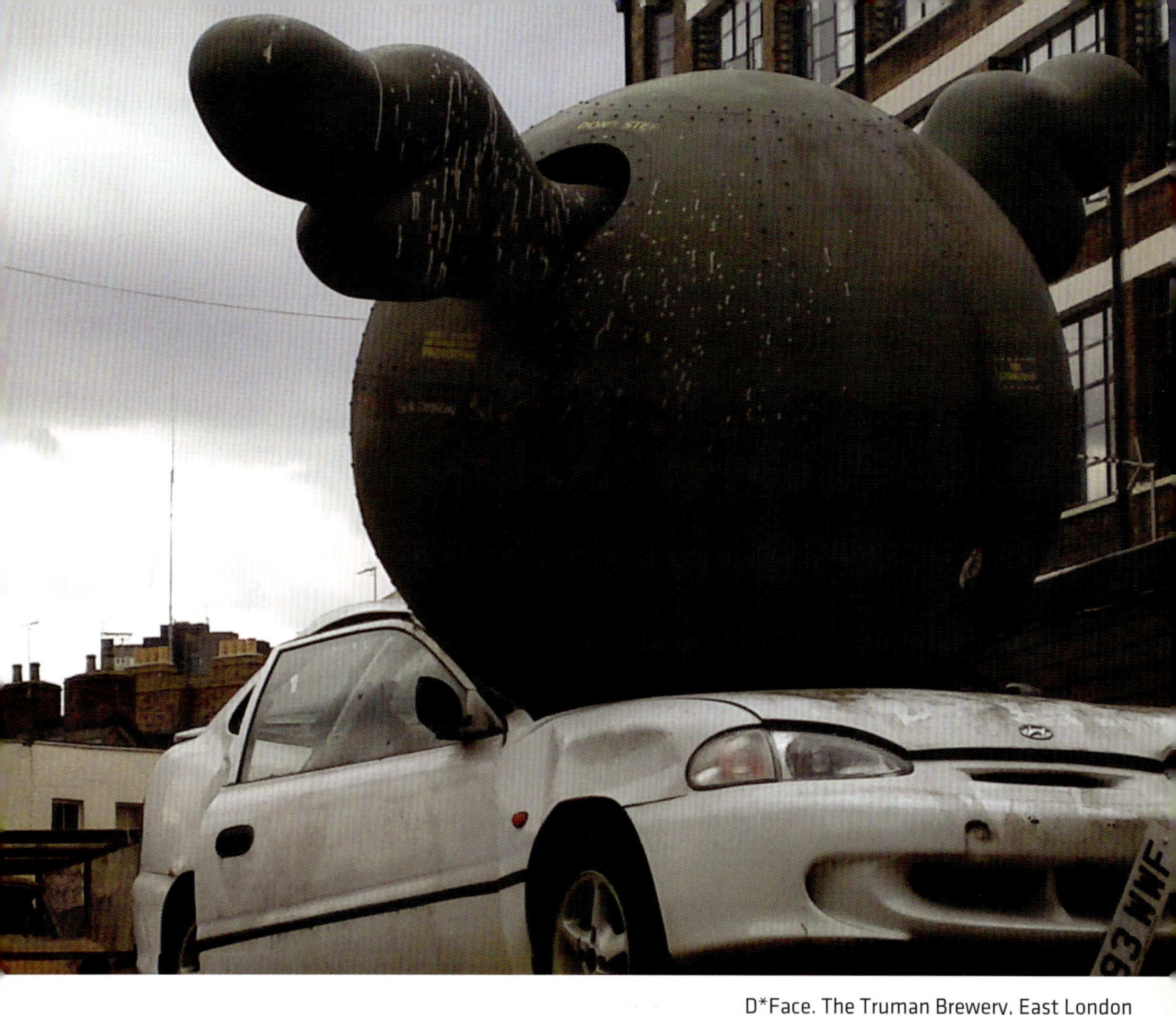

D*Face. The Truman Brewery, East London

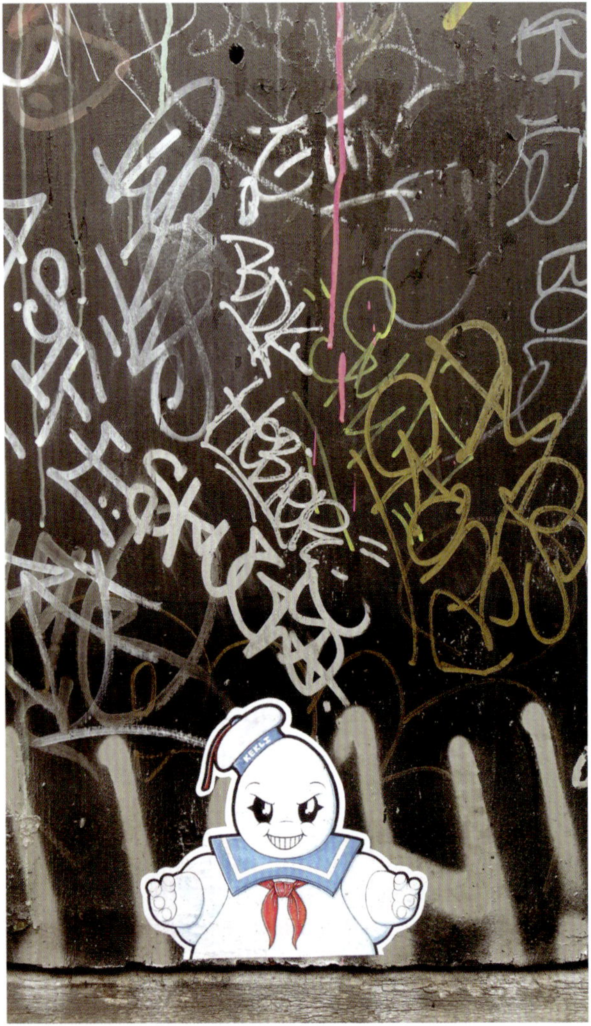

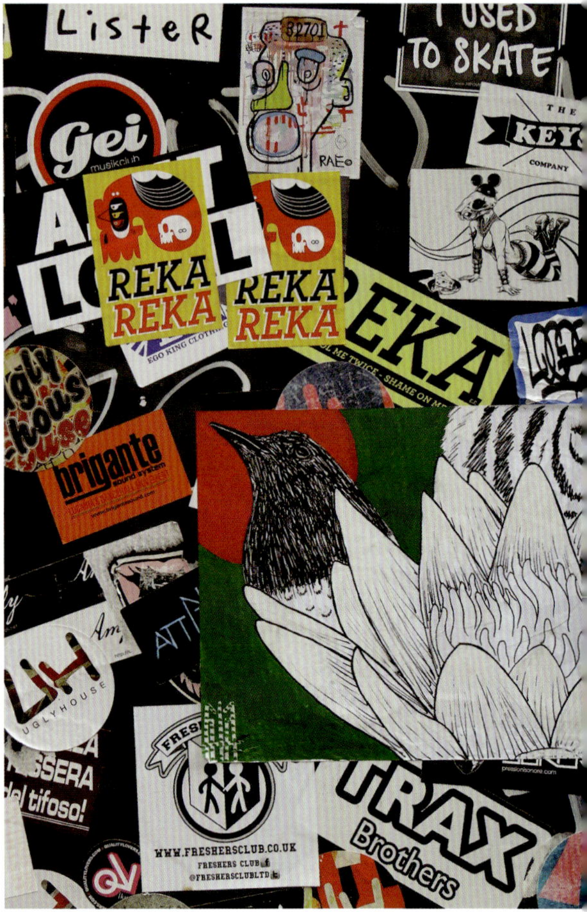

Sticker artists often come from diverse design, illustrative and artistic backgrounds. Stickers are also commonly used by graffiti writers to swap their outlines and letter designs.

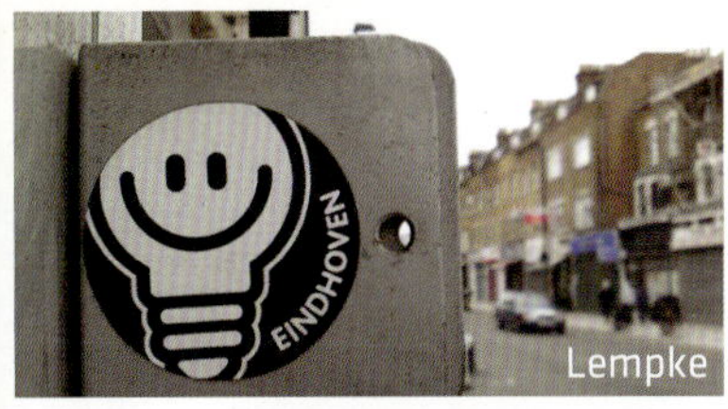

Lempke

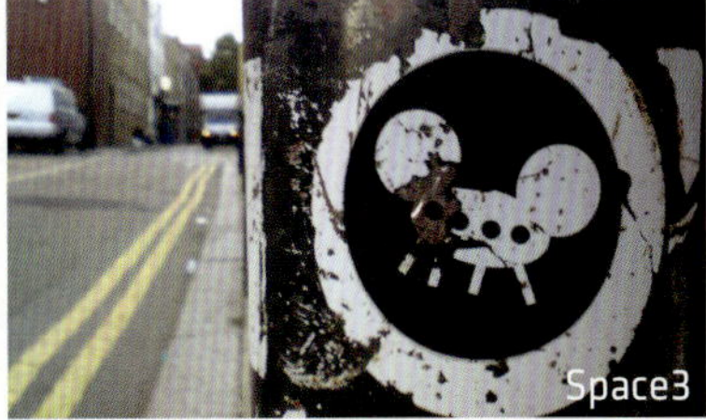

Space3

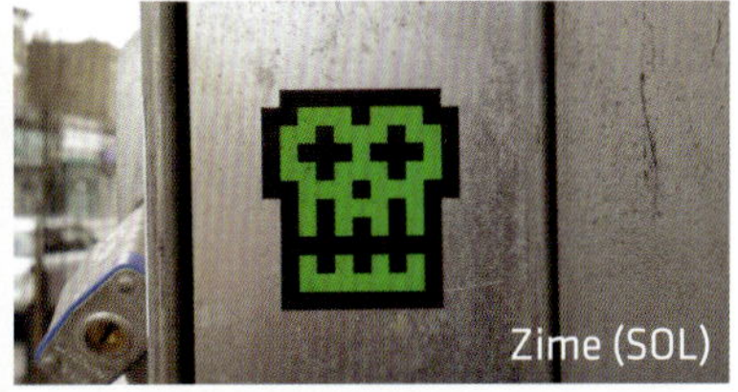

Zime (SOL)

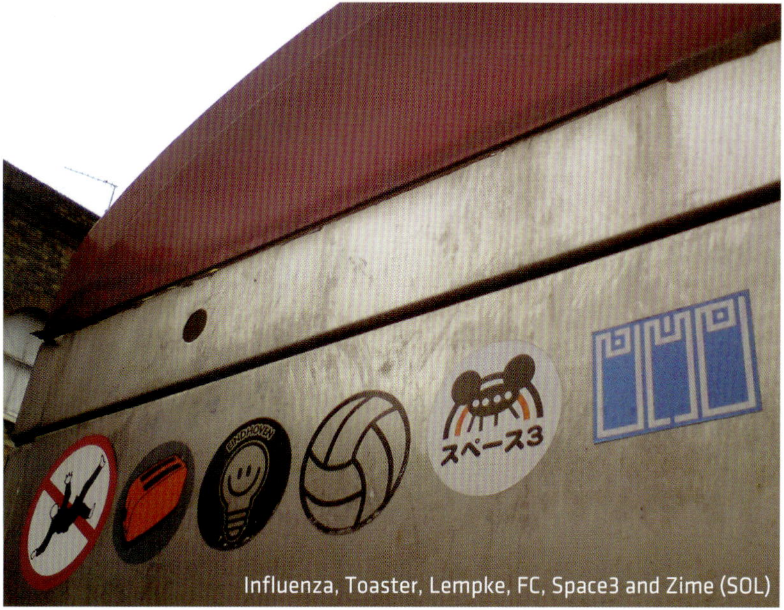

Influenza, Toaster, Lempke, FC, Space3 and Zime (SOL)

"London means having fun, meeting (new) friends, drinking beer in a nice pub, go to a football match, sightseeing, and do street art!" - **Lempke Eindhoven**

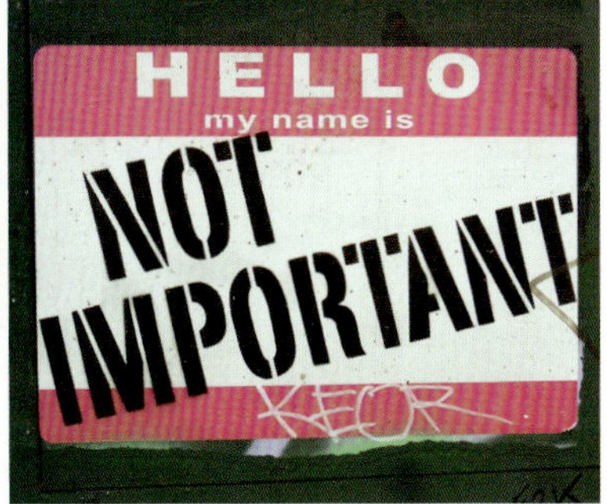

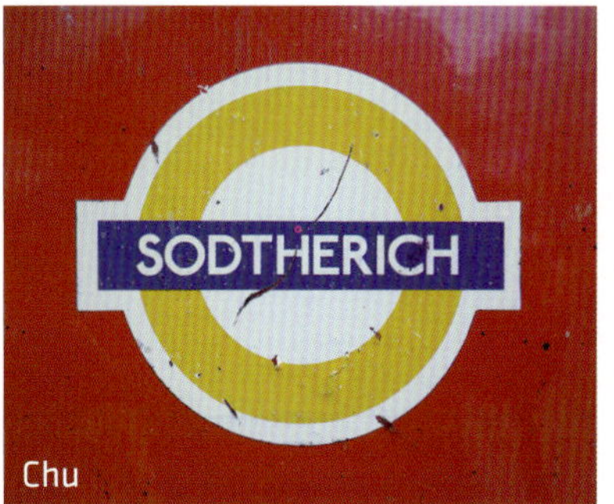

Chu

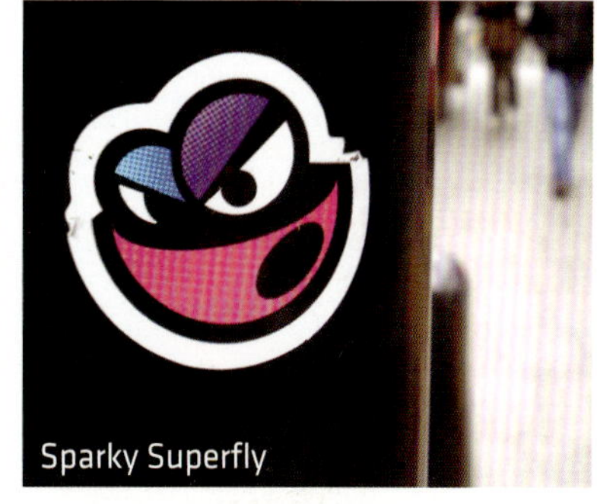

Sparky Superfly

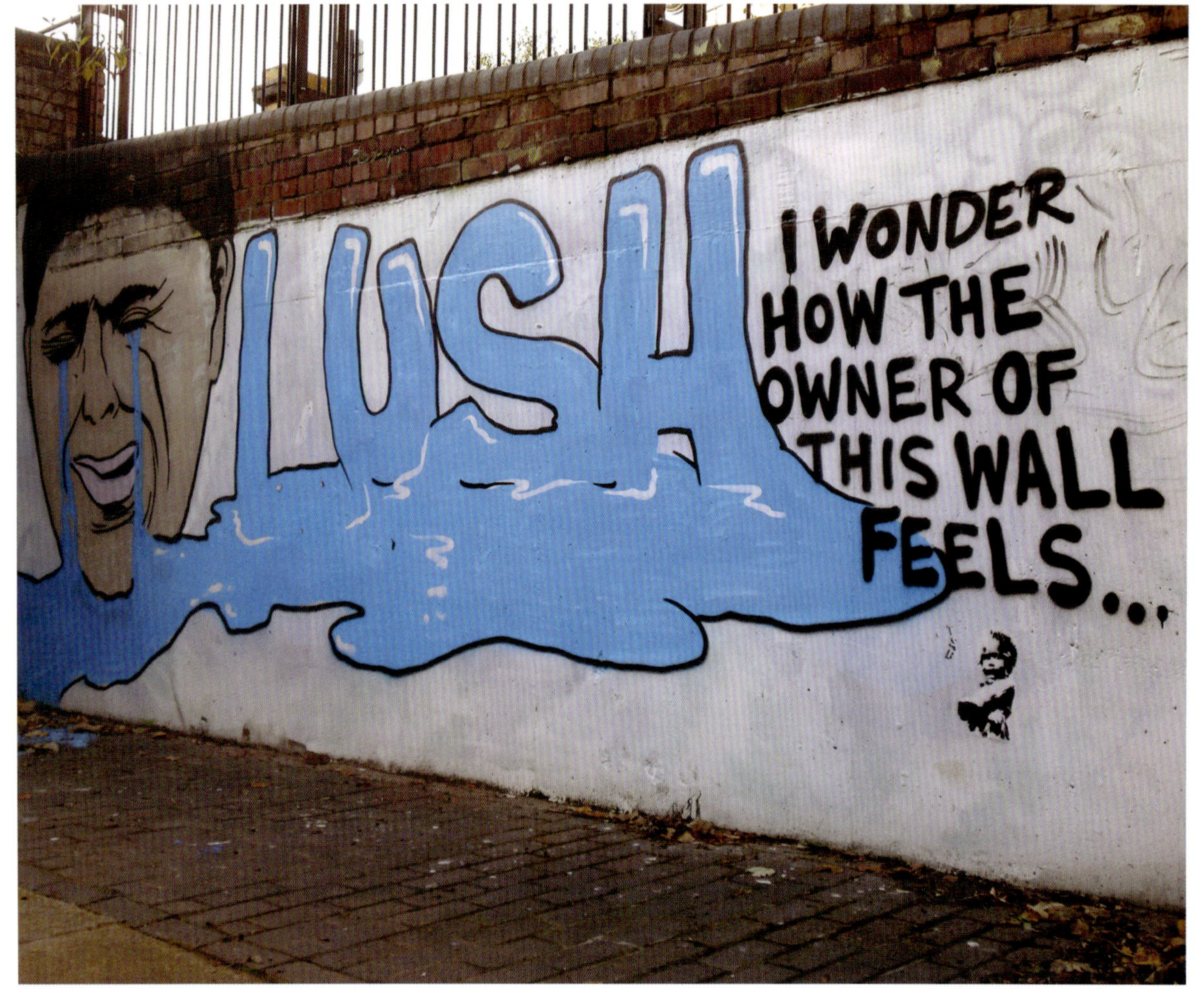

"A miserable shithole filled with miserable shits. Until the sun shines that is." - **Lush**

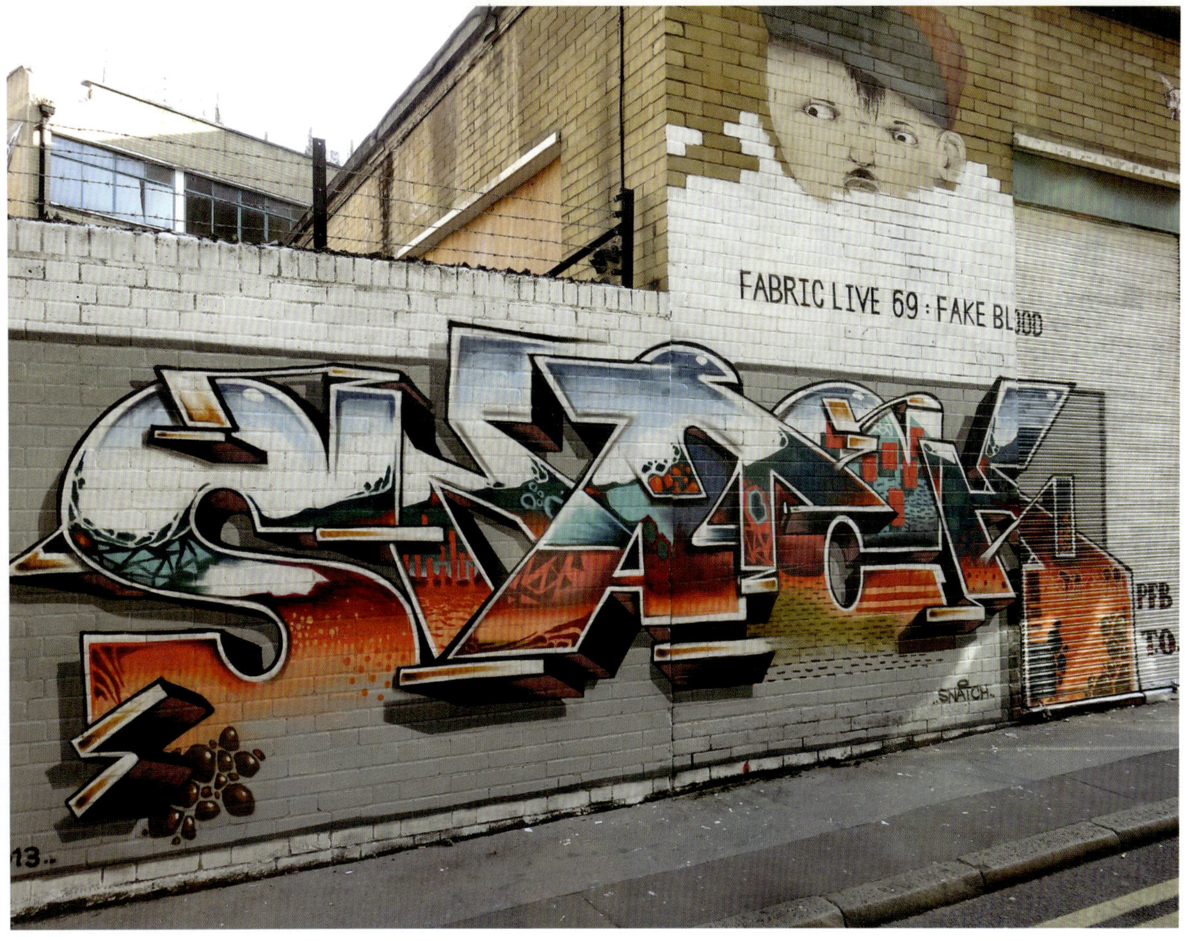

"London. Always creating/always ingesting. Always moving forwards - while occasionally looking backwards. Worldwide inspiration/international feeding through. Bricks, basslines, silver dubs, clubs. Home of the (b)rave." - **Snatch PFB/The Others**

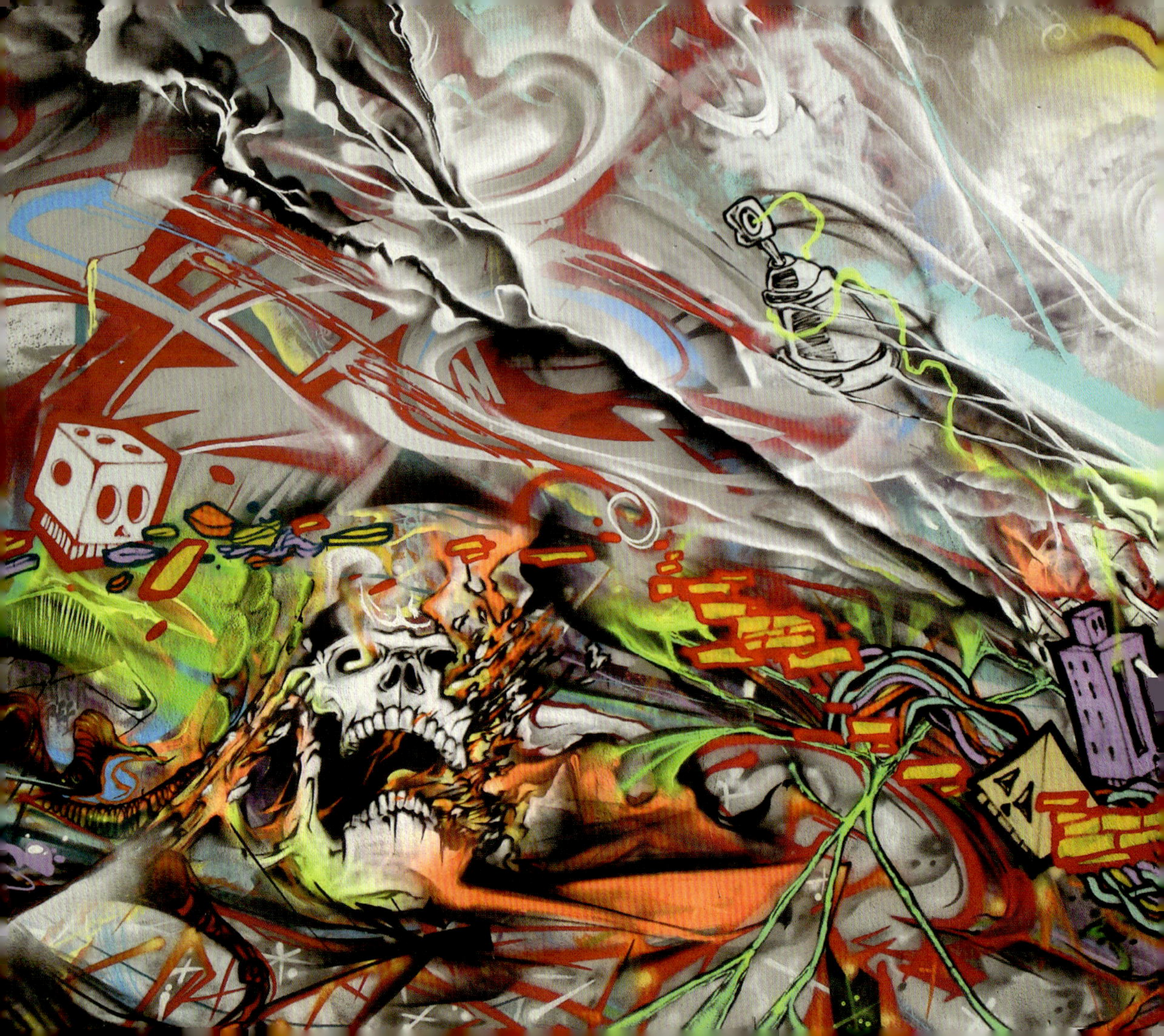

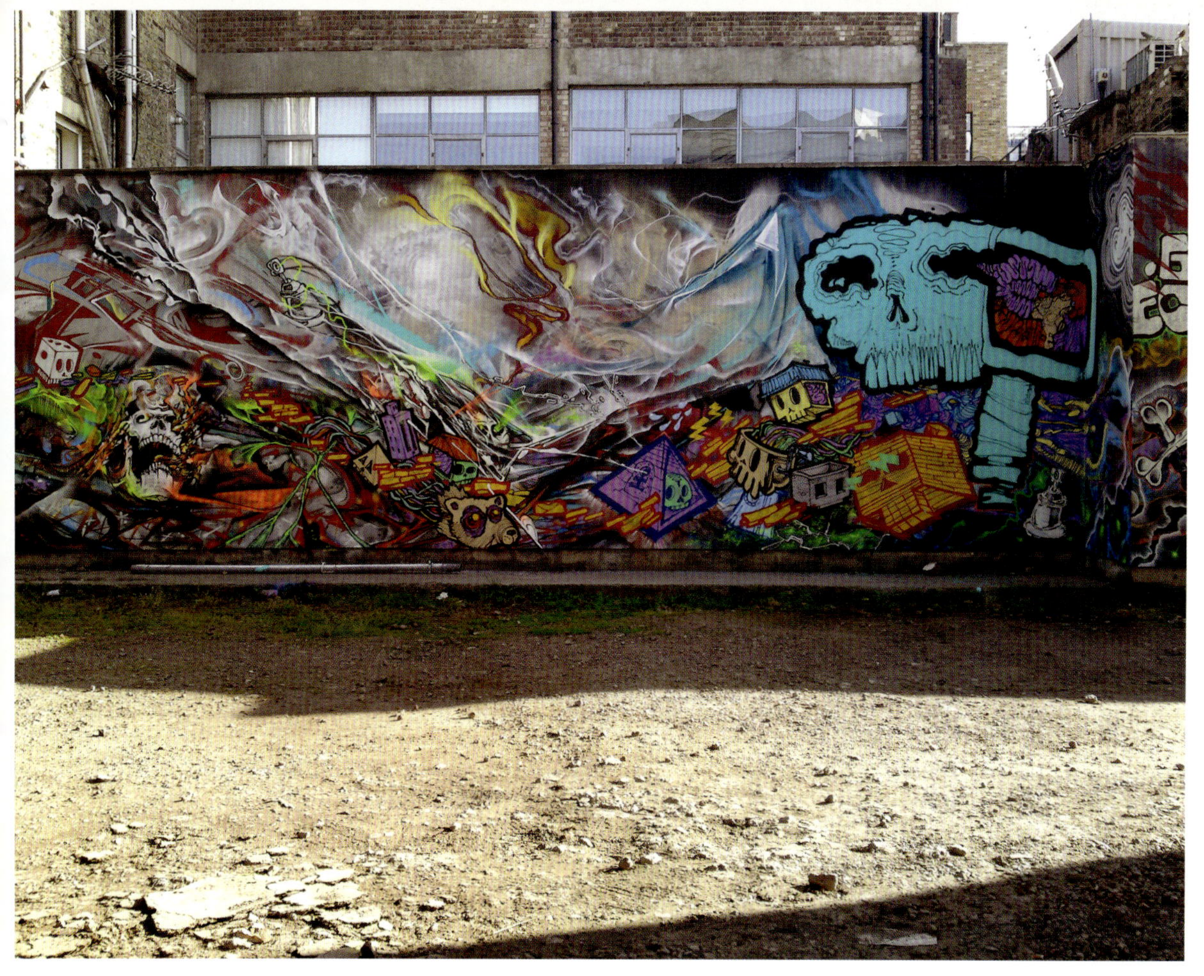

Aseb, Cemo & Neist (Eighties Conspiracy), Kloz, and Fan77 & Rems (Ghetto Farceur).

"Rebirth Tenacious Success Future." -
Cemo - Eighties Conspiracy

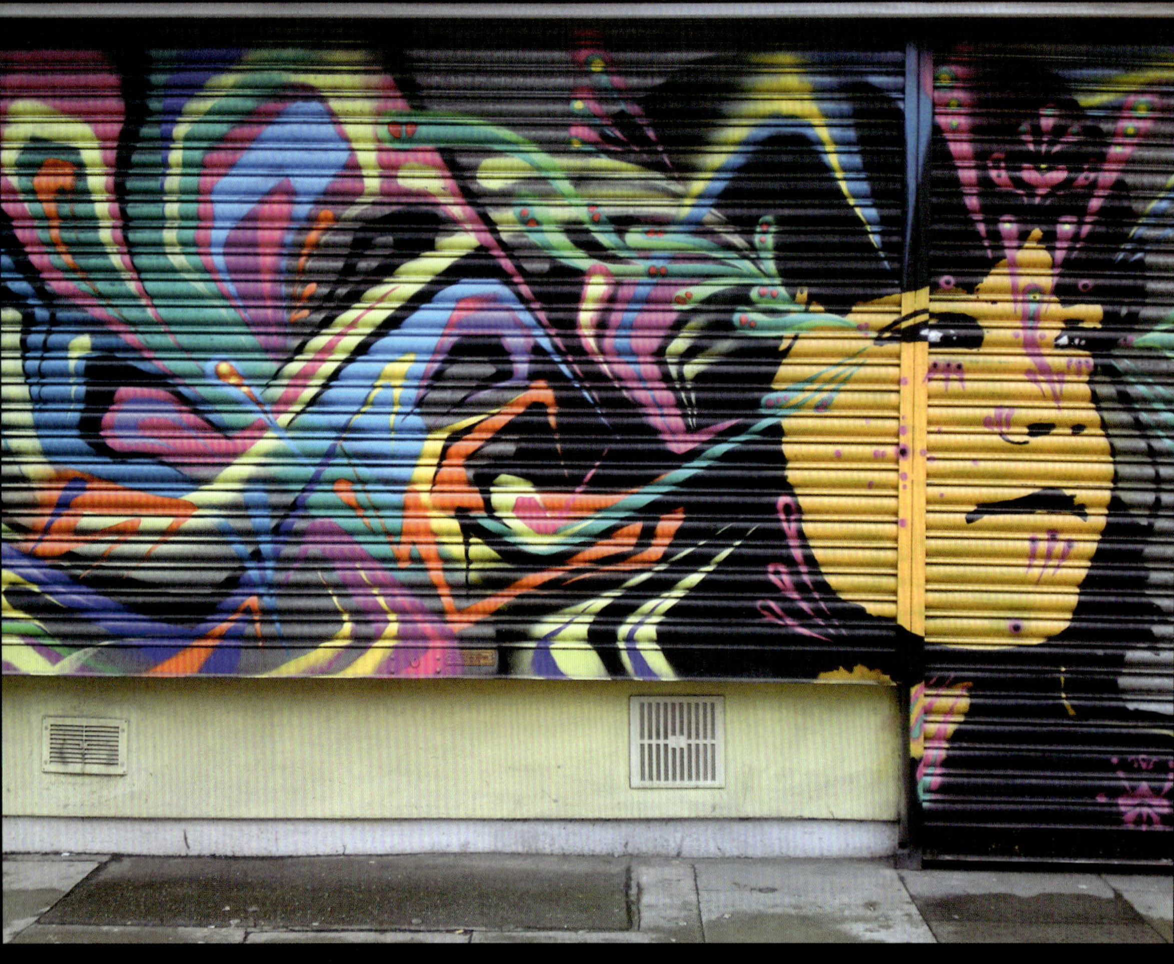

"World wide street action." - **Stinkfish**

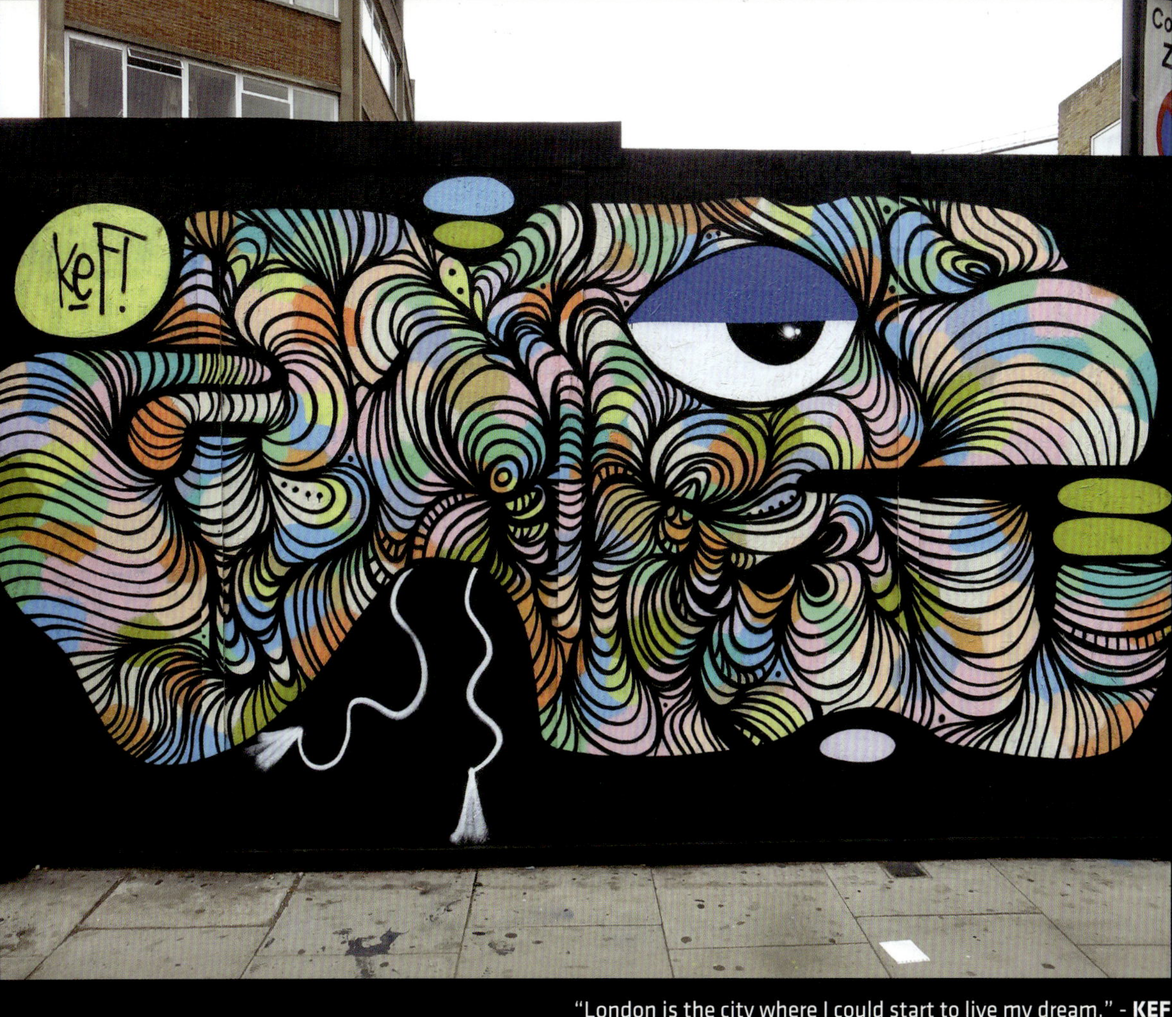

"London is the city where I could start to live my dream." - **KEF**

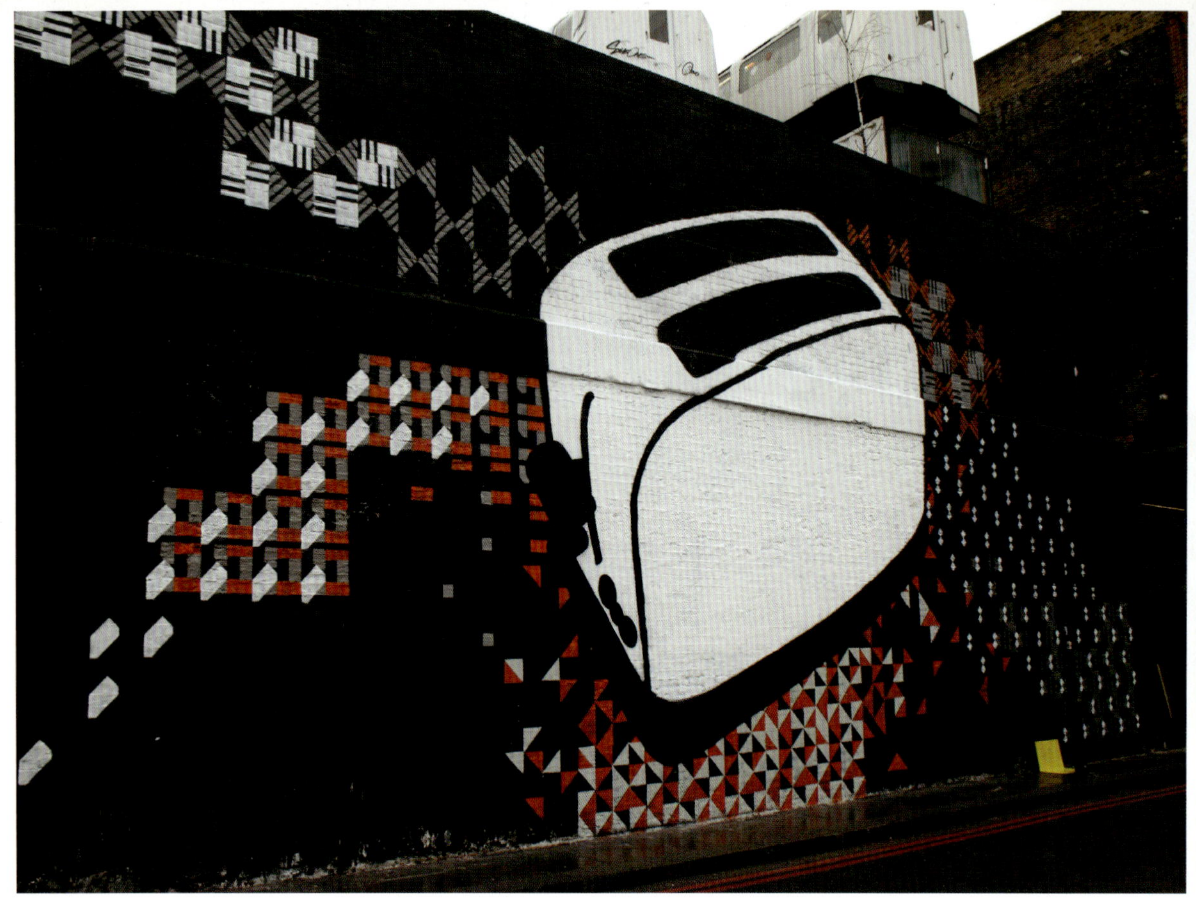

"London is about opposites. One day you are buzzing from its vibrancy, another day you are getting trampled in the stampede. It's dirty but refreshing, congested yet energising, lonely though you're never alone. With so many people in one city, it's a great place for your art to become noticed. Thankfully, it's easy as the person creating the art to go unnoticed." - **Toaster**

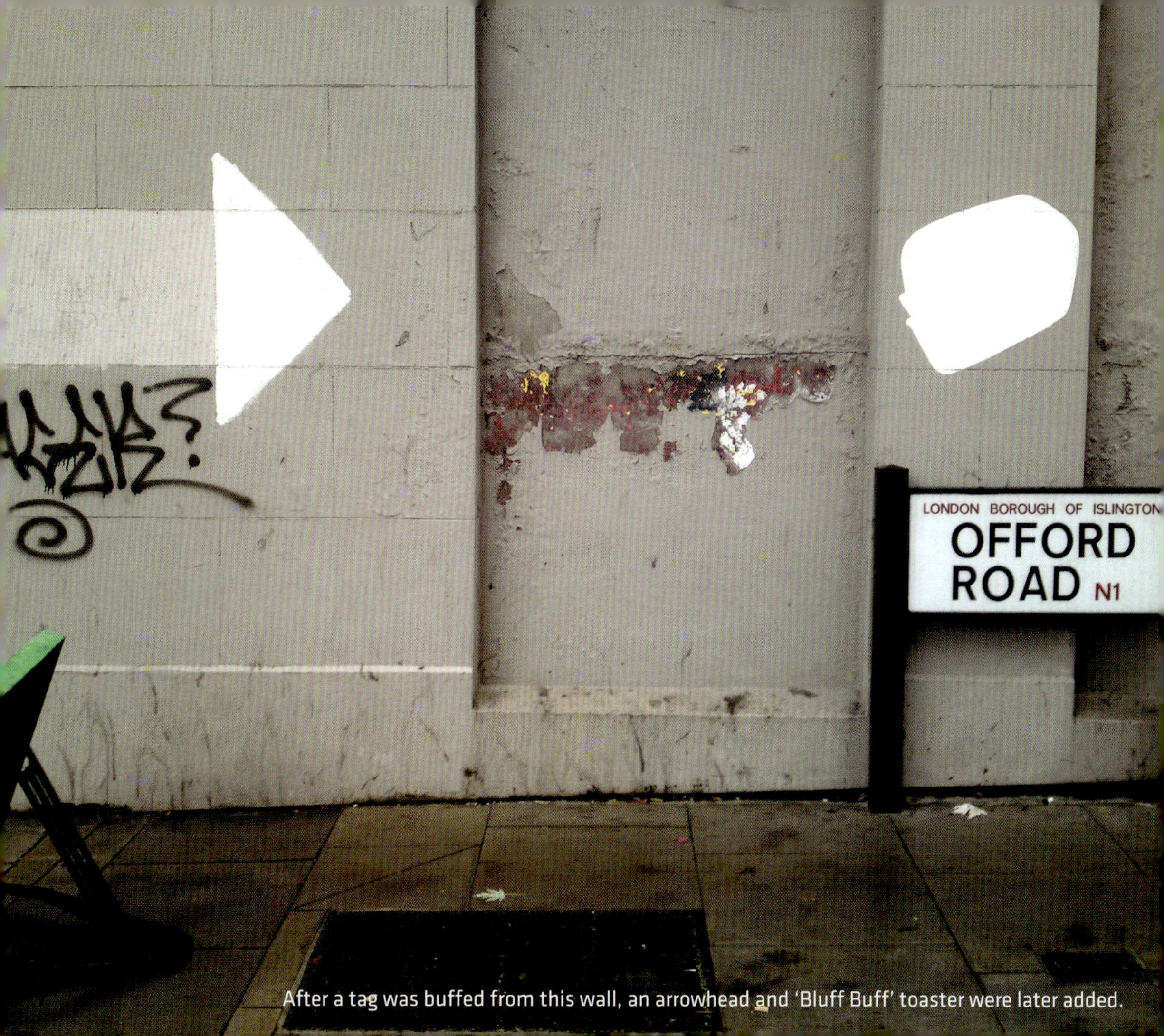

After a tag was buffed from this wall, an arrowhead and 'Bluff Buff' toaster were later added.

'Buff This?' - MOBSTR. Holywell Lane, East London

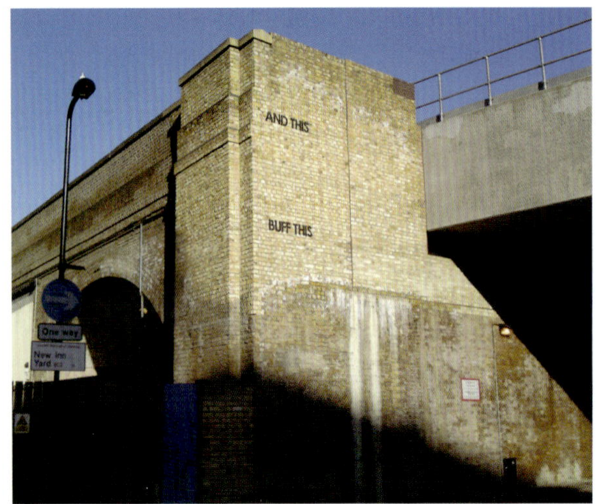

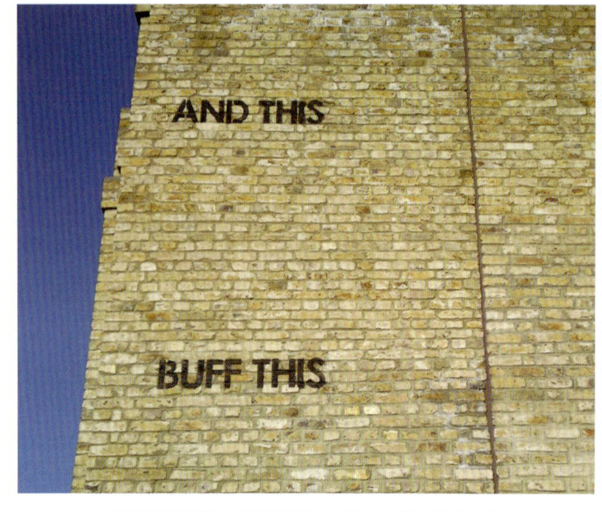

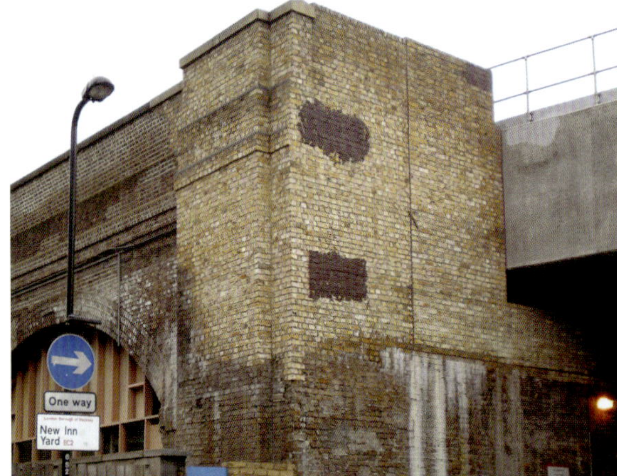

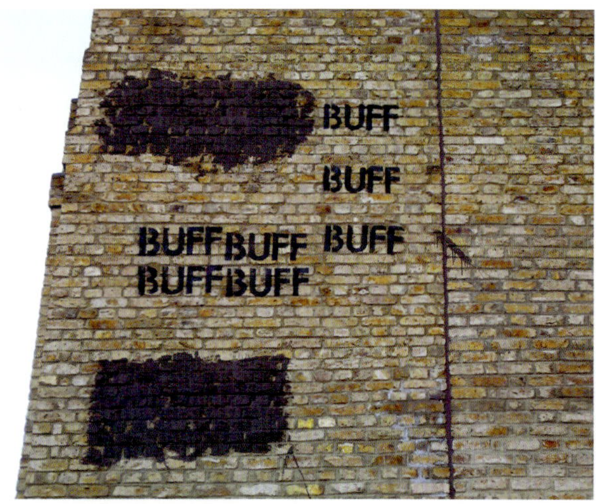

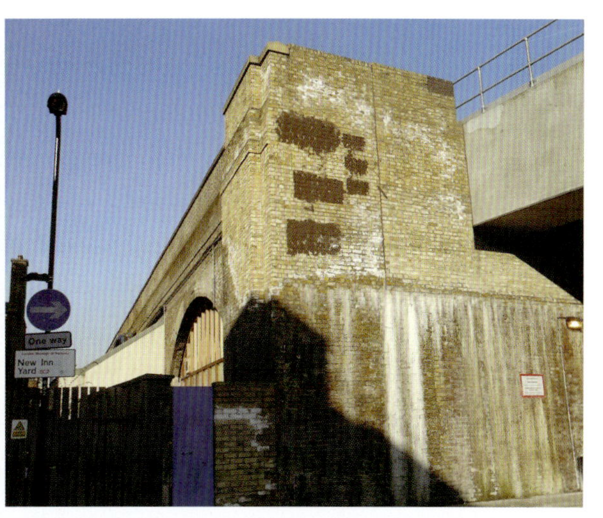
One way
New Inn
Yard EC2

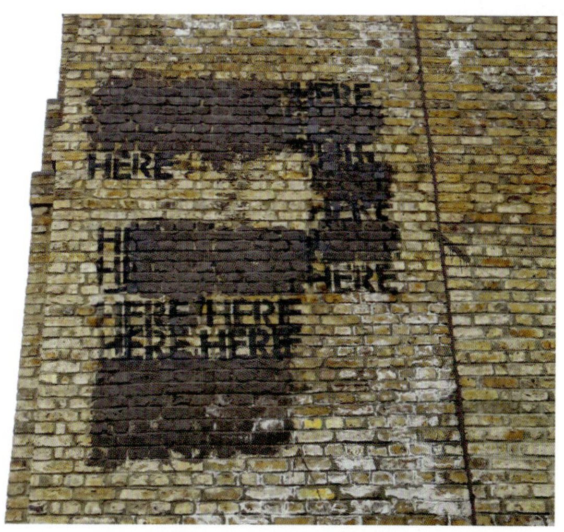
HERE
HERE
HERE HERE

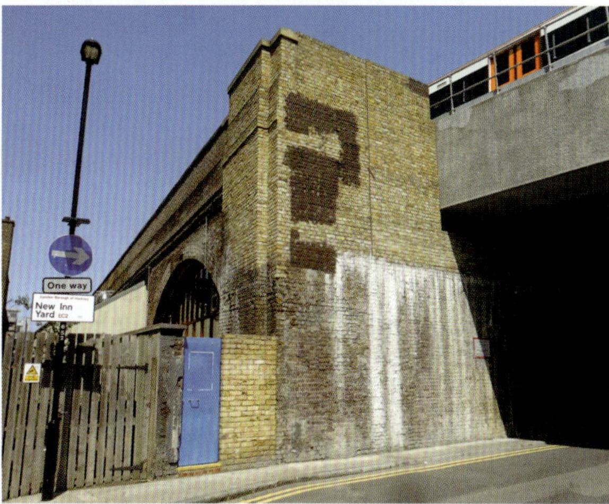
One way
New Inn
Yard EC2

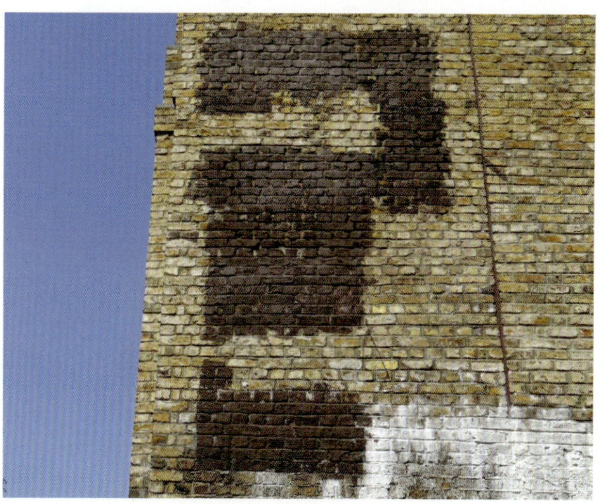

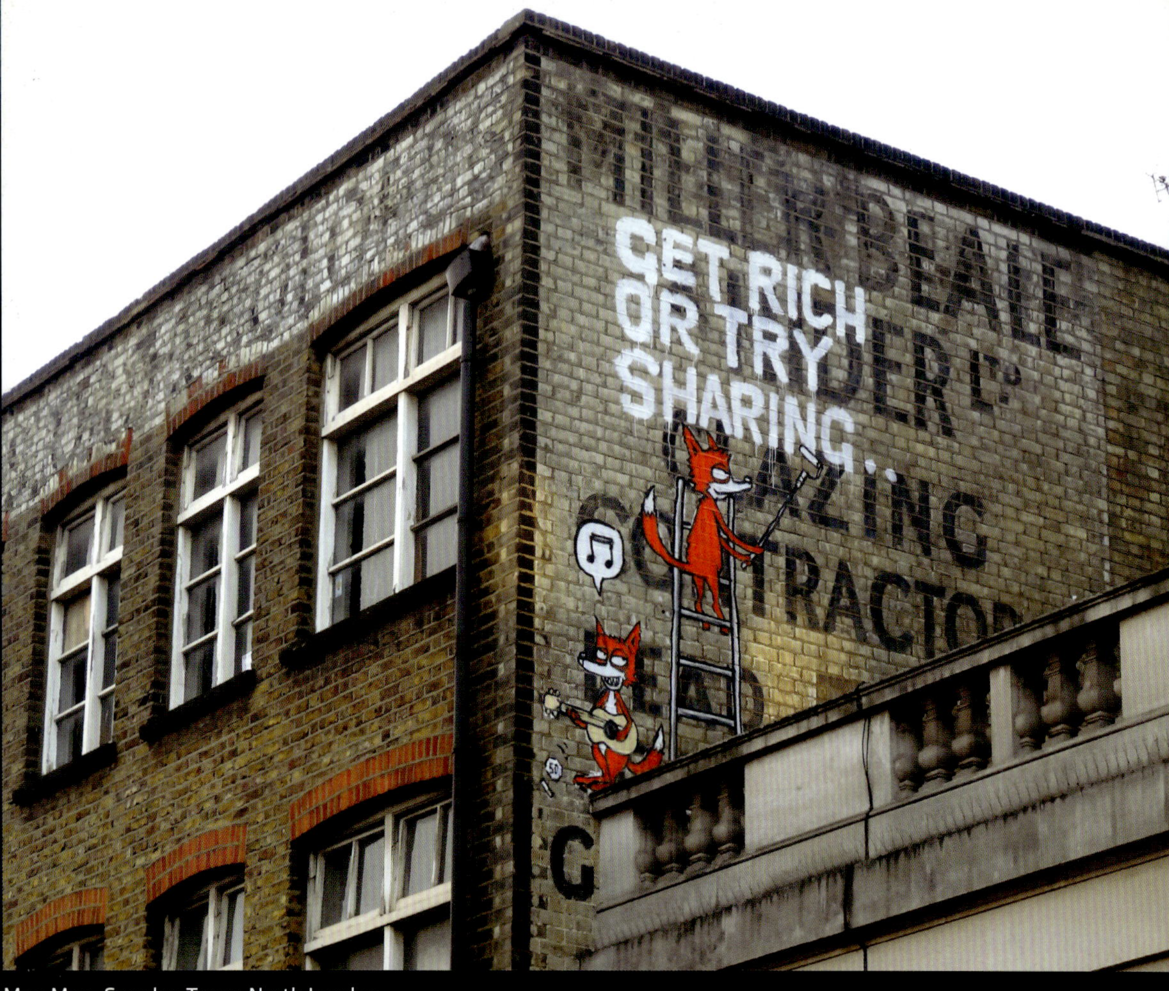

Mau Mau. Camden Town, North London

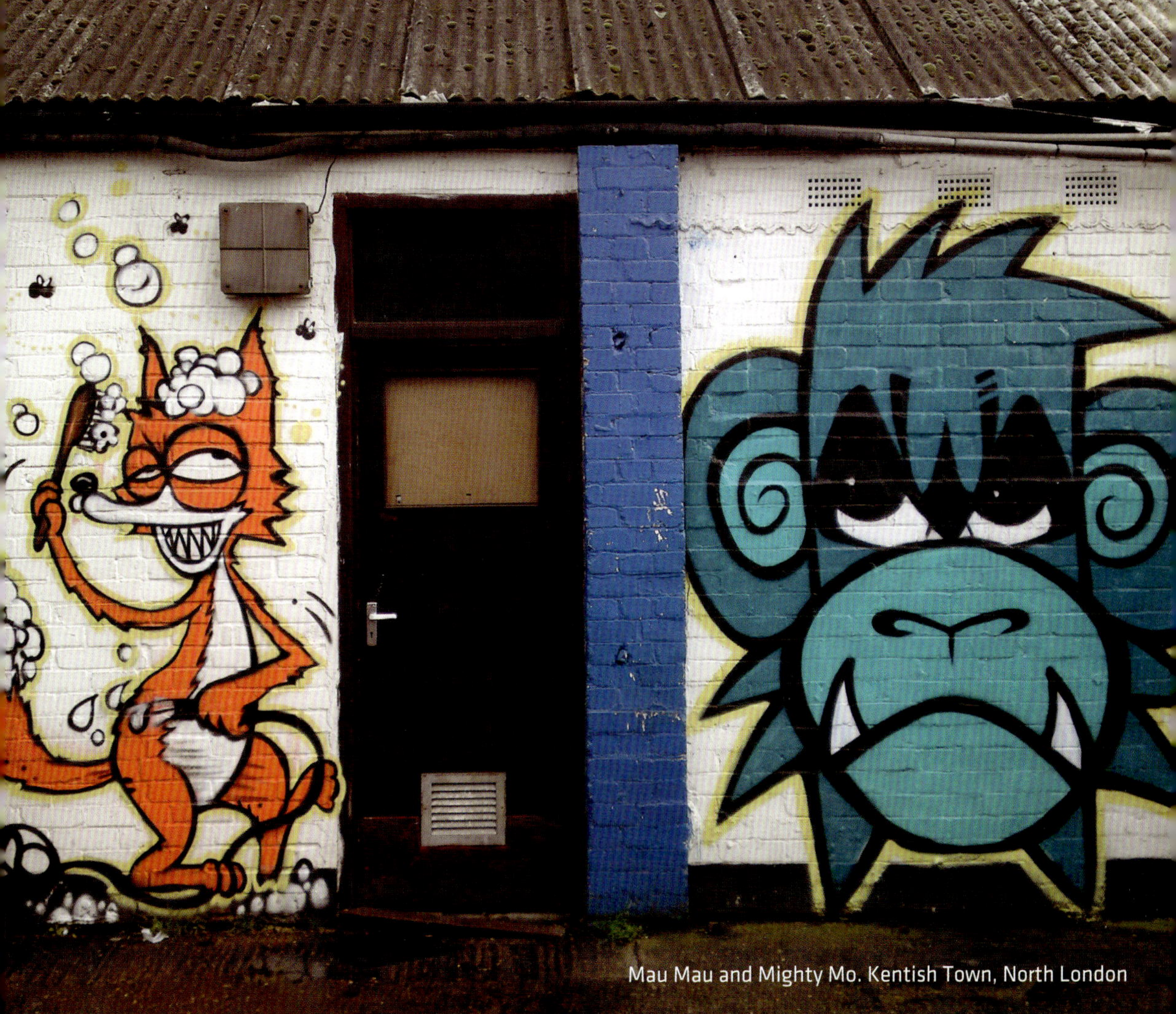

Mau Mau and Mighty Mo. Kentish Town, North London

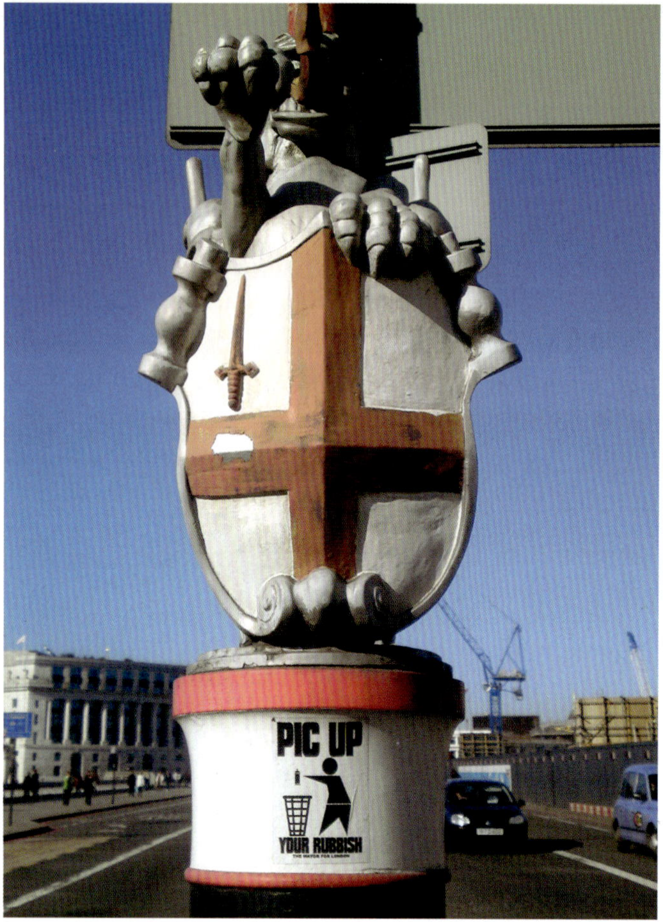

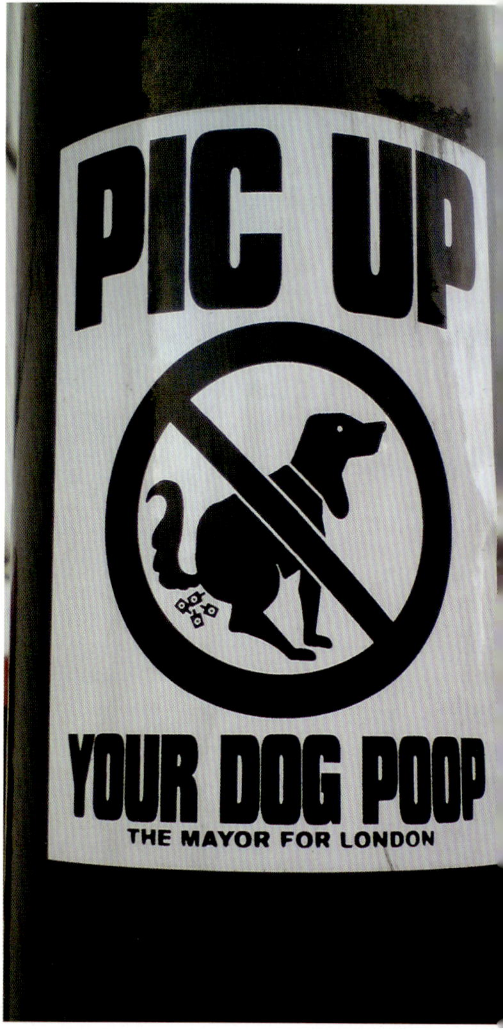

"My Roots, culture, movement and energy. I'm proud to be from this diverse city. Camden Town, North West One, Born & Bred, North London." - **P.I.C.**

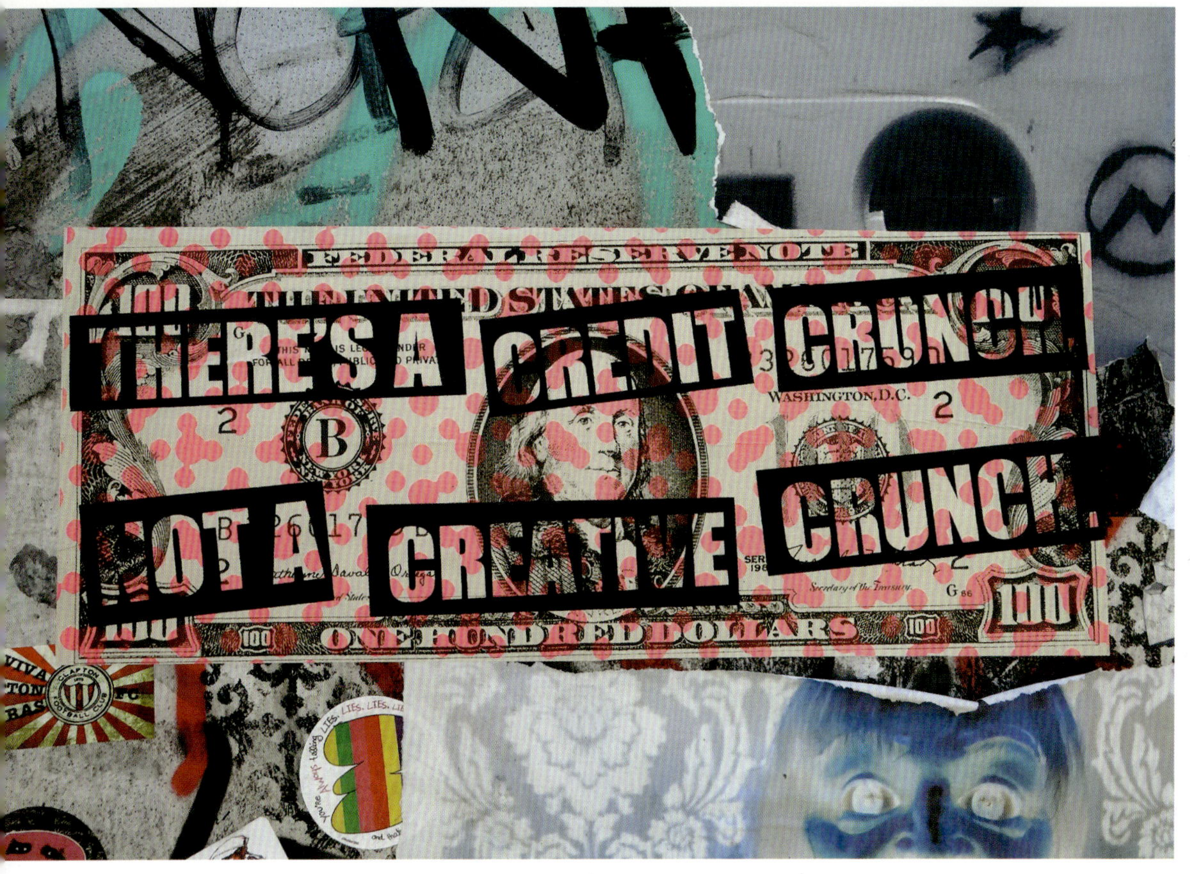

"I resented the fact that I was reluctantly made to move to London by my family when I was a teenager. I often think about how my life would have turned out if we had stayed in Sunderland or even Iran, come to think of it. I think fate has a mysterious way of working out and if I hadn't been in London, I probably wouldn't have had the career that I have now, the good friends and colleagues that I have met through the years, and the inspiration and opportunities that this wonderful metropolis has created for me. Thank you LDN." - **Aida**

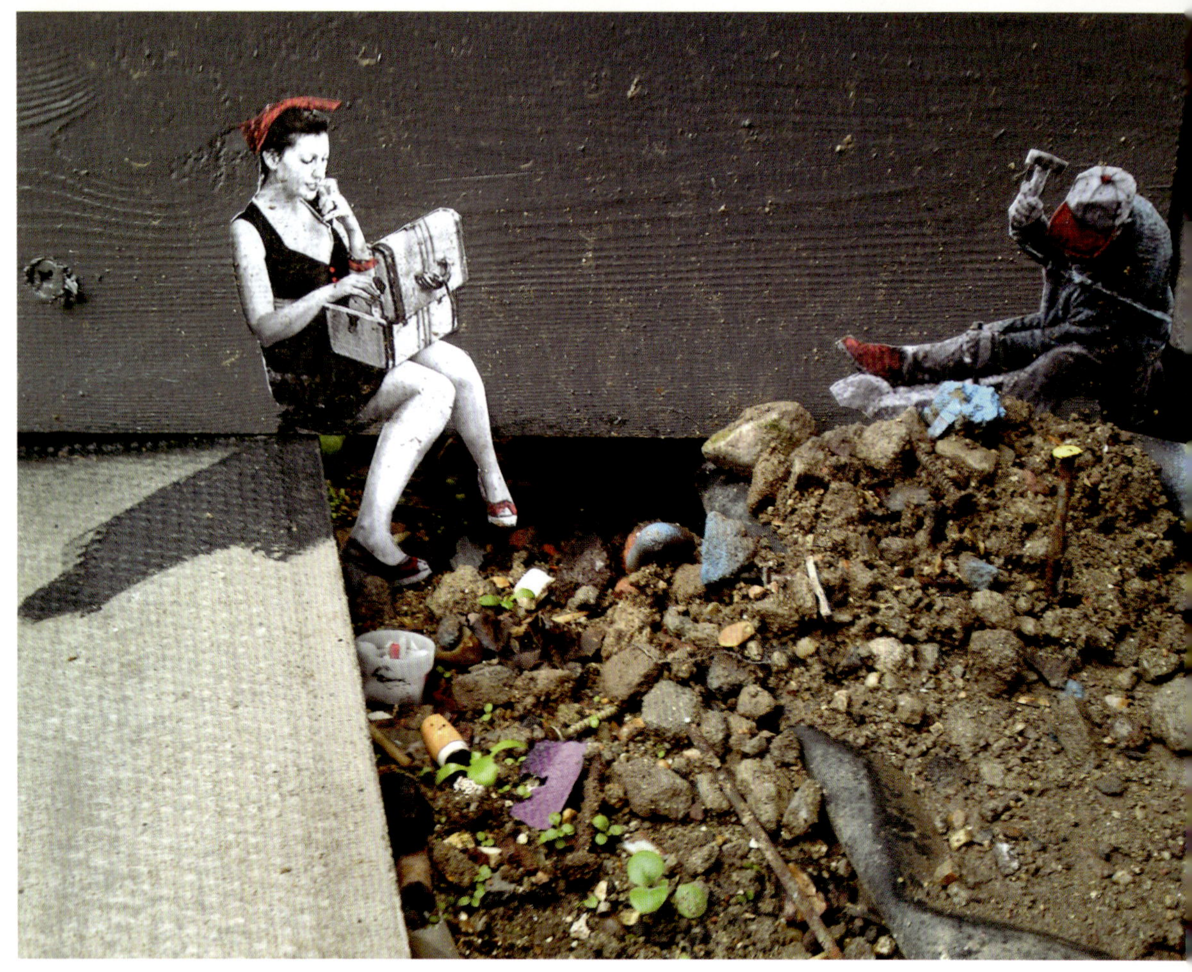

"London, for me, represents an unsteady place where things happened to live for a moment, to then vanish in a way to perdure. It provokes ephemoral life and it's evolving constantly." - **Pablo Delgado**

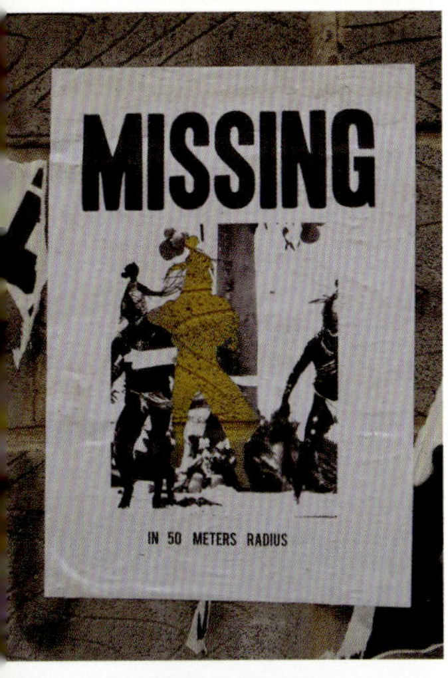
MISSING
IN 50 METERS RADIUS

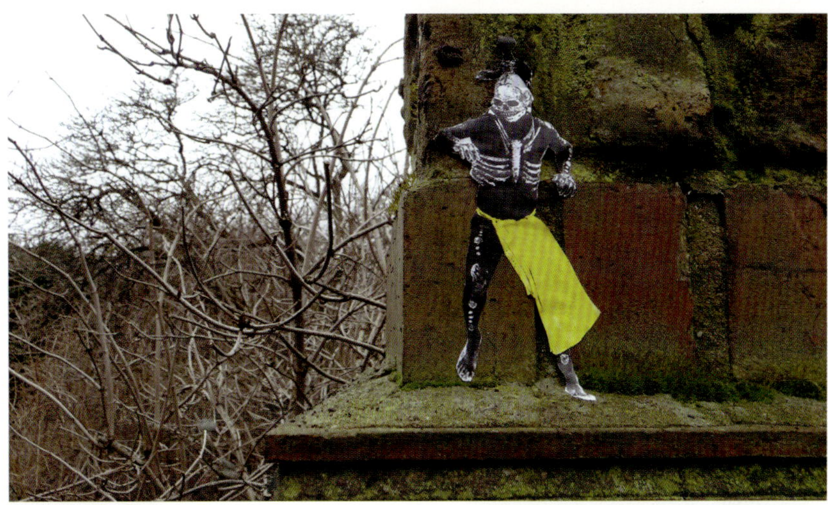

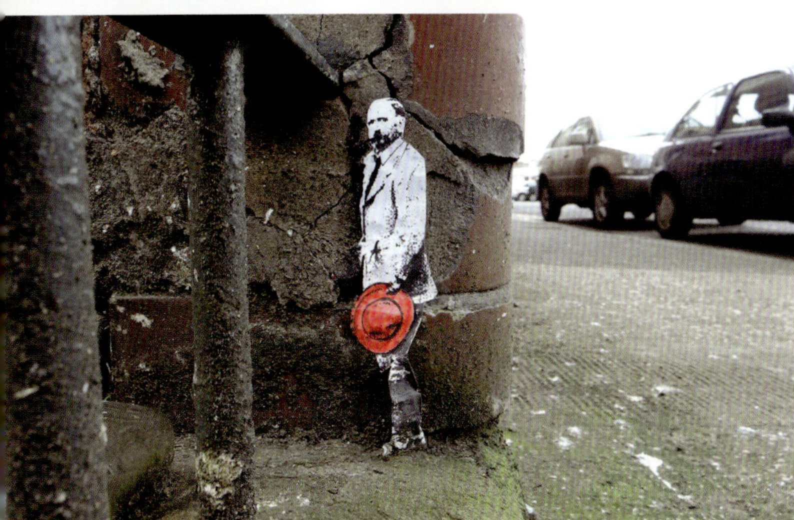

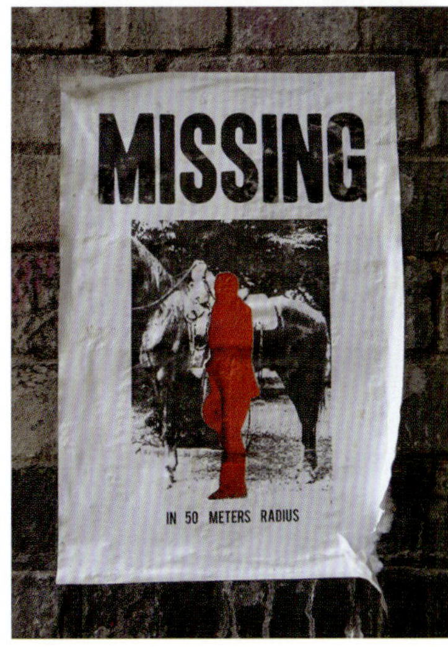
MISSING
IN 50 METERS RADIUS

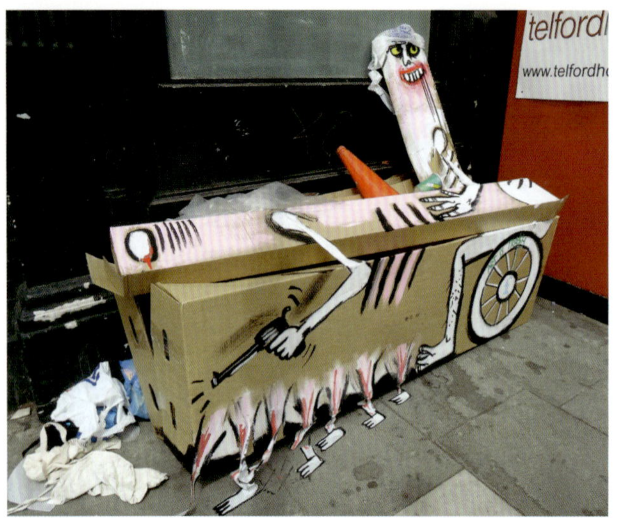

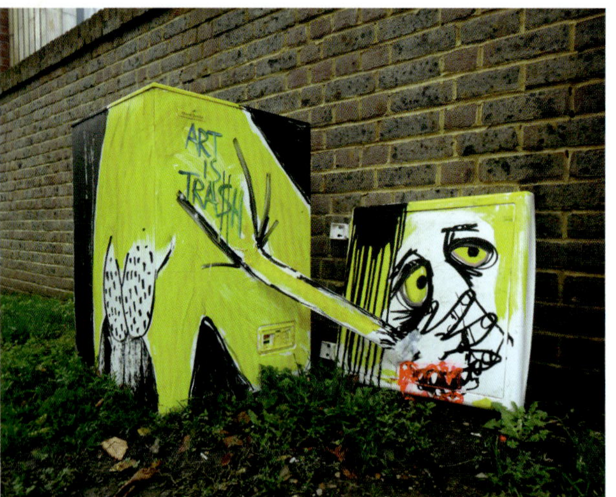

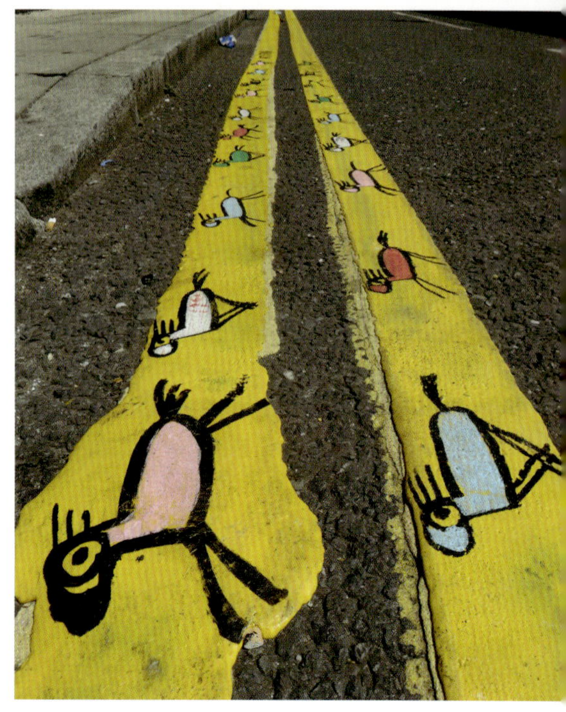

"The streets and trash of London have been, for me, a new city to explore and to create. A cared-for city that's sensible about art and culture. 'Art is Trash' action was born with my freedom of expression chained, in a city with political repression and police brutality. To create in London has liberated me from my chains, has given me the opportunity and freedom that I needed to be able to create without having a heart attack. In Barcelona I feel like an urban criminal, in London I feel like an artist." - **Francisco de Pájaro**

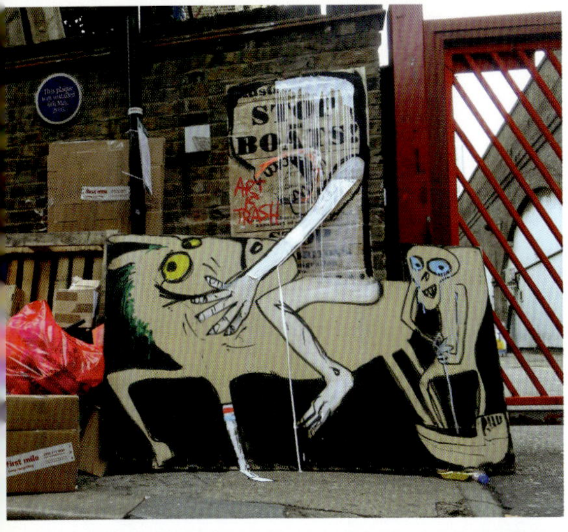

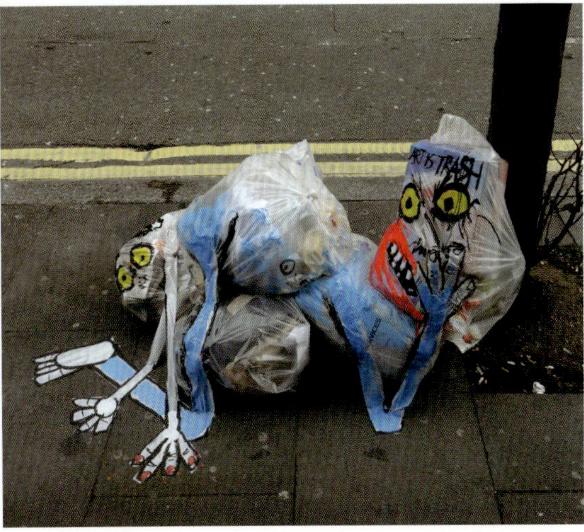

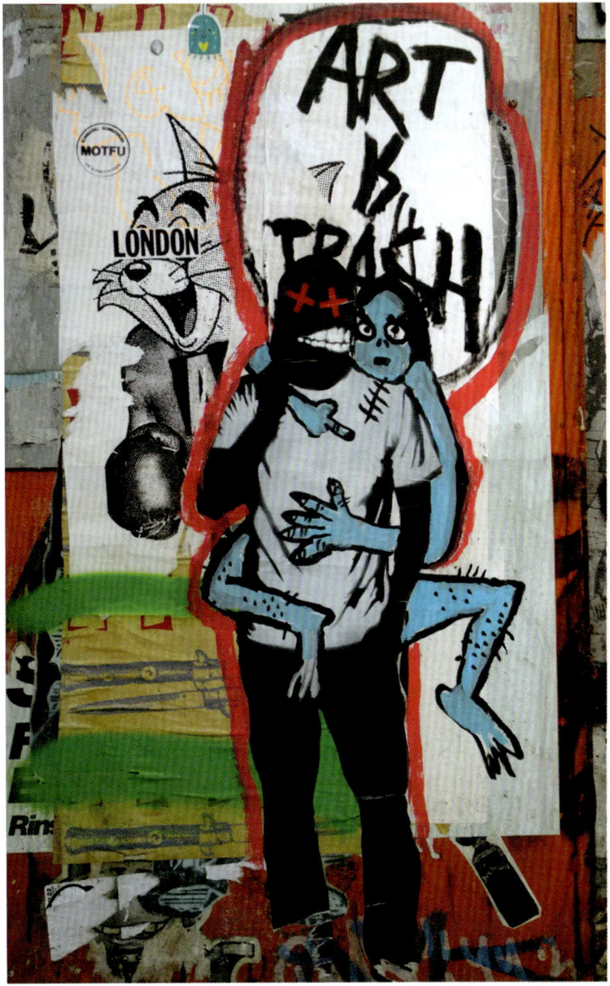

A.CE, Id-iom and Francisco de Pájaro. East London

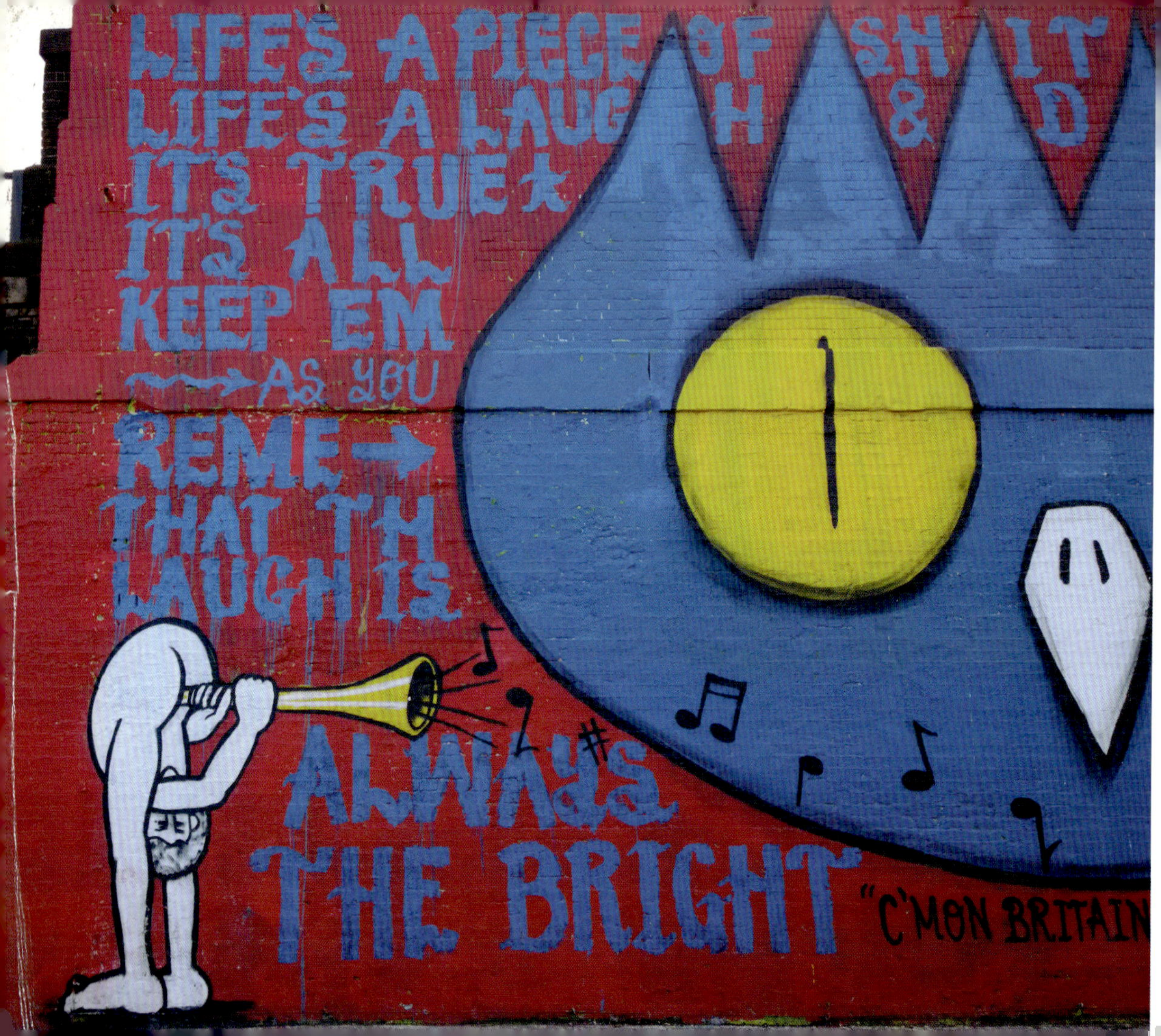

LIFE'S A PIECE OF SH IT
LIFE'S A LAUG H & D
IT'S TRUE
IT'S ALL
KEEP EM
AS YOU
REME
THAT TH
LAUGH IS
ALWAYS
THE BRIGHT
"C'MON BRITAIN

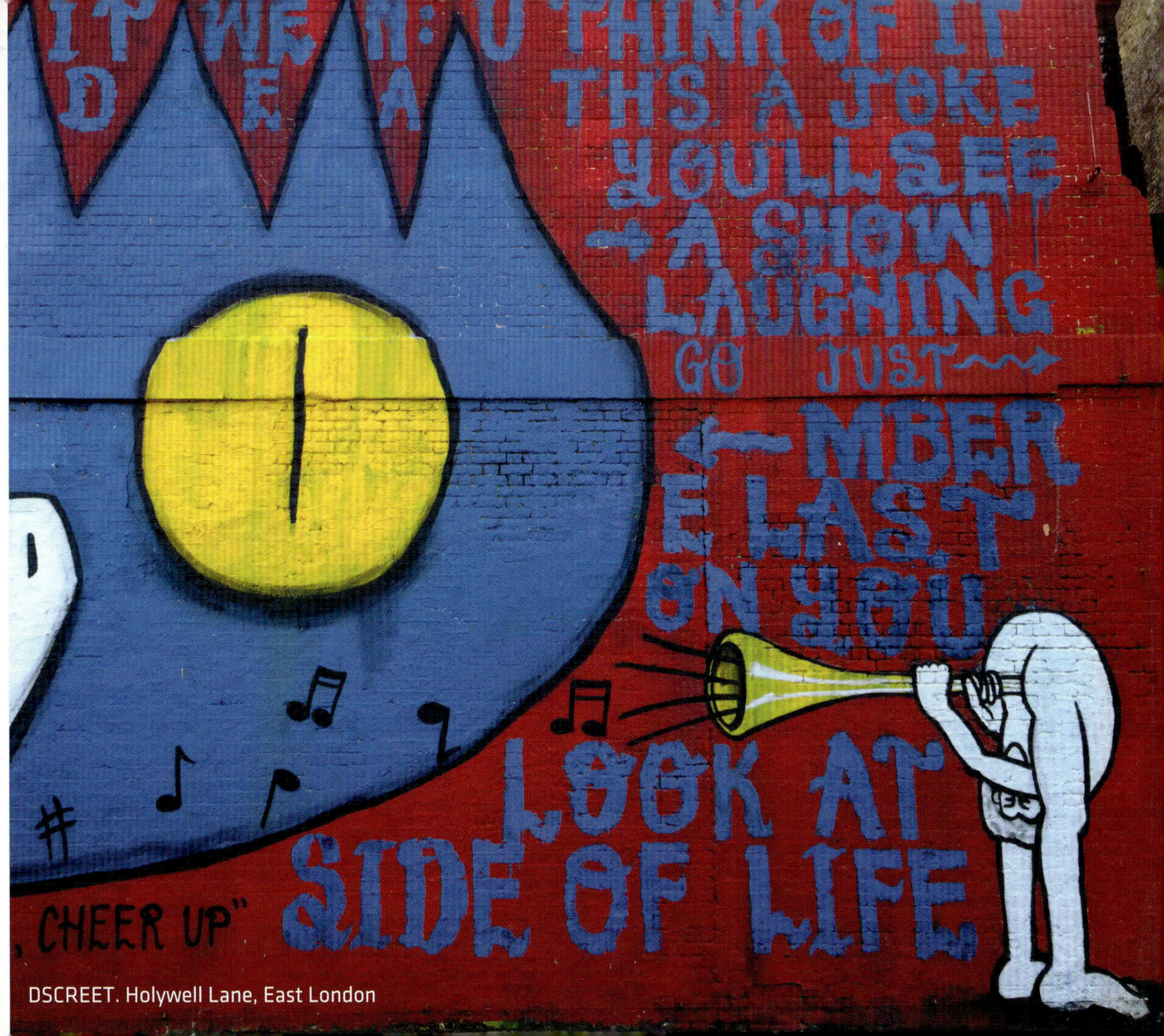

DSCREET. Holywell Lane, East London

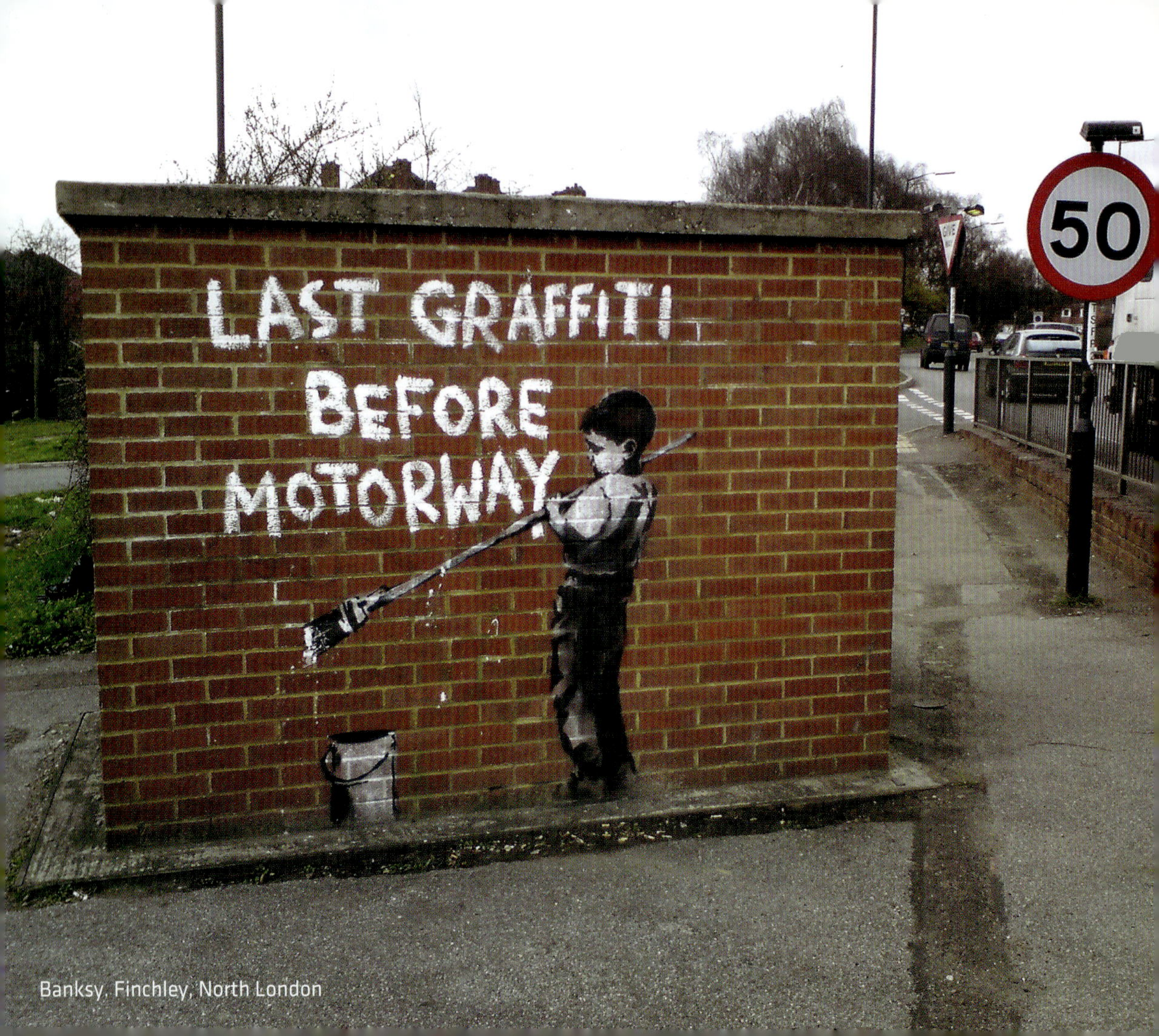

Banksy, Finchley, North London

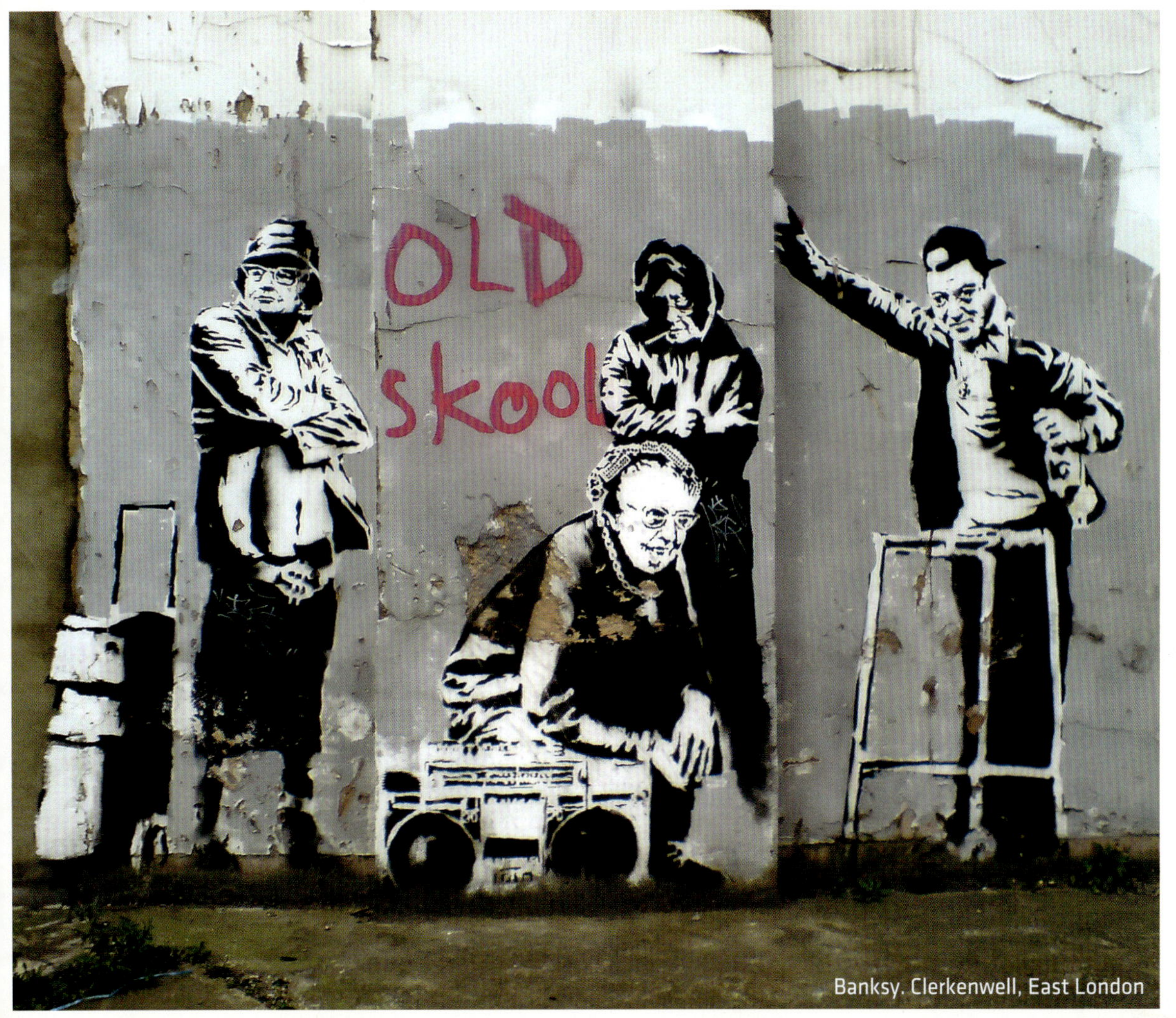

Banksy. Clerkenwell, East London

ENDWORD: LOVE YOUR CITY!

We've got it all: Taggers, Piecers, Bombers, Toys, Kings and everything in-between. London stands up as one of the greatest cities to embrace and cultivate this culture, which we have made ours for the last 30+ years. Graffiti.

Over the last three decades London has produced some of the best graffiti writers in the world, from the 80s onwards this city has been responsible for being an inspiration for the train writers, street bombers and hall of fame artists to do it good, and to do it right.

We have the oldest underground Tube system in the world, an intricate network of main-line trains running above and through the city, centuries old streets, alley ways and waste-grounds, football pitches, basketball courts, empty buildings, tracksides – space for your London Graffiti Adventure to be set and captured.

As time has gone on over these three decades, we have experienced crippling recessions, sell-out governments, public property becoming private, and less and less space to paint. Halls of fame that have been tolerated, permission granted or just not cared about by local councils for the last 30 years have started to be taken away, knocked down, painted clean and arrests have been made.

I've been involved in this culture for 20 years and when I started painting in '95 the scene was a whole lot different. I caught the end of a different London. I experienced and witnessed the changes throughout the city and the things that effected our culture from then to now; we've lost a lot but also have gained a lot, maturing with it.

We are Londoners, London's people, London's Writers, Bombers and Artists. We know how to overcome and deal with many situations, figure out ways to get that painting done, find that spot and do the do. Our city now admittedly does not have as many bombed up streets city-wide, painted trains don't run and prison sentences are harsh but we still paint and the halls of fame that are left (and they are blossoming every week as you can see with this great book) with hundreds of Writers hitting the walls city-wide alongside some supremely talented street artists.

This culture is ours and is developing every day, so in the words of London's Hip Hop Kings Taskforce: "If your back's against the wall turn around and write on it!"

David Samuel/RareKind

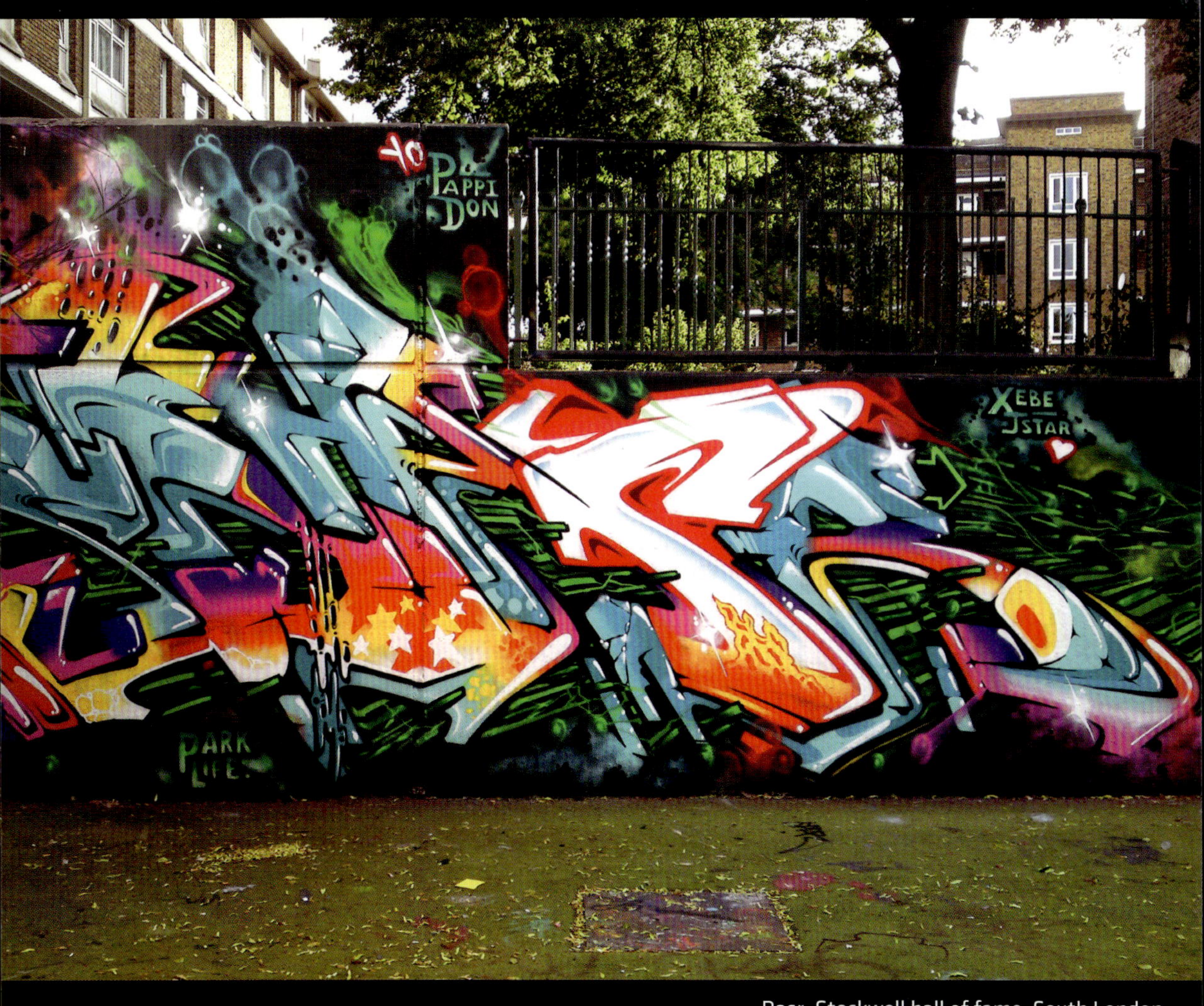

Dasr. Stockwell hall of fame, South London

ARTIST CREDITS

Many thanks to everyone who features in and supported the book – thanks also for the opportunity to photograph the work, wherever I found it! Here's an alphabetical list of the writers and artists I have managed to include.

*616, A.CE, Aeon Fly, Aero, Aida, Alex Senna, Alo, Alternative London, Andrrea, Anthony Lister, Aroe, Art Under The Hood, Aseb, Aser, Aset, ATG, Audio57, Bailon, Banksy, Basik, Beau Stanton, Ben Slow, Best Ever, Blavoe, Boe, Born, Brave1, BRK, Busone, C215, Cadi, Captain Kris, Catch, CBM, Cemo, Cept, Chil, Choci Roc, Chrome & Black, Chu, Clepto, CodeFC, Colt45, Corze, Cranio, Crept, Crimo, Crome, D*Face, Dabs Myla, Dale Grimshaw, DALeast, Dan Kitchener, Daps, Dasr, David Walker, DDS, Ders, Deus, Don, Donk, Dowta, Doze, Dr Cream, Dr Zadok, Drax, DSCREET, Dyelck, Dyet, Eaz RIP, Edwin, Erk, Eska, Fan77, Faver, Fels, Fenza, Fin DAC, Francisco de Pájaro, Frank Malt, Fuel, Fun Factory, Funk, Gee, Global Street Art, Gnasher, Gold Peg, Graffi ti Life, Grose, Heato, Hero32, Hin, Hooked Blog, Hozae, Hunto, Hush, Id-iom, IFC, InkFetish, Insane, Irony, ITS, Jadell, Jim Vision, Jim2, Jive, Jobs, Jonesy, KEF, Kekli, Kesh, King Robbo, Kloz, Klue, Koar, LB, Lempke, LiskBot, Lone, Louis Masai, Lovepusher, Ludvig, Lush, MadC, Malarky, Masika, Math, Mau Mau, Mean, Merc, Midge, Mighty Mo, Millo, MOBSTR, Morsa, Mr Cenz, Mr Met, Muro & Matem, My Dog Sighs, Nathan Bowen, Nehs, Neist, Neka, Nemo, Neyec, Nychos, Obit, Olas, OPD, Owed, Ozone RIP, P.I.C., Pablo Delgado, Panik, Parkers, Parlee, Part2ism, Paul Insect, Pedro, Pez, Phlegm, Phorm, Prime, Prize, Props, Pure Evil, Reka, Rems, Revert, Roa, Roan, Roe, Ronzo, Roten, Rowdy, Run, Sares, Seks, Sexy, She One, Shu2, Si Mitchell, Sian E, Sickboy, SkyHigh, Slam, Snatch, Snoe, Soleo, Solo One, Space Invader, Space3, Sparky Superfly, Spat, SPZero76, Squirl, Steve ESPO Powers, Stik, Stinkfish, Street Art London, Sweet Toof, Taskforce (Chester P & Farma G), Teach, Team Robbo, Temp32, The Krah, Thierry Noir, Tizer, TML Stars, Toaster, Tope, Toxic, Trev, TRP, Tune, Twesh, Txemey, Uhuh, Vega, Vents, Vibes, Vinnie Nylon, Virus, Wisher, Word to Mother, WOT, Yeah, Zaki Dee, Zerx, Zime, Zina, Zomby.*

With so many talented people working in London today, it was impossible to feature them all in this book, for which I am sincerely sorry, to them and to you! Visit my website to see an extension of this book and the many more photographs, and resources it has to offer!

LDNGraffiti.co.uk/Follow me @LDNGraffiti

LDNGraffiti? I made all of this for my mum, my dad, Line and, most of all, Joshua X
Joe_LDNGraffiti

BACK COVER: Boe & Irony. East London

Pojo & Joeppo. LDNGraffiti

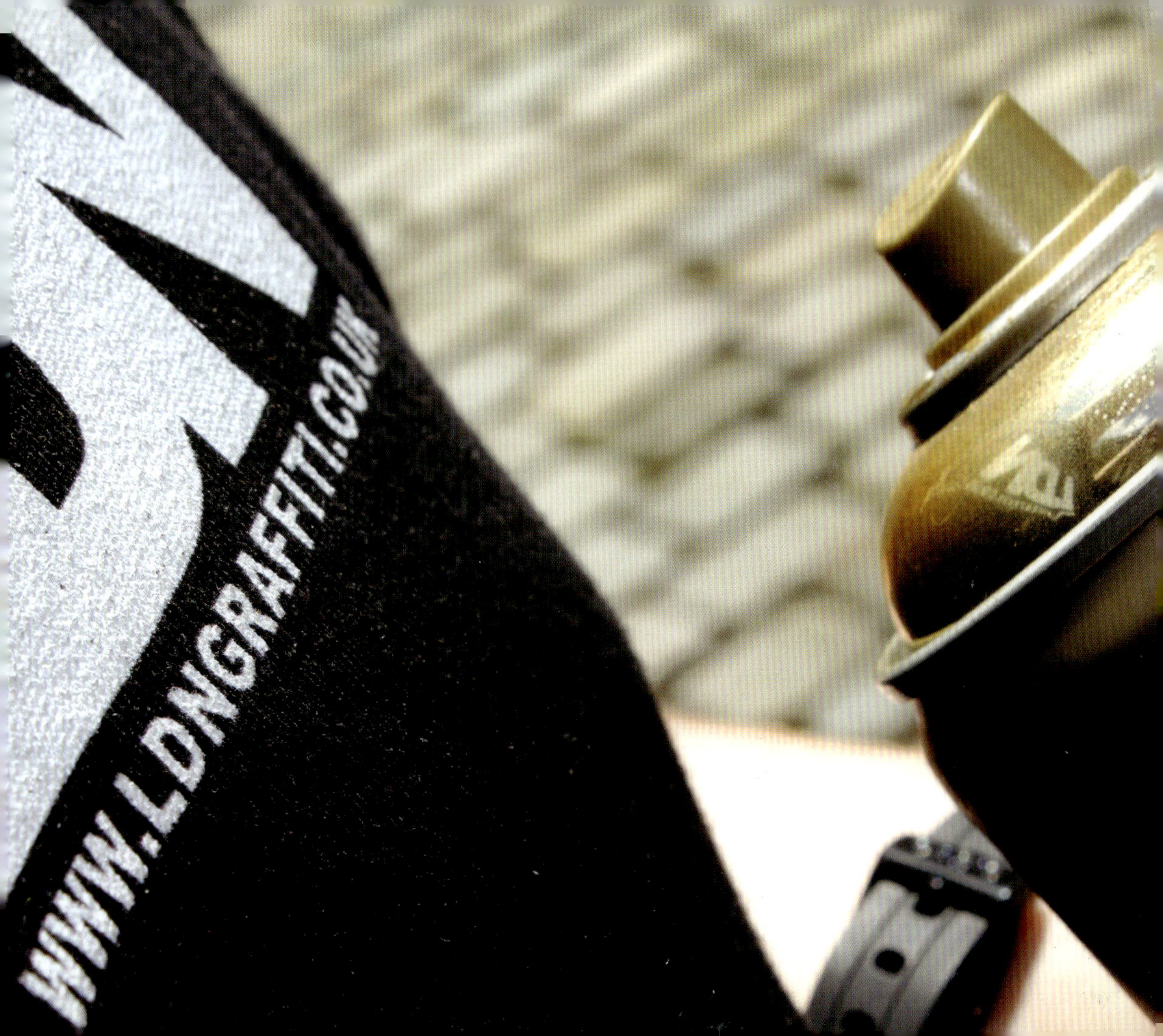
WWW.LDNGRAFFITI.CO.UK

3 5 7 9 10 8 6 4 2

First published in 2014 by Ebury Press, an imprint of Ebury Publishing
A Random House Group company

The Random House Group Limited Reg. No. 954009

Addresses for companies within the Random House Group can be found at www.randomhouse.co.uk

A CIP catalogue record for this book is available from the British Library

Penguin Random House is committed to a sustainable future for our business,our readers and our planet.
This book is made from Forest Stewardship Council® certified paper.

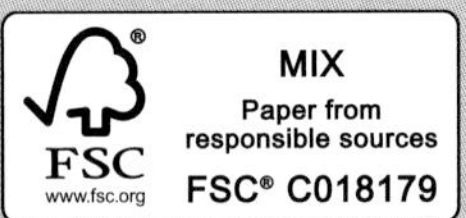

Printed and bound in China by C&C Offset Printing Co., Ltd
Typeset by www.envyltd.co.uk
Design by Joe Epstein

ISBN 9780091958688

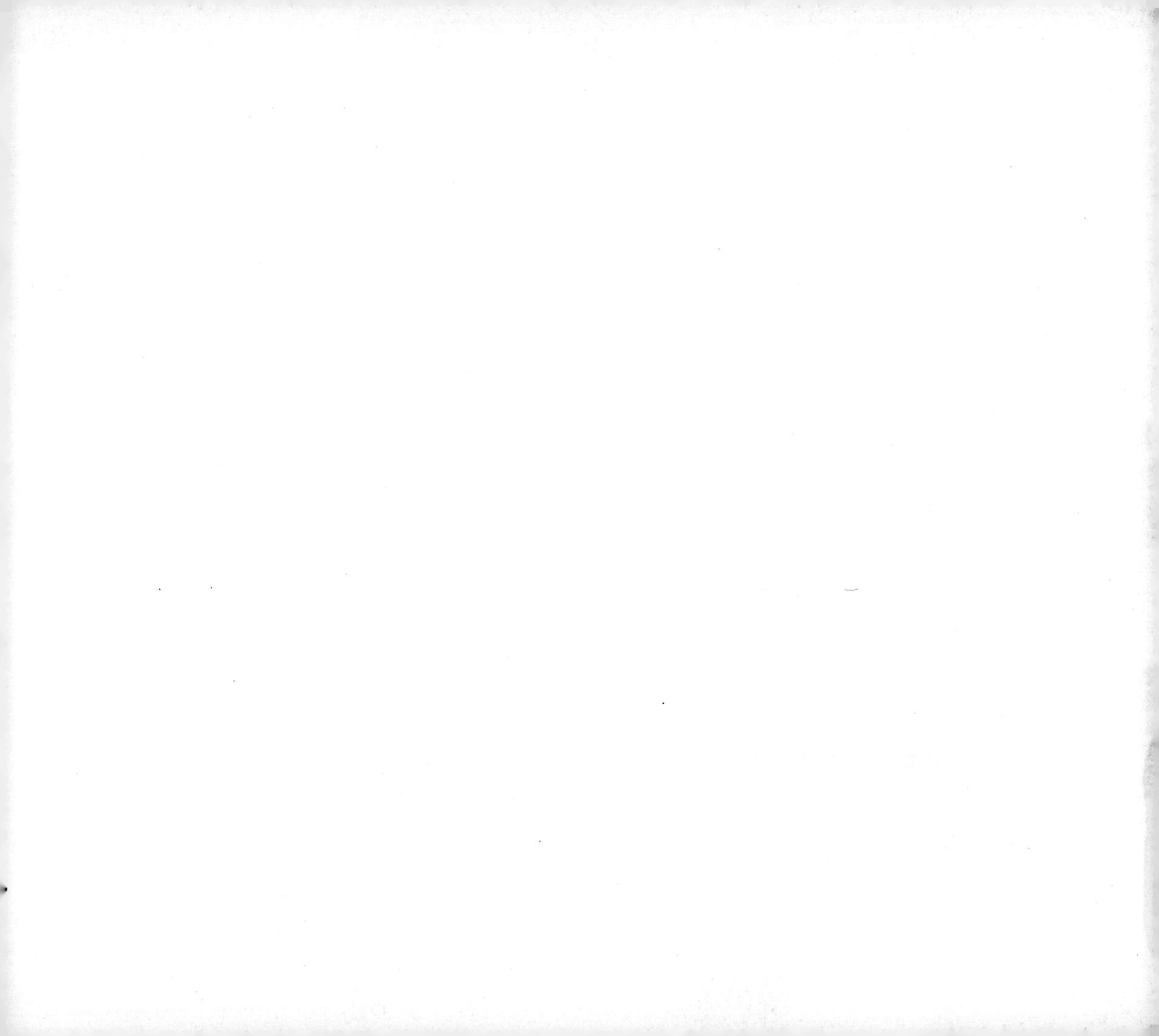

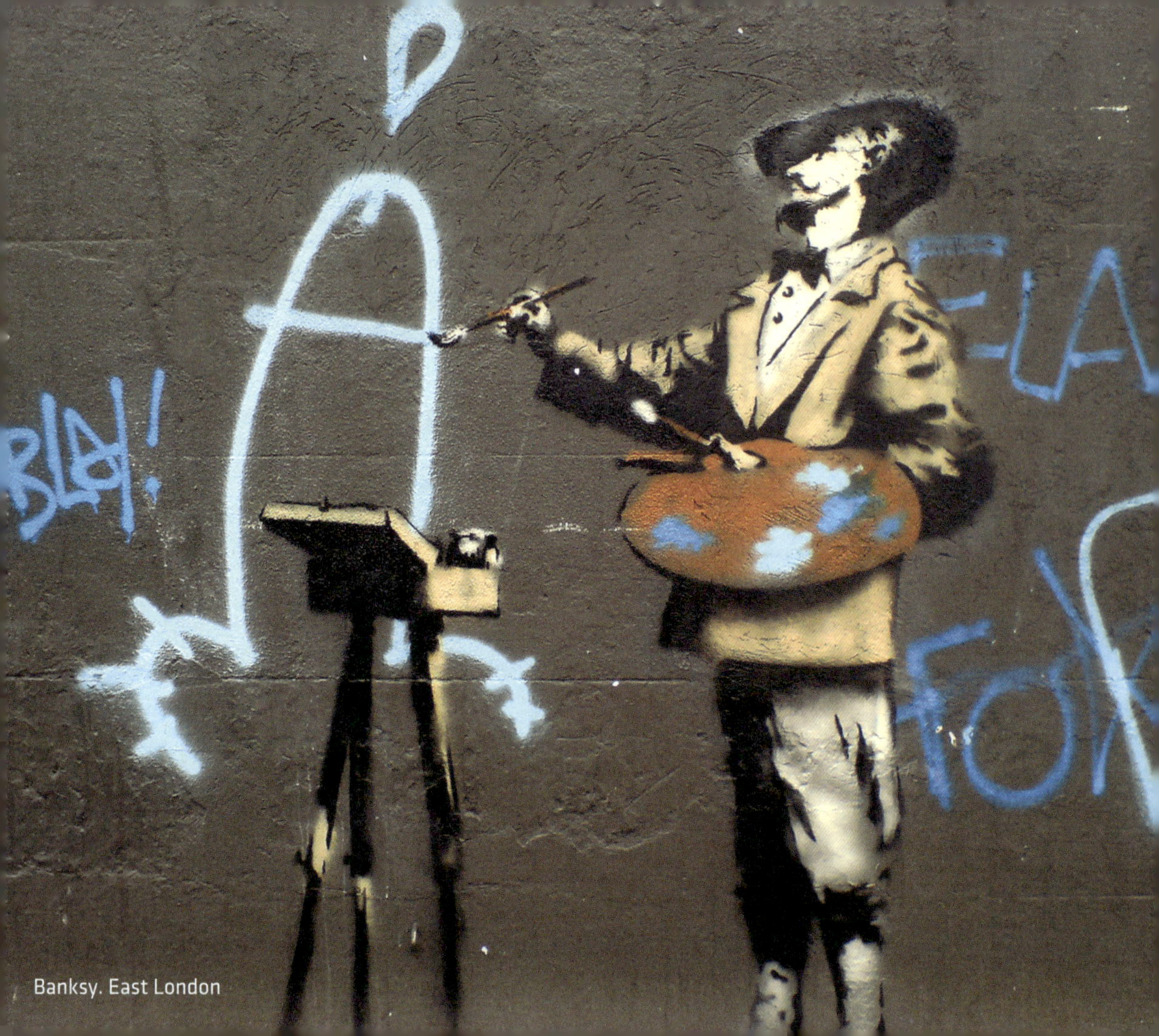

Banksy. East London